D1570178

JOURNAL FOR THE STUDY OF THE OLD TESTAMENT
SUPPLEMENT SERIES
277

Sheffield Academic Press

The Religion of the Patriarchs

Augustine Pagolu

Journal for the Study of the Old Testament
Supplement Series 277

Dedicated to the memory
of Anand Doron (1981–96)

BS
573
,P340
1998

Copyright © 1998 Sheffield Academic Press

Published by
Sheffield Academic Press Ltd
Mansion House
19 Kingfield Road
Sheffield S11 9AS
England

Typeset by Sheffield Academic Press
and
Printed on acid-free paper in Great Britain
by Bookcraft Ltd
Midsomer Norton, Bath

British Library Cataloguing in Publication Data

A catalogue record for this book is available
from the British Library

ISBN 1-85075-935-9

CONTENTS

PREFACE

I am grateful to Sheffield Academic Press, and particularly to Professor David Clines, for accepting my thesis for publication in their JSOT Supplement Series. Except for some minor corrections the present work is the same as the dissertation that I submitted for my PhD to the Open University (UK) through the Oxford Centre for Mission Studies in 1995.

A number of trusts and funding agencies helped me during the course of my research. My special thanks are due to Tyndale House, Cambridge, where I did all my work, the Overseas Council (UK), the Ulting Trust, the Oxford Centre for Mission Studies, the South Asia Institute of Advanced Christian Studies (Bangalore) and the Langham Trust.

I am grateful to the Revd Dr John Goldingay, director of my research, and Dr Gordon Wenham, my supervisor, who guided and encouraged, and commented meticulously on my work at every stage. For initial editing, I thank Drs Jason Bray, Ted Herbert and Philip Johnston, especially the latter who also read the entire thesis and made many helpful comments on style and content. I am grateful to Dr Alan Millard, University of Liverpool, for his additional suggestions and improvements.

I thank also Nigel Ajay Kumar for preparing the indices of modern authors and extra-biblical texts, and Mrs Beulah Wood for proofreading the manuscript before it went to press.

Finally, I thank my wife and children for their unfailing love and understanding throughout the duration of the research and especially recently when I had to isolate myself to check the proofs and correct the manuscript. I am especially grateful to my wife Sumathi for translating a number of French articles needed for my research.

ABBREVIATIONS

AAA	*Annals of Archaeology and Anthropology*
AB	Anchor Bible
ABD	David Noel Freedman *et al.* (eds.), *The Anchor Bible Dictionary* (New York: Doubleday, 1992)
ABR	*Australian Biblical Review*
AfO	*Archiv für Orientforschung*
AJA	*American Journal of Archaeology*
AnBib	Analecta biblica
ANEP	James B. Pritchard (ed.), *Ancient Near East in Pictures Relating to the Old Testament* (Princeton, NJ: Princeton University Press, 1954)
ANET	James B. Pritchard (ed.), *Ancient Near Eastern Texts Relating to the Old Testament* (Princeton, NJ: Princeton University Press, 3rd edn, 1969)
AnOr	Analecta orientalia
AOAT	Alter Orient und Altes Testament
AOS	American Oriental Series
ARTU	J.C. de Moor, *An Anthology of Religious Texts from Ugarit* (Leiden: E.J. Brill, 1987)
ARW	*Archiv für Religionswissenschaft*
ASOR	The American Schools of Oriental Research
ASTI	*Annual of the Swedish Theological Institute*
BA	*Biblical Archaeologist*
BARev	*Biblical Archaeology Review*
BASOR	*Bulletin of the American Schools of Oriental Research*
BDB	Francis Brown, S.R. Driver and Charles A. Briggs, *A Hebrew and English Lexicon of the Old Testament* (Oxford: Clarendon Press, 1907)
BHS	*Biblia hebraica stuttgartensia*
Bib	*Biblica*
BibOr	*Biblica et orientalia*
BJRL	*Bulletin of the John Rylands University Library of Manchester*
BR	*Bible Review*
BSac	*Bibliotheca Sacra*
BSC	Bible Student's Commentary
BSS	Biblical Seminar Series

BWANT	Beiträge zur Wissenschaft vom Alten und Neuen Testament
BZ	*Biblische Zeitschrift*
BZAW	Beihefte zur *ZAW*
CAD	Ignace I. Gelb *et al.* (eds.), *The Assyrian Dictionary of the Oriental Institute of the University of Chicago* (Chicago: Oriental Institute, 1956–)
CBQ	*Catholic Biblical Quarterly*
CBQMS	*Catholic Biblical Quarterly*, Monograph Series
CBSC	Cambridge Bible for Schools and Colleges
CM	*Classica et Mediaevalia*
CML	J.C.L. Gibson, *Canaanite Myths and Legends* (Edinburgh: T. & T. Clark, 2nd edn, 1978)
DB	J. Hastings (ed.), *Dictionary of the Bible* (Edinburgh: T. & T. Clark, 1900–1904)
DBSup	*Dictionnaire de la Bible, Supplément*
DISO	Charles-F. Jean and Jacob Hoftijzer (eds.), *Dictionnaire des inscriptions sémitiques de l'ouest* (Leiden: E.J. Brill, 1965)
EAEHL	M. Avi-Yona (ed.), *Encyclopedia of Archaeological Excavations in the Holy Land* (London: Oxford University Press, 1975)
EB	*Encyclopaedia Britannica*, VI (Chicago: University of Chicago Press, 1945)
EBib	Etudes bibliques
EnBib	T.K. Cheyne and J.S. Black (eds.), *Encyclopaedia of the Bible* (London: A. & C. Black, 1899–1903)
EncJud	*Encyclopaedia Judaica*
EI	*Ereṣ Israel*
ER	M. Eliade (ed.), *The Encyclopaedia of Religion* (New York: Macmillan, 1987)
ERE	J. Hastings (ed.), *Encyclopaedia of Religion and Ethics* (Edinburgh: T. & T. Clark, 1908–26)
ES	A. Even-Shoshan, *A New Concordance of the Bible* (Jerusalem: Kiryat-Sefer, 1993)
EvQ	*Evangelical Quarterly*
EvT	*Evangelische Theologie*
ExpTim	*Expository Times*
FOTL	The Forms of the Old Testament Literature
FRLANT	Forschungen zur Religion und Literatur des Alten und Neuen Testaments
HAT	Handbuch zum Alten Testament
HKAT	Handkommentar zum Alten Testament
HSM	Harvard Semitic Monographs
HSS	Harvard Semitic Studies
HTR	*Harvard Theological Review*
HUCA	*Hebrew Union College Annual*

ICC	International Critical Commentary
IDB	George Arthur Buttrick (ed.), *The Interpreter's Dictionary of the Bible* (4 vols.; Nashville: Abingdon Press, 1962)
IDBSup	*IDB*, Supplementary Volume
IEJ	*Israel Exploration Journal*
Int	*Interpretation*
JAOS	*Journal of the American Oriental Society*
JBL	*Journal of Biblical Literature*
JBR	*Journal of Bible and Religion*
JCS	*Journal of Cuneiform Studies*
JEA	*Journal of Egyptian Archaeology*
JHS	*Journal of Hellenic Studies*
JJS	*Journal of Jewish Studies*
JNES	*Journal of Near Eastern Studies*
JNSL	*Journal of Northwest Semitic Languages*
JPOS	*Journal of the Palestine Oriental Society*
JQR	*Jewish Quarterly Review*
JSOT	*Journal for the Study of the Old Testament*
JSOTSup	*Journal for the Study of the Old Testament*, Supplement Series
JSS	*Journal of Semitic Studies*
JTS	*Journal of Theological Studies*
KAI	H. Donner and W. Röllig, *Kanaanäische und aramäische Inschriften* (3 vols.; Wiesbaden: Harrassowitz, 1962–64)
KAT	Kommentar zum Alten Testament
KD	*Kerygma und Dogma*
KHAT	Kurzer Hand-Kommentar zum Alten Testament
KlSchr	O. Eissfeldt, *Kleine Schriften*, I–V (Tübingen: J.C.B. Mohr, 1962–79)
KTU	M. Dietrich, O. Loretz and J. Sanmartín, *Die keilalphabetischen Texte aus Ugarit* (AOAT, 24.1; Neukirchen–Vluyn: Neukirchener Verlag, 1976)
KUB	*Kelschrifturkunden aus Boghazi* (42 vols.; Berlin: German Academy of Sciences)
LCL	Loeb Classical Library
NBD	J.D. Douglas *et al.* (eds.), *New Bible Dictionary* (Leicester: IVP, 2nd edn, 1982)
NCBC	New Century Bible Commentary
NEAEHL	E. Stern (ed.), *New Encyclopedia of Archaeological Excavations in the Holy Land* (4 vols.; New York: Simon & Schuster, 1993)
NEB	New English Bible
NICOT	New International Commentary on the Old Testament
OBT	Overtures to Biblical Theology
OECI	Oxford Editions of Cuneiform Inscriptions

OECT	Oxford Editions of Cuneiform Texts
OLA	Orientalia lovaniensia analecta
Or	*Orientalia*
OTG	Old Testament Guides
OTL	Old Testament Library
OTS	*Oudtestamentische Studiën*
PEQ	*Palestine Exploration Quarterly*
PRU	*Le palais royal d'Ugarit*
RA	*Revue d'assyriologie et d'archéologie orientale*
RAC	*Reallexikon für Antike und Christentum*
RB	*Revue biblique*
REJ	*Revue des études juives*
RelSRev	*Religious Studies Review*
RGG	*Religion in Geschichte und Gegenwart*
RHA	*Revue Hittite et Asianique*
RHR	*Revue de l'histoire des religions*
RLA	E. Ebeling and B. Meissner (eds.), *Reallexikon der Assyriologie* (Berlin, Leipzig: W. de Gruyter, 1928–)
RSV	Revised Standard Version
SBL	Society of Biblical Literature
SBLDS	SBL Dissertation Series
SBLMS	SBL Monograph Series
SBT	Studies in Biblical Theology
SH	*Scripta Hierosolymitana*
SOTSMS	Society for Old Testament Study Monograph Series
ST	*Studia theologica*
StudOr	*Studia orientalia*
TDOT	G.J. Botterweck and H. Ringgren (eds.), *Theological Dictionary of the Old Testament*
THAT	Ernst Jenni and Claus Westermann (eds.), *Theologisches Handwörterbuch zum Alten Testament* (Munich: Chr. Kaiser Verlag, 1971–76)
ThWAT	G.J. Botterweck and H. Ringgren (eds.), *Theologisches Wörterbuch zum Alten Testament* (Stuttgart: W. Kohlhammer, 1970–)
TNSI	G.A. Cooke, *A Text-Book of North-Semitic Inscriptions* (Oxford: Clarendon Press, 1903)
TOTC	Tyndale Old Testament Commentaries
TSSI	J.C.L. Gibson, *Textbook of Syrian Semitic Inscriptions* (Oxford: Clarendon Press, 1971–82)
TY	*Tantur Yearbook*
TynBul	*Tyndale Bulletin*
TZ	*Theologische Zeitschrift*
UF	*Ugarit-Forschungen*
Ug.	C.F.-A. Schaeffer *et al.* (eds.), *Ugaritica* (Paris: Imprimerie

	Nationale–Paul Geuthner, 1939–)
UL	C.H. Gordon, *Ugaritic Literature* (Rome: Pontifical Biblical
	Institute, 1949)
UM	C.H. Gordon, *Ugaritic Manual* (AnOr, 35, Rome: Pontifical
	Biblical Institute, 1955)
VE	*Vox Evangelica*
VT	*Vetus Testamentum*
VTSup	*Vetus Testamentum,* Supplements
WBC	Word Biblical Commentary
WMANT	Wissenschaftliche Monographien zum Alten und Neuen
	Testament
YOS	Yale Oriental Series
ZA	*Zeitschrift für Assyriologie*
ZAW	*Zeitschrift für die alttestamentliche Wissenschaft*
ZDMG	*Zeitschrift der deutschen morgenländischen Gesellschaft*

Chapter 1

INTRODUCTION

1. *A Brief Survey of Research on Patriarchal Religion*

The aim of this book is to describe the religion of the patriarchs from Israel's own understanding of her traditions.[1] However, it is important to give a brief survey of descriptions of patriarchal religion from other perspectives in order to show how they contribute to, or differ from, the present study. It has long been observed that the patriarchal religion portrayed in Genesis has elements both peculiar to itself and common to the Yahwistic religion of later times. The clearest example of this is the idea of God portrayed in the narratives, which makes no distinction between the God of the patriarchs and Yahweh, the God of Israel. Genesis thus assumes that Yahweh, the God of Israel, was the God of the patriarchs as well. Consequently a number of scholars have argued that patriarchal religion was both a prelude to, and continuous with, the Mosaic religion, thus essentially accepting the historicity of the patriarchs.[2] But Wellhausen and many following him contest the historicity of the patriarchs and, with it, their religion. They maintain that the patriarchal traditions were retrojections of the monarchic period reflecting the time the stories arose in Israel, not historical knowledge of the patriarchs. Thus, for them, there is no such thing as a patriarchal period or patriarchal religion.[3]

However, with Alt's seminal essay 'Der Gott der Väter' in 1929, not only was the issue of the historicity of the patriarchs brought into sharp focus again, but also the question of the probability of their religion being distinct from that of later Israel was raised (Alt 1989a: 1-77). Alt

1. For a discussion of method to be followed here, see below.
2. Dillmann, Gunkel, Gressmann, Kittel; cf. Weidmann 1968: 46-64.
3. Wellhausen 1885: 318-19; Hoftijzer 1956: 6-30; Thompson 1974; Van Seters 1975; 1980: 220-33.

began his search with the assumption that the God or gods of the patriarchs must be different from the God of Israel, because certain traditions of Israel state that Israel's fathers worshipped other gods beyond the river (Josh. 24.2-14)[4] while other traditions insist that Yahweh, the God of Israel, is to be identified with the God of the fathers (Exod. 3.13-15; 6.2-3). As Alt pursued his study, he came to the conclusion that the patriarchs worshipped different gods of their own clans, but the editors of Genesis identified them with Yahweh, the God of Israel. This identification took place, according to Alt, in the course of historical development. Patriarchal groups, being semi-nomadic, settled independently with their own clan gods on the fringes of the plains. These wandering groups eventually came into contact with sedentary dwellers and worshipped at the local shrines, thus identifying their gods with the local shrines' deities. (Alt took the *Elim* of Genesis as local *numina*.) Thus distinction can be seen between 'the God of Abraham', 'the God of Isaac' and 'the God of Jacob': these were different clan gods which were later merged into 'the God of the fathers' (Alt 1989a: 25-30). In Alt's words: 'The gods of the fathers were the παιδαγωγοί leading to the greater God, who later replaced them completely' (Alt 1989a: 62). Further, Alt thought that the patriarchal gods were originally anonymous gods who were later identified with the local Canaanite gods. Their oldest names were 'Fear of Isaac', 'Mighty One of Jacob', 'God of Abraham', and so on. Alt also thought that patriarchal nomadism was a stage in the process toward sedentarization. He drew possible religio-historical parallels from Nabataean and Palmyrene inscriptions in Greek and Aramaic dating from the first century BCE to the fourth century CE. These reflect a people who, like the patriarchs, were nomadic tribes and worshipped the gods of the heads of their clans (Alt 1989a: 32-44). However Alt's conclusions are evaluated, since his work the majority of scholars have acknowledged that an inquiry into patriarchal religion before the exodus and the settlement in the land is possible.

However, Alt's thesis has been found untenable in a number of aspects. Alt's parallels from the early Christian era are thought to be too remote to be applied to the patriarchal era. It is questioned whether there was anything distinctively nomadic about the mode of designating gods, for all the inscriptions quoted come from settled peoples, and the

---

4.   Cf. Kittel 1925: 39; contrast Sarna 1989: 396-97.

people named were not the founders of the cults in question.[5] The biblical evidence Alt adduced was shown to be weak, for his conjectures that the cult of 'the god of Abraham', 'the fear of Isaac' and 'the bull of Jacob' existed among the tribes of Caleb/Judah, Judah/ Simeon and Joseph respectively has been found to be baseless (Haran 1965: 51 n. 34; cf. Wenham 1980: 166-67). Alt's view that the patriarchs worshipped anonymous gods who were identified only by their worshippers is also rejected on the basis of the old Assyrian texts from nineteenth-century Cappadocia, where a high god is described in terms similar to the patriarchal narratives; it is argued that the real name of the patriarchal god was El Shaddai.[6] Further, the designation 'god of my father' only expresses the relationship of the worshipper to the deity, and such a description is found to be very common in relation to the named gods throughout the ancient Near East.[7] It reflects not the name of the deity, but the relation of that deity to the worshipper, comparable to 'God of Israel' (Westermann 1985: 108).

Despite the problems raised by Alt's thesis, for some scholars it led the way toward an inquiry into the nature of the 'God of the fathers' behind the divine names found in Genesis,[8] while others turned toward the social and legal practices reflected in the patriarchal narratives. The aim of both these trends was to unravel the distinctive features of the religion of the patriarchs before the exodus and the settlement in

5.   Lods 1938: 201; cf. May 1941a: 127; Cross 1962: 229-31; Lods thought that the patriarchs were deified ancestors, a view that was previously refuted by Dillmann 1897: 3-8.

6.   Lewy 1934: 50-64; cf. Albright 1935: 188-90; May 1941a: 123-26.

7.   Cf. the various examples given by Cross 1962: 228-29, 231; 1973: 10-12.

8.   These are formed by the well-known Semitic word for god, El, which occurs in the construct state and is followed by a genitive or an attributive noun supplemented to it. Thus the appellations focused upon were: *El Elyon* (Gen. 14.18-22), *El Roi* (Gen. 16.13), *El Olam* (Gen. 21.33), *El Elohe Israel* (Gen. 33.20), *El Bethel* (Gen. 31.13; 35.7) and *El Shaddai* (Gen. 17.1; 28.3; 35.11; 43.13; 48.3; 49.25 [*we'el Shaddai* should be read here instead of *we'et Shaddai*]). Cf. Haran 1965: 47 n. 10. It must be pointed out that the title 'God of the father' is another designation peculiar to patriarchal traditions and times. Haran (1965: 36-37) argues that this is a 'crystallized expression reflecting a religious concept of another period', probably indicating a household god of a small clan. Several scholars also argue that the name YHWH is also a remnant of pre-Mosaic traditions, and that it is not justified to interpret it entirely from post-Mosaic concepts only: Rowley 1950: 149-50; Hyatt 1955: 133-36; Cross 1962: 251-59; Maclaurin 1962: 439-63; Kosmala 1963: 103-106.

Canaan. The former concentrated on the precise determination of the designation for God, assuming that this would clarify the nature of the patriarchal religion. Soon the conclusion that the patriarchal religion was a type of El-religion gained wide currency among scholars.[9] This may be partly because these designations are used only in relation to patriarchal times, suggesting that it was a distinct phase in the religion of Israel.[10] However, it is still disputed whether these designations were inherited from Canaan or known by the Hebrews from their ancestors and brought with them into Canaan.[11] Further, with the discoveries of the Ugaritic texts, where El is described so colourfully as the father of the gods and the head of the Canaanite pantheon, subsequent scholarship has tried to see a connection between the different designations used for God in Genesis and the El of the Ugaritic texts (cf. Pope 1955: 82-89). Thus one could accept with little difficulty that the god El could be described as 'the god of my father' or as El Elyon, El Shaddai or El Olam, the different divine designations used in Genesis. This line of argument has been followed by F.M. Cross (1962; 1973: 3-75).

Cross made a thorough analysis of the ancient Near Eastern parallels in order to compare the divine epithets in Genesis with the known characteristics of El from Ugarit and elsewhere in the Near East. He assumed that if El can be described by these titles, then patriarchal religion may be described as a form of El religion. Certain titles like *El Elohe Israel* and *El Elohe abika* (Gen. 33.20; 46.3) have an undoubted affinity to the Canaanite El. But the other titles, *El Olam*, *El Elyon* and *El Shaddai*, also fit the known character of El, because of their meaning and their context in Genesis. Cross finds difficulty only with *El Shaddai*, to which he attributes an Amorite origin and which he suggests was brought by the patriarchs from Mesopotamia. Thus, for Cross, the different divine names of Genesis do not represent the gods

9.   Lewy 1934; Albright 1935; Rist 1938: 289-303; May 1941b: 155-58; Hyatt 1955: 130-36; Gemser 1958: 1-21; Cross 1962: 225-59; 1973; Manley 1964: 3-7; Haran 1965: 30-55; Eissfeldt 1968: 79-91.

10.   It may be pointed out, however, that this idea was also held by several scholars even before Alt, e.g. Gunkel 1902; Gressmann 1910; Kittel 1925: 41-45; Baudissin 1925; cf. Westermann 1985: 106.

11.   Gunkel (1902), Gressmann (1910: 8-9, 28-29), and Haran (1965: 33-35) hold that it was a direct Hebrew heritage, while Eissfeldt (1956: 25-37), Weippert (1961: 42-62) and Cross (1962: 244-47), following Alt, argue that it was inherited from Canaan. Cf. Haran 1965: 47 n. 13.

of different clans before they adopted Yahwism, as argued by Alt,[12] but they were different titles of El during the pre-Mosaic period. This also explains why these titles of El were more readily acceptable to later Yahwism than those associated with the Baal cult. Cross plausibly suggests a basic continuity between the patriarchal religion, a form of El religion, and the Yahwism adopted later by the tribes of Israel. Not surprisingly, Cross's thesis has been accepted by many scholars, not only because of the brilliant way he handled the comparative materials but also because his parallels were much closer in time and place to the patriarchal times (cf. Wenham 1980: 170). Nevertheless, several scholars challenge Cross's identification of *Elyon*[13] and *El Shaddai*[14] with the Canaanite El, while others point out that the patriarchs probably knew El before they entered Canaan.[15]

The other trend resulting from Alt's essay was that which focused on the personal names, people movements and religious, political, social and legal practices of the patriarchal traditions. Certain assumptions and legal concepts reflected in the patriarchal stories either are inexplicable by the conditions of later Israel or openly contradict the various laws of the pentateuchal codes. Yet these customs and practices are surprisingly similar to the social and legal ideas reflected at Nuzi, Mari and Alalakh.[16] This combination of similarity with second-millennium

12. Cross (1973: 4 n. 3) comments: 'For Alt these contacts [with local deities] were not so much in the Patriarchal, i.e. the pre-Mosaic period, as in the era of the entry into Canaan in "Israelite" times. In our view, this is a fundamental weakness in Alt's historical stance, a position increasingly untenable in view of our present knowledge of the movements in Palestine in the second millennium B.C.'

13. Pope 1955: 55-58. However, Lack (1962: 44-64) argued that Elyon was once an epithet of El and only later became a title for Baalshamen and that this explains why Elyon is mentioned alongside El in the Sefire texts. It is part of a long process in which El was displaced by Baal as the latter took over the position and titles of the former. Cf. Koch 1976: 299-332; Wenham 1980: 170.

14. Ouellette (1969: 470-71) points out that El Shaddai probably refers to Amurru, the god of the steppe, while Bailey (1968: 434-38) and Abel (1973: 48-59), drawing attention to several features of the patriarchal narratives, argue that El Shaddai may be identified with the moon god of Haran. Cf. Wenham 1980: 170-71.

15. Haran 1965: 42; Roberts 1972: 34; Wenham 1980: 171.

16. Albright 1940: 80-112; 1968: 47-95; Rowley 1952: 299-303; Cross 1962: 225-59; 1973; Bright 1981: 67-103; some scholars, however, argue that the patriarchal traditions cannot go back beyond the Amarna period, that is, the fourteenth century BCE, e.g. Gordon 1954: 56-59; 1963: 77-84; cf. Fisher 1973: 59-65. But

practices outside Israel and dissimilarity with first-millennium Israelite customs has led scholars to reconsider the antiquity of the patriarchal traditions. This would accord with the observation that the divine appellations in the patriarchal narratives, whether the heritage of Canaan or Mesopotamia, belong to the patriarchal age, and with the conclusion that the traditions of Genesis preserve a genuine memory of patriarchal religion before the exodus. Thus the thesis that patriarchal religion was more at home with the form of society and the lifestyle of the patriarchs portrayed in Genesis than with the religion of the monarchic period was affirmed.

However, with the studies of T.L. Thompson (1974; 1987; cf. Goldingay 1980: 35-40) and J. Van Seters (1975; 1980: 220-33), who revive the earlier thesis of Wellhausen that the patriarchal stories are retrojections of the monarchic period, the whole idea of a patriarchal period and therefore a patriarchal religion has once again been questioned. Thompson and Van Seters have reacted against the way the archaeological evidence was used by the so-called Albright school in support of biblical traditions.[17] The studies of both the Albright school and its critics have shown how a particular datum can be used to support both an early and a late date of a particular practice or a custom in the patriarchal narratives. For instance, while parallels were drawn by Speiser between the Nuzi tablets and biblical traditions about adoption contracts and other social and family customs in order to explain various patriarchal practices from a second-millennium setting,[18] similar parallels from the first millennium were drawn by Van Seters to explain the same practices.[19] Such opposing conclusions may simply reflect differ-

Gordon's view has been criticized by several scholars, see Thompson 1974: 196-297; Selman 1976: 114-36; 1980: 95.

17. Albright 1950: 3; 1963: 1-2; Wright 1962: 40; Bright 1981: 80. Cf. Bright's confident assertions in the second edition of his *History of Israel* (1972: 79) about the value of archaeological evidence as proof for the historicity of patriarchal life and times. This confidence is less assertive but still present in the third edition (1981: 80). It is against such confidence that one has to evaluate the studies of Thompson and Van Seters.

18. Speiser 1955: 252-56; 1963b: 15-28; 1964: xxxvii-xliii; cf. Albright 1932: 138, 209; 1961: 36-54; Gordon 1940: 1-12; 1954: 56-59. It must be pointed out that these three scholars proposed three different dates for the age of the patriarchs. For a critique of their positions, see Weippert 1971: 407-32; Dever 1977: 91-96; de Vaux 1978: 241-56; Selman 1980: 94-103, 109-112.

19. Van Seters 1968: 401-408; 1969: 377-95; 1975: 65-103; cf. Tucker 1966:

ent methodologies. Besides, these studies have reflected, as has been rightly pointed out by Millard, 'an air...of search for proof, of an attempt to support a view or a hypothesis by choosing the most suitable evidence—and this applies to those who invoke texts for a first-millennium date as much as to those who invoke others for a higher date' (1980: 47). On the other hand, social customs probably survived basically unchanged for centuries, and therefore cannot form a basis for dating the patriarchal period (Freedman 1961: 205; Selman 1980: 125). Social and legal customs form just one aspect of the patriarchal lifestyle, and their comparative study may not necessarily point to a precise date of the patriarchal period. This in turn has led to a rethinking of methodological presuppositions by various scholars.[20] The question is: how can different scholars arrive at widely divergent conclusions despite using the same source material? The answer is not too far to seek. From Alt onwards the study of patriarchal religion has been pursued in a historical framework despite the fact that the sources in Genesis stand at a considerable historical remove from the patriarchal period they depict. As a result, scholars are not in a position to date patriarchal traditions accurately and to relate them to a wider historical context.[21]

The 'quest for the historical patriarchs' has been thoroughly pursued by scholars. However, on the one hand, the evidence is not sufficient to date the patriarchs accurately, and, on the other hand, neither Thompson's argument that the patriarchal narratives are unhistorical nor Van Seters's use of first-millennium parallels has proved to be satisfactory. Nevertheless, the enormous efforts spent on comparative studies of patriarchal customs in order to ascertain the historicity of the patriarchal stories, though in my view a misplaced emphasis, have not been entirely fruitless.[22] One of the significant results of these studies has been

77-84. For a critique of Van Seters and others, see Selman 1980: 115-17. Also cf. the different opinions on dating of patriarchs on the basis of the personal names found in the Near Eastern texts: Gordon 1953: 102-104; Thompson 1974: 22-52.

20. E.g. Miller 1977, Luke, Talmon, Warner, Millard and Selman.

21. It is unnecessary for my purpose here to go into the details of discussions over the use, misuse or non-use of comparative social customs in order to establish the historicity of the patriarchal narratives.

22. E.g. the inheritance rights of a slave, or the son of a slave-girl. While these customs may reflect certain aspects of the patriarchal lifestyle, they are not the overriding concern of the narrator who was probably transmitting what his traditions, oral or written, contained. The narrator himself does not intend to draw any

the clarification of the methodological confusion of previous studies and the establishment of guidelines for comparing external data with the patriarchal narratives (cf. n. 20 above). Secondly, the distribution of the parallels over a wide period of time does not disprove the historicity of the patriarchal stories, but they paint a general picture of the ancient Near Eastern family and social practices and thereby the historicity of the patriarchal narratives has been placed in a wider context (Selman 1980: 114-15; Westermann 1985: 74, 85, 86). This insight may be combined with the biblical tradition's own testimony, which places the patriarchs in the period before the exodus and sojourn in Egypt.[23] As Selman rightly notes, to seek parallels in the first half of the second millennium 'is not due to prejudice but is based on a recognition of the biblical scheme. Unless this pattern is rejected as being entirely unhistorical, it is in the earlier material that contacts might initially be expected to be found, although any proper study of the chronological setting of a Patriarchal Age must include consideration of alternative periods' (Selman 1980: 121; cf. Millard 1980: 51). Westermann's epoch-making commentary on Genesis has led the discussion in this direction.

Westermann extensively surveys various literary-, form- and traditio-historical studies of the patriarchal narratives and the archaeological studies that focus on the lifestyle, practices and customs of various peoples of the world of the patriarchs (1985: 23-86). His conclusions are very revealing. He observes that the patriarchal stories are the product of a long process of tradition, and were probably transmitted orally in their earliest stages. 'We will never achieve complete certainty as to which texts in Gen. 12–50 come from the patriarchal period…', Westermann notes. 'We can, however, be quite certain that one cannot contest the possibility that texts, narratives, and motifs in Gen. 12–50 reach back into the patriarchal period.'[24] It is not possible to fix the patriarchal period by historical data or by the nomadic lifestyle or by

conclusions from them. For this very reason, it is possible that they are valuable for historical information.

23. This is based on the consistent testimony of the genealogies, the chronological data and the historical narratives of the Old Testament. Warner 1977: 59; Selman 1980: 121; cf. Bimson 1980: 81-85.

24. Westermann 1985: 40 cf. 34; cf. Moberly 1992: 198; Albertz 1994: 28. Sarna (1989: xv-xvii) argues that the internal evidence of Genesis itself is sufficient to suggest that Genesis reflects an authentic picture of early historical traditions.

customs and practices from the surrounding world because of the nature of the data and its diffusion into an extended period of 2200 to 1200 BCE. Thus 'it was possible to revive J. Wellhausen's hypothesis, or even to outdo it, by contesting any talk of a patriarchal period at all' (Westermann 1985: 85). Nevertheless, the political, economic and religious life presented in the narratives is so distinct from that of later Israel, as known to us from the rest of the Old Testament, that 'there remains no alternative but to set the group with the form of community presented in the patriarchal stories prior to the period of the tribes' (Westermann 1985: 86).

For Westermann, the issue of patriarchal religion cannot be resolved as long as the debate is restricted to the designations or names of God used in Genesis.[25] If the patriarchal narratives received definitive shape in the period of the early monarchy, and if the Yahwist made his indelible mark on the traditions, not only is it not always possible to distinguish whether a particular text is speaking about Yahweh or the God of the fathers, as J makes no distinction between them, but also it is impossible to know to what extent the theology of the Yahwist has affected other aspects of the patriarchal religion and the final form of the text.[26] But this need not lead us to despair because one can still identify certain traits peculiar to patriarchal religion, such as the personal relationship between the patriarchs and their God,[27] the unconditional promises relating to the patriarchal situation,[28] the lack of priesthood and temple, the lack of holiness relating to God, the lack of the concept of sin and judgment, and the family-based patriarchal society (Westermann 1985: 108-13; Moberly 1992b: 84-87). Westermann argues further that there are different forms of religion within patriarchal religion; for instance, we find that the form of worship in Genesis 12–25 is characterized by building altars and calling upon the name of Yahweh, but in Genesis 25–36 by raising pillars and anointing them.[29] However,

25. This point was already noted by Wenham 1980: 160; later by Moberly 1992a: 79.

26. Similar methodological questions are raised by Moberly 1992a: 83.

27. Fohrer 1973: 35-42; Westermann 1985: 109; Heimerdinger 1992: 41-55; Albertz 1994: 29, 33, 34; cf. Cazelles 1975: 141-56.

28. Alt 1929; Eissfeldt 1968: 50-62; Westermann 1985; Wenham 1980: 172-75; 1994: xxxiv-xxxv; Mettinger 1988: 63. Contra Hoftijze 1956; Rendtorff 1979; Van Seters 1980; Blum 1985.

29. Westermann 1985: 107. This factor was already observed by Dillmann 1897: 227-28.

these and other distinctive features of patriarchal religion have not been pursued further by Westermann. They are only mentioned in the introduction to his commentary and commented on briefly, often with special reference to their distinctiveness, but they are not treated in a comprehensive way.

With Köckert's recent work, *Vätergott und Väterverheißungen*, the whole post-Alt debate about patriarchal religion receives a major analysis and appraisal. As Moberly rightly points out, Köckert for the most part focuses his attention on the agenda set by Alt, giving extensive discussion of pre-Yahwistic divine appellations, possible religio-historical analogies, the promises to the patriarchs and their relationship to the election of the fathers. Unlike Westermann, Köckert rejects Alt's hypothesis of patriarchal nomadism which is based on an assumed polarity between the desert and the arable land, between nomadism and sedentarism. He contends that various references to *'El* in Genesis are not in themselves homogeneous, referring to a distinctive type of deity and his worship, and that customs described in Genesis cannot be read off as reliable indicators of second-millennium religious practices. Even if the individual elements within the patriarchal traditions can be seen as much earlier, they do not form a basis for constructing a detailed history of the patriarchal period, still less of the type of religion in which the patriarchs may have engaged. Köckert's view of patriarchal religion hinges primarily on his dating of the patriarchal narratives to the seventh or sixth century BCE. Building on the work of Albertz,[30] he argues that the practices they depict are not distinct from the popular religion prevalent alongside the official Yahwism of that period.[31] Further, Köckert rejects Alt's view that the promises to the fathers are evidence for the idea of their being chosen. This idea was based on two pre-requisites—an understanding of the sovereignty of God, and the special position of Israel in regard to this God of all nations. But neither of these featured either during Israel's early history or in any kind of clan religion. 'It was not Israel's nomadic ancestors, but their descendants in the exile and afterward who interpreted their ancestors in relation to God in such a way, thus learning for themselves that they were

---

30. Albertz 1978: 77-91. However, Albertz (1994a: 187) suggests that popular piety changed in the late monarchy under Assyrian and Deuteronomistic influence.

31. Köckert 1988: 141-47, 309-11. A similar view has already been posited by Van Seters (1980), who thought that the Genesis material originated in Israel's popular piety before the Deuteronomic reform.

chosen in their forefathers' (Köckert 1988: 198, cf. 163-64). However, while Köckert's own theory is less convincing, as we shall see below, he gives little attention to the distinctive traits as outlined by Westermann and others.[32]

Moberly pertinently counters this approach in his recent work, *The Old Testament of the Old Testament*:

> If patriarchal religion was in reality popular or family piety contemporary with but outside the mainstream of official Mosaic Yahwism, it is difficult to see why the pentateuchal writers, who are effectively the definitive exponents of official Mosaic Yahwism in Exodus-Deuteronomy, should have done what such a hypothesis requires. They have given traditions depicting non-Yahwistic ethos and practices the considerable luster of inseparable association with the ancestor of Israel's faith, Abraham, and the eponymous ancestor of the whole nation, Jacob/Israel. They have refrained from all adverse comment. And they have gone to considerable lengths to relate such material to Mosaic Yahwism... One would have thought that straightforward suppression would not only have been easier but also more in keeping with the generally exclusive and polemical nature of Yahwism in Exodus–Deuteronomy (1992a: 195).

Further, he argues that, while it is difficult to reconstruct patriarchal religion in accordance with the canons of modern historiography, 'an explanation of patriarchal religion as a disguised form of non-Yahwistic religion in the seventh or sixth centuries [is] extremely implausible', for three important reasons: the Yahwistic respect for patriarchal religion, its coherence and distinctiveness within the pentateuchal traditions, and the undoubted antiquity of the divine, human and geographical names compounded with El (1992a: 195-97). On the other hand, 'a clear general presumption in favour of an early and historically rooted context for the patriarchal traditions as a whole' emerges from the traditions themselves, although some elements in them may be recognized as 'originating from their interpretation and use in the context of the Exile' (1992a: 198). Thus Moberly attempts to unravel 'a tradition of a distinctive patriarchal religion' (1992a: 84) preserved by all the pentateuchal writers in order to reconstruct its distinctive features. Accordingly he highlights: patriarchal monotheism which is completely devoid

32. Since my main focus will be on the latter aspects, to which Köckert gives only a passing comment (1988: 160-61), his conclusions will not affect my hypothesis. Cf. Moberly 1992a: 195-96.

of the polemic or exclusivism of later Mosaic Yahwism; cultic practices featuring pillars and trees which were condemned in later Yahwism; and the lack of priests and prophets, of moral content and of the
notion of holiness, all of which are distinctive features of the Mosaic
Yahwism. Moberly admits that one cannot offer a comprehensive picture of patriarchal religion but can only show what is distinctive to it. In
this book, however, an attempt will be made at attaining a comprehensive picture of the distinctive cultic practices of the patriarchs, such as
altars, prayer, pillars, tithes, vows and purification rites. It is hoped that
such an attempt will show not only the religious ethos of the patriarchs
but also its distinctiveness in relation to both the ancient Near Eastern
and later Israelite religions.

2. *Method*

The chief aim of this study, therefore, is to describe in detail the various
cultic practices performed by the patriarchs according to the patriarchal
narratives. In other words, the primary sources for this study are the
patriarchal narratives themselves, as preserved in Genesis 12–50, because these practices are mentioned only in these narratives and not
outside them. In this case, it is necessary to ask certain fundamental
questions concerning the origin, history and nature of the texts at hand,
and the best way to handle them to achieve my objective of describing
the 'religion of the patriarchs as portrayed in the patriarchal narratives'.
This objective necessarily betrays an assumption that there is such a
thing as the religion of the patriarchs portrayed in the texts. That this
assumption is compatible with the nature of the texts themselves has
already been shown above and will be further discussed below. Whereas
it is beyond the scope of this book to go into the details of the origin
and history of the text of Genesis, a survey of the methods used so far
reveals the problems involved in such a study.

However, it appears that no single method has an exclusive claim to
the explication of the texts. Those who follow the source-critical
approach have generally assumed that the ideas and people portrayed in
the narratives originated with the texts, and the texts that purport to
describe events of periods earlier than the monarchy are generally considered retrojections. Thus the patriarchal narratives have little historical value in them.[33] The form and traditio-historical methods, however,

---

33. Wellhausen 1885: 9 and other literary critics accepted that the documents

assume that the narratives have a historical kernel and that many texts and ideas go back to the patriarchal period.[34] Similarly, the archaeological approach assumes the essential historicity of the patriarchs. Literary criticism, on the other hand, focuses solely on the literary aspects of the narratives, giving little or no attention to their history or theology.[35] While it is legitimate to pursue this kind of inquiry, it does not do complete justice to the intentions of the authors. It is true that attention to the language, style and all the artistry of composition focuses on the given text rather than the supposed background (Muilenburg 1969: 7; Alter 1981: 12, 21 cf. 14), but this does not necessarily discern the overall purpose of the author. Like other methods which were preoccupied with origins and historicity, this method might become bogged down, this time with literary form.

However, the Genesis authors seem to be concerned more with content and purpose than with the form of the materials they were handling.[36] I will focus on the overall content and purpose of the Genesis authors in the present book. This may be better achieved by a synchronic approach to the Genesis texts, rather than by the diachronic approach followed by traditional source, form and traditio-historical methods. The latter basically assume the composite nature of the texts and attempt to recover the original text behind the present one. Perhaps inevitably, these methods result in conflicting theories about the origin and date of the texts and the ideas contained in them (cf. Westermann 1985: 30). This is one of the chief reasons why literary critics have been dissatisfied with them.[37] But by a synchronic approach one takes the given text or book as a unit despite the disparate materials brought together by the final author. This has the merit of allowing one to look at the patriarchal narratives as they stand before one. It assumes that the final author or editor has an overall plan and purpose for their present

were ultimately based on some pre-literary oral traditions, but these were completely transformed in the documents which thus have no historical value. Cf. Whybray 1987: 22-28.

34. Gunkel 1902; Alt 1929 = 1989; von Rad 1965; Westermann 1985; 1986.

35. This is plainly admitted by several structuralists, e.g. Jacobson 1974: 157; cf. Exum 1973: 47; Boadt 1973: 20-34, though this was not the aim of the early critics, e.g. Muilenburg 1969: 1-18. For a representative sample of this approach and further bibliography, see House 1992.

36. For instance, Gen. 12.1-3, 17; 13.8-13; 14.24; 15.6; 17.1-2 and 22.1, 17, 18 state or imply that the author has a definite purpose for including these traditions.

37. Alter 1981: 14; Gunn 1987: 69-70; Clements 1989: 11-12; House 1992: 8.

form and place in their present context. It does not attempt to discover the texts behind the present ones and the various intermediary stages.[38] In this regard I follow the literary-critical approach, but unlike the literary approach, I will not study the patriarchal narratives for their artistic worth as literature, however legitimate this may be. At the same time I do not discard insights provided by any of the methods mentioned above. For this reason, I frequently discuss the issue of sources in this book and evaluate critical findings. I am chiefly concerned with the perspective of the final author for several reasons: first, it is the synchronic approach that allows one to look at Genesis as a whole in its final form. This is a more certain basis than are the supposed sources and their redaction. The final author intended these sources to be read in their present order. The Jewish and Christian communities have read the Bible in this manner for over two millennia. Any attempt to bypass the final author is to suppress his voice and intention. Secondly, to date there has been little study of patriarchal religion from such a perspective, though several studies from this perspective have appeared on different themes of Genesis.[39] Thirdly, only the final author's perspective allows one to see the patriarchal life and religion as a unified whole, since there is a consistency about his portrayal of the patriarchs in regard to their social life, beliefs and customs.

A further feature of my approach is a comparison of the ancient Near Eastern and later Israelite cultic practices with the patriarchal practices. There are two reasons for this. First, it is universally agreed that the patriarchal traditions were written from the perspective of Yahwism, the official religion of the Israelite nation. Hence, one may safely presuppose that the patriarchal traditions were coloured by the ideas and perspectives of Yahwistic authors. Therefore it is logical to expect parallels to patriarchal cultic practices in Israelite traditions. A comparative analysis of Israelite cultic practices might throw light on the patriarchal practices and thus becomes imperative. At the same time, the assumption that the patriarchal traditions were coloured by later Yahwistic authors will be constantly tested in the present work. At the very outset it may be noted that the Yahwistic authors of Genesis presup-

---

38. Traditio-historical critics follow this approach, which is considered to be more hypothetical than the source-critical approach. Whybray 1987: 138.

39. Redford (1970) and Coats (1976) on the Joseph story, and Fokkelman (1975) and Fishbane (1979) on the Jacob stories. Wenham (1987: xxxii-xxxvi) and Sarna (1989: xvii-xviii) are among the few commentators to follow this approach.

posed a basic continuity between the faith of the patriarchs and their own only in certain aspects, such as belief in Yahweh, promises to the patriarchs and circumcision, but not in regard to their cultic practices such as building altars, planting trees, calling upon the name of Yahweh, raising pillars, tithing, making vows and performing purificatory rituals. Each of these aspects will be discussed in detail in separate chapters in the body of this work. Thus there is a tension between the beliefs and practices of the patriarchs and that of the authors who portrayed them. The authors of Genesis probably left much unsaid concerning patriarchal cultic practices because of this tension and perhaps also because of their unfamiliarity with these practices. A comparative study of patriarchal and Israelite cultic practices thus becomes important, in order to show the distinctiveness of the former more clearly.

Secondly, a comparative study of patriarchal worship and cultic practices alongside ancient Near Eastern practices becomes equally imperative for several further reasons. First, Israel was not an isolated entity in Canaan. Its historical, cultural, linguistic and religious affinities with neighbours such as Egypt, Assyria and Babylon are undeniable. Many of these aspects can be demonstrated from both the biblical and the archaeological records (Walton 1989: 13, 14; cf. Albertz 1994: 28-29). Therefore the distinctiveness or commonalty of Israel's religion can only be understood or appreciated when set against the religions of its neighbours. Secondly, if the patriarchal lifestyle, beliefs and practices belong to pre-Mosaic and pre-Yahwistic times, one may find parallels from the wider context of the ancient Near East. This is not to prove the historicity of the patriarchs or their beliefs but to see whether non-Yahwistic elements of patriarchal religion have anything in common with the ancient Near East, and how such parallels might help one understand the religion of the patriarchs. This leads me to define the focus of the present study.

3. *Focus and Aim*

Obviously it is impossible to focus on all aspects of patriarchal religion in the patriarchal narratives. As I noted above, only those religious aspects that are distinctive to the patriarchal lifestyle, such as building altars, calling upon the name of Yahweh (praying), planting trees, raising pillars, paying tithes, making vows and performing purification rites will be dealt with in the present volume. The patriarchs are described as engaging in these cultic practices in order to maintain their religious piety. There is a consistent portrayal about these aspects as being distinctive to their religion and lifestyle. The distinctiveness is not in the aspects themselves but in the way the patriarchs were involved in these practices. Altars and sacrifices were common to ancient Near Eastern and Israelite religions, but altars were not built by individuals nor were sacrifices offered by lay people like the patriarchs. Altars were largely if not entirely present in the organized or popular cult in which priests and sanctuaries occupied the pre-eminent place. Similarly, planting trees or raising pillars in order to worship God is not just unattested in later Israel but explicitly prohibited, yet the writers of Genesis portray these patriarchal practices as normal and even approved by the same God whom they themselves worshipped. They were attested in the ancient Near East, but in the organized cult. Thus patriarchal actions associated with these practices are distinct from the customs of both the ancient Near East and Israel.

Similarly, prayer, tithing, vow-making and purificatory rituals were common in the ancient Near East and Israel, but in the latter they largely took place at sanctuaries with the aid of the priests. Moreover, nearly every religious practice had detailed legislation. In contrast, there is no legislation on any of these practices in the patriarchal narratives. Most of them were carried out voluntarily by the patriarchs, except that Abraham and Jacob were each asked once to build an altar. In most of the cultic activities the patriarchs themselves were the officiants, but this was not condemned or disapproved by the later writers, although contrary to their own beliefs. These distinctive patriarchal cultic practices have hardly been studied so far, and only Westermann, Wenham and Moberly have given any attention to them. Moberly in particular devotes a chapter especially to highlighting the distinctive character of the religion of the patriarchs. He contends that all the major pentateuchal writers in Genesis, that is, J, E and P, portrayed a distinctively pre-Mosaic or non-Yahwistic character of the patriarchal period in lifestyle, beliefs, customs and values. As Moberly's approach is theological, he takes his cue from the Priestly writer's claim that God was not known to the patriarchs by the name of Yahweh. From this he goes on to demonstrate that all the other authors of Genesis maintained a distinct pattern of God's dealings with the patriarchs from that of Israel.[40] He especially focuses on patriarchal monotheism (despite the

40. However, only P seems to be a true Yahwist, J and E do not seem to share

different divine names used in the patriarchal narratives and later Israelite traditions), cultic practices, holiness and morality (Moberly 1992a: 87-104). But he does not deal in any detail with the patriarchal religious and cultic practices, though these probably represent the core of their religion. Even with other aspects, he does no more than highlight the distinctive nature of these elements in contrast to their portrayal in later Israelite religion. Thus there is a serious gap in relation to research on patriarchal religion. The present work undertakes to bridge this gap by dealing with the patriarchal religious and cultic practices in detail. What I propose to do is to demonstrate the distinctive character of patriarchal religion from its religious and cultic practices as portrayed in Genesis. For the reasons given above, my focus will be limited to these aspects.

Other aspects, such as the nature of the God of the fathers, the promises to the patriarchs and the rite of circumcision, will not receive attention in this book, partly due to constraints on space and partly due to the excessive attention already given to them. Further, these do not count as religious or cultic aspects in which the patriarchs were engaged in order to maintain their religious piety. These aspects are related to the aspect of the patriarchs' faith, which is a necessary corollary of their religion. Although the authors of Genesis portrayed God's dealings with the patriarchs and his unconditional promises to them as distinctive, the authors made no distinction between the God of the patriarchs and the God of Israel. Even P, who states that Yahweh was not known to the patriarchs, believed this.[41] Similarly, the significance of circumcision as the sign of the covenant remained the same for both the patriarchs and Israel. Therefore these aspects may be considered not as religious acts but as the theological basis for patriarchal or Israelite faith.

To this end I will deal with the following aspects of the religion of the patriarchs: altars and sacrifices (Chapter 2), prayer or calling upon the name of Yahweh (Chapter 3), pillars or *maṣṣēbôth* (Chapter 4), tithes (Chapter 5), vows (Chapter 6), ritual purification (Chapter 7). As already noted above, there is a coherence about the theme of the first three aspects, as together they constitute patriarchal worship. Building

the Yahwistic ethos, at least in the Genesis account of the patriarchal narratives. See Chapter 2 n. 68.

41. P consistently avoids using the name Yahweh in the patriarchal narratives (except twice in the framework); Wenham 1980: 161-62.

altars, praying and raising pillars (Chapters 2–4) are usually a response to theophanies, thus suggesting that they form a patriarchal pattern of worship, while the other three aspects (Chapters 5–7) may be described as patriarchal religious practices. The presence of certain sacred trees in Genesis and the significance of Abraham planting a tamarisk will be dealt with under altars and prayer (Chapters 2 and 3). This is appropriate here because of Abraham's frequent camping and building altars at places where the holy trees were supposed to have been, and Abraham's calling upon the name of Yahweh following the planting of a tamarisk tree. A tree appears once in the Jacob cycle but with little or no religious significance. In each chapter, the ancient Near Eastern and Israelite backgrounds will be dealt with first, then the patriarchal traditions will be dealt with comparing or contrasting with the former's traditions wherever relevant.

Chapter 2

ALTARS AND SACRIFICES

1. *Introduction*

As mentioned above, I shall first deal with those aspects related to the
patriarchal pattern of worship such as altars and sacrifices, prayer and
pillars. Among these, however, altars and sacrifices deserve to be
treated first because they are not only attested in all the patriarchal
cycles but also they appear to form the core of their worship. Prayer
will be dealt with next, because it naturally follows the building of
altars in the patriarchal narratives. Thus the idea of prayer embraces the
connotation of both worship and the general concept of petition in this
book. Pillars will be dealt with next because they appear only in the
Jacob cycle, though they also indicate Jacob's pattern of worship.

As in Canaan, the places where the patriarchs erected altars and
offered sacrifices were usually the same places where they experienced
theophanies (cf. Alt 1989: 20-21). However, one may also find both
Mesopotamian and Israelite elements in patriarchal worship, since Mesopotamia was the original home of the patriarchs and since the authors
were Yahwists themselves. Therefore it is necessary to paint a broader
picture of the ancient Near East and of later Israelite practices in order
to see which ones elucidate the patriarchal practices most. My approach
will be, for each of these cultures and for Israel, first to examine the
various occasions when sacrifices were offered and the types of sacrifices presented, and then to seek to explain their nature as to how
they were viewed and what they were expected to achieve for the
worshipper.

However, the occasion, types of sacrifices and ritual procedures in
both the ancient Near East and Israel are much more varied and elaborate than in patriarchal narratives. Furthermore, the context of sacrifices in the latter is radically different from that of the former, where
the places of sacrifices are usually temples and the officiants usually the

appointed priests. Consequently, how the sacrifices were viewed and what they were intended to achieve in these cultures is also different from that of the patriarchal narratives. In contrast, sacrifices in the patriarchal narratives occur in two contexts, namely formal worship and special occasions. While the former followed a theophany, movement to a new place or long-term encampment, the latter were occasioned by a covenant, a command of God or thanksgiving. Thus my focus on Near Eastern and Israelite materials will be limited to those aspects that will illuminate the occasion and types of sacrifices in the patriarchal narratives, while other aspects may be touched upon in passing.

2. *Sacrifice in the Ancient Near East*

In what follows, I shall examine the occasion, types and nature of sacrifice in Mesopotamian, Egyptian, Hittite and Canaanite cultures in order to compare how they relate to each other and what light they can throw on Israelite and patriarchal sacrifice. The notion behind sacrifice in the ancient Near East seems to be 'offering' or 'giving' something as gift or tribute to a deity.[1] There are close similarities between the words used for 'incense offering', 'animal sacrifice', 'ritual slaughter' and 'libation' in the Akkadian, Phoenician, Ugaritic, Hebrew and other cognate languages.[2] Whether terminological similarity indicates borrowing from one culture to the other or not, it certainly suggests that the practice of sacrifice is common to all these cultures.

a. *In Mesopotamia*
Occasion and Types. Sacrifices in Babylonia were offered on various occasions, such as the dedication of a temple,[3] which probably included the dedication of altars; before battles; after battle in order to give thanks for the help of the gods (Jastrow 1898: 224; 1905: 234; Oesterley 1937: 56); and for healing of the sick. In the last case either

---

1.   Gray 1925: 3-4; cf. Smith 1927: 244-45; Yerkes 1953: 25-26; van Baal 1976: 161-78.

2.   *KAI*, 214: 15-22; *DISO*, 71; *Ug.*, V: 586-88; *TDOT*, IV: 11; Milgrom 1991: 713-14. It may be pointed out here that the Deuteronomic use of the word זבח may refer to the festive meal where sacrificial meat is consumed (Deut. 12.15, 21; 15.21).

3.   Jastrow 1898: 215, 663; 1905: 225; Oesterley 1937: 56. Incidentally, this has parallels in both the Ras Shamra tablets and the Old Testament (1 Kgs 6–8, Solomon's dedication of the temple).

sympathetic magic was carried out on the sacrificial animals by removing their inward parts, symbolizing the removal of sickness (Jastrow
1905: 350), or they were presented as substitutionary offerings, especially to the gods of the underworld to cause them to give up their
claims on the sick. If the king was sick, a human substitute was installed in order that he might draw to himself the evil that had threatened the king, and thus deliver the king 'through his own natural or
otherwise induced death' (von Soden 1994: 193). Von Soden rightly
observes that the ritual sometimes presents a disguised form of human
sacrifice.[4]

While elaborate sacrifices were offered during festivals (Jastrow
1898: 676-77), daily sacrifices,[5] *sattûku* and *ginû* (both terms meaning
'fixed', 'perpetual') were attested only for larger cult centres, such as
Babylonia, Borshippa, Sippar, Cuthah and Nineveh.[6]

The most common type of sacrifices among the Babylonians were the
gift-offerings, which included animal sacrifices, libations and offerings
of farm-produce. Both kings and commoners made these offerings at
sanctuaries on special occasions, either as a direct act of worship to a
god or to fulfil a vow. Sometimes the statues of the gods were offered
to the temple as gifts, along with costly wood, precious stones and
garments (Jastrow 1898: 669-75; Oesterley 1937: 56-57). Frequent
references to oil and wine in sacrifice suggest that such items represented some sort of sacrifice. Stones in temples, palace foundations,
and stones bearing commemorative or votive inscriptions were often
anointed with oil, wine or honey (Jastrow 1898: 664-65). Jacob's
anointing of a pillar, which in the context may suggest the founding of
a temple, has close parallels here (see Chapter 4).

Certain texts also suggest that the one who offered the sacrifices was
expected to be 'bright' or 'resplendent', probably indicating ethical concerns.[7] Offerings and sacrifices were made even by laymen, although
before making an offering they had to wash their hands in ordinary

---

4.   Von Soden 1994: 194. Cf. Jastrow 1898: 662; *TDOT*, IV: 17.

5.   Presented each morning and evening, but there is only one reference to a
noon meal; Oppenheim 1964: 188.

6.   Cf. the Pentateuchal institution of the *tamîd*, and its technical usage in Dan.
8.11. However, the number of sacrifices vary according to the popularity of the
deity and its temple; Jastrow 1898: 667.

7.   *CAD*, XXI: 106. Cf. Jacob's call for purification before sacrifice (Gen. 35.1-
4).

water, whereas the priests washed theirs in running water.[8] As in Israel, certain portions of the sacrificial animal, such as the right thigh or shoulder, the loins and hide, the rump and tendons, and part of the stomach, were reserved for the priest (Sayce 1902: 472).

Nature of Sacrifice. Sacrifices were commonly viewed as a food to the gods in Old Babylonian and Neo-Assyrian texts (e.g. the hungry gods in the Epic of Gilgamesh),[9] and mankind was created to provide for their food (e.g. Sumerian and Akkadian myths; Lambert-Millard 1969: 15). It was believed that gods, like men, died and needed nourishment to continue in the afterlife.[10] The idea that offerings had to be pure, holy and of first quality is also present in Mesopotamia.[11]

There is no clear concept of a 'burnt offering' (*CAD*, XXI: 105; *TDOT*, IV: 17) since the sacrificial meat was usually cooked before it was offered.[12] The deities were viewed in some mysterious way as consuming the offerings, either by looking at them or by having them waved in front of their eyes (Oppenheim 1964: 191-92). Further, the sacrifices were usually described as pleasing to the gods (*CAD*, XXI: 105). It is, however, disputed among scholars whether those who offered sacrifice thereby had table fellowship with the gods.[13]

b. *In Egypt*
Occasion and Types of Sacrifice. The most common of the Egyptian sacrifices were the daily sacrifices[14] and incense offerings[15] to both

---

8.   Oesterley 1937: 58. Cf. the patriarchal practice, the lay Israelite also assisted (Lev. 3) the priests while offering sacrifices.

9.   Lambert-Millard 1969: 99; cf. Tigay 1982: 224-27; Hallo 1983: 165-80, esp. ll. 375-76; Lambert 1993: 194.

10. Jastrow 1905: 511; cf. Oesterley 1937: 58, 59; *TDOT*, IV: 16; von Soden 1994: 188.

11. *CAD*, XXI: 105; *TDOT*, IV: 17; Jastrow 1898: 661-62; Sayce 1902: 466-67, 471-72; von Soden 1994: 188-89.

12. Cf. the Arabs who rarely offer fire-sacrifices. They simply smear the blood of the sacrificed animal on the sacred stone or pour it into the receptacle, *ghabghab,* for the offering; Wellhausen 1897: 116.

13. *CAD* (XXI: 105) implies; Oppenheim (1964: 191), *TDOT* (IV: 17) deny; *ERE* (IX: 33), Dhorme (1949: 231-32), Oesterley (1937: 58) and Frankena (1961: 199-207) claim.

14. The rituals include the daily services, from opening the temple doors and

gods and deified pharaohs.[16] Texts from the tenth century BCE and earlier describe daily sacrifices of incense, libations and all sorts of food at Karnak, Thebes and Dendera (*ANET*, 325; Lichtheim 1980: 106-108). Public festivals were important occasions when many sacrifices were offered including 'elevation of offerings' (Nelson 1949: 327-29, 331; cf. Lev. 23.9-21). Sacrifices were also offered at the time of the king's accession to the throne (*ERE*, XI: 32).

The sacrificial materials represent both domestic and wild animals and birds, besides various kinds of foods and fruits (*TDOT*, IV: 14; *ERE*, XI: 32). The foreleg of an ox is the choicest offering, and geese are the most commonly sacrificed birds (cf. Faulkner 1969: 26-27).

Offerings to the dead form a special feature of the Egyptian sacrifice. A number of tomb inscriptions from the Fifth and Sixth Dynasties (twenty-fifth–twenty-fourth centuries BCE)[17] describe daily and seasonal (festivals) offerings, but it is not clear if they were meant for the care of the dead or were offered to a deity. The concern of the inscriptions, however, appears to be to pray for their good reception in the land of the dead (Lichtheim 1973: 15-27). The texts aim to promote the resurrection and ascension of the dead in order for them to join the company of the immortal gods. The texts are also concerned with the purification of the dead (*ANET*, 325; Faulkner 1969: 7, 20, 21). Besides choice food and drink, the offerings include perfume, eye-paint and sandals for the journey of the deceased. Most, if not all, suggest that they are part of a daily care for the dead (Faulkner 1969: 21-40).

Nature of Sacrifice. Like the Babylonians, the Egyptians viewed sacrifices as food for the gods. Frequently sacrifices were also viewed as representing the enemies of the gods. At festivals persons representing the enemies of the gods were beaten nearly to death and prisoners of war were slaughtered regularly before the gods.[18] In most cases

awakening the deity to the feeding and disposal of the left-overs and finally to closing the doors; Nelson 1949: 201-32; 310-45.

15. It is technically called 'the utterance for striking the fire'.

16. Notable among them are Imhotep and Amenhotep; Lichtheim 1980: 104.

17. Funerary texts also occur in the pyramid of King Ibi of Eighth Dynasty, and in the *maṣṣēbāh* tombs of several nobles of the middle kingdom and, sporadically, in tombs of the New Kingdom and the Late Dynastic period down to the Thirtieth Dynasty; Hayes 1953: 82-83; Lichtheim 1973: 29.

18. In the civilized cults of later times many of these barbarities were preserved only in symbolic form; Hayes 1953: 78.

the victim represents both nourishment and the enemy of the god (*TDOT*, IV: 15).

With regard to the sacrifices to the dead, there is a clear distinction in presentation between offerings to the dead and offerings to the gods. While there is confession of innocence and affirmation of purity when offering to the gods, offering to the dead contains no such description of the servitor. On the contrary, some of the offerings to the dead were expected to effect purification in order for the recipient to attain resurrection (Faulkner 1969: 62, 103, 104 *passim*; Lichtheim 1973: 33-34). So the view that the Egyptians did not venerate their dead commends itself so long as the offering to the deified pharaohs does not suggest in itself a cult of the dead.[19]

c. *Among the Hittites*
Occasion and Types of Sacrifice. Public sacrifices were offered to different gods when the foundations of a new palace were laid (*ANET*, 358). The significance of the animal species for the particular gods is, however, not stated. Sacrifices were also made during the festivals, especially a seasonal festival Puruli, and the New Year Festival (Gaster 1966: 245-46; Gurney 1977: 32). The congregation received a share of food and drink after it had been blessed by the king (Gurney 1977: 33-34).

There were three semi-public occasions when the Hittites offered sacrifices. The first was when substitutionary offerings were made to purify the god, temple and the royal family who were suspected to be contaminated by evil or impurity (*ANET*, 346; cf. the Day of Atonement [Lev. 16] in Israel). The second was when people were dying of pestilence, substitute offerings were made of a ram or a bull or a ewe or even a human substitute and were sent to the enemy land in order to carry away the infection[20] and to appease the enemy gods.[21] The third occasion was before battle (*ANET*, 354-55). Occasionally, human sacrifice, along with the animals, was made in the case of military defeat.

19. *ERE* (XI: 32), *TDOT* (IV: 15) and Hayes (1953: 81) imply a cult of the dead among the Egyptians, while Morenz (1973: 204) denies it.

20. In one of the rituals the infection was transferred to the animal by laying on of hands by the performers.

21. In some rituals the technical word for 'scapegoat', *nakkuš*, 'let go, dispatch', was mentioned. Gurney 1977: 48, 49, 51; cf. *ANET*, 347.

The procedures of such sacrifice are surprisingly similar to the covenant sacrifice in Gen. 15.9-18:

> If the troops have been beaten by the enemy they perform a ritual 'behind' the river, as follows: they 'cut through' a man, a goat, a puppy, and little pig; they place half on this side and half on that, and in front they make a gate…and in front of the gate they light fires on this side and on that, and the troops walk right through, and when they come to the river they sprinkle water over them (Gurney 1952: 151).

Human substitution for pestilence and human sacrifice for defeat in a battle may suggest the community's view that extreme calamity requires the costliest sacrifice.

Besides these, private sacrifices were offered on various occasions according to the needs of the individuals, such as against sickness (*ANET*, 348-49), for moral offences and for the dead. In the case of sickness, a fir tree was planted either side of the temple gate, and the priestess asked the god to deliver the individual from the evil sickness (cf. Abraham in Gen. 21.33). In a ritual against impotence, libations and sacrifices were offered, and the priestess made vows to give a house, a pillar or a statue to the deity if the patient became well (*ANET*, 349-50).

With regard to moral offences, a bird and a lamb were offered as a peace offering for sin, imprecation and false testimony.[22] Some texts also mention silver, gold and valuable articles, probably offered as the price for a 'guilt-offering' (*ku-iš du-at*),[23] either in place of or in addition to the animal sacrifices, and finally with a declaration of atonement (Weinfeld 1983: 106-107).

As in Egypt, sacrifices to the dead are also attested in Hittite rituals. In a 14-day ritual carried out when the king or queen died, an ox was slaughtered and a goat was waved over the body and a libation was poured for the soul of the deceased. Silver, gold and precious stones were weighed in the scales as a price to appease the chthonic deities.[24]

22. Weinfeld 1983: 105-106, 106 n. 51; for transliteration and interpretation of the text (KUB, xli: 11), see Hoffner 1973: 86-87.

23. Hoffner (1973: 88), translates it as an offering to 'make it good'. This probably corresponds to the biblical אשם offering of restitution; cf. Milgrom 1973: 299-300.

24. Sacrifices were also directed toward chthonic deities during a ritual for absolving a house from guilt; Weinfeld 1983: 110.

The sacrifices were primarily propitiatory in order that the dead might not pose a threat to the living (Gurney 1977: 62).

Nature of Sacrifice. As in other ancient Near Eastern religions, Hittites viewed sacrifices as food to the gods: the daily, monthly and New Year sacrifices may not be stopped (*ANET*, 399), and the food and drink dedicated to the gods may not be shared with laymen (Gurney 1952: 150).

The gifts and propitiatory offerings often formed part of ritual healing by magic. First fruits of fields and yearlings of flocks were especially dedicated to the gods, probably suggesting that the Hittites' fields and flocks belonged to their gods. Animals were to be without blemish and deformity, and they were more valued if they had not yet mated, again suggesting the gods' requirement for purity (cf. Lev. 22.17-25). Animals were sacrificed by cutting the throat and the blood was poured out on the ground. Bread and cheese were broken, but the exact implication of this is uncertain (Gurney 1952: 151; 1977: 28). However, shedding of blood in certain sacrifices became both an offering to the chthonic deities and an agent to absolve a house from blood guilt (Gurney 1977: 29), and in some rituals the blood functioned as part of the sharing of a meal to sanctify a covenant (Gurney 1977: 30).

d. *At Ugarit*[25]

Occasion and Types of Sacrifice. A well-preserved ritual text from the Baal-cycle 'prescribes'[26] instructions about the offerings during the New Year festival when various types of sacrifices to Baal and numerous other gods were made.[27] More importantly, these texts also indicate a 'system of classification that specified not only the class of the [required] animal but also its sex' (Levine 1963: 110).

25. With the discovery of a fully developed cult at Ugarit, the Wellhausenian hypothesis that Israel's highly developed cultic system was the mere product of postexilic theocracy has been severely shaken; see Gray 1957: 142. Cf. Weinfeld 1983: 95-129; *ABD*, V: 874. For a detailed argument for the antiquity of P, see Milgrom 1991: 3-12.

26. For a distinction between 'prescriptive' and 'descriptive' rituals, see Levine 1963: 105-11.

27. *KTU*, 1.41; translation from *ARTU*, 157, 158-65. Several copies of this text are extant, suggesting its importance; Levine 1963: 105.

While a Hittite ritual describes sacrifices to be offered when the troops had been defeated, a Ugaritic ritual prescribes sacrifice for averting an enemy's attack on the city:

> O Ba'luma, please chase away the strong one from our gate, the warrior from our walls! The bull, O Ba'lu, we shall consecrate, the vows to Ba'lu we shall fulfil, the firstlings of Ba'lu we shall consecrate, the ḫitpu-sacrifice of Ba'lu we shall fulfil, the tithe of Ba'lu we shall pay, we shall ascend the sanctuary of Ba'lu, the paths of the house of Ba'lu we shall walk.[28]

Only vows, firstlings and tithes are mentioned here. These offerings probably include animal sacrifices. Unfortunately, we cannot be certain what the *ḫitpu* sacrifice means. It may mean just 'offering' or 'food offering' (Boyd 1986: 64 n. 24). One may recall an actual situation when Samuel offered a suckling lamb as a whole burnt offering at the time when the Philistines were attacking Israel (1 Sam. 7.9-10). The text seems to draw attention to the time of attack and the sacrifice, as in the Ugaritic text. Further prayer is also mentioned in both the texts. There seems to be no antecedent or prescription on this matter in Israel. It is possible that Israel adapted this practice from the Canaanites.

Sacrifice by individuals with regard to childlessness is attested in the legends of Keret and Aqhat. In the former legend, El asked Keret, who was bereaved of all his wives and children, to offer sacrifice in order to receive children. The text mentions ritual cleansing prior to sacrifice and the raising of hands, a symbolic gesture in prayer, and then goes on to prescribe sheep, fowl, bird, wine and honey as sacrificial materials.[29] Though it is uncertain if a libation offering is meant here (Gray 1957: 145; Gordon 1965: 413-14), it is rather unlikely that wine would have been mentioned with no motive of a drink offering. Bread loaves and wine are often mentioned in relation to drink offering in the Old Testament.

---

28. *KTU*, 1.119, 26-35; translation from *ARTU*, 173-74.

29. *KTU*, 1.14.ii, 6-26; *ARTU*, 194-95. Cf. *ANET*, 143. The same process is repeated later in the legend, when Keret awakes to perform the actual sacrifice (*KTU*, 1.14.iii, 50-53; *ARTU*, 198-200). Slaughter and sacrifices also occur again in Keret's funeral banquet, which was ordered by the goddess Athiratu who was angered over Keret's broken vow. He promised (probably to the goddess) gold three times the weight of his would-be bride, Hariya, the Tyrian princess, if he would obtain her in marriage.

In the legend of Aqhat, on the other hand, the childless king Dan'el himself offered to the gods 'food', *ylḥm*, and 'drink', *yšqu* (*KTU*, 1.17, 2-3), which were probably 'consecrated oblations',[30] in order to find favour with them so that he might obtain a son who would perform, among other things, funerary rites to his ancestral gods. When the gods granted his wish, Dan'el probably offered sacrifices of thanksgiving for seven days.[31] Later in the legend Dan'el offered sacrifices to the dead ancestors and also to the gods once again, apparently to seek their help to bring Aqhat back from the dead (*ARTU*, 262-63, 267-68, 272).

We have a number of references to sacrifices and offerings, gifts and presents in the myth of Baal and Anath, but all of them were either demanded by one god/goddess on behalf of another god, or offered by one god or group of gods to another.[32] Most of these are undoubtedly related to banquets or drinking parties of the gods and seem to have very little to do with the concept of sacrifice from the human point of view.

Sacrifices to the dead at Ugarit are mainly concerned with the royal ancestral cult in which the king and the priests invoked the spirits, or 'shades' of the dead, the king sacrificed to the seven invoked spirits as they disappear, and the priest finally offered a bird (*ARTU*, 167-68). Sacrifices to the dead are also attested during the New Year festivals, during which the spirits of the deified kings would rise along with Baal the saviour (*KTU*, 1.41, 35-36; *ARTU*, 163, 98 n. 428). Surprisingly, another text, concerned with the care and honour of the deified ancestors, mentions a peace-offering (*KTU*, 1.43, 4-5; *ARTU*, 169). The significance of these offerings, however, is uncertain, although the food

---

30. *ARTU*, 225; cf. *ANET*, 149-50: 'oblation'.

31. *ARTU*, 232. Cf. the biblical peace offerings in Lev. 3; 7.11-12.

32. For instance, the god Radmanu serves to Baal a suckling, a fatling and wine; *ARTU*, 3. Anathu tells El that all other gods must bring gifts and presents to Baal because he is the Almighty; *ARTU*, 18, 53. But Anathu also offers sacrifices at the funeral of Baal; and finally she offers bread and wine to Kotharu on the victory of Baal over Motu; *ARTU*, 83, 98. But Baal also offers sacrificial meal and wine to his brothers and other goddesses, such as the throne gods, chair gods, vase gods and bowl goddess; *ARTU*, 60-61. Even El, the head of the pantheon, sacrifices in his house after advising Yammu to occupy the palace that was originally built for Baal; *ARTU*, 26. On another occasion El says that Baal must bring tribute and gifts to Yammu; *ARTU*, 33. Presents and bribes were offered to Athiratu by other gods; *ARTU*, 50.

for a three-day journey suggests that the sacrifices were concerned with the care for the soul's journey in the afterlife.

Sacrifices for moral offences were signified by the two expressions, *ap* and *npš*, 'offerings concerning anger and (sin of the) soul respectively' (Weinfeld 1983: 108), that occur alongside number of offerings at Ugarit. The context in which they occur refers to the ceremonial ablutions of the new moon day:

[*bym ḥd]t slḥ npš..., slḥ ap w npš*[33]

Both in Ugaritic and biblical ceremonies, the prince was the officiant for this ritual (Ezek. 48.18-25) (Weinfeld 1983: 108-109). Another Ugaritic text that mentions expiatory offerings was concerned with the transgression, *ḥt'*, of the people, who had sinned with anger, *ap*, and impatience, *qṣrt npš*, and asked for forgiveness for themselves, their king, their queen and the strangers living among them.[34]

Nature of Sacrifice. Sacrifices at Ugarit were probably viewed as food for the deities, since the deities themselves were involved in arranging banquets for one another. Besides, the idea of sacrifice both as gift and thank offering is similar to the biblical view of sacrifice.

There are many close similarities between the Ugaritic and the Hittite offerings on the one hand, and the Ugaritic and the biblical offerings on the other. As in the Hittite rituals, Ugaritic texts describe burnt-offerings (*šrp*), peace-offerings *(šlm<m:>)*, and bird-offerings along with silver and gold, though the latter in the Hittite rituals appear to be the price for a guilt-offering. As in the Priestly code, Ugaritic lists of offerings often make specific mention of 'two birds' (*'ṣrm*), 'doves' (*ynt*), and also 'turtledoves' (*tr*), which remind one of the various occasions when birds and doves were offered within the Israelite cult.[35]

---

33. *KTU*, 1.46, 1-2; Weinfeld 1983: 108. Cf. the biblical ritual for the new moon day, Num. 28.11-15; 1 Sam. 20.29.

34. *KTU*, 1.40, 18-19; cf. the similar biblical idea in Num. 15.22-26; Weinfeld 1983: 109.

35. Cf. the burnt offering of the birds in Lev. 1.14, the dove offered for sin offering, burnt offering, and for the woman's purification after childbirth (Lev. 5.17; 12.6); the two birds offered for the lustration of the person with צרעת, and the house cleansed of צרעת (Lev. 14.4-9, 49-53); and those offered for the purification of זב (Lev. 15.14, 19), and the two doves for the *nazir* (Num. 6.10). For other categories in Ugarit whose nature cannot be established, see Hillers 1970: 42; Weinfeld 1983: 109; cf. Urie 1949: 79.

Besides *'āšām* and *ḥaṭṭā't*, the two types of purificatory offerings also known in Israel, many categories were present in Ugarit, suggesting that these were not 'peculiarly Israelite innovations'.[36]

3. *Sacrifice in Israel*

Sacrifice in Israel is too broad a subject to deal with in any detail here. Only an outline of the main occasions, types and nature of sacrifice will be sketched as a basis for comparative analysis between the ancient Near East and Israel on the one hand and between Israel and patriarchal sacrifice on the other.

The various sacrificial offerings in the Old Testament are: the 'burnt offering', עלה; the 'peace offering', שלמים; the 'cereal offering', מנחה; the 'purification offering', חטאת; and the 'guilt offering', אשם. The non-sacrificial offerings which did not involve either slaughter or burning are the tithe, מעשר, the first fruits, בכורים, the wave-offering, תנפה, and the heave-offering, תרמה. In this section I am concerned only with the sacrificial offerings that involved slaughter and partial or complete burning.

Primary attention will be given to the Priestly texts, since the concept of sacrifice and the rules of its performance are the chief concern of them. However, I shall examine other texts at relevant points.

Besides Leviticus, the so-called Priestly texts are found in Exodus 25–40 and in Numbers. The final form of these texts suggest that the priestly regulations were given within the framework of the Sinai Covenant and in the context of the tabernacle (*ABD*, V: 877). The rituals associated with the sacrifices are described in minute detail as to the type of animals required at each occasion, the place of slaughter and the distribution, consumption or disposal of their various parts. This suggests that the entire section comes from a 'Handbook for Priest' (Rainey 1970a: 487; cf. Milgrom 1991: 2).

a. *Occasion and Types of Sacrifice*
Leviticus 1–7 (also Num. 5.5-8; 15.22-31) comprises basic rules for how each sacrifice was to be performed, while other Priestly texts describe how these rules were to be applied to different sacrificial rituals performed on different occasions. These different occasions may be

36. Weinfeld 1983: 109. But Urie (1949: 72, 80) is doubtful about the nature of *ašm* at Ugarit.

categorized, starting from the initiation rituals of the clergy, into: (1) sacrifices at the ordination of the priests and the Levites (Lev. 8, 9; Num. 8); (2) sacrifices at the dedication of the tabernacle (Lev. 8.10-11; Num. 7); (3) daily, monthly, weekly and yearly sacrifices, *tāmīd* (Num. 28–29); (4) sacrifices at festivals (Lev. 16, 23); (5) individuals' sacrifices on various occasions (Lev. 1–7; 12; 13–14; 15) (cf. *ABD*, V: 877).

(1) Sacrifices at the ordination of priests are unattested outside Israel, while the other occasions have many parallels in the ancient Near East. (2) Sacrifices and gifts of cultic furnishings of various kinds on the occasion of the dedication of the temple resemble the dedication of temples in the ancient Near East (Levine 1993: 247, 259-66). (3) The sacrifices, following a cultic calendar (Num. 28–29), describe the regular sacrifices, in the order of their frequency—daily, weekly, monthly and yearly—required by God at the tabernacle/temple right through the year.[37] The opening verses, especially 28.2b, suggest that these offerings were viewed as God's food, as in the ancient Near East: קרבני לחמי לאשי ריח ניחחי, 'my offering, the food for my offering by fire, my pleasing odour'.[38] But other texts emphatically deny that Yahweh needed food (e.g. Ps. 50.7-15).[39] (4) The various festivals and special occasions when Israelites offered sacrifices were the New Moon festival (Num. 28.11-15), the Passover (Num. 28.16 cf. Exod. 12; Lev. 23.5-8; Num. 9.1-14; Deut. 16.1-8), the feast of Unleavened Bread (Num. 28.17-25 cf. Lev. 23.5-8), the Day of First-fruits (Num. 28.26-31; cf. Exod. 34.22; Deut. 16.10), the Day of Atonement (Lev. 16)[40] and the Festival of Tabernacles. (5) Besides these, Leviticus 1–7 (cf. Num. 29.39) clearly presupposes that the individual Israelite on various occasions offered sacrifices, such as votive offerings, free-will offerings, burnt offerings, grain offerings, guilt offerings, well-being offerings and offerings after purification from various defilements described

37. A helpful chart categorizing the type and number of animals required for each sacrifice on each occasion is given in Wenham 1981: 197; Ashley 1993: 563. However, the quantity of cereal and drink offerings required for each animal is missing in these lists. Probably the tithes provided for the daily sacrifices, while the princes provided sometimes (Mal. 3.10; Ezek. 45.18–46.15).

38. Also cf. 'my sacrifices and my offerings' and 'my table' in 1 Sam. 2.29; Ezek. 44.16.

39. Cf. Eichrodt 1961: 141-44; Haran 1961: 286; de Boer 1972: 27-47.

40. For Hittite and Mesopotamian parallels, see above. Further examples may be found in Wright 1987: 15-74; Milgrom 1991: 1072-79.

in Leviticus 12–15. I will not go into details of these sacrifices, but I shall discuss them briefly here.

Burnt Offering, עלה *(Leviticus 1).* עלה, literally 'that which ascends', suggests that the whole[41] is turned into smoke, והקטיר. Sacrifices include a male without blemish from the herd or flock, prepared and made עלה אשה ריח־ניחוח ליהוה, 'a burnt offering by fire, a pleasing odour to Yahweh' (v. 9). The Ugaritic parallel to this sacrifice is *šrp* which occurs 15 times with *šlmm*, probably equivalent to the Hebrew שלמים. While the Ugaritic *šlmm* differs from its Hebrew counterpart, in that the offering can be a bird, cluster of grapes, or oil, the *šrp* is limited to animals as the Hebrew עלה (Milgrom 1991: 172). The burnt offering is also attested in the Syrian and Hittite rituals. That the purpose of עלה is clearly propitiatory and expiatory is suggested both in the biblical and the Hittite texts.[42]

Cereal Offering, מנחה *(Leviticus 2).* מנחה can mean 'gift' or 'tribute' for showing reverence or homage and, in political contexts, friendship or submission.[43] A similar meaning is also implied in a Babylonian text: 'Did it bring its flour offering to appease the goddess's anger?' (Lambert 1960: 75; cf. Milgrom 1991: 196-97). מנחה included both bloody and unbloody sacrifices, which were probably 'whole burnt offerings',[44] but the Priestly code later limited מנחה to vegetable offerings only, although the old idea of offering it by fire on the altar was still maintained (Lev. 2.1-2; 2.2; 6.7-8; 10.12). The cereal offering usually followed the burnt offering. It probably meant to appease or retain favour with God, who granted forgiveness through the burnt offering (Wenham 1979: 70).

41. Milgrom (1991: 172-73) suggests that at an earlier stage עלה was designated by the כלל, 'whole, entire', but this word fell out of use because later the skin of the victim was awarded to the priest. Cf. Urie 1949: 70-71.

42. Judg. 20.26; 1 Sam. 7.9 cf. Jer. 14.12; 1 Sam. 13.12; Wenham 1979: 63; Milgrom 1991: 175-76.

43. Gen. 32.14, 19, 21; Judg. 3.15, 17; 1 Sam. 10.27; 16.19; 2 Kgs 20.12; also at Ugarit, *UT*, 120.1, 4; 137.28; in Akkadian *PRU*, IV: 29; Milgrom 1991: 196.

44. Gen. 4.3, 4; 8.20, 21; 15.9-17 (? probably a burnt offering); 22.13; cf. Milgrom 1991: 197-98.

Well-being Offering, זבח שלמים (*Leviticus 3*). זבח is 'the general term for animal sacrifice whose meat is eaten by the offerer;[45] שלמים refers to the specific motivation that prompts the sacrifice, a feeling of "well-being"' (Milgrom 1991: 204). שלמים may be offered as a thank-offering,[46] votive offering or free-will offering (Ps. 56.13-14; Exod. 35.29). They were presented on solemn occasions of various kinds, such as festivals (Exod. 32.6, 8; 1 Kgs 8.63-64; 9.25; Amos 4.4), victory in battle (1 Sam. 10.8; 13.9), the election of a king (1 Sam. 11.13-14), before war, and at thanksgiving (Josh. 8.31; cf. Ps. 56.13-14; Deut. 12.7; 27.7). The priest received the breast and the right thigh while the rest went to the offerer and his family who consumed it in a state of ritual purity within a stipulated period (Lev. 7.11-21; 34, 35).

The purpose of שלמים is variously explained as 'fellowship offering' (Snaith 1967: 37), 'concluding sacrifice' (Rendtorff 1967: 133), or 'gift sacrifice' (from the Akkadian root *šulmānu*; Levine 1974: 16, 29-30). It probably means that the sacrifice is offered 'to obtain peace between the worshipper and the deity' (Urie 1949: 77), but is not a mystical communion with the deity (contra Smith 1927: 265), since this is difficult to establish in the Old Testament.[47]

Purification Offering, חטאת (*Leviticus 4*). חטאת, derived from the verb חטא, 'to purify', is synonymous with טהר and כפר. It always means 'to cleanse, expurgate, decontaminate' (Milgrom 1991: 232, 253). It is required when an individual or a community commits inadvertent sin (as in Lev. 4), or when a person is under the influence of severe impurity (Lev. 12–15). The flesh of חטאת offerings whose blood is not taken into the tent of meeting for atonement must be eaten by priests in the holy precincts, because it is most holy, like the cereal offering. The blood of the victims is used to purge the most sacred parts of the sanctuary on behalf of the inadvertent offenders, and even persons (seriously unclean) and objects which cannot have sinned. This suggests that the very status of impurity in some and the inadvertent sins in others caused the contamination of the sancta and hence the need for its cleansing and so this offering.[48]

---

45. 1 Sam. 3.14 implies that זבח and מנחה have atoning effect.

46. 'Thank offering', תודה, is presented for deliverance from distress and the sphere of death, or as thanksgiving in festivals (Pss. 107.22; 22.27; 23.5).

47. Cf. Num. 8.7; 19.19; Ezek. 25.26; 43.22, 26; Ps. 51.9; Milgrom 1991: 221.

48. Milgrom 1991: 254-55. For another type of purification offering prescribed

Reparation Offering, אשם *(Lev. 5.14-26;*[49] *Num. 5.6-8).* Traditionally
אשם has been rendered as 'guilt offering', but 'reparation offering'[50] or
'compensation offering'[51] is more accurate with regard to its function.
אשם is prescribed for 'sacrilege', מעל, in relation to the holy things of
Yahweh' (vv. 14-19),[52] and/or 'sacrilege in relation to oaths' (vv. 20-
26).[53]

The אשם therefore logically constitutes the restitution of the thing to
the owner plus one-fifth of its value, and a ram without blemish, con-
vertible into silver by the sanctuary weights,[54] for a guilt offering to
Yahweh. The restitution and sacrificial offering alone will not, however, expiate the sinner from the false oath, for which the normal penalty is death.[55] But confession will reduce one's intentional crime to
inadvertent crime and restitution and sacrifice will expiate the sinner
(Num. 5.5-8). The idea of confession and the reduction of punishment
is evident also in the ancient Near Eastern literature.[56]

b. *Nature of Sacrifice*
Among the various types of sacrifices in Israel, the burnt offering,
which was totally consumed on the altar, comes very close to being

in Lev. 5.1-13, sometimes called 'graduated purification offering', see Milgrom
1991: 307-308; others regard it as a poor man's 'purification offering', de Vaux
1961: 419-21; 1964: 92. Rendtorff (1967: 207-10) assigns 5.1-6 to 5.14-26 to make
it part of the 'reparation offering', and 5.7-13 to 4.27-31.
    49. 5.14–6.7 in English.
    50. Milgrom 1976: 13-14.
    51. Snaith 1965: 73-80.
    52. For מעל and holy things of Yahweh, see Milgrom 1976: 17-18; 44-55;
1991: 321; Wenham 1979: 106. For the Hittite parallels of sacrilege, see *ANET*,
207-10; Milgrom, 1991: 322; 1976: 29-35.
    53. For offences in relation to oaths, see Lev. 19.13; Deut. 24.6, 14, 15, 17;
Ezek. 18.12; Prov. 20.16; for discussion, see Milgrom 1976: 84-98. For parallels in
the ancient Near East, see Driver and Miles 1952: 80-81; Yaron 1988: §§40, 49;
Milgrom 1991: 101.
    54. For various interpretations of the idea of the sacrificial animal convertible
into silver, see Milgrom 1991: 326-27. Reparation offerings are prescribed also in
the case of the cleansing of a leper (Lev. 14.10-28), sexual crime with a slave-girl
betrothed to another man (Lev. 19.20-22), and for the purification of a nazirite
(Num. 6.12).
    55. Oath violations are punishable by the deity in all ancient Near Eastern
cultures; Brichto 1963: 71-76.
    56. *ANET*, 395; from a letter of Amarna, *ANET*, 486, EA, no. 254.

viewed as nourishment to Yahweh, but this is difficult to ascertain from the biblical texts. The well-being offering suggests a fellowship of the worshippers with the deity, but not a mystical communion with him (Kraus 1966: 114). The purification offering provided cleansing to an average Israelite who might be defiled in various ways, and enabled him to access the holy things of Yahweh. The reparation offering achieved similar purification in the realm of the individual's ethics. Thus purification and atonement were ideas common to all the sacrifices so that the worshipper could have continual access to the sanctuary and a 'living intercourse' with God (Pedersen 1940: 359; cf. Kraus 1966: 123).

c. *Comparative Analysis*
Occasion. With few variations, the occasions for sacrifice in all the Near Eastern cultures are similar. As in Israel, there are daily sacrifices and those that take place on special occasions, such as festivals, dedication of temples, laying palace foundations, before and after battles, averting pestilence and healing the sick. There are also sacrifices on various occasions by individuals, such as for thanksgiving or votive purposes, and sacrifices for the dead at regular intervals and on special occasions. However, by contrast, sacrifices for the dead in Israel were condemned, implying that these were viewed as lapses on a popular level. As will be observed, most of these occasions are not relevant to the patriarchal sacrifices, except those offered on special occasions and by individuals for thanksgiving, peace-making and votive purposes.

Nature and Purpose. The most common view in the ancient Near East and in Israel was that sacrifice was a gift to the deity (cf. Evans-Pritchard 1956: 282; Bourdillon and Fortes 1980: 23) with the motive being physical or spiritual blessing (Milgrom 1991: 441). In the physical realm blessing could include victory/success, fertility/posterity or healing/protection. In the spiritual realm it could include ritual purity and moral justice—for example, the Hittite guilt offering and Ugaritic offering for anger. In the Israelite ritual, however, every offering can be labelled as a gift to God, since this was the dominant motive behind all of them. The burnt offerings and libations were especially so, since they were totally turned into smoke or poured into the ground. The motivation in all types of offerings was not only to gain favour from God but also to seek peace with him and to enact atonement. The שְׁלמִים, חטאת and אשׁם sacrifices dealt especially with the moral problems of the worshipper as well as being sacrifices, gifts to God. So the idea of inducing the deity by a gift is largely absent in the official cult.

Sacrifice was commonly regarded in the ancient Near East as food for the gods (cf. Sauneron 1960: 84-85; Oppenheim 1964: 187-93). Except at Ugarit,[57] no texts describe sacrificial materials as actually having been eaten by the gods (cf. the story of 'Bel and the Dragon'). They were only waved or presented in front of them before being distributed. The idea of sacrifice as food to God is not entirely absent in Israel. Israel probably understood that in some way sacrifices were appropriated by God, but not physically, since God was not allowed a material form (Eichrodt 1961: 143; cf. Milgrom 1991: 440).

The idea of sacrifice as a communion meal with God was developed particularly by Robertson Smith, who argued that Arabs, Canaanites and Semites in general believed that god and the worshippers were *commensals* in the sacrificial meal (Smith 1927: 226-27, 269-70). This is doubtful among Babylonians, and possible among the Hittites only in festivals.[58] Sacrifices within banquets were certainly shared together at Ugarit; these were primarily arranged by, and shared among, the gods themselves. In Israel, language and procedures suggest that such views were present, especially at the time of covenant making,[59] where the meal that followed was probably concerned with the presence and fellowship with God, but not in any magical sense. Rather, as Eichrodt notes:

> the consuming holiness of his nature constantly breaking into human life further excludes any thought of presuming on the bond of blood-brotherhood... The power of sacral communion mediated by the sacrifice rests rather on God's declaration that he is prepared to enter into a special relationship with his people and to give them a share in his own life.[60]

57. Ugaritic texts describe gods, even El, as drunken and wallowing in urine and excrement.

58. But here there is no suggestion of a communion with the deity.

59. At Sinai, Exod. 24.9-11; at the time of the king's accession to the throne, 1 Sam. 11.15; 2 Sam. 15.12; 1 Kgs 1.9; 3.15; when the ark was brought to Zion, 2 Sam. 6.17; 1 Kgs 8.63; on all these occasions a communion with Yahweh was probably sought by the worshippers, but it was not made possible without the sacrificial atonement for the people.

60. Eichrodt 1951: 157. The meal itself was eaten 'before him', not with him; Exod. 18.12; Deut. 27.7; 1 Sam. 2.13-16; Milgrom 1991: 441. Even the meal that

The sacrifice was only a symbol and an occasion for celebrating such a communion. Further, in certain sacrificial accounts any 'union with the deity is expressly denied' (Judg. 6.18-21; 13.16; Milgrom 1991: 441).

The idea that the substitute took the place of the offerer was prominent in the ancient Near East, and some scholars have applied this to Israel also (cf. James 1938–39: 151-55; Rodriguez 1979: 257-60). Others have argued that the scapegoat which carried off the sin did not even die (*pace* Rodriguez 1979: 73-74, 303-308) and so cannot be a sacrifice, and that the most important part of the ritual, in which a bull and a goat were sacrificed in the sanctuary, was intended to purify the sanctuary and the cultic system rather than the offerer.[61] Further, Israel's substitutionary offerings were not to the chthonic or enemy gods as in the ancient Near East, but to Yahweh, suggesting that there was no realm that was not controlled by Yahweh and that no sacrifice was required for anyone else (cf. Wright 1987: 32-45). But the idea of substitution and the elimination of evil from the community is similar in both systems.

Sacrifices for moral offences attested at Ugarit and among the Hittites are similar to the biblical אשם. Not only the offences, such as sin, sacrilege, imprecation and false testimony, but also the offering prescribed, such as a bird for sin, and another bird for imprecation, a lamb and a bird for false testimony, besides silver, gold and valuable articles as a price for guilt offering, either in place of, or in addition to, the animal sacrifices, are very similar to the way guilt was dealt with in Israel. Further, both in Hittite ritual and in Israel, confession of sin reduced the punishment, the significant difference being that confession was mandatory in Israel.

The above analysis suggests that Israel was aware of the ancient Near East cultic practices, with regard to their time (occasion), category (various types of sacrifices) and their general purpose (gift). However, Israel is significantly different in its motivation and in what it expected the sacrifice to achieve. In this sense, sacrifice as atonement for sin is unique to Israel. Sacrifices to the dead and the underworld gods are absent in Israel. It is also evident that temples and priesthood played an important role both in the ancient Near East and Israel and, except in

followed the Nuer sacrifice has only a 'social significance', Evans-Pritchard 1956: 214-15.

61. Milgrom 1971: 56; 1991: 41; cf. Steinmueller 1959: 556-67; de Vaux 1964: 93-94.

Babylon, that there is hardly any instance where a lay person offers sacrifices in an informal setting. In sharp contrast, sacrifices by lay persons dominate in the patriarchal narratives, with no priest even mentioned. But do patriarchal stories suggest an established cult and other aspects of sacrifice found in the ancient Near East and Israel?

4. *Altars and Sacrifices in the Patriarchal Narratives*

The word זבח/זבחים, sacrifice(s), occurs only twice in the patriarchal narratives (Gen. 31.54; 46.1). In neither instance were the type of sacrifices, the animals used and the procedures followed specified, though in both cases the officiant was apparently Jacob himself. There are also two occasions in which Abraham is said to have offered a sacrifice.[62] In Gen. 22.1-14 it is referred to as a 'burnt offering' in which a ram was offered,[63] and in Gen. 15.7-21 a ritual is described in which a heifer, a she-goat and a ram, each three years old, a turtledove and a young pigeon were apparently slaughtered by Abraham to seal a covenant with God. There are 11 further references to altars built by patriarchs (12.7, 8; 13.4, 18; 22.9 [twice]; 26.25; 33.20; 35.1, 3, 7),[64] presumably for the purpose of offering sacrifices, though this is not explicitly stated. I shall examine each of these sets of references in the order of their occurrence in the narratives. Thus I will analyse the idea of sacrifice first in the Abraham cycle, then in the Isaac cycle, and finally in the Jacob cycle, in order to see if patriarchal worship, though in some respects similar to worship in the ancient Near East and Israel, is distinct from both, being compatible only with the lifestyle of the patriarchs as portrayed in the narratives.

a. *Sacrifice in the Abraham Cycle*
Sacrifice in the Abraham cycle was probably offered on two types of occasion, namely, during formal worship when Abraham built altars at various places he had chanced to camp, following or preceding a theophany, and on special occasions when he had been directed by God to do so. In the former case only altars are mentioned, although sacrifices

62. No distinction is made in this book between 'Abram' and 'Abraham'.

63. Further in the story 'wood for burnt offering' and a 'lamb for a burnt offering' are mentioned, suggesting that burnt offerings were a common form of sacrifice with the ancients.

64. Actual reference to building altars occurs only seven times.

were most probably involved, but in the latter not only the type of
sacrifice but also the place (in Gen. 22) and underlying intention are
explicitly stated. I shall deal with these separately.

Altars. There are four occasions when Abraham is said to have either
built an altar or used an existing altar for the purpose of conducting
normal worship. The context and the circumstances surrounding the
activity of building altars suggest that sacrifices were involved here and
that they were occasions of regular worship compatible with the lifestyle of the patriarchs. I shall examine these different occasions more
closely in order to understand how patriarchal worship is distinct from
both ancient Near Eastern and later Israelite worship.

1.　　Gen. 12.7

וירא יהוה אל־אברם ויאמר לזרעך אתן את־הארץ הזאת ויבן
שם מזבח ליהוה הנראה אליו:

2.　　Gen. 12.8

ויעתק משם ההרה מקדם לבית־אל ויט אהלה בית־אל
מים והעי מקדם ויבן־שם מזבח ליהוה ויקרא בשם יהוה:

3.　　Gen. 13.4

אל־מקום המזבח אשר־עשה שם בראשנה ויקרא שם אברם בשם יהוה:

4.　　Gen. 13.18

ויאהל אברם ויבא וישב באלני ממרא אשר בחברון
ויבן־שם מזבח ליהוה:

On three of these occasions Abraham is said to have built an altar,
ויבן מזבח, and on the other to have used the one that he had previously
built. While in the ancient Near East and Israel the occasion and purpose of sacrifices were usually 'prescribed', and often the whole process of a particular sacrifice was elaborately 'described', in the case of
patriarchs, except on two occasions (with Abraham), no prescription of
materials or occasion is mentioned. This makes it difficult to determine
the nature and purpose of sacrifice in the patriarchal narratives. Consequently many scholars deny that sacrifices were involved with patriarchal altars, although the very word for 'altar', מזבח, meaning 'place
of slaughter', suggests that sacrifices were probably involved with the
patriarchal altars. So the following basic questions with regard to these
texts are in order: Why did Abraham build altars? What did he do with
them? What did the author of Genesis think that he did?

Why Did Abraham Build Altars? The text states that Abraham built altars at a place near Shechem, between Bethel and Ai, and by the oaks of Mamre at Hebron. Assuming for the present that Abraham built altars for the purpose of offering sacrifices, we seek the occasions and the reasons for Abraham as an individual to have undertaken such an action. At least two occasions may be found when Abraham built altars: in response to a 'theophany' (12.7), and when he 'moved his tent' (12.8; 13.18), but there appears to be no reason for Abraham to have done this if he had been visiting an existing cult place.

Although it was commonly thought in the ancient Near East that the place where a deity manifested itself was hallowed by its presence (*ERE*, XI: 34; Alt 1989: 20-21), this point should not be emphasized so sharply here, since Abraham is not said to have built an altar in Haran where the narrative implies that Yahweh had appeared to Abraham and made extravagant promises (12.1-2). There is also no mention of theophany when he built altars at Bethel and Hebron (12.8; 13.18). In these instances it appears that it was because Abraham moved to a new place that he built altars. On the other hand, he did not always build altars when he moved to a new place. For instance, there is no mention of an altar either when he first moved to Shechem before God appeared to him or when he moved his tent to Egypt, presumably in stages, since he made several stops on the way to and from Egypt (13.3). He probably would have stopped at Hebron, where he would later build an altar, at Beer-sheba and elsewhere. This suggests that movement to a new place was not in itself the reason for building altars, but probably rather the intention to settle down for a longer period was (cf. Albertz 1994: 36). Alternatively, building altars may have established a claim to the land promised, since there is no evidence of patriarchs building altars outside Canaan, even though they often moved and dwelt outside it. Thus there is no strict pattern that theophany or movement to a new place was always followed by building altars. Nevertheless, it may be generally true to say that theophanies made people respond in some way to their experience. Responses varied, but in most cases some means of honouring the deity was involved: either building an altar, raising a pillar or offering a sacrifice.[65] It is of course probable that sacrifices were also offered in the first two situations.

---

65. Cf. Isaac's identical response to theophany, 26.23-25; but Jacob's response was a pillar, not an altar, Gen. 28.17, 18; 35.9-14; and Gideon's and Manoah's

When the patriarchs intended to settle down at a place for a long period they built altars. This suggests that patriarchal altars followed their tents (Westermann 1985: 156-57), that is, their worship pattern was adapted to their wandering lifestyle. There is no suggestion here, contrary to the assumption of many scholars (see below), that patriarchs made use of existing Canaanite cult centres or that they founded new cult centres, though it is true that some of these places were indeed Canaanite cult centres during the second millennium or became important cult centres in later Israel. In the ancient Near East either places of theophany tended to become established cult centres, or it was at cult centres that theophanies were usually expected, while the patriarchs seem to have attached no permanent importance to these locations as they kept moving from place to place. In what follows, I shall examine the claim that the patriarchs made use of existing cult centres or founded new ones.

Some have argued that the places where Abraham built altars (Gen. 12.6-7; 13.4, 18) were already sacred places, as suggested by the use of מקום, 'the place', אלון מורה, 'the oak of Moreh', or אלני ממרא, 'the oaks of Mamre'. This assumption has carried the day from the time of Gunkel onward,[66] probably for two reasons. First, these scholars were working within the framework of the 'history of religions' school which assumed that Mosaic religion evolved from an inferior, if not animistic, religion that preceded it. The second reason, which gives credence to the first and is suggested by the biblical texts themselves, is that Yahweh was not known by the patriarchs (Exod. 6.3 P). For these two reasons it appeared legitimate to scholars to seek a type of primitive religion behind patriarchal practices, and מקום and אלון provided possible hints to confirm their assumptions. However, it has not been explained so far how P, claimed to be the latest source, knew that Yahweh was not known by the patriarchs while the earlier sources—J (and E)—assume that they did. On the other hand, if P was early, why did J (and E) not follow his cue? This indicates the problem of dating and of the interrelationship between the sources (Wenham 1980: 162). If P was late, the most plausible explanation may be that it was P's theological judgment that Yahweh was not known to the patriarchs

response to theophany was neither an altar nor a pillar but a sacrifice on a rock at the place of theophany, Judg. 6.18-24; 13.19-23.

66. Gunkel 1902: 147; Procksch 1924: 98; Skinner 1930: 246; Kidner 1967: 115; Westermann 1985: 153-54.

because the cultic practices in which the patriarchs were involved did not conform with the Yahwistic norms. P saw that J believed that Yahweh was also the God of the patriarchs. Thus P shared the theological position of J and E but not their historical view that the patriarchs knew Yahweh.[67] This may explain P's avoidance of patriarchal cultic practices, except circumcision, in his account of patriarchal history (cf. Wenham 1980: 163). If J was entirely responsible, according to the source-critical analysis, for recording the cultic practices of the patriarchs (cf. Wenham 1980: 163), and made no distinction between the patriarchal God and Yahweh, did he believe or know that the places where the patriarchs built altars were already cult centres? I shall turn to this issue now.

Though it is possible that מָקוֹם suggests a holy place, it is not certain that the author used it in a technical sense. In Gen. 22.3-4 it probably has such a meaning, suggested both by the context and the identity of the specific 'place' where Abraham was to offer sacrifice, and in the Deuteronomic expression, 'the place that Yahweh will choose', the word almost certainly had this sense. In itself, however, מָקוֹם may not necessarily carry a sacred connotation, for it is also used in its basic sense of *a place* in Gen. 39.20 and 40.3. The word is found in a similar construction in the immediate context of Gen. 13.4: אֶל־מְקוֹם הַמִּזְבֵּחַ אֲשֶׁר־עָשָׂה שָׁם, 'to the place where he had made an altar'. If the author had meant a sacred place, it would have been sufficient to say 'between Bethel and Ai, to the מָקוֹם', since the altar, which was as good as a sanctuary, was already there (cf. Cassuto 1964: 323-24; Wenham 1987: 279). Further, the fact that the author describes Abraham as building an altar suggests at least that there was no existing altar, or that the existing altars were not good enough for the wayfarer to offer his worship. In any case, a cult place without an altar or with a

<hr/>

67. Cf. Moberly 1992a: 79-104. Moberly thinks that all the writers of Genesis, J, E and P, were aware of the fact that the patriarchs did not know God as Yahweh, but these writers did not make a distinction between Yahweh and the God of the fathers because they believed that Yahweh was the God of the fathers. However, the Genesis sources themselves do not suggest that J and E knew the distinction between the God of the patriarchs and Yahweh. This raises another query of whether J and E, as revealed in Genesis, really shared the Yahwistic ethos; if so, they would not have been so casual in their use of the divine name in relation to the patriarchs who had not known Yahweh. Only P could be said to have been a true Yahwist who was consistent with his knowledge that the patriarchs knew God only as El Shaddai. Cf. Wenham 1980: 161-62.

defunct one was an anomaly. This is further confirmed by Gen. 13.4, where Abraham is said to have 'called upon the name of Yahweh', a technical expression for normal worship (cf. Gen. 4.26), which I shall discuss more fully in the next chapter. The author, however, suggests that there was no need for Abraham to build an altar because the previous altar was still there and he could conduct his worship there. Further, even in Gen. 12.8, Abraham is said to have 'called upon the name of Yahweh' immediately after building an altar, which may indicate that he prayed to God or, more likely, that with the altar in the background he conducted worship, probably with sacrifices. If this was the case, then Abraham acted here as priest, which again suggests that the place was not equipped with any cultic personnel. While the situation of cult in early second-millennium Canaan is unclear, the later Ugaritic texts indicate a highly organized cult, with the king or royal family firmly in control. It is possible to think that this may have also been the case during Abraham's time, if the story of Melchizedek has any historical value. It thus seems unlikely that the author used מקום as a technical word for a sacred place.[68] If the places where Abraham built altars lay outside the settled townships, as the author portrays it, the other details of patriarchs pitching their tents where they intended to settle for a while fits well with the whole story, suggesting that this was a family altar compatible with the lifestyle of the patriarchs. I shall consider the implications of the archaeological data for this matter below.

The presence of the oak, אלון, at places where the patriarchs often camped, is claimed as further evidence to indicate the prior sanctity of the place. This probably has more claim to religious connections than the word מקום. *Targum Onqelos* renders אלון as 'plain', 'valley', in all of its occurrences in Genesis,[69] probably to suppress the idea that the patriarchs engaged in what was later associated with pagan cults. מורה literally means 'teacher', thus the phrase, אלון מורה may mean 'oak of the teacher' or 'the oak where oracles may be obtained' (cf. 'the palm of Deborah', Judg. 4.5). In six references to oak-like trees in Genesis, three different Hebrew forms, אֵלוֹן, אֵלָה and אַלּוֹן, are used,[70] but only in two instances were altars associated with these trees, while twice burial

68. So Delitzsch 1888: 381; Cassuto 1964: 323-24; Aalders 1981: 271-72.
69. 12.6; 13.18; 14.13; 18.1. The Vulgate follows this rendering in 12.6 only.
70. אֵלוֹן: 12.6; 13.18; 14.13; 18.1; אֵלָה: 35.4; אַלּוֹן: 35.8; there is only one other form, אֵלָה which occurs only in Josh. 24.26. RSV renders all these forms as 'oak(s)'.

occurred under them (foreign gods and Deborah's body). Nevertheless, the form אֵלוֹן seems to have had religious associations in all its occurrences in Genesis and Judges.[71] In Judg. 9.6 the leaders of Shechem make Abimelech king by the אֵלוֹן and מַצֵּב at Shechem. The association of the 'pillar', מַצֵּב, with the oak and the crowning ceremony of Abimelech suggests the existence of a tree-shrine, still with the practice of receiving oracles, outside the city. Opinion is divided concerning whether it is the same tree that is mentioned in Gen. 12.6.[72] In view of the presence of a number of temples in and around Shechem, it is not always easy to correlate the biblical texts with the archaeological evidence (cf. Terrien 1970: 315-18; Soggin 1987: 189-93). The earliest settlement at Shechem is attested in the Chalcolithic period (4500–3200 BCE). By the early Middle Bronze period (1900–1750 BCE), Shechem had become an important strategic and political centre according to certain Egyptian inscriptions, with the temple area an open place outside the city, but there is no archaeological evidence of an open-air shrine in this period.[73] If Abraham is to be dated during this period he could not have used an already existing open-air shrine. In the light of these many possibilities, our best guide is a plain reading of Gen. 12.6, which may be taken to indicate that Abraham built his own altar at the place where he camped, that is at the oak near Shechem. The text does not assign any importance to the oak.

Abraham also built an altar at a spot between Ai and Bethel, where he also pitched his tent. Here, unlike on previous occasions, Abraham is said to have 'called on the name of Yahweh' (Gen. 12.8). As I have argued above, his building of an altar suggests that there had been no altar beforehand, which in turn suggests that there had also been no shrine there. Further, the author specifically states that the place where Abraham pitched his tent and built his altar was neither in Bethel nor in Ai but between them, with Bethel on the west and Ai on the east. While

---

71. This form occurs ten times in all, four times in Genesis (as shown above) and twice in Judges. In the other four occurrences it refers to a landmark or boundary marker, Deut. 11.30; Josh. 19.33; Judg. 4.11; 9.37.

72. Haran (1978: 50-51 n. 12) and von Rad (1961: 157) think it is not the same. But the majority of commentators and archaeologists think that the tree of Gen. 12.6, 35.4, Deut. 11.30, Josh. 24.24 and Judg. 9.6, 37 are the same; cf. Westermann 1985: 154.

73. *NEAEHL*, 1351; *ABD*, V: 1174-86, esp. 1179-81; cf. Wright 1968: 1-35.

there have been problems with the identification of Ai,[74] Bethel is usually identified with Beitin, ten miles north of Jerusalem. An open-air shrine from the mid fourth century BCE, a pillar *in situ* from MB I and II, and a temple from the nineteenth century BCE have been found at Beitin, suggesting that Bethel was already a cult centre during patriarchal times. There is also evidence that it was continuously occupied until the late sixth century BCE (Kelso 1968: 1-3, 20-21, 45-46), but it is not appropriate to identify the place where Abraham pitched his tent with Beitin, nor is it possible to think, with Gunkel (1902: 142), that Abraham went from Shechem to Bethel to found another cult centre. Unlike Shechem, there is no mention of any form of oak at this place during the time of Abraham, but in Jacob's time an oak, אַלּוֹן, is said to have existed near Bethel, for Jacob is said to have buried Deborah, Rebekah's nurse, there. I shall discuss this when I come to discuss the Jacob cycle.

Abraham also built an altar 'by the oaks of Mamre at Hebron', בחברון באלני ממרא אשר. As in earlier cases, the building of an altar suggests that there was no shrine already established at this place. As at Shechem, however, this place is identified by the 'oaks[75] of Mamre'. While the single oak in 12.6 is qualified by 'Moreh' ('teacher'), here they are qualified by 'Mamre'. Genesis 14.13 implies that they either belonged to, or were named after, an Amorite called Mamre. But elsewhere Mamre is identified with Hebron or a place nearby (Gen. 18.1; 23.17, 19; 25.9; 35.27; 49.30; 50.13). Since no reference to Mamre occurs outside Genesis, it is difficult to elucidate these references. It is possible that the name Mamre was originally that of a person, a tribal

---

74. Usually identified with Et-Tell, one and a half miles east of Beitin, although its identity has been disputed since it contained no remains between the Early Bronze Age and the Iron Age; Mazar 1990: 331-32.

75. LXX has the singular, 'oak', τὴν δρυν, so also Syriac. Procksch thinks that the plural in the MT is a rabbinic correction in order to hide the sacred tree. This is possible in view of 14.13; 18.1. However, the same logic should apply to Deut. 11.30 where the plural is used. But Deut. 11.30 refers to the oak at Shechem which is singular at 12.6 and 35.4. Then, why did the scribe leave them uncorrected when they certainly give sacred associations to the tree? De Vaux (1965: 292) thinks that the story in 18.4, 8 demands a singular 'oak', but if we accept that 'oaks of Mamre' was a grove named after Mamre, the singular 'oak' in 18.4, 8 could be explained as the particular tree under which the transactions took place.

chief, after whom the grove of trees was named,[76] and it later survived as a place name. It is doubtful, however, that its absence outside Genesis reveals that later authors suspected it of being associated with a syncretistic cult. The growth of legends around the name/ place of Mamre does not prove that it was a sacred site during patriarchal times (*pace* de Vaux 1965: 292-93). There is no archaeological evidence of occupation at Mamre in the first half of the second millennium.[77]

Of the three places where Abraham is said to have built altars, only Bethel shows clear evidence of a shrine existing before and during the time of the patriarchs, but Gen. 12.8 clearly denies that Abraham built his altar at Bethel. There is therefore insufficient evidence to assert that the places where Abraham built altars were already sacred places.

An alternative view is that the places where the patriarchs built altars later became sanctuaries, so that the patriarchs may be viewed as founders of ancient cult centres.[78] Those who follow this line of argument obviously affirm, directly or indirectly, that the places were not already sacred. However, the patriarchal stories themselves provide witness to the fact that the places where patriarchs built altars were considered special or awesome in some sense by the patriarchs themselves. This is implied in Abraham's return to the place where he had previously built an altar. In Jacob's case, he first recognized the 'awesomeness' of the place, then promised to build a temple there, and finally was directed by God to return to Bethel where God had first appeared to him. Thus the patriarchs built altars following a theophany or at places to which they had newly moved. From the authors' point of view, Israel regarded these places as sacred because their fathers had received revelations there. It is quite possible that some of these places were Canaanite cult centres when Israel took them over, but the sanctity attached to them was not seen (at least by the authors of Genesis) as having derived from their having been Canaanite cult centres but from the fact that their patriarchs had already worshipped in those places.

---

76. Speiser 1964: 97; Aalders 1981: 280; Haran 1978: 53-54; cf. Driver 1948: 154.

77. At Hebron, however, there is evidence of occupation from 3000 BCE, a city wall throughout the Middle Bronze period, and some traces of Late Bronze Age activity, and later again in the Iron Age. At Mamre there is nothing of Iron Age date. But remains of the late Roman and Byzantine period were found in both places. *NEAEHL*; cf. Mazar 1990: 332-33; Vos 1977: 174-75.

78. Keil 1878: 167; Dillmann 1897: 15; Cassuto 1964: 325-26.

In summary, the occasions for building altars are very different for the patriarchs from those apparent in the ancient Near East and in Israel. In the latter case, sacrifices were largely corporate, and were made chiefly during festivals and other public occasions; individual sacrifices were mainly for/after healing, occasionally votive and sometimes for sin or guilt. Further, the place of sacrifice was always at the sanctuary, except for certain healing rituals, and usually by a cult functionary. In this way, patriarchal altars were unique. They are, however, compatible with Abraham's wandering lifestyle, since there was no established cult or priest involved. But what about the nature of the altars, that is, what did Abraham do with his altars?

What Did Abraham Do with his Altars? Opinions are sharply divided here. Some think that patriarchal altars were memorials,[79] while others believe that the patriarchs offered sacrifices on them as part of their worship.[80] The word altar, מזבח, occurs about 400 times in the Old Testament and there are very few instances where its purpose is ambiguous. For instance, the 'altar of wood' in Ezek. 41.22 is later described as 'the table that is before Yahweh', השלחן אשר לפני יחוח. It is not certain if this was an altar, the altar of incense, the 'table of the Presence', or more probably 'an altar-like table'.[81] Nor is its function clear. Two other instances, where מזבח probably means a 'memorial altar', occur in Exod. 17.15 and Judg. 6.24. In the former case, it certainly stood for the memory of Israel's critical victory over the Amalekites, and the naming and the sign on it (v. 16) suggest that it was intended as a memorial. But it is unclear why it was called an altar, since elsewhere memorials were usually stones (e.g. Josh. 24.25; 1 Sam. 7.12).[82] Gideon's altar in Judg. 6.24 was probably intended as a witness to the fact that there was still peace between him and God, and

79. Delitzsch 1888: 382, 393; Procksch 1924: 98; Cassuto 1964: 328-29; Aalders 1981: 175, 271-72; for Westermann (1985: 255-56) they are memorials as well as nomadic journey markers. For Skinner (1930: 246), following Procksch, there is no sacrifice in J.

80. König 1919: 452; Rowley 1967: 24; Wenham 1987: 280. *ABD*, I: 164 implies that, except in Gen. 33.20 and 35.7, sacrifices were offered on other occasions.

81. Cf. 1 Kgs 6.20; Exod. 30.1-10; Lev. 24.5-9. Cooke 1936: 451-52; Taylor 1969: 262.

82. 'Whether these constructions were memorials which the author calls "altars" or whether they were altars which later authors attempted to legitimize by

that he would not die even though he had come into direct contact with the divine being (this altar probably commemorates sacrifice). There is only one other case (Josh. 22.10, 34) where it is explicitly stated that a particular altar was not meant for the usual sacrifices and offerings. The whole narrative in Josh. 22.10-34, however, only proves that altars were usually meant for offering sacrifices (cf. Snaith 1978: 331). None of these cases can be compared to the patriarchal altars. Haak includes two of the patriarchal altars (Gen. 33.20; 35.7) with the memorial altars just discussed, but this is unhelpful (*ABD*, I: 164). Further, on two occasions (12.8; 13.4) it is explicitly stated that Abraham 'called upon the name of the Lord' when he built an altar or visited one previously built. This phrase, ויקרא בשם יהוה (see Chapter 3 §4), is considered to be a technical term for worship as in Gen. 4.26.[83] It is doubtful, however, whether the author meant that pronunciation of the name exerts a mystic influence on the deity (*pace* Skinner 1930: 127), or that it represented a petition or praise to the deity.[84] More probably it was 'an umbrella phrase for worship', suggesting that 'Abram worshipped in a regular formal way', including 'most obviously prayer and sacrifice'.[85] Further, archaeological evidence from the Chalcolithic period at En-Gedi (Ussishkin 1971: 29) and from Bronze Age Megiddo (several levels), Ai, Shechem, Hazor and Gezer (Ottosson 1980: 63-65; 99-101; 128-30; cf. *ABD*, I: 165-66) amply show the remains of ashes and animal bones at *all* places where different kinds of altars were identified. Therefore the cryptic statements that the patriarchs built altars and called upon the name of the Lord most probably suggest that they not only offered sacrifices but also worshipped God in accordance with their lifestyle.

Sacrifices. Abraham's sacrifices, however, on two other occasions (Gen. 15; 22) appear to be similar to those in the ancient Near East and Israel. The occasion, the species of victims and the procedures of offering were all prescribed by the deity himself.

assigning an acceptable function is not clear', *ABD*, I: 164. Cf. Snaith 1978: 330-35; Van Seters 1980: 232.

83. Gunkel 1902: 148; Aalders 1981: 272; Westermann 1985: 156-57; Hamilton 1990: 378.

84. The phrase is used to seek an answer from the deity in 1 Kgs 18.24; 2 Kgs 5.11; Isa. 64.6; Joel 3.5; Zech. 13.9; Ps. 116.4; Lam. 3.55. It is used in doxology in Isa. 12.4; Zech. 3.9; Pss. 80.19; 105.1; 116.13, 17; cf. Hamilton 1990: 378.

85. Gen. 4.26; 21.33; 26.25; Zeph. 3.9; cf. Wenham 1987: 116, 281.

Genesis 15.7-12, 17. There is no consensus on the origin, composition and date of the material in Genesis 15.[86] In keeping with my main aim, I shall look into the occasion and nature of the sacrifice apparently offered by Abraham. The occasion clearly seems to relate to Abraham's present situation of childlessness and may be compared to those of Keret and Dan'el in Ugaritic texts that I have considered above. Even Abraham's worry seems less about land than about childlessness, an 'unmitigated disaster in the ancient world' (Wenham 1987: 334; cf. *ANET*, 149-50). This was certainly true with Keret and Dan'el, for whom having no son meant no heir to the throne and no fertility or prosperity in the land, since the king, being sacral, mediated divine blessings to humanity. Further, no son meant no care-taker in old age, and more importantly none to perform the funerary rites, since this was the son's responsibility. The presence of these ideas in Israel is doubtful, but the idea that one's name must continue after death and that only a son could facilitate this is commonly assumed, and is reflected in the law concerning levirate marriage.[87] Abraham's problem, however, clearly concerned his need for an heir to his property, and probably also someone to carry on his name after his death. The sacrificial ritual that Abraham performed, however, was unlike those of Keret and Dan'el which concerned the need for children, being rather concerned with the promise of land (Westermann 1985: 216-17). Both the species and ages of the victims were carefully prescribed as in the Priestly texts of Leviticus: a heifer, a she-goat and a ram, each three years old, a turtledove and a young pigeon. Was this ritual a legal formality, or does it reveal something about Abraham's religion? Are there parallels to it either in Israel or in the ancient Near East?

There are no complete parallels to Genesis 15 in any known ancient Near Eastern text, but different aspects may be found in texts from various periods from the first and second millennia BCE. In a Neo-Assyrian text concerned with a treaty between the Assyrian king Asshur-nirari V and Mati'-ilu, vassal-king of Arpad, the latter cuts up the sacrificial lamb and says:

---

86. The majority of scholars, following Wellhausen, have assumed that Gen. 15 was composed of two independent narratives, vv. 1-6 and 7-21, and have given up attempts to assign the material to any known sources. For a history of exegesis of Gen. 15, see Kaiser 1958: 107-26; Van Seters 1975: 249-53.

87. Gen. 38.8-10; Num. 27.4; Deut. 25.5-10; 2 Sam. 18.18.

The head is not the head of a spring lamb, it is the head of Mati'-ilu, it is the head of his sons, his magnates and the people of [his lan]d. If Mati'-ilu [should sin] against this treaty, so may, just as the head of this spring lamb is c[ut] off, and its knuckle placed in its mouth, [...] the head of Mati'-ilu be cut off, and his sons [and magnates] be th[rown] into [...] (Hess 1993: 62).

A comparable Aramaic text from Sefire states:

[Just as] this calf is cut in two, so may the wives of Matî'el be cut in two, and may his nobles be cut in two! (Hess 1993: 61-62).

In both these examples, dismemberment of the victims, though only one in each case, forms part of the treaty that the vassal makes before his overlord. The divided animal illustrates the fate of the vassal if he violates the words of the treaty.[88] These examples are probably more relevant to Jer. 34.17-20, where a similar substitutionary principle operates for those who disobey the terms of Yahweh's covenant.[89] In Genesis 15, however, there is neither the idea of substitution nor the implication that Yahweh accepts the possibility of being torn into pieces if he failed to keep his promise to Abraham (Snijders 1958: 271-72; Hess 1993: 62-63). On the other hand, divine oaths generally take the form: 'As I live, says Yahweh'. Thus there is no idea of a self-imprecatory oath on the part of God as has been assumed by several scholars.[90] Only the dismemberment of the victims yields any parallel with Genesis 15.

However, the Alalakh Tablets from the first half of the second millennium BCE contain two parallels which have closer similarities to the ritual in Genesis 15. Both texts describe the swearing of an oath in the context of a covenant-making:

Abba-AN swore an oath of the gods to Yarimlim and he cut the neck of one lamb (saying): (May I be cursed) if I take what I have given you. The neck of the sacrificial lamb in the presence of Niqmepuh was cut.[91]

88. McCarthy 1978: 94; Hamilton 1990: 432; Hess 1993: 61-62.
89. A Hittite ritual, which has already been noted above, tells of a similar procedure when the army was defeated in a battle. Except for the dismemberment of the victims, it is hardly relevant to this text. Cf. Hamilton 1990: 432.
90. Speiser 1964: 112-13; Westermann 1985: 228; Hasel 1981: 61-78.
91. Hess 1993: 57, 58; cf. Wiseman 1958: 124-29; Draffkorn 1959: 94-97; Hamilton 1990: 430-31.

Several parallels have been drawn between Genesis 15 and the Alalakh texts. First, both texts concern land grants. Secondly, the grants involved an obligation of a servant to his master, and it is the granter taking the oath. And thirdly, the sacrifice of animals and their dismemberment formed part of the property grants (Weinfeld 1970: 184-203; Hess 1993: 57-58). Thus, despite the common theme of land grants, the animal rite in the latter is unique. Many aspects of the ritual, such as the number of animals, Abraham's driving away of the birds of prey hovering over the carcasses, his sleep during the ritual, and the smoke of fire that passed through between the dismembered parts of the animals, have no known parallels in any ancient Near Eastern texts (cf. Wenham 1987: 333). Consequently, clues to the interpretation of the biblical rite must be sought elsewhere, probably from Israel herself, that is from the general categories of Israel's rituals, as suggested by Wenham. Thus the slaughtered animals may represent Israel, the birds of prey the enemies of the pagan nations, Abraham's actions his attempts to protect his people, and God's walk his commitment to the covenant to preserve Israel (Wenham 1982: 134-37; 1987: 332-33; cf. Hamilton 1990: 433-34).

The meaning of the ritual, therefore, is not confined to a legal understanding of a treaty between two parties. Rather, it probably also has religious significance for the relationship between Abraham and God and between Abraham's descendants and their God. The occasion for the ritual probably also has more than one purpose, namely Abraham's childlessness and his landlessness about which God had been making promises, though not yet with an oath as here. Therefore it appears reasonable to suggest that this ritual was a ratification of that oath, a once-for-all action, and that it probably forms part of Abraham's religion, not in the sense of a cultic practice that Abraham would repeat often, but of a common cultic practice that was used for the specific purpose of ratifying a relationship. A sacrifice may be assumed here, but there is no hint of worship; indeed, the devotee falls asleep during the ritual!

Genesis 22.1-19. The story of Isaac's sacrifice is problematical historically, ethically and theologically (for a review of research and literature, see Westermann 1985: 351-54). But I shall focus only on the occasion and the nature of sacrifice from the perspective of the final author and see how these throw light on the religion of Abraham.

This is the clearest instance of a 'burnt offering' sacrifice of a ram in the patriarchal narratives. The occasion, created by God himself in the form of a testing (נסה) of Abraham, was special, because it involved a human victim—there was never a prescription of human victims for a burnt offering or, for that matter, any other type of offering in Israel. There are, however, several instances of human sacrifice in Israel (Judg. 11.31-40; 21.6), and there could have been many at the popular level of worship, especially during the reigns of some kings who openly encouraged pagan worship (2 Kgs 17.17). Perhaps the rejection of the human sacrifice already lies behind the law of redemption of the firstborn son by animal sacrifice (Exod. 22.28; 34.20). But in any case Genesis 22 is not a polemic against human sacrifice, marking the transition from human sacrifice to animal substitution (Westermann 1985: 354; Sarna 1989: 392-93). It is clear from the earliest biblical stories that animals from the flock or products from the field were the natural materials for sacrifice (Gen. 4.3-4; 8.20). Even Isaac's innocent query assumes that a lamb was an appropriate animal for a burnt offering. It is uncertain whether the narrator added this note to increase the tension in the story or whether it really reflects Abraham's normal practice with which Isaac was familiar. Further, as noted above, pagan human sacrifices were usually offered at the worshipper's own initiative, in an extreme emergency or in order to appease an angry or inattentive god (cf. 2 Kgs 3.26-27). None of this, however, is suggested in the text. The occasion for this sacrifice therefore remains an unusual one, that is, to test Abraham, this motif pervading the whole story (Westermann 1985: 354-55).

Further, this is the first time that a burnt offering is prescribed in the patriarchal narratives. At Ugarit, the victims are varied, including a bird, a cluster of grapes and oil, but again, no human victims were prescribed. In Hittite rituals, however, human victims were prescribed on two occasions—namely, defeat in a battle and pestilence. In both cases, the human victims were sacrificed or sent away (in the case of pestilence) along with other animal victims, but in neither case were they called a burnt offering. Thus there are no real parallels to Abraham's attempted sacrifice of Isaac either in Israel or in the ancient Near East. Once again, therefore, this reveals the distinctiveness of Abraham's religion.

As to the nature of sacrifice, the author describes Abraham as if preparing for a normal sacrifice of a burnt offering, suggested by the wood, fire and knife. These things were not mentioned on earlier occasions, probably because the sacrifice took place in family surroundings, so there was no need for such preparation. But now this sacrifice to God was to involve a three-day journey (cf. Gilgamesh; *ANET*, 75) from home to a 'place', מקום, which God would show him. מקום is mentioned thrice (vv. 3, 4, 9) and 'worship', 'altar'[92] and the 'mount of Yahweh' (vv. 5, 9, 14)[93] associated with it suggest that it was a familiar place, possibly considered to have been sacred to the author and his reader. But the fact that Abraham needed to take wood and fire and had to build an altar suggests that there was no existing or functioning sanctuary there. So once again the preparation, the place and the manner of sacrifice offered suggest that it was peculiar to the patriarchal lifestyle and inextricably related to their personal piety. The non-mention of Sarah in the whole episode reinforces this point. Also the direct command of God to Abraham and the intervention of the angel are typical of God's dealings with the patriarchs elsewhere in the narratives. Westermann's suggestion that the story arose during the later period of monarchy, when the idea of the 'fear of God' or 'testing of the people of God' acquired significance for the people of God (Westermann 1985: 355-56), is possible but uncertain, since it involves importing foreign ideas into the text while leaving several aspects inherent in the text unexplained. The author of the story wanted to portray how God tested Abraham and how Abraham obeyed God, in spite of the fact that all God's promises depended upon Isaac's survival.

Thus Abraham's building of altars and calling upon the name of Yahweh, though sounding comparable to worship anywhere with the ancient Near East or in Israel, was in fact different from any such pattern of worship. The texts of Genesis suggest that there were no established cult or cultic personnel involved at the places where he built

92. It is only here in the patriarchal narratives that an altar is described with a definite article. Does it suggest a restoration of an existing altar? So Sarna 1989: 392.

93. While the 'mount of Yahweh' can be identified with Zion (2 Chron. 3.1; *Jub.* 18.13; Josephus, Targums and Talmud; cf. Isa. 2.3; 30.29; Mic. 4.2; Zech. 8.3; Ps. 24.3), the 'land of Moriah' where this mount was located could not be identified with any certainty. The etymology of 'moriah' is uncertain as 'none of the ancient versions transliterates *moriah*'. And Jerusalem is not a three-day journey from Beer-sheba; Sarna 1989: 391-92.

altars. Neither the presence of the 'oak-like' trees nor the use of מקום in these contexts require that they were already 'sacred sites'. On the other hand, the occasion for building altars and the intention behind them suggested by the texts reveal a pattern in which the patriarch built these altars either in response to a theophany or as a result of moving places, which in turn suggests that these altars were for the purpose of worshipping God in accordance with his wandering lifestyle as an alien in the land. This is very different from the cultic practices of both the ancient Near East and Israel, in both of which sacrifices were highly organized, largely corporate, and offered chiefly during festivals and other public occasions; individual sacrifices were mainly for or after healing, and occasionally votive or for removing sin and guilt. Further, the place of sacrifice was always the sanctuary, except at certain healing rituals, and it was usually conducted by a priest. In these ways patriarchal altars were unique.

Abraham's apparent sacrifice in Genesis 15 and the special sacrifice in Genesis 22 must be regarded as special occasions. Though the specification of sex and types of animals and sacrifice on these occasions resemble the Israelite and ancient Near East practices, the pattern is still compatible with the patriarchal lifestyle. On both these occasions neither a priest nor an established cult place was involved. The transaction was between God and the patriarch only. Both represent a specific relationship of the patriarch with God and do not reflect the patriarch's pattern of worship. It is possible that some of the concerns expressed in them were from the editors and not truly patriarchal, but their identification depends more on speculation than firm evidence.

b. *Altars in the Isaac Cycle*
There is only one reference to building an altar in the Isaac cycle (Gen. 26.25). The majority of scholars consider Genesis 26 to be a unity, probably coming from J (Westermann 1985: 423; Wenham 1994: 188). The story of Isaac is eclipsed in Genesis by the Abraham narratives on the one hand and the Jacob narratives on the other. Indeed, most scholars regard the whole of the Isaac story as an introduction to the Jacob–Esau cycle (Wenham 1994: 172), as suggested by its starting with the struggle between Jacob and Esau in their mother's womb (25.22-23). Thus Isaac appears to be insignificant compared to the figures of Abraham and Jacob, but nevertheless forms an indispensable link between them. The story-line is firmly linked to the two larger

narratives of Abraham and Jacob. The introduction of Laban into the
story of Isaac's marriage already anticipates Jacob's future relationship
with Rebekah's family. As for lifestyle, religion and the patriarch's
relations with others, there are many parallels between Abraham and
Isaac which suggest that the traditions arose from a similar milieu. For
instance, the famine and wife-sister motif (26.11 // 12.10-20), wealth
and quarrels between the patriarch's herdsmen and others (26.12-22 //
13.2-10), separation (26.23 // 13.11-12), divine promise of descendants
(26.24 // 13.14-17), moving and altar building (26.25 // 13.18), good
relations with foreigners (26.26-31 // 14) and a foreign king blessing
the patriarch (26.29 // 14.19-20) (Wenham 1994: 187).

Thus the religious activities of Isaac, though not as numerous as
those of Abraham, are quite compatible with his lifestyle as portrayed
in the narratives (Westermann 1985: 426). He prays for his barren wife
(25.21) (see Chapter 3), and builds an altar at Beer-sheba following a
theophany and a move to a new place (26.25). The occasion for
building an altar is similar to that of Abraham who built altars during
his wanderings through the land (12.7, 8; 13.3, 18). Like Abraham,
Isaac builds an altar and 'calls on the name of Yahweh' after a
theophany and a move to a new place, from Gerar to Beer-sheba. Patriarchal altars followed their tents with Isaac as with Abraham. However,
unlike Abraham's case where the use of מקום or the presence of 'oak-
like' trees suggested the prior sanctity of the places, here there is no
suggestion that there was a Canaanite sanctuary at Beer-sheba.[94] But
in view of Abraham's earlier associations with Beer-sheba (21.33;
22.19)[95] and of Jacob's receiving a theophany later at this place and

---

94. Smith 1927: 181-82 suggests that among the Semites a special sanctity was
attached to the place of 'seven wells', Beer-sheba. However, whether the tradition
was about the place of 'seven wells' or 'well of the oath' is not clear. In the light of
Abraham's treaty with Abimelech (Gen. 21.27-32) the latter meaning seems more
likely. Cf. Dillmann 1897: 136-37; Westermann 1985: 349.

According to archaeological studies, the deepest stratum represents an unwalled
settlement during the time of the judges. A fortified city appears only during the
period of the monarchy, so that the 'city of Beer-sheba' in Gen. 26.33 must be
regarded as an editorial note. If there was a settlement during the time of the
patriarchs, it should have been in the valley near the water source, but the
patriarchal stories themselves do not suggest a Canaanite settlement prior to their
arrival there. Cf. Aharoni 1973: 110-13; *EAEHL*, 162, 168; Herzog 1980: 12-28;
Fowler 1982a: 7-11.

95. Abraham planting a tamarisk tree at Beer-sheba is discussed in Chapter 3.

responding with sacrifices (46.1-4), it is reasonable to assume that this place had a tradition as a patriarchal sanctuary. That Abraham not only made his home at Beer-sheba but also 'called upon the name of Yahweh' there suggests that Abraham conducted formal worship as he had previously done elsewhere. Abraham's action here differs only in respect of his 'planting a tree' instead of 'building an altar' as in earlier cases. The lack of the mention of an altar, however, probably suggests that no sacrifices were involved. The fact that Isaac built an altar clearly suggests that there was no altar existing, and the fact that Isaac called upon the name of Yahweh suggests that formal worship with sacrifices was involved. The two questions asked above in relation to Abraham's altars, namely 'why did Abraham build altars?' and 'what did he do with them?', are relevant even here. Apart from a formal act of worship, compatible with the patriarchal lifestyle being involved here, it is possible to suggest that building an altar at Beer-sheba, the southernmost border of the promised land,[96] may have represented not only a claim to the land but also a legitimation of the sanctuary for later Israel.[97]

Therefore, as in the case of Abraham, Isaac built an altar following a theophany and with the intention of staying there for a while. As there is no evidence of a Canaanite settlement prior to Isaac's arrival there, and since Isaac himself was the officiant in the cult, it is reasonable to think that Isaac's worship is compatible with the patriarchal wandering lifestyle. While the idea of worship itself is common with that of the ancient Near East and Israel, the pattern of patriarchal worship is distinct from both the ancient Near East and Israel, where temples, priests and cultic calendars played an important role.

c. *Altars and Sacrifices in the Jacob Cycle*

Not only altars but also pillars are frequently associated with Jacob. I shall, however, focus on his altars and sacrifices, pillars being considered in Chapter 4. On two occasions Jacob is said to have built altars (Gen. 33.20; 35.7) and on two other occasions he is said to have offered sacrifices. If the latter occasions presuppose the building of altars, do the former presuppose sacrifices? I shall deal with these questions

96. Cf. the expression 'from Dan to Beer-sheba', Judg. 20.1; 1 Sam. 3.20; 2 Sam. 3.10; 17.11; 24.2, 15; 1 Kgs 5.5.

97. Pilgrims resorted to oracles from Beer-sheba in eighth-century Israel (Amos 5.5; 8.14); Skinner 1930: 327.

separately and see how these cultic practices reveal the nature of the patriarch's religion.

Altars (Genesis 33.20; 35.1, 3, 7). The verb used previously for building altars, בנה, is replaced by נצב, 'to erect', in 33.20, and עשה, 'to make', in 35.1, 3, though the author returns to בנה in 35.7. Some scholars think that the change of verb in 33.20 indicates that Jacob had originally erected a pillar as he did on other occasions (28.18; 31.45; 35.14, 20), but that a later hand changed it to מזבח because pillars were proscribed in later Israel. It is further argued that only בנה and עשה referred to altars, never נצב,[98] but others think that the use of נצב does not prove that Jacob erected a pillar. Further, נצב is also used for setting up a pile of stones elsewhere (2 Sam. 18.17) (Delitzsch 1850: 217; Wenham 1994: 301). However, given the similarity of the form between מצבה and מזבח, it is more probable that a scribe mistook one for the other than that he made an intentional correction. In any case מזבח would not have entirely removed Jacob's association with pillars, since Jacob elsewhere is clearly described as having raised pillars. While it is possible that מצבה was original, the context in 33.20 suggests a more formal worship with a period of settlement, for which מזבח would be more appropriate than מצבה. In view of Jacob's settlement at Shechem, Westermann's remark on Gen. 12.8 that altars and tents went together with patriarchs also holds good here (1985: 156-57). In view of Jacob offering sacrifices on other occasions (31.54; 46.1), it is plausible to think that Jacob offered sacrifices on this altar.

Once again, the previous observation that patriarchs built altars when they intended to settle down at a place for a while is confirmed by Jacob's actions at Shechem. The text clearly states that Jacob built his altar in the place he had bought from the natives to erect his tent. For the author this altar was none other than Jacob's own, just as were Abraham's and Isaac's. It is not clear, however, if Jacob had intended to offer sacrifice on this altar—Abraham and Isaac 'called upon the name of Yahweh' when they built altars, but this phrase is significantly lacking here. On the other hand, it is said that Jacob named the altar in Gen. 33.20 as אל אלהי ישראל. What is the meaning of naming the altar? Is it compatible with the life and experience of the patriarch? What did the author think of it?

---

98. Dillmann 1897: 293; Procksch 1924: 378; Skinner 1930: 416; de Pury 1975: 442; Westermann 1985: 529; *BHS*, note.

In the light of the practice of Abraham and Isaac, it is reasonable to think that Jacob built this altar in order to worship God, because it followed a theophany and a movement to a new place, despite the temporary stop at Succoth. Thus the naming of the altar does not necessarily undermine the function of the altar as a place of sacrifice. But it probably adds an extra element to it, in that Jacob had a special reason for building this altar besides using it for formal worship. The immediate context suggests that the name of the altar was to reflect Jacob's own experience with the God who met him in his crisis and even changed his name (32.29). Such naming of altars was not unusual in Israel.[99] In this sense, this altar may also have represented a 'memorial' of Jacob's experience, and 'Israel' in the name may refer to Jacob and not to the people 'Israel' (Cross 1973: 49; Sarna 1989: 232). If the combination אלהי ישׂראל refers to 'the God of Israel' as in other cases, then it should be noted that 'the God of Israel' usually refers to Yahweh, not El. Therefore it is doubtful, as some scholars have argued,[100] that the naming was programmatic for an author who was describing the religious struggles of Israel after the settlement when the worship of the God of Israel had replaced the cult of El, since after the settlement El, as the supreme God of Israel, was less an issue than was Israel's loyalty to Yahweh. In any case, El's importance was already waning in the Canaanite pantheon toward the end of the second millennium, and El was never as serious a contender to Yahwistic faith as was Baal. Thus it is more plausible to think that the patriarch, who did not know Yahweh, affirmed that El was his God, than to attribute this statement to later Israel. If the author was Yahwistic, it would contradict his faith to describe a religious stage in Israel when the Canaanite El was the God of Israel. Therefore Jacob's altar at Shechem should be regarded as compatible with the lifestyle of the patriarch and as having been intended not only for a memorial, but also for offering worship and sacrifices.

Both archaeological evidence (cf. Wright 1965: 123-38; Campbell and Wright 1969: 104-16) and biblical tradition indicate that there was more than one shrine at Shechem during the time of Israel's settlement (Josh. 24.26; Judg. 9.4, 6, 37, 46). The present text, however, states that Jacob camped 'before the city', פני העיר (33. 18), as was the usual practice with other patriarchs. As I have argued above, there is no

99. Cf. Gen. 35.7; Exod. 17.15, Judg. 6.24; Ezek. 48.35. Sarna 1989: 232 n. 15.
100. Kapelrud 1966: 46-47; cf. Eissfeldt 1956: 35; Westermann 1985: 529-30.

evidence of a shrine outside the city during the patriarchal period, and it is difficult to prove that the patriarchs worshipped at an existing shrine (cf. n. 73 above).

Jacob is also said to have built an altar in Bethel at the direction of Yahweh (35.1-7). Three issues may be immediately identified in this passage: the occasion, preparation and building of the altar. First, the occasion for building an altar is clearest here of all the patriarchal altars. Although Abraham was commanded to offer his son as a burnt offering, which inevitably assumes the building of an altar, only here is there an explicit command to a patriarch to build one. So Abraham, Isaac and even Jacob built altars as part of their practice of worshipping God, but here the occasion was prompted by God and the text suggests that it was associated with the specific theophany to Jacob at Bethel.[101] Thus both the place to build this altar and the occasion are made clear to Jacob as never before. Nevertheless, there are some features shared with the previous occasions, for which the texts presuppose that there were no altars already existing there and that the patriarchs were the sole cultic officiants. Further, if the occasion was to fulfil Jacob's previous vow at Bethel, the context and the circumstances fit quite well with the overall Jacob story, Jacob having already been reminded of his forgotten vow while still in the service of Laban (31.13) and commanded to return to his native country.[102] Jacob's initial response to this reminder (35.3) is also suggestive of a recollection of his vow and God's part in it, as God had kept Jacob safe from the wiles of Laban and the attacks of both Esau and the Shechemites. Jacob returns to the promised land, but not to Bethel, to fulfil his vow. In fact when Jacob finally arrived at Bethel to worship God, there is no mention of a fulfilment of the vow.

Secondly, the ritual preparation of purification and parting from foreign gods before worship, though not part of God's direction, is unique to this particular instance. That such preparation was not only a necessary preliminary before presenting oneself at the sanctuary but also a very common custom in the ancient Near East, has already been observed regarding Keret and others.[103] Here my focus will remain on

101. Cf. Dillmann 1897: 302-303; Westermann 1985: 551-53; Wenham 1994: 321-23.
102. Here Jacob may be compared to Keret who forgot his vow to Anath. Cf. Skinner 1930: 423; Wenham 1994: 323.
103. Cf. Gunkel 1902: 336; Procksch 1924: 381-82; von Rad 1961: 331-32.

Jacob's altar and whether it is compatible with his lifestyle and religion as portrayed in the Genesis account. The occasion and the circumstances described in the story suggest that the altar built by Jacob was compatible with the lifestyle of Jacob. If so, what did Jacob do with his altar? This leads me to my third point, the altar.

When Jacob arrived at Bethel, 'he built an altar there and called the place "El Bethel"' (ויבן שם מזבח ויקרא למקום אל בית־אל). But unlike at Shechem, where the altar received the name, here it is the place that received the name, אל בית־אל. Such a place name, which had already been given by Jacob on his earlier visit, is strange, and the reason given, that it was because God had revealed himself to him there when he had fled from his brother, does not help much either.[104] However, God's reminder to Jacob of his encounter with him at Bethel, together with Jacob's recollection of the incident, confirms that this altar was the result of the vow made by Jacob when he had first met with God (28.20-22) (for Jacob's vow, see Chapter 6 §4), though this is not stated explicitly. The elaborate preparations before they reached Bethel also suggest that this was not only for presenting themselves before God but also to worship him. Altar building in relation to fulfilling a vow certainly suggests sacrifices. Thus, as in the case of Shechem, the naming of the place only adds an extra aspect to the worship, but does not conflict with its sacrificial aspect. Therefore it is legitimate to suppose that Jacob's altar involved sacrifices.

The place of Bethel has an unbroken tradition of having a shrine from the third millennium BCE. As argued in Chapter 4 below, the place of Jacob's altar should be distinguished from the site of the traditional shrine, which had previously been called Luz. The new name given by Jacob to the place of his altar was probably extended to the traditional site so that the name Bethel then applied to the whole place.

Sacrifices (Genesis 31.54; 46.1). While Jacob's altars implied sacrifices, there are two occasions when Jacob is explicitly said to have offered sacrifices—one following a covenant between him and Laban, and the other when he heard that Joseph, whom he thought was dead,

104. Among the suggested are: 'Bethel', LXX, Syriac, Vulgate, Westermann; 'El is in Bethel', Jacob 1934: 662; a similar title, 'Ilu-bayt-ilī' is also found in an Assyro-Tyrian treaty, Speiser 1964: 244. But Sarna's (1989: 240) suggestion, ' "the God of Bethel", that is, the one whose associations with Jacob were repeatedly bound up with Bethel', is probably more appropriate to the context.

was still living. In the covenant between Jacob and Laban, it was Laban who sought to make this treaty, probably because it was his interests that were under threat. We have parallels to such treaties in Genesis itself. Abimelech had sought to conclude a covenant with Abraham (Gen. 21.22-24) because he realized that Abraham was a force to reckon with since God was with him (Wenham 1994: 92), but Abraham seized this opportunity to settle the dispute in which Abimelech's servants had seized Abraham's wells, probably violently or illegally. The covenant took the form of swearing and exchange of gifts, as was customary in treaties and covenants (1 Kgs 15.19; Wenham 1994: 93). Though not mentioned, it is quite likely that the covenant ended with a meal just as was the case later when Abimelech sought to make a similar covenant with Isaac (Gen. 26.26-31 cf. Exod. 24.11; 2 Sam. 3.20-21). These are similar to the Jacob–Laban covenant, in that in each of them a superior recognizes the rising power of the inferior, the superior seeks a treaty, the inferior accepts the terms, both parties swear an oath of mutual non-aggression, and they share a meal together (cf. McCarthy 1964: 182; Sarna 1989: 221). By contrast, there is no mention of sacrifice in the covenant ceremonies of either Abraham or Isaac, though it is possible that Isaac's feast might allude to it (so McCarthy 1964: 184). The practice of holding sacrificial meals is widely attested in the second millennium BCE in the ancient Near East and among Semitic nomads. Thus one cannot assume with Gunkel and others that the Genesis covenants are etiological stories (McCarthy 1964: 182, 185).

The covenant between Jacob and Laban, like most covenants in the ancient Near East, is of a religious nature, in which each swears by his own deity, who is called to act as judge if either of them should violate the treaty. Only Jacob is said to have offered sacrifices on this occasion, probably because Laban at that time would not have had the where-withal to do so. The word used for sacrifice here and in 46.1 is זבח, which is a general term for sacrifice. The priestly regulations apply this term, combined with שלמים, to the particular sacrifice of 'well-being offerings' (Lev. 3; 7.11-21, 34, 35) which are made as thanksgiving, votive and free-will offerings (cf. Driver 1948: 289). As I have noted, the Ugaritic *šlmm* probably refers to the 'peace between the worshipper and the deity', and the priestly שלמים has a similar meaning that 'peace is meant to be achieved' through it. The context of the Jacob–Laban treaty certainly fits such a meaning. It is, therefore, likely that a שלמים זבח was involved here.

The other occasion when Jacob offered sacrifices was when he was about to go down to Egypt after hearing that his beloved son was still living. As in 31.54, זבח is used on this momentous occasion. If the priestly זבח שלמים is any guide here, it is quite likely that Jacob offered sacrifices as a thanksgiving for Joseph whose life had been preserved, the plural זבחים possibly suggesting the number of sacrifices made. Usually building or erecting an altar or pillar followed a theophany, but here the order is reversed. Thus it is probable that Jacob sought guidance through his sacrifices before leaving for Egypt.[105] 'Such a move as Jacob is undertaking requires divine sanction, the more so in that to leave Canaan is to retreat from the promised land' (Wenham 1994: 440). It is possible that the patriarchs sought guidance within their usual worship which included sacrifices, though not by examining the parts of the sacrificial victims as in Babylon.

Thus Jacob's altars at Shechem and Bethel seem to have had more than one purpose, but only the altar at Shechem was similar to those of Abraham and Isaac, because they were built either in response to a theophany or due to a move to a new place. Yet Jacob's altar at Shechem had an extra feature, namely that it was also named, probably as a memorial to Jacob's recent experiences.

Jacob's altar at Bethel is unique among the patriarchal altars, since it was demanded by God, promised by Jacob as part of his vow, and marked by unusual ritual preparations on the part of the patriarch and his family. It was also unique in the sense that the naming of the place was added to the ceremony, suggesting that this altar, besides being used for sacrifices, was also used as a memorial to Jacob's renewed allegiance to God.

Of all the patriarchs, only Jacob is said to have offered 'sacrifices' twice, once to seal the covenant between Laban and him, and once to thank God for Joseph's life and to seek guidance for his move to Egypt. In all this, Jacob's altars and sacrifices, while having certain parallels in the ancient Near East and Israel, are unique and compatible only with his wandering lifestyle and with the religion of the other patriarchs. Yet among the patriarchs, Jacob's religious practices are distinct from those of others. Further, unlike Abraham and Isaac, Jacob's usual response to theophany was not to build an altar, but to erect a pillar.

---

105. Cf. Balaam's (Num. 23) and Babylonian sacrifices as a means for guidance.

d. *Cult of the Dead*
Several scholars argue that certain of the patriarchal sacrifices, funerary and burial customs imply a practice of the cult of the dead as in the ancient Near East and Israel. It is important to examine this issue to present a comprehensive picture of patriarchal religious practices.

A cult of the dead in the ancient Near East, as discussed above (§2), involved propitiating the deceased through sacrifice, ritual and magic. These practices reflect a belief that the dead seek an afterlife which their living kin can provide through these rituals. Further, the rituals were also intended to ensure that the deceased would be benevolent, not malevolent, to their descendants. Thus, in practice, the deceased are treated as part of the family and community, and their approval is sought on important matters of the life of the family or community (Levine 1993: 472). It is necessary, at this point, to examine the biblical evidence, especially the patriarchal narratives, to see if any of their sacrifices or funerary and burial customs involved a cult of the dead.

Death, מות, is spoken about and described as normal and apparently thought of as the cessation of life and activity and a discontinuity of relationships with the living.[106] Burial is recorded for Sarah (Gen. 23), Abraham (25.9), Deborah (35.8), Rachel (35.19 cf. 48.7), Isaac (35.29) and Jacob (50.13). All except Deborah and Rachel were buried in the family grave at Machpelah, as were also Rebekah and Leah (49.31). The family graves and the desire to be buried with one's ancestors may indicate not only a belief in a kind of afterlife but also in an 'ongoing communion with one's deceased relatives' (Spronk 1986: 240-41). The formulaic phrase 'gathered to his people', נאסף אל-עמיו, added in the case of Abraham, Ishmael, Isaac and Jacob (25.8, 17; 35.29; 49.33), and elsewhere used only of Moses and Aaron, might indicate joining one's relatives in the afterlife.[107] Thus the burial practices of the patriarchs suggest that they believed in some kind of continuation of life after death. For this reason the texts seem to be interested more in a proper burial than in any cult of the dead. This is confirmed by the

106. מות in its verbal and nominal forms occurs 67 times in the patriarchal stories. Cf. Gen. 23.2; 37.33-35; 38.12, etc. Cf. Bailey 1979: 47-61; Alexander 1986: 41-46.
107. Some scholars argue that this phrase meant secondary burial, e.g. Meyers 1970: 2-29; cf. Alfrink 1948: 118-31; Illmann 1979: 43-45; Johnston 1993: 88-90.

family tombs[108] and the desire for proper burial in later Israel.[109] The archaeological studies of Early, Middle and Late Bronze Age tombs seem to suggest the idea of family tombs (Mazar 1990: 98-99, 213-14, 277-78). Do family tombs mean care or veneration of the dead? Many scholars think that the presence of jewellery, clothes, weapons, sometimes furniture, pottery and especially bowls and jars connected by a hole outside indicate probable care for the dead, but others strongly contest this interpretation.[110] A t Ebla, possibly also at Hazor and Byblos, royal cemeteries were found connected to the temple dedicated to Reshep, a god of the nether world, suggesting not only the care for the dead but also their veneration (Spronk 1986: 139-41). Occasionally bones of domestic animals and fish were also found (Horwitz 1987: 251-55). It is possible, as many scholars think, that these grave-materials either originally belonged to the deceased[111] or were supplied later by their relatives who believed that the dead must be gratified with food and some of their most cherished possessions (*ERE*, IV: 428, 443-44). It is possible that certain grave-materials and installations of pipes or conduits suggest the nourishing of the dead or even the cult of the dead in Palestine, but some think that archaeological evidence is inconclusive 'without additional literary evidence' (Spronk 1986: 141, 258) as we have in case of Ugarit and Mesopotamia. In the latter case the offerings were intended to be a nourishment to the dead as well as to secure favours or blessings for their relatives.[112] In the light of these observations, I shall examine the relevant Genesis texts.

Genesis 23; 37.34, 35; 42.38; 44.29, 31. Although Genesis 23 is mainly concerned with Abraham's purchase of the cave of Machpelah for Sarah's burial, some scholars interpret it as Abraham's stake in the

108. Josh. 24.30, 32; Judg. 8.32; 16.31; 1 Sam. 25.1; 2 Sam. 2.32; 17.23; 21.12-14; 1 Kgs 2.34; Isa. 22.16.

109. 1 Kgs 14.11; Isa. 14.4-23; Jer. 16.4; 22.19; Ezek. 29.5; cf. de Vaux 1961: 56-57; Spronk 1986: 238.

110. At Ugarit besides such tomb installations, a special term for the pipe or conduit, *arūtu*, or *knkn* is attested; Pope 1981: 161; cf. Astour 1980: 228; Spronk 1986: 142-45; Lewis 1989: 97; Bloch-Smith 1992a: 108; 1992b: 220-24. Contrast Johnston 1993: 83-84; Pitard 1994: 20-37.

111. 1 Sam. 28.14 and Ezek. 32.27 may indicate that the dead were buried fully clothed.

112. Spronk 1986: 145-49; *KTU*, 1.161; 1.6.vi, 45-49; 1.113; cf. Finkelstein 1966: 95-118; Bayliss 1973: 115-24; Lewis 1989: 7-10, 31.

promised land.[113] Others see here a link between burial, land ownership and ancestral cult (Brichto 1973: 9-12). Still others argue that it is the Priestly writer's polemic against the ancestral cult 'as there are no ritual acts, no future hope of an after-life: death is regarded as a [*sic*] impenetrable frontier' (Bray 1993: 72). However, the last mentioned view seems to be an overstatement. First, it is doubtful if Genesis 23 can be unequivocally established as from P, since scholars widely differ on this matter.[114] Secondly, it is almost impossible to think that there were no ritual acts at the death scene (23.2). ספד is used almost exclusively for mourning for the dead, and בכה is used both for weeping in general and for mourning for the dead. For Westermann, the use of these two words together is probably 'based on a fixed expression (also in Ezek. 24.23)'. He continues: 'The further addition of the verb ויבא ("he went in") designates what takes place as a ritual action' (1985: 373). This might involve other traditional mourning customs, such as rending garments, dishevelling hair, cutting the beard, scattering dust on the head, fasting and refraining from washing and perfumes.[115] Therefore it is almost certain that ritual mourning was involved in Genesis 23.

But does this mean that the cult of the dead is also implied here? Lewis argues that the usual mourning rites which lasted for seven days (Gen. 50.10; 1 Sam. 31.13; 1 Chron. 10.12) involved a ritual descent into the underworld in order to bring back the dead from the clutches of death or to invoke the ancestral shades (Lewis 1989: 43-46). Thus Jacob's mourning for Joseph (Gen. 37.34, 35) and David's for his son (2 Sam. 12.15-24) indicate a ritual descent into the underworld, as portrayed in *KTU* 1.161, 21-22. However, this is unlikely, even though Jacob seemed to have been engaged in full mourning rituals as he tore his clothes, put on sackcloth and 'mourned' for his son (as in Gen. 23.2 both ספד and בכה are used here). Lewis's argument is based on the interpretation of ירד in the *KTU* text where, although the ritual is obvious, the 'subject and nature of the descent to *arṣ* is unclear' (Johnston 1993: 158). In its biblical usage ירד in relation to death usually means 'a descent to the place of death', which is variously described as pit,

113. Von Rad 1965: 245; Eichrodt 1967: 218; Westermann 1985: 376.

114. Skinner 1930: 335; Speiser 1964: 173; von Rad 1965: 249; McEvenue 1971: 22; Wenham 1994: 124-25.

115. Josh. 7.6; 1 Sam. 4.12; 2 Sam. 12.20; 15.30; 19.5; Isa. 22.12; Jer. 16.6; 41.5; Ezek. 7.18; 24.15-24; Amos 8.10; Job 1.20; 2.12; Neh. 9.1; cf. de Vaux 1961: 59; Spronk 1986: 244; Wenham 1994: 126.

sheol, grave, silence, dust, death, people of old, and so on. This is a place of no return; only Yahweh could raise them up.[116] Thus the ritual mourning of Jacob indicates only his overwhelming grief over his beloved son Joseph. A similar sentiment is also expressed later at the thought of Benjamin's death (42.38; 44.29, 31). In both these instances it probably means that Jacob 'will remain mourning until his death' (Westermann 1986: 44; cf. Wenham 1994: 357). It is equally unlikely in David's case to mean a ritual descent into the underworld. Indeed, his words, 'Can I bring him back again?', and his pleading with God indicate the reverse (cf. Emerton 1991: 384; Johnston 1993: 159). Therefore there is no suggestion of a ritual descent here.

Thirdly, it is doubtful that there is no hope of afterlife in the texts. As noted above, the desire for a proper burial, the desire to be buried in the family grave and the stereotyped phrase 'gathered to his people' suggest some belief in the afterlife. Moreover, this formula is used only for the patriarchs and for Moses and Aaron. It could not have meant burial in the family grave since this is mentioned after the record of death and before burial in the case of the patriarchs, except that for Jacob 'died' and for Ishmael 'buried' is omitted; and in any case it cannot be applied to Moses and Aaron as they were not buried in their family grave (Johnston 1993: 90).

If ritual mourning does not necessarily imply a cult of the dead, does family burial imply it? Bloch-Smith argues that the biblical pattern of family burial suggests the belief that the dead ancestors possessed certain powers since they maintained the intimate contact with God that they had during their lifetime, and 'it is important for the supplicant to know the location of the burial in order to petition the deceased' (1992a: 111; cf. *ABD*, II: 106-108). However, it is recorded that only six people (Abraham, Sarah, Isaac, Rebekah, Jacob and Leah) were buried in the cave of Machpelah (Gen. 49.31; 50.13 cf. 25.9, 10; 35.29), and the cave was certainly important as a burial place for the family line of Abraham, but it is not certain whether an ancestral cult was practised at Machpelah. First, the burials of Rebekah and Leah are not described, but simply reported later. If this place was so important for ancestral cult, their burial would surely have been recorded along with its mourning customs. Even Isaac's burial in the first instance is recorded without a mention of the cave of Machpelah. This is simply

116. Num. 16.30, 33; 33.24; Isa. 38.18; Ezek. 26.20; 31.14; Pss. 22.29; 28.1; 55.23; 115.17; Job 7.9; etc. Cf. *TDOT*, V: 319-20; Westermann 1986: 44.

assumed. By contrast, burial was not recorded for several major Old Testament figures such as Ishmael, Aaron, Othniel, Ehud, Shamgar, Deborah, Eli, Jeroboam, Ahab, Jeroboam II, Hezekiah in Kings and Jehoakim. On the other hand, burial of some minor figures (Rebekah's nurse, Asahel, Ahithophel) is recorded, but not that of many others. 'Thus burial was not so important that it was necessarily recorded whenever a death was narrated or, in pre-literary tradition, that it formed a necessary part of any tradition' (Johnston 1993: 85). Secondly, important people in the clan, such as Ishmael and Rachel, were not buried at Machpelah (Gen. 25.17; 35.19). Conversely, Joseph's bones were buried at Shechem where none of the patriarchal family members seems to have been buried (Josh. 24.32).[117] Thus mourning practices are apparently more important than burial places in the patriarchal texts. Thirdly, there is no implication of any sort, either in the patriarchal stories or elsewhere, that the famous dead ever maintained intimate contact with God, and that people petitioned at their graves. The most suitable candidate to have maintained intimate contact with Yahweh after his death would have been Moses, but his burial and grave are surrounded with mystery (Deut. 34.5-6), and there is no record of any petition to him by anyone later in history. Human mediators have their part (Jer. 15.1), but not after their death. 'The only recorded consultation of a famous person (Samuel) occurred far from his burial place' (Johnston 1993: 87). And even here Samuel was not the ancestor (אב) of Saul, and the texts do not condone the actions of the latter (cf. Johnston 1993: 129). Therefore, while proper burial and family burial were desirable during patriarchal times and later, and mourning rituals were part of the burial practices in general, there is no indication of a practice of the ancestral cult in the patriarchal narratives. Thus Albertz sums up: 'while the significance attached to the tombs of paternal and maternal ancestors in the patriarchal narratives and formulas like "be gathered to his fathers"…still indicate that there was emotional solidarity between the living members of the family and their dead ancestors, there are no references whatsoever in the patriarchal narratives to a regular cult of the dead of the kind evident, for example, in the *kispu* ritual of Mesopotamia, and elsewhere they are scanty…' (1994a: 38; cf. Bailey 1979: 35-36).

117. Bloch-Smith (1992a: 114-15), wrongly assumes that Joseph was interred in the family grave. She probably means at Shechem, but there is no record of a family grave prior to Joseph's interment there.

However, several scholars think that a cult of the dead can be seen in certain other practices in patriarchal stories, such as the Bethel episode where Jacob vows tithes to God, and the Jacob–Laban treaty and the communal meal that followed. I shall examine these texts in turn.

Genesis 28.22; 31.44-54. Following Halevi, Bloch-Smith translates אלהים, בית אלהים and אלהי אביהם in these texts as 'divine beings' (referring to the deified ancestors), 'shrine to the deified ancestors' and 'their ancestral deities' respectively. She argues that אלהים is 'unequivocally used for the dead Samuel' in 1 Samuel 28; that Isa. 8.19 provides another example of this use; that the tithe offered in Gen. 28.22 was the same tithe prohibited to the dead in Deut. 26.14; and that the anointing of, and pouring drink offerings to, the מצבה and the sacrifices on the hill-tops in Gen. 31.52-54 are all part of the cult of the dead (1992a: 123-24, 127-28; 1992b: 220-22). Most scholars, however, take אלהים in 1 Sam. 28.13 as 'supernatural being or spirit'[118] following Akkadian, Ugaritic, Hittite, Egyptian and Phoenician parallels, although it could also mean 'deceased children and ancestors' in Akkadian, 'dead and deceased kings' at Ugarit, and 'dead and deified kings' in Hittite and Egyptian sources.[119] אלהים in Isa. 8.19 may mean 'spirits of the dead' or simply 'spirits' (see discussion in Johnston 1993: 10-15). It is possible, though not unequivocal, that אלהים in these two occasions refers to the dead. But it is unlikely that it has the same meaning in Genesis 28 and 31. The context in the former case clearly demands some meaning such as 'spirits' or 'gods', but there is no justification to read the same meaning in the latter, since Jacob was nowhere near the graves of his ancestors, and the place where he lay had no significance for the story prior to his lodging. Further, Jacob was taken totally by surprise in the story as he was not expecting an encounter with God, let alone with an ancestor. By the same reasoning it would be impossible to establish that Jacob and Laban were involved in a cult of the dead in Gen. 31.44-54. Bloch-Smith sees the stone 'pillar', מצבה, probably also the 'cairn', גל, the sacrifices on the hill, בהר זבח, and the phrase אביהם

118. Elsewhere it could mean 'household gods', 'judges' or 'rulers', 'supernatural beings' and occasionally 'specific man'. Gen. 31.30, 32 cf. vv. 19, 34, 35; Exod. 21.6; 22.7-8; Pss. 8.6; 82.1, 6; Gordon 1935: 140; Johnston 1993: 110.

119. Cf. variously *RLA*, III: 543; Bayliss 1973: 117 n. 19; Kitchen 1977: 132; Spronk 1986: 147 n. 4; Knoppers 1992: 114-15; Hornung 1983: 156; Johnston 1993: 110-15.

אלהי ('their ancestral deities' according to her) in their oath, as evidence for a cult of the dead. However, the language in the context and the names given to the pillar and cairn suggest a treaty among the non-literary cultures. Thus a majority of scholars see the transaction between them as a 'non-aggression pact' and the communal meal as the sealing and 'conclusion of the dispute' (Buis 1966: 399; Westermann 1985: 498-500). The sacrifices by Jacob in v. 54 also must be seen as part of the covenant (Wenham 1994: 281-82). Therefore there is no suggestion here of an ancestral cult as assumed by Bloch-Smith. Similarly, Bloch-Smith's assumption that the tithe vowed in Gen. 28.22 is the same tithe prohibited as an offering to the dead in Deut. 26.14b is impossible to maintain. The latter text says that an Israelite presenting his tithe must declare that he has 'not eaten it in mourning, or carried it while unclean or given to the dead'. Some scholars have interpreted the meaning of the last phrase 'to the dead', למת, as that which is given for the refreshment of the mourners or the grave food for the dead spirits (Reider 1937: 241; de Vaux 1961: 60). This is possible in view of the Deuteronomic concern for the poor and the needy, but it is not convincing. On the other hand, the text implies that only tithed food, not food in general, was denied to the dead. Since the tithe was an offering to God, presenting it to the dead probably implied their veneration, hence the Deuteronomic editors prohibited the practice, but they probably allowed the 'grave food'[120] for the normal care of the dead,[121] which was thought to be harmless in later Jewish traditions.[122] It is possible that the patriarchs were involved in such activities, but the texts themselves are silent about it. On the other hand, the story of Jacob at Bethel has no hint of any mourning or even any memorial of an ancestor. Jacob's tithe is clearly related to the vow, which he made not to an ancestor but to Yahweh, whom he has just met. Therefore Bloch-Smith's assumption has no basis in the text.

120. To call it 'grave offerings', as it is often done, is 'potentially misleading' because of the term's sacrificial connotation; Johnston 1993: 136 n. 16.

121. Von Rad 1966: 160; Spronk 1986: 248; Johnston 1993: 136-37. Contra Driver 1895: 292; Lewis 1989: 103.

122. Tob. 4.17; Ecclus 30.18 (this text could even be a ridicule of the practice, so Driver); 2 Macc. 12.45.

Other Proposed Reference to the Cult of the Dead. Several scholars claim that burial markers such as Rachel's grave-stone in Gen. 35.19-20 (cf. Absalom's memorial stone, 2 Sam. 18.18), and the oak at Bethel where Deborah, Rebekah's nurse, was buried served as loci for death cult activities in Israel.[123] Apparently Rachel's grave remained significant in the preserved tradition (Gen. 48.7; 1 Sam. 10.2; Jer. 31.15-17; Mt. 2.17-18), but the view that Rachel's tomb became a place of pilgrimage for generations is based on a dubious interpretation of the word בצלצח as 'in the shade of a shiny rock' in 1 Sam. 10.2. Luker argues that the tombstone became smooth and shiny because of the continual anointing of it by pilgrims (*ABD*, V: 609). However, none of the traditions suggests cultic activity at Rachel's tomb. On the contrary, the last two texts cited indicate a prophetic imagination that Rachel was weeping for her children, the exiled Israelites, because her tomb was situated on the border of Benjamin and Ephraim. There is no suggestion of grave activities or of someone pleading at the ancestress's grave to help the exiles return. Therefore Rachel's grave stone is to be regarded as a memorial stone, like Absalom's monument (Graesser 1972: 40), about which Johnston comments: '[the cult of the dead] involved nourishing and feasting with the departed, and a pillar could hardly do this. If this cult was prevalent, Absalom would probably have adopted a son or commissioned a priest to conduct it (cf. Egyptian practice). If anything, erecting a monument suggests the unnecessariness of an ancestral cult' (1993: 159). Similarly, it is unlikely that the grave of an insignificant character like Deborah, unknown elsewhere in the Old Testament, should become a place of the cult of the dead. Oak trees are sometimes associated with theophanies and cultic activities (Gen. 12.6; 13.4, 18; 18.1) of the patriarchs, but there is no such suggestion here. And there is not even a memorial except for the once-for-all activity of mourning, which gave rise to the name 'oak of weeping'.

5. *Conclusion*

A distinct pattern of patriarchal worship emerges from investigation into altars and sacrifices within the patriarchal narratives. Unlike in the ancient Near East and Israel, where worship was highly organized with an established cult and cultic personnel and with the occasion, purpose

---

123. Albright 1957b: 251, 257; Lewis 1989: 119; Bloch-Smith 1992a: 113-14; cf. Eliade 1958: 217-19.

and procedures of sacrifices elaborately prescribed, the patriarchal cultic practices were informal with no fixed cult place or cult personnel and with no prescribed sacrifices or procedures. The places of their altars were usually outside the settled communities and probably distinct from their public shrines. At Shechem and Beer-sheba there was no evidence of a Canaanite shrine during the patriarchal period. At Bethel, it is uncertain whether the wandering patriarchs used the Canaanite shrine or not. The occasions for their sacrifices were usually a theophany and moving to a new place, or covenant and guidance. Unlike in the ancient Near East and Israel, they had no festival or sacrifices for healing. Battles are recounted in the text, but there is no hint of the patriarchs offering sacrifices or invoking God for help on these occasions. The nature of their sacrifice is less certain. It was probably mainly part of their worship, but also served to fulfil vows or for thanksgiving. But there is no evidence of a cult of the dead nor a hint of caring of the dead.

Thus, patriarchal altars and sacrifices are depicted not so much as offerings in fulfilment of a requirement, as was the case in both ancient Near Eastern and Israelite cult, but as a spontaneous act of worship in response to God's dealings with them. Thus they appear not only to be living as aliens in the land but also as aliens to the native cult. Their social and political relations with the indigenous inhabitants were harmonious, but only on the basis that they were still aliens. This means that their ethnic difference made them distinct as much as their religious practices. This probably had a large effect on their religious observances. The problem of religious syncretism became an issue only after Israel claimed the land as her own and wanted to become like the native inhabitants, but this does not seem to have been a problem for the patriarchs. Thus their religion was probably less syncretistic than that of Israel at other periods.

Chapter 3

PRAYER

1. *Introduction*

That prayer and the patriarchal altars went together is evident from the frequent phrase, 'called upon the name of Yahweh', that accompanied the patriarchal actions of either building altars or planting a tree. Though the idea of prayer is implicit in sacrifice, the former may still exist on its own as one of the most effective forms of drawing God's attention to human needs. It is the motivation, form and results of prayer that reveal not only the religious ethos of the patriarchs, but also their theology of prayer.[1] It is the task of this chapter to explore the form and theology of patriarchal prayer as portrayed in Genesis. The fundamental occasion for any prayer is a situation of dire need in which a person cannot cope without help (cf. Buck 1975: 61). The most common such situations are childlessness, natural calamities, disease and other evil forces, danger from enemies and threat of war, and a host of other real or imagined dangers. It will be argued that, as with the patriarchal altars, the situation and theology of patriarchal prayer is compatible with patriarchal lifestyle portrayed in Genesis.

At least five different forms of prayer may be identified: (1) prayer of petition, (2) thanksgiving and praise, (3) intercession, (4) penitence and confession, and (5) curses and blessing. Not all these forms are prominent in every culture, but in one way or another most of these elements are reflected in prayer. Since prayer may fall into one or other of these forms, I shall focus on each of them separately and see how in the ancient Near East and Israel particular forms were used and what religious ideas and theology of prayer were reflected by them. Finally, I

---

1. Cf. Greenberg's (1983) view that biblical prose prayer is a window to Israel's popular religion, and Miller's (1994) view that the form of prayer reveals its theology.

shall focus on the patriarchal forms of prayer, and then compare them with the ancient Near East and Israel in order to see whether they are distinct or similar and in what ways they reflect the patriarchal religious ethos. However, before we look into the forms of prayer in different cultures it will be helpful to explain certain general characteristics of these different forms.

a. *Types of Prayer*
Petitionary Prayer. This is the most common form of prayer, and usually assumes a situation of distress or trouble. Sometimes it takes the form of a lament, as often in the psalms. The basic form of this prayer consists of three elements, namely address to the deity, petition for help and motivation clauses (cf. Heiler 1958: 15-40). Sometimes other elements such as a complaint, a statement of confidence and trust or a vow of praise are also present, mostly in psalmic prayers. The aim of the address is to make contact with the deity by identifying the deity by name or titles or by describing the relationship of the petitioner to the deity, thereby establishing a basis for seeking help. Sometimes the address may include praise and exaltation which is motivational, at other times self-deprecation, which facilitates the petition.[2] The heart of the petitionary prayer, however, is the petition for help. While the address focuses on the deity, the petition focuses on the suppliant by describing in specific terms the suppliant's situation. Once this is secured, the petitioner makes specific requests usually in the words 'deliver/save/help' or 'forgive/heal' (Miller 1994: 91-92). The motivation clause gives reasons for the deity's intervention by using explicit and direct motivational expressions. These describe the deity's nature and character, such as his justice, faithfulness and goodness, or highlight the petitioner's affliction and helplessness or his faithfulness, loyalty and relationship to the deity.[3] Such motivation may already be initiated in the address itself, but it is made secure by explicit and direct motivational expressions.

There is no suggestion in any prayer that following these steps will automatically secure the desired results, except in some magical rituals (Walton 1989: 148-51). At the same time, petitioners assume that the deity can be persuaded and moved to act in their favour. Even in Israel

---

2.   Greenberg 1983: 11; Aejmelaeus 1986: 54-59; Miller 1994: 65.

3.   Gerstenberger 1980: 40-42; Greenberg 1983: 8-18; Aejmelaeus 1986: 59-84; Miller 1994: 114-24.

the 'impassability and immutability of God' were not part of the under-standing of prayer (Miller 1994: 126).

Thanksgiving Prayer. This prayer presupposes an answered petition or a received favour, and indeed in most cases it is a natural and spon-taneous response, but sometimes it can be organized and formal. Three features usually appear in this prayer: expressions of praise and thanks-giving, report of deliverance to others and vows of sacrifice (cf. Miller 1994: 184-98). The last aspect sometimes may be spiritualized as 'vow of praise', at other times it takes the form of votive altars and inscrip-tions (Hermisson 1965: 45; Miller 1994: 197-201).

Confessional or Penitential Prayer. This often forms part of petitionary prayer. Sometimes it is found independently but still follows the pattern of petitionary prayer, with confession, petition, motivation and renun-ciation of sin. These elements are more obvious in biblical prayer than in the ancient Near East. The heart of this prayer contains the charged expressions, 'I am sorry' or 'I have sinned', which form the first cru-cial step towards pardon and reconciliation. The form of this prayer is probably adapted from the pattern of inter-human speech in social rela-tions.[4]

Intercessory Prayer. Prayer becomes intercessory when an individual or community or even one deity addresses another for the needs of others (cf. Balentine 1984: 162). The notion of personal god probably arose in Sumer for the purpose of mediation (Kramer 1955: 171 n. 3). Though biblical intercession is often made by leaders of family, tribe and community or by prophets, elders and kings, the principle that familiarity can influence remains the same. This is true regardless of Israel's belief in her special relationship with God. Often biblical inter-cessors drew God's attention to this relationship as a basis for his action.

Blessing and Curse. A prayer of blessing is usually a prayer wish on the part of the one who blesses. This kind of prayer is often occasioned by separation before a journey, marriage, a new job, daily greeting or imminent death. On these occasions the one who blesses normally

4.   Greenberg 1983: 19-37; cf. Gerstenberger 1980: 17-63; Miller 1994: 244-45.

commits the fortunes of the one being blessed into the care of the deity. Prayers of cursing, on the other hand, are directed toward enemies, sorcerers and any other malevolent force that disrupt the peace of the individual.

While any form of prayer mentioned above may be found in either prose or poetry, the function of a prayer need not change with its genre. However, prayers set in poetry may not necessarily reflect the life setting of the petitioner. The best example of this is the biblical Psalms (cf. Westermann 1989: 13-16). This will help to delimit this enquiry into prayer in Israel, where psalmic material forms the substantial part of prayer texts. Since there are sufficient texts of prose prayers in Israel to form a suitable background for prayer in the patriarchal narratives, where prayer is largely if not entirely in prose, I shall leave out of consideration the psalmic texts of Israelite prayer.[5] Since this is not possible with the ancient Near Eastern material where very few prose prayers are preserved, I shall examine the most significant examples of prayer, whether prose or poetic.

2. *Prayer in the Ancient Near East*

a. *In Mesopotamia*

Most of our information comes from the hymns and prayers often preserved in the records or inscriptions of kings and rulers, and from objects related to prayer found in temples (cf. Falkenstein and von Soden 1953). In most cases the latter type of evidence was also largely controlled by the rulers, so one is not always certain whether it deals with the popular religion, or with the official cult of which the king was often the patron. Nevertheless, it still reflects human piety from the earliest known records.

Petitionary Prayer. The Sumerian 'letter prayers' as votive objects left in the cella of the deity are the best examples of petitionary prayers in Mesopotamia.[6]

5. For specialized works on the Psalms, see Gunkel and Begrich 1933; Westermann 1980b; 1981; Anderson 1983; Aejmelaeus 1986; Broyles 1989.
6. 'Letter prayers', which originated during the periods of Agade, Ur III and Isin I, were organized into the scholarly curriculum in the Old Babylonian period; Hallo 1968: 73.

Though the form of 'letter prayers' was originally modelled on a letter, it gradually developed into a more poetic form like the laments of the individual in the Bible.[7] Most of the letter prayers contain two or three of the recognizable elements mentioned above, namely the salutation or address with which they begin, the body or the petition, and the conclusion of the letter. The salutation invariably modifies the name of the god with longer or shorter laudatory epithets, which were chosen not as a matter of convention but to signify the qualities of the deity and often related to the requests that followed. For instance, the letter which prayed for health praised the therapeutic skills of the deity; one which asked for legal redress emphasized the unchangeable character of the divine command; one of those concerned with scribal problems praised Enki as the lord of wisdom.[8] Whether the laudatory epithets are conventional or not, that they are inherently motivational is obvious from the various letter prayers (Hallo 1968: 75-76). The body of the letter containing the petition is more elaborate and consists of complaints of social, economic and family adversities,[9] and protests, petitions and formal reinforcements of the appeal, and even confession of sins. These elements may be seen clearly from a Sumerian letter prayer addressed to the personal god Enki by a scribe named Sin-šamuh (Hallo 1968: 85-87):

Address with typical laudatory epithets:

> To Enki, the outstanding lord of heaven and earth whose nature is unequalled...
> The omniscient one who is given intelligence from sunrise to sunset,
> The lord of knowledge, the king of the sweet waters, the god who begot me...

Petition prefaced with complaints and protestations:

> I have not been negligent toward the name by which you are called, like a father...
> I did not plunder your offerings at the festivals to which I go regularly...[10]

7. For a detailed analysis of the genre, see Hallo 1968: 77-80; Jacobsen 1976: 153-54; Miller 1994: 10-21. For a discussion of lament prayers organized in terms of Sumerian and Akkadian categories, see Dalglish 1962: 18-55.

8. Hallo 1968: 77; with respect to hymnic prayers, cf. Dalglish 1962: 44.

9. Van der Toorn 1985: 64; cf. Job 9.15; 19.7, 15; Pss. 22.6-8; 55; 69; Miller 1994: 16.

10. It is implied that the piety and the loyalty of the suppliant are incompatible

I am (still) young,[11] must I walk about thus before my time? Must I roll around in the dust?...

Damgalnunna, your beloved wife,
May she bring it to you like my mother, may she introduce my lament before you[12]
Asalalimnunna, son of the abyss,[13]
May be [*sic*] bring it to you like my father, may he introduce my lament before you...

Vow of praise:

When you have turned my dark place into daylight,
I will surely dwell in your gate of Guilt-Absolved,[14] I will surely sing your praises!...
(Then) I will surely appear to the people, all the nation will verily know![15]

In some prayers, the petitioner's personal distress is described graphically as one eating and drinking with tears and sighing, and walking through marshes and falling into mud, crushed with pain and covered with gloom, weary and trembling.[16] Similar complaints of anxiety, panic and embarrassment can be seen also in *Namburbi* and *Šuilla* prayers (Mayer 1976: 72-75).

with the sufferings being experienced; Hallo 1968: 79. Claims to moral innocence or ignorance are ubiquitous in many of the letter prayers, so also the petitioner's piety and loyalty, or social and political status; Miller 1994: 18.

11. It is assumed in other prayers that gods would be lenient towards sins of youthful ignorance; van der Toorn 1985: 96.

12. The idea of gods as intercessors will be discussed below.

13. Most of the deities addressed in letter prayers are connected with the underworld or with healing, indicating the threat of death to the petitioner of sickness, enemy or other evil forces; Miller 1994: 13.

14. In addition to vows of praise, the petitioner sometimes makes other attractive offers, such as to become a slave of the deity or a sweeper of the temple, or to bestow a new title based on the latest kindness: 'when I have been cured, I will rename my goddess the one who heals(?) the cripples'; Hallo 1968: 79.

15. Sometimes the petitioner calls upon others, such as the land, the nation, heaven and earth and even other gods, to join in praise of the greatness and the wonderful deeds of the deity who delivers; Mayer 1976: 327-34; cf. Pss. 40.9-10; 52.9; 66.16; 116.14, 18; 118.17, etc.

16. Widengren 1937: 104, 121; Dalglish 1962: 25; cf. Pss. 42.3; 28.1; 30.3; 69.15; 102.29.

Thanksgiving Prayer. There is very little evidence of thanksgiving by individuals for favours received from the deity. With few exceptions, Mesopotamian hymns are 'almost entirely general descriptive praise of the deity' (Miller 1994: 26; cf. Gunkel and Begrich 1933: 285-86). However, several names given to children express the idea of thanks and gratitude to the deity who heard their prayers. Names such as 'Assur is great', 'Sin heard my prayer' (cf. Ishmael), and 'My god has dealt compassionately with me' are clear examples of thanksgiving prayer. These are similar to the names apparently given by Leah and Rachel to their children (Gen. 30).[17]

Confessional Prayer. Confession forms part of the petition, but its intention seems to be more motivational than moral rectitude (Walton 1989: 152). The meaning of some lines is unclear, but the confessional aspect is clear:[18]

> My fate has come my way, I am lifted onto a place of destruction, I cannot find an omen.
> A hostile deity has verily brought sin my way, I cannot find (?) its side.
> On the day that my vigorous house was decreed by Heaven,[19]
> There is no keeping silent about my sin, I must answer for it...
> When I have verily brought (my) sin to you, cleanse (?) me from evil!...

The first line suggests that the petitioner has felt that his personal deity, having withdrawn his protection, no longer guides his affairs. On the other hand, he was probably misguided or troubled by evil demons.[20] The last two lines suggest that the petitioner's only way out from his problem was to confess his sin and be cleansed. Such an attitude is also clear from other Sumerian poems from about 2000 BCE in which it was believed that man's misfortunes were the result of his sins and that confession of the latter would result in deliverance from the former (Kramer 1955: 180; cf. van der Toorn 1985: 97).

The Sumerian Ershahunga prayers similarly focus on confession of sin and guilt. The meaning of *ershahunga,* 'to appease the heart of the deity', suggests this (Michalowski 1987: 44). Further, confession of sin is also found in public laments over the destruction of the many ancient

---

17. Miller 1994: 9; cf. *RLA*, III: 162-63; Albertz 1978: 49-76, 101-19; Fowler 1988. Cf. the matriarchal prayers in §4.c below.

18. Hallo 1968: 76. The quotation is from the same Sin-šamuh's prayer.

19. It is not clear if this refers to a judgment on the body of the petitioner.

20. Cf. van der Toorn 1985: 64-65; Jacobsen 1976: 153; Saul in 1 Sam. 28.5, 6.

cities (e.g. Ur, 2000 BCE) (Miller 1994: 24, 25). The significant place given to confession in Mesopotamian prayer is an indication that there is a gradual shift of focus from the sufferings to the underlying sins that caused them, and this shift marked an increasing move towards a closer relationship with the deity.[21]

However, there are several other texts in which knowledge of sin and guilt is simply denied. This is most openly expressed in the 'Prayer to Every God' (*ANET*, 391-92; Hallo 1968: 79). At other times its seriousness is played down (Lambert 1974: 281, 283; cf. Kramer 1955: 179). Furthermore, gods were blamed for not revealing their purposes to man (*ANET*, 435), and even for human sinfulness (Lambert 1960: 89).

Intercessory Prayer. In Mesopotamia, this was often presented to one deity by another, often of a lower rank, on behalf of the petitioner. This worked in three ways. First, the individuals usually requested their personal deities to intervene on their behalf to one of the high gods not only to enjoy the latter's good will, but also to find help in times of need (Jacobsen 1976: 159-60; cf. Miller 1994: 22). Secondly, it worked sometimes the other way round when petitioners appealed to one of the high gods to mediate and help restore their strained relation with the personal god who had withdrawn his protective hand (Mayer 1976: 231, 234). Thirdly, there are certain specific 'intercession deities' who, by some magical means, provided immediate access to the great gods who in turn settled matters with the personal god. However, petitioners depended largely on their personal gods rather than on the great gods, who were called upon primarily to influence the former.

b. *In Egypt*
Petitionary Prayer. A petitionary prayer of a poor man who experiences injustice in the law court itself is attested from the late Nineteenth Dynasty (c. 1230 BCE):

> O Amon, give thy ear to one who is alone in the law court, who is poor... The court cheats him (of) silver and gold for the scribes of the mat and clothing for the attendants. May it be found that Amon assumes his form as the vizier, in order to permit [the] poor man to get off. May it be found that the poor man is vindicated (*ANET*, 380).

---

21. Hallo 1968: 81-82; Miller 1994: 21; cf. Jacobsen 1976: 147-64.

The Mesopotamian letter prayers have their parallels among the Egyptians in their letters to dead relatives seeking their help in different circumstances. We have an example of a demotic letter prayer, probably from the late sixth century BCE, to the necropolis deity Thoth by his servant Efou. The petitioner requests deliverance from his fellow worker who inflicts severe persecution on Efou by stealing everything he had and killing his servants. Further, Efou's words in his appeal to Thoth, 'I have no human master', suggests that there were no social structures existing either to redress the injustice or to protect him from his persecutor.[22] There is little difference in the form of prayer between the second-millennium Mesopotamian and the first-millennium Egyptian prayers.

Thanksgiving Prayer. Thanksgiving and gratitude may be found in the votive stele of an artisan, Neb-Re, of Nineteenth Dynasty Egypt (thirteenth century BCE). It seems that Nakht-Amon the son of Neb-Re acted irreverently with regard to a cow belonging to the god Amon-Re and thus became ill. The prayer on the stele is a fine example of not only thanksgiving, but also adoration, praise and intercession:

> when he was (under) the power of Amon because of his cow[23]... He rescued the Outline Draftsman... I shall make this stela in thy name, and I shall establish for thee *these* adorations in writing upon it, because thou hast rescued for me the Outline Draftsman Nakht-Amon.[24]

Confessional Prayer. The various claims to innocence found in the Book of the Dead, especially in ch. 125, have been viewed as suggesting that Egyptians had no sense of sin and its consequences, but this view has been refuted by Morenz. He argues that the fact that the editor of the chapter had given the claims to innocence the most appropriate title 'So that he may be separated from every sin (*ḥww*) which he hath done' suggests the opposite. The assurance in ch. 125 testifies to the Egyptians' deep anxiety to avoid sin (Morenz 1973: 132). Further, the exhortation of the sage Amenemope, 'Say not: "I have no wrongdoing"' (Morenz 1973: 132), and confession of sins to god elsewhere

22. Hughes 1958: 5-6; Miller 1994: 367 n. 27. Cf. Gen. 32.11; Exod. 17.14; Josh. 7.9; Judg. 16.28; Neh. 4.5; 2 Chron. 20.11.
23. This is probably a temple cow designated for the particular deity, like the many sacred cows attached to Hindu temples in India. The nature of the offence, however, is unclear. Cf. *ANET*, 380 n. 7.
24. *ANET*, 380-81; cf. Assman 1975: 349 ll. 10-13; Miller 1994: 14, 27.

by individuals suggest that there was both consciousness of sin and a moral accountability to god. This is also evident from the stele of Neb-Re quoted above and from other texts.[25]

Intercessory Prayer. In contrast to Mesopotamia, the Egyptian intercessors were not gods but the deified kings and other important office bearers represented by statues installed in the temple precincts. The petitions were tied to these statues, which bore them perpetually before the gods (Sweeney 1985: 229 n. 103; cf. p. 219). The statues in many temples often bear invitations to the petitioner saying, 'I am the messenger of this or that god, I will pass on your petition to those gods' (Morenz 1973: 102).

However, intercessory prayer is also attested in the Late Ramasside Letters (1100–1070 BCE), where a community, friends, relatives and family members prayed for a man Dhutmose, who was summoned on a dangerous mission by the king. The man asked for their prayers when he wrote home while he was on his journey (Sweeney 1985: 213-14). On another occasion colleagues prayed for a recently appointed official: 'May Pre' Harakhte grant you a long spell of life in the post of your father!'[26] Such prayers were carried out anywhere and were not part of the cult, but intercession for the king was part of the cult, and the royal duties themselves involved praying for the people in general and for the family's future rule in particular. King Ramses III, for instance, prayed for the peaceful succession of his son to his throne after him (Sweeney 1985: 217).

c. *Among the Hittites*
Petitionary Prayer. Petitionary prayer among the Hittites has similar features to that of Mesopotamia and Egypt. The 'daily prayers of the king' recited on his behalf by the scribe/priest at the temple have the familiar form: the prayer opens with adoration and praise and goes on to petition for blessings on the royal family, the people and the land, especially for its fertility. Interestingly the congregation shouts in response, 'Let it be so!' (*ANET*, 396-97). Besides this formal prayer, we have examples of individual petition in times of sickness and misery.

25. Morenz 1973: 32; cf. Dalglish 1962: 15-16; Lichtheim 1976: 104-10.
26. Sweeney 1985: 217. This may appear as a good wish on the part of the colleagues, but Sweeney argues that the idea of intercession in Egypt may be found in a gratitude, blessing, wish or even in a greeting.

Kantuzilis, a member of the royal family, petitions for healing from sickness which had become misery and oppression to him (*ANET*, 401).

There are no clear examples of thanksgiving prayer among the Hittites.

Confessional Prayer. One of the best examples of confession is found in the plague prayers of Mursilis, which are in fact intercessory prayers for the people dying of a severe plague (*ANET*, 395-96). The address declares that the king had worshipped all the gods. This is followed by a protestation of personal innocence and a general statement that man is sinful, though the king accepted no responsibility for the plague. Then the prayer asks for an oracle to establish the causes of the plague. Interestingly the king, like David, interprets the plague as a judgment because of the Hittites' breach of a treaty with Egypt under an earlier king (cf. 2 Sam. 21.1-14; Roberts 1988: 36). This is followed by a confession of the misdeeds of the fathers which were particularly thought to be the cause of the plague. Finally follows the reparation and appeal to the justice and reputation of the name of the gods. Almost every aspect of the prayer attempts to motivate the gods. The theology of sin and retribution are similar to Israel's understanding of them, but this is only the king's interpretation, and there is no divine decree as in Israel. Further, the basis for appeal is not an established relationship such as the covenant in Israel, but the ritual acts of confession and restitution which have an almost magical effect.

Intercessory Prayer. Hittite intercessory prayers contain some of the best examples in the ancient Near East for comparison with Israelite prayers. There are both human and divine intermediaries, but it is the humans, in common with the biblical examples, who take it upon themselves to intercede for others; other gods are addressed only to pass on the prayers and to influence the great gods to whom the petition was ultimately addressed. The Hittite queen and consort of Hattusilis took advantage of her sex,[27] and pleaded for the life of her husband who had fallen ill. Her prayer was primarily to the Sun-goddess Arinna, but she also invoked other gods to mediate on her behalf to the Sun-goddess. To many of them she promised gold and silver statues and ornaments as inducements (*ANET*, 394). The finest Hittite intercessory

27. She says, 'Among men there is a saying: "To woman in travail the god yields her wish"'.

prayer was probably the plague prayer of king Mursilis, which we have already seen above.

d. *In Canaan*

Though the fragmentary prayer texts at Ugarit are not very significant compared to Mesopotamian sources (Roberts 1988: 36; Miller 1994: 27-28), a number of Phoenician and Aramaean votive inscriptions add to the Ugaritic information on Canaanite prayer.

Petitionary Prayer. The legend of Keret provides a good example of this prayer. There is no mention of prayer here, but it is obvious in the expression 'to lift one's hands up to heaven' and in the act of sacrifice associated with it. The ritual sacrifice which Keret was asked to make is probably the normal way of invoking God.[28] Further, the prayer may be implicit in the dialogue between Keret and El in the night vision (*ANET*, 143, 144; cf. Miller 1988: 150, 151; Ps. 6.7, 10). This is obvious in the context of Keret's bereavement of wife and children, and of his vow to Athirat.

We have another petitionary prayer from the ritual texts couched in the form of a vow, prescribed to be used when an enemy attacked the city. Once again prayer is not explicit, but is obvious from the elaborate description of the vow (*KTU*, 119, 26-35; cf. Chapter 2 §2.d and Chapter 6 §2.d) followed by an assurance, probably by a priest: 'So Ba[al has hea]rd your prayer. He will drive the strong one from your gates, the warrior from your walls' (Miller 1988: 139-55; 1994: 28-29). There are no formal features here because it was probably a ritual prayer in stock available for times of need.

Petitionary prayer is also attested in two votive inscriptions from the ninth and eighth centuries BCE, erected in memorial of the answered prayers:

> I am Zakir,[29] king of Hamat and Lu'ath. A humble man I am... I lifted up my hand[30] to Be'elshamayn, and Be'elshamayn heard me... [spoke] to me through seers and... [said]...Do not fear, for I made you king, and I shall stand by you and deliver you from all [these kings who] set up a siege against you (*ANET*, 655; Miller 1994: 28).

---

28. Cf. the patriarchal altars along with the invocation of the name of Yahweh, suggesting the normal way of worship.

29. This name is now known to be more correctly Zakkur; Millard 1990: 47-52.

30. Cf. Keret.

The petitioner describes himself as a 'humble (*'nh*) man',[31] which probably served as a motivation for the god to act (cf. Ps. 34.6). His god answered his prayer by an oracle of salvation.

Thanksgiving Prayer. The prayer of gratitude seems to be a universal phenomenon, although not many have been found in Canaan. The idea of thanksgiving is implicit in the legend of Keret, where the goddess Anath attempts to take revenge on Keret because he failed to fulfil his vow. This suggests that gratitude was expected for received favours. Similarly the Zakkur stele is an example of a thanksgiving prayer of which few have survived in non-biblical records (cf. Miller 1994: 28). While the prayer is a petition, the stele probably represents the performance of a vow and thanksgiving.

Blessing. The Ugaritic root *brk* means 'to give the power of the gods (to a man)', or 'to commend someone to a deity for a blessing'.[32] In the legend of Keret, El blesses Keret at the request of Baal saying, 'The woman you take...shall bear seven sons to you' (*ANET*, 146). In many Phoenician-Punic consecratory inscriptions the phrase 'A blessed B' occurs as a concluding formula, and it expresses the idea of 'granting happiness, vitality and success' in a similar way to that of biblical usage, for instance, 'May Melqart bless my successor with life', or 'may the gods bless my way'.[33] The formula also occurs as a social greeting as in Ruth, but the biblical formula 'blessed be so-and-so' does not occur in these inscriptions. It is always understood, as in the biblical blessing, that it is the deity who bestows these blessings even when he is not explicitly mentioned.

3. *Prayer in Israel*

As Clements notes, biblical prayer is 'portrayed in a great variety of forms, sometimes with extraordinary simplicity and at others with great complexity and formality' (1986: 2). However, biblical material on

---

31. This designation, however, is disputed; Millard 1990: 47-50.

32. Cf. similar meanings for the root in Akkadian, Phoenician, Aramaic and South Arabic; *TDOT*, I: 282-84.

33. The identical biblical formula, however, occurs in the Aramaic texts of the tomb inscriptions and graffiti from Egypt; *TDOT*, I: 282.

prayer is too extensive to deal with in any detail here.[34] As I said earlier, I will focus mainly on prose prayers, of which there are no less
than 140 in the Bible (cf. Greenberg 1983: 59 n. 3; contrast Miller
1994: 233), and will deal with the various forms of biblical prayer to
understand its content and theology. But before doing so, it is
appropriate to look briefly at the language of prayer.

The context and range of words that describe the act of prayer suggest that prayer in Israel was primarily dialogical and could be carried
out in both formal cultic, or informal mundane circumstances, by any
one at any time, and through verbal and non-verbal communication.

Very general terms such as אמר 'to say' or דבר 'to speak' are used to
introduce most petitionary prayers in the Bible, suggesting that prayer
is an address to someone in a conversation.[35] Thus what Abraham,
Jacob and Eliezer 'said' (Gen. 17.18; 24.12; 32.9) or what David
'spoke' (2 Sam. 22.1) to God was their prayer (Miller 1994: 32-33; cf.
Heiler 1958: 9). However, not every dialogue between God and man is
a prayer, but only that which has an explicit purpose with an intention
to achieve it (Balentine 1993: 31). There are, however, other more technical words used which suggest that biblical prayer has a more formal
side to it. The most frequent among them are תפלה (77 times) and its
verb פלל (84 times), which means 'to place a case or situation before
God for consideration or assessment'.[36] While the examples where this
root appears indicate that it is used for both prayer and intercession,[37]
the idea behind it assumes God as a righteous judge who assesses every
case 'graciously' (תחנה/התחנן).[38] Among other technical words not so

34. For an overview of previous scholarship and the form and theology of
biblical prayer, see Balentine 1993; Miller 1994.

35. Such ordinary words are also used to introduce prayers of intercession,
thanksgiving and blessing: Gen. 17.18; 24.12, 26-27; 32.9 cf. Num. 14.13; 16.22;
22.34; Judg. 6.39; 10.15; 21.3; 1 Sam. 7.6; 2 Sam. 15.31; 24.10, 17; 1 Kgs 3.6;
8.23; 18.36; 2 Kgs 6.20; Amos 7.2, 5; Ezra 9.6; 2 Chron. 20.6; Miller 1994: 374 n.
2. For a discussion on other general words, such as בקש, 'seek', שאל, 'ask', and
דרש, 'inquire', which are not so frequently used for prayer, see Westermann 1960:
2-16; Buck 1975: 71; Balentine 1984: 167-68; Miller 1994: 34-37.

36. Blank 1948: 337-38; Speiser 1963a: 301-306; Ap-Thomas 1956: 230-38.

37. Gen. 20.17; Num. 11.2; 21.7; Deut. 9.26-29; 1 Sam. 7.5; 12.19; 1 Kgs 8.30;
2 Kgs 4.33; 19.15-19; 20.1-3; Pss. 17.1-3; 80.4; Jer. 29.7; 37.3; 42.2, 4, 20; Dan. 9;
Jon. 2.1; 4.2.

38. The heaviest use of the latter word is apparent in the prayers of Solomon
and Daniel, 1 Kgs 8–9; Dan. 9; Miller 1994: 43.

frequently used is עתר, 'entreat' or 'intercede' (22 times). While its particular focus is on God's response to prayer, it is most frequently used in Moses' prayer to avert the plagues (Exod. 8.8-9, 28-30; 9.28; 10.17-18), and it is also used in contexts of formal ritual acts of sacrifice (2 Sam. 21.1-14; 24.25) (Balentine 1984: 163; Miller 1994: 41-42). Besides these, there are certain general words which virtually became technical terms for prayer: קרא, used to call upon the name of the Lord in worship, or more specifically to cry to God in times of need; and צעק and זעק used interchangeably for the 'outcry' of the oppressed.[39] Therefore, prayer in Israel, besides being formal and informal, emphasizes God's character as a righteous judge who assesses every case and deals kindly with his creatures in trouble.

a. *Forms of Prayer*
Petitionary Prayer. As in the ancient Near East, petitionary prayer in Israel has the basic features of address, petition and motivational clauses, plus expressions of confidence and vow of praise. One of the best examples of petitionary prayer is the prayer of Hannah which is preserved in the form of a vow (1 Sam. 1.11):

Address:	O Yahweh of hosts,
Petition in the form of vow:	if thou wilt indeed look on the affliction of thy maidservant, and remember me, and not forget thy maidservant, but wilt give to thy maidservant a son,
Motivation clause:	then I will give him to [Yahweh] all the days of his life, and no razor shall touch his head.

As can be observed, the address, in contrast to the ancient Near Eastern practice, is very brief. It identifies the deity by name and by the title צבאות,[40] but there are no laudatory epithets. The petition is focused, not just on the affliction, but on the petitioner's self-deprecation which is

39. E.g. Abel, Gen. 4.10; Sodom and Gomorrah, 18.21; 19.13; the Hebrews in Egypt, Exod. 2.23; 3.7, 9; the poor, widow and orphan, Exod. 22.23, 27; the Israelites during the time of Judges, Judg. 3.9; 4.3; 6.6; 10.10, 12, 14; several times in Psalms; the sailors, Jon. 1.14; and sometimes there is simply the exclamation: 'Violence!', Job 19.7; Hab. 1.2; Boyce 1989; Miller 1994: 45.
40. Probably refers to Yahweh's 'celestial and/or terrestrial hosts, the divine council, the luminaries of the sky, and the totality of creation'; *ABD*, III: 304.

evident in the thrice-repeated description of the petitioner as 'maidservant'. While this in itself can be a motivation, an even stronger motivational clause is added in the form of a vow. What Hannah asks is not for her own sake, but so that she might give it back to the deity totally and permanently. Thus it is the deity who stands to gain if the request is granted. What the petitioner gains as a by-product is the removal of the stigma of barrenness. There can be no greater motivation for the deity to act in favour of the request. By comparison, the requests of Abraham, Keret and Dan'el may be less attractive to the deity.

The prayers of Hezekiah are much more elaborate and resemble the prayers of the ancient Near East. His prayer in the face of the enemy's attack (2 Kgs 19.15-19) reflects one of the most common occasions in the ancient Near East when people turn to their gods for help, although it lacks ritual accompaniment as at Ugarit. The address precisely identifies the deity's name, the country whose patron he is and the location, and then goes on to describe him with extravagant epithets[41] as the only God in the world, and the maker of everything. The petition describes both the immanence (anthropomorphic description) and transcendence (he is not the work of men) of God and the motivation demands that this is the opportune time for this God to show himself as sovereign over the world's greatest power. The religion of this prayer is clearly monotheistic as it does not acknowledge the existence of any other god.

Similarly, Hezekiah's personal prayer for his own healing also reveals his personal religion (2 Kgs 20.3). This prayer has a very brief address, and the petition is adapted into the motivational clause in which the petitioner's loyalty to God, not any ritual, is put forward as the ground for his favourable action.

Thanksgiving Prayer. Some scholars have thought that there was no independent concept of thanksgiving in Hebrew thinking (cf. Westermann 1965: 27 n. 13, 87-90), probably because of the considerable overlap in the meaning of the two biblical words, תודה 'thanksgiving or confession of what God has done', and תהלה, 'praise'.[42] However, several other scholars have argued convincingly that, though these words are closely related, they refer to genres or types of prayers and are

41. They are more of historical experience than flattery.
42. Pss. 34.1-6; 40.1-2 are the best examples of confession of what God has done and praise to God as thanksgiving.

capable of being distinguished (Miller 1994: 402 n. 2; cf. Crüsemann 1969).

A third word, ברכה, is also used for thanksgiving to God as well as in interpersonal relations. About two-thirds of its occurrences refer to gratitude for favours received (cf. Blank 1961: 87-89). The form of the blessing is consistent and the gratitude is normally found in the expression 'Blessed be the LORD', followed by a description of God's kindly acts.[43] The structure of this blessing in the Old Testament consists of a *qal* passive participle of ברך, followed by the subject, God, who is the recipient of praise, and finally the reasons for the blessing. The setting of most of these blessings is non-cultic, while the reasons for them are always the saving acts of God (Balentine 1993: 204-205). One of the best examples may be found in Jethro's spontaneous thanksgiving when he heard from Moses all about Israel's deliverance from Egypt (Exod. 18.8-12):

> Blessed be [Yahweh], who has delivered you out of the hand of the Egyptians and out of the hand of Pharaoh.

Sometimes the occasion is turned into a communal thanksgiving with sacrifices and offerings, for example, the songs of Miriam (Exod. 15), Deborah (Judg. 5) and Hannah (1 Sam. 1.28–2.11). However, this formula of thanksgiving seems to be very common as it is also expressed in very informal circumstances by women, men, kings and commoners alike (1 Sam. 25.39; 2 Sam. 18.28; 1 Kgs 1.48; Ruth 4.14, 15). These examples suggest that the idea of thanksgiving for God's saving acts is so integral to both the communal and individual religious ethos of Israel that this formula is said to be found even in the mouths of pagan queen and kings who were favourably disposed towards the affairs of Israel (1 Kgs 10.9; 5.7; Dan. 3.28).

Confessional Prayer. This prayer is characterized by the charged expression, 'I have sinned', חטאתי, or 'I/we have sinned against the LORD', often followed by an acknowledgment of God's justice. The fact that this form is found even with the Pharaoh of Egypt confirms Morenz's contention (above) that the Egyptians indeed had the sense of

---

43. At least 18 narrative occurrences of this form may be identified in the Bible: Gen. 14.20; 24.27; Exod. 18.10; 1 Sam. 25.32, 39; 2 Sam. 18.28; 1 Kgs 1.48; 5.21; 8.15, 56 (= 2 Chron. 6.4); 10.9; Zech. 11.5; Ruth 4.14; Dan. 3.28; Ezra 7.27; 1 Chron. 29.10; 2 Chron. 2.11; 6.4; *THAT*, I: 374; cf. Balentine 1993: 204.

sin and a desire to avoid it. Pharaoh says to Moses (Exod. 9.27-28 cf. 10.16, 17):

confession:	This time I have sinned;
elaboration:	[Yahweh] is in the right, and I and my people are in the wrong.
	Entreat [Yahweh]; (petition)
motivating reason:	for there has been enough of this thunder and hail;
renunciation of sin:	I will let you go, and you shall stay no longer (cf. Miller 1994: 252-53).

A similar form is found in the confessions of Balaam (Num. 22.34), the Israelites (Judg. 10.10; 1 Sam. 12.10) and Saul (1 Sam. 26.21), and in David's classic confession (2 Sam 12.13; cf. 24.10; Ps. 51.1-17). In all these confessions elaborate motivational clauses acknowledging the justice of God are added. This shows that a moral dimension is inherent in biblical prayers of confession in which the guilty not only acknowledged the responsibility for his sin but also accepted God's judgment as just (Gerstenberger, 1988: 213-14; cf. Miller 1994: 252). Miller thinks that the confession in Ezra, Nehemiah and Daniel (Ezra 9.5-10; Neh. 1.4, 7; Dan. 9.3, 11) characterized by 'extreme acts of contrition and humbling oneself, such as weeping and fasting, and tearing of garments' is peculiar to later Israel (Miller 1994: 256-57). However, such attitude in prayer is by no means confined to the later period. It is evident in the prayers of Abraham (Gen. 17.3; 18.2), Moses (Num. 16.22; Deut. 9.25), Samuel (1 Sam. 7.6), David (2 Sam 12.16, 21) and Hezekiah (2 Kgs 19.1, 2) as well.

Intercessory Prayer. As has been already stated, the intercessors in Israel were often people of responsibility, such as leaders of family, tribe and community, or those prophets specially appointed by God to carry his message to his people. More than any others, it was Israel's prophets who were deeply engaged in intercessory prayers,[44] probably because of their very close acquaintance with God's plans and actions. Moses is especially described as repeatedly interceding for others.[45]

---

44. Cf. Balentine's (1984: 169-73) reservations about this view and contrast Miller's affirmation (1994: 421 n. 18).

45. For example, to avert the Egyptian plagues (Exod. 8.8-9, 28-31; 9.28; 10.16-17) and God's wrath on Israel, Aaron and Miriam (Exod. 32.11-13, 30-32; Num. 11.2; 12.13; 14.13-19; 16.22; 21.7; Deut. 9.7, 20, 25-29). Probably for this

Most intercessory prayers are in the form of dialogue with a very simple address. Their content reveals the character of God and of the intercessor, as well as God's relationship with the people for whom the intercession was made. First, the most significant presupposition behind every intercession was that God can be persuaded to change his mind and relent from judgment (e.g. Moses, Exod. 32.12; Jon. 4.2). This is further confirmed by God's own desire to seek intercessors/mediators, and his susceptibility to the pleas of 'his servants, the prophets' (Ezek. 22.30-31; Jer. 7.16; 11.14; 14.11, 12).[46] Secondly, the character of intercessors, especially the prophets, as unselfish and sacrificial comes out clearly. Thirdly, the basis of all intercession is God's promised relation with the people and his revealed character of 'steadfast love' (Exod. 32.13; Num. 14.19).

Blessing and Curse. The prayer of blessing, which is to be distinguished from the thanksgiving-blessing, appears to be one of the most common prayers in the Bible, and seems to take place in every day circumstances of family and community life in Israel.[47] The most common informal occasions were when family members or friends separated from each other (Gen. 24.59-61; 31.55; 1 Sam. 20.13; Ruth 1.8-9), when people got married (Gen. 24.60; 28.1-5; Ruth 4.11, 12), in the context of meeting and greeting during a day's routine work (Ruth 2.4, 5), or when people realized that they were about to die (Gen. 27.1-4, 27-29, 39-40; 48.8-22; 49.1-29; Deut. 33.1-29). Blessing was also pronounced for those who showed loyalty to others (Ruth 2.12; 3.10 cf. 4.14). The informal blessings were pronounced in serious as well as mundane situations, and when there was no cult involved. The form is usually jussive, 'May the Lord do so and so', suggesting that God is the source of all blessing, and the content is a prayer-wish for continuing welfare or a committing of the fortunes of the ones who had been blessed into God's hands (Miller 1994: 282, 291).

reason Ps. 90 was ascribed to him as 'a prayer of Moses'. Cf. Freedman 1985: 56-59.

    46. Miller (1994: 277) pertinently notes that the changing or not changing of God's mind is especially related to his 'acts of punishment or judgment, not to acts in general'. For the theological questions raised by God's changing of his mind, see Greenberg 1977–78: 21-36.

    47. *TDOT*, II: 304: The 'oldest and most persisting setting' for blessing in the Old Testament is the family.

The formal blessings, on the other hand, were pronounced in the cultic context of worship and thanksgiving by the priests and the Levites.[48] The clearest and most explicit priestly blessing is the so-called 'Aaronic blessing' (Num. 6.22-27).[49] It has also been found on two silver amulets of the seventh/sixth centuries BCE, showing its significance in Israel (Yardeni 1991: 176-85). The form and content of this blessing are the same as in the informal blessing, except that the formal blessing is more comprehensive and lacks reference to a specific occasion. Like other blessings, its source is God and its nature a prayer-wish. Its function, however, is to sustain the hopes of God's people in the providence of God (Miller 1994: 298).

Curse prayers are the corollary of blessing in the Bible, but they do not occur in the patriarchal narratives, and hence they need not occupy our attention much. They are not as numerous as the blessings, but are nevertheless present especially in the Psalms.[50] While the form of these prayers is the same as the blessing, the content is just the opposite, in that they passionately seek the harm or destruction of enemies. As with the blessing, the divine source of the curse is not always mentioned, but is assumed and often made explicit, especially in the Psalms where the prayers are directly addressed to God (e.g. Ps. 139.19-22). Miller rightly notes that the overriding concern of these prayers was to 'turn the issue of justice over to God rather than taking vengeance into one's own hands' (Miller 1994: 303).

b. *Comparative Analysis*
There is little variation in form, content and setting of prayer between Israel and the ancient Near East. The address in Israel was simple and short, while in the ancient Near East it was prefaced with long intro-ductory sections of praise. The content in both was the same with simi-lar problems of childlessness, sickness, sin, enemies, and so on. The

48. Deut. 10.8; 21.5 cf. Lev. 9.22-23. Exceptions are David and Solomon, 2 Sam. 6.18; 1 Kgs 8.14, 55; and the psalmist, Pss. 29.11; 67.1, 7; 115.14, 15. But the context in all these is probably cultic.

49. For an extended treatment of the priestly blessing, see Miller 1975: 240-51; Freedman 1975: 35-48; Fishbane 1983: 115-21.

50. Sometimes they are embedded in the blessing, Gen. 9.25; 27.29; 37.22; the curses will come upon Israel also if they disobey God's commands, Deut. 28; other texts where curses occur: 2 Sam. 3.29, 39; Jer. 18.21-22; Mal. 2.12; Pss. 35.4-6, 8, 26; 58.7-8; 69.22-28; 109.6-19; 139.19-20; 140.9-11. For a comprehensive treatment of the subject, see Brichto 1963.

setting in Israel was both formal and informal, while it was largely formal and cultic in the ancient Near East. However, there are significant differences in how they viewed prayer, as to what they expected of it and how they achieved it. While the Mesopotamian incantations and ritual prayers were largely intended to manipulate, coerce and appease the angry god (cf. Walton 1989: 157), the Sumerian letter prayers and some Hittite petitionary prayers often relied on seducing the deity with gifts and presents, expecting almost mechanical if not magical results. In contrast, the Israelite prayers are largely an appeal to God's promises to the patriarchs and his obligations to Israel.[51] These were declared or recalled time and again by God through Israel's leaders and prophets so that Israel knew what it was that pleased her God and what aroused his anger. Therefore national or personal calamity, disaster, defeat or disease was always traced back to a disobedience to, or violation of, a law prescribed by God. Thus Israel knew in such situations that God would be pleased not by ritual or sacrifice but confession of disobedience and renewal of the covenant obligations.[52]

Further, not all prayer in the ancient Near East reveals the personal piety behind it. The Mesopotamian and Hittite healing rituals especially are fixed in regard to place, time, the offerings and incantations. The priest performs the ritual and the accompanying gestures with little variation, expecting magical results. However, the presence of theophoric personal names and the idea of a personal god in Mesopotamia and the concept of a patron deity for royal families elsewhere suggest that there exists an assumed or inherited relationship between the deity and the petitioner, although it is not clear what this implies for the individual or the deity. Sometimes the personal relationship is entirely dependent on the need of the petitioner, and could be strained even without the knowledge of the petitioner. The petitioner had to approach a higher god to mediate between him and his personal god who had abandoned him. There is no declared relationship between the petitioner and the deity in the ancient Near East as can be found in Israel. In contrast,

51. Cf. Walton 1989: 157. However, there are occasions when prayer and ritual were closely associated in Israel (1 Sam. 7.8-10; 2 Sam. 24.25; Job 42.8), and at times the ritual was almost magical (Lev. 14). Nevertheless, these exceptions only prove the rule that magical rituals have no place in the official cult of Israel.

52. Nevertheless, prayer in Israel often degenerated into mere ritual, to the extent of expecting magical results. But this was sharply criticized by the prophets (Isa. 1.11-16; Amos 5.21-25).

Israel approaches God almost as a right, on the basis of such a bond. This is even more evident in the case of Israel's intercessors who make the covenant relationship the basis for their intercession. Further, no intercession is made by a dead person or ancestor however great he might have been. Thus prayer, besides being a means of asking and receiving from God, is primarily a relationship, sometimes an intimate relationship, between God and the petitioner. Intercessory prayer adds a new dimension to this relationship, in that the intercessor was allowed to enter into the divine council in order to warn people to change their ways, or to persuade God to change his mind and relent from judgment. This kind of prayer is alien to the ancient Near East.

4. *Prayer in the Patriarchal Narratives*

About 20 times in all prayer is either mentioned or alluded to in the patriarchal narratives. In six of these instances it is only the allusion to prayer that is recorded and not the prayer itself (Gen. 20.7, 17; 25.21; 30.6, 22; 47.31 [see *Targum Neofiti*]). However, in other texts all the types of prayers that are found in Israel occur, except the imprecatory prayers. Thus there are some general references to prayer, such as 'calling on the name of Yahweh', and to prayers of petition, thanksgiving, intercession and blessing. I have already touched upon some of these instances in the discussion of prayer in Israel. We shall look at them more closely in the context of the patriarchal narratives.

a. *General Reference to Prayer*

As noted above, קרא, 'to call', is one of the general terms used for prayer in Israel which virtually became a technical term. This term occurs four times with בשם יהוה in the patriarchal narratives, all in the context of either building an altar or planting a tree (Gen. 12.8; 13.4; 21.33; 26.25), which were in themselves strong tokens of worship. Though this word occurs over 700 times in the Scriptures, it occurs only about 24 times with בשם יהוה,[53] and with אל יהוה or יהוה about another 70 times. But the latter cases usually refer to crying to God for help in different situations, and hence their relevance for the present

---

53. Gen. 4.26; 12.8; 13.4; 21.23; 26.25; Exod. 34.5; 1 Kgs 18.24, 25, 26; 2 Kgs 5.11; Isa. 12.4; 41.25; 64.6; Jer. 10.25; Joel 3.5; Zeph 3.9; Zech. 13.9; Pss. 79.6; 80.19; 105.1; 116.4, 12, 17; 1 Chron. 16.8; Balentine 1984: 165-66.

investigation is not very great.[54] However, its occurrence with בשם יהוה
in the Bible probably throws light on one's understanding of its relation
to prayer or worship in the patriarchal narratives. Of the 20 occurrences
outside the patriarchal narratives, it refers 11 times to worship in general.[55] In the others it refers to prayer for help in different situations.[56]
Interestingly, in two of these instances it is the prophets of Baal that
pray for help using the similar expression, 'they called on the name of
Baal'. Therefore, it is reasonable to suggest that קרא בשם יהוה is a
common expression for both prayer in a specific situation and worship
in general, and it is the context that determines the meaning in each
situation. The context where this expression occurs in the patriarchal
narratives gives no suggestion that the patriarchs are crying to God in
some specific need. On the other hand, since it occurs in the context of
building altars and planting a tree, it probably refers to their worship in
general (Gunkel 1902: 48). Westermann sums it up well:

> One can conclude...that J wanted to describe worship in the patriarchal
> period by this two-part event. The expression קרא בשם יהוה stands for
> the *word* in worship while the building of the altar (or some other action,
> like the planting of a tamarisk) indicates the *action* in worship. The
> background of 12.8...is the awareness that the two basic elements of
> word and action are already part of worship in its simplest form. The
> designation of the word element gives notice that the indispensable
> presupposition for worship is the union of man with God which takes
> place with the invocation of the name of God (1985: 156).

It is not clear, however, what Westermann means by 'union of man
with God' in the above quotation. But as I have observed above, the
invocation of the name of the deity in the address enables the worshipper to make contact with the deity. This may be just as true in
prayers of petition, where the petitioner being in some dire need wants
to assure himself that such a deity exists and that he is not pleading in
vain, as in worship, since in the patriarchal narratives this expression of
'calling on the name of Yahweh' is found in relation to formal worship

54. This conveys the cry of the poor when mistreated (Deut. 15.9; 24.25); the
cry of others in need, e.g. Samson (Judg. 15.18; 16.28), Samuel (1 Sam. 12.17, 18),
David (2 Sam. 22.7) and Job (12.14); and the call to God for help in many Psalms.
Miller 1994: 44.
55. Gen. 4.26; Isa. 12.4; Jer. 10.25; Zeph. 3.9; Zech. 13.9; Pss. 79.6; 80.19;
105.1, etc.
56. Exod. 34.5; 1 Kgs 18.24, 25, 26; 2 Kgs 5.11; Isa. 41.25; Joel 3.5; Ps. 116.4.
The meaning in Exodus and Isaiah is ambiguous.

probably accompanied by sacrifice (cf. Wenham 1987: 280-81). Such an occasion did not seek to make contact with the deity, but it assumed that such relation already existed and on the basis of this the worshipper simply paid his homage to the deity in a formal or customary way.

However, in Gen. 21.33 two new elements are added to the expression יהוה קרא בשם, namely the planting of a tamarisk, אֶשֶׁל, and אֵל עוֹלָם (אֵל occurs with Yahweh only here in the patriarchal narratives). It is not clear what is the relation of these actions with calling on the name of Yahweh. Neither is the planting of a fir tree on either side of the temple gate in the Hittite healing ritual relevant here (cf. Chapter 2 §2c above). Several scholars think that Abraham planted a sacred tamarisk at Beer-sheba and worshipped the pre-Israelite local *numen* called אֵל עוֹלָם, and that the cult was transferred to Yahweh with the arrival of Israel.[57] But Jacob asks pertinently, 'Can one plant a sacred tree?' He then goes on to suggest that it was 'meant to be a lasting landmark' of a pastoral nomad (Jacob 1934: 489-90). Others think that the planting of the tree is analogous to building altars on earlier occasions, since worship followed both types of actions (Sarna 1989: 149; Wenham 1994: 94). Westermann implies this in the above quotation. Hitherto, Abraham has been associated with oak-like trees, at which he either pitched his tent or built an altar for worship. As I have argued in Chapter 2 §4, the author did not view the places or the tree as sacred prior to Abraham's activity. It is uncertain if he implied sanctity of the tamarisk here. The tamarisk plant in which a tree spirit is believed to live is frequently used in Babylonian healing rituals, but it is not planted or associated with worship (cf. Chapter 7 n. 10). Further, עוֹלָם אֵל need not refer to the local deity of Beer-sheba. The Hebrew, as Sarna argues, 'does not allow the use of a proper name in the construct state joined to a noun. Hence, *'el* in the phrase *'el 'olām* can no longer be the proper name of a god but means simply "God"' (Sarna 1989: 150). Thus it may be a logical epithet of a deity called upon to witness the formal treaty between Abraham and Abimelech.[58] In view of the latter's granting of rights to water, it is appropriate for Abraham to memorialize the event by planting a tree and worshipping God (cf. Wenham 1994: 94).

57. Gunkel 1902: 207; Skinner 1930: 327; Jenni 1952: 197-248; 1953: 1-35; *THAT*, II: 236.

58. Dillmann 1897: 138; Pope 1955: 14-15; Speiser 1964: 159.

b. *Prayer of Petition*

Prayers of petition in the patriarchal narratives may be categorized as individual and community laments and pleas for help. Pleas for help, unlike laments, do not mention personal distress or danger to life. Otherwise all prayers of petition could be referred to as prayers for help. While the prayers of Abraham, Hagar[59] and Jacob may be called individual laments in which personal discomfort or an immediate threat to life is the utmost concern, the 'outcry' that had risen to God from Sodom and Gomorrah may be categorized as a community lament in which the threat to the community is the utmost concern. I shall deal with them each in turn.

Abraham's Lament. Abraham's first recorded prayer in Gen. 15.2-8 may be called a lament in the form of a complaint. Though Abraham is said to have called upon the name of Yahweh on several occasions previously, it is only here that we find him talking to God almost like a man to his friend. The address is introduced by the simple words, ויאמר (twice) אברם, indicating the character of this prayer as an informal dialogue with no cultic setting assumed (*pace* Westermann 1985: 219; cf. n. 81). This is clear from the previous verse where Yahweh has initiated the dialogue. There are no laudatory epithets as in the ancient Near East, except אדני.

Then follows the petition, in the form of a complaint:[60] 'I continue childless, you have given me no children, and my heir will be Eliezer of Damascus'. There is no suggestion here that this is a 'factitious narrative' (cf. Westermann 1985: 215; Wenham 1987: 325-26). Abraham's childlessness and the dialogue are similar to Keret's situation and dialogue with El at Ugarit (*ANET*, 143, 144). Their complaints are similar; while Keret says, 'What need have I of silver and gold? Grant that I may beget children', Abraham says, 'What will you give me, for I

59. It is not certain if Hagar's words in Gen. 21.16 can be counted as an address to God. The form of the words suggests that she was talking to herself, but the context suggests that she may have uttered a prayer to God; so Miller 1994: 235. In any case since this is not one of the prayers by the patriarchs we shall leave it out of consideration.

60. Greenberg's analysis does not include laments as part of prose prayers because it is generally assumed that the lament is a special characteristic of psalm prayers. However, its presence in prose prayers is undeniable, and where it is present 'it is almost entirely in the form of *complaint* to or against God'; Miller 1994: 69, 86.

continue childless?' Both are drawing attention to their problem. While Keret's question presupposes El's immediate promise of silver and gold, Abraham's question presupposes God's earlier promises of children (Gen. 12.7; 13.16). Otherwise the second part of the complaint, 'you have given me no offspring', makes little sense (cf. Westermann 1985: 219-20; Wenham 1987: 327-28). They are protests, not requests.[61]

The third element, the motivation clause, sets reasons for God's intervention. Indeed, enough of a reason has already been made implicit in the complaint itself, where God has been squarely blamed for doing nothing either about Abraham's situation or the promises already made. Those reasons are further reinforced by the motivational clause, 'and the heir of my house is Eliezer of Damascus, a slave born in my house'. Exegetical problems associated with these clauses are particularly difficult,[62] but it is plain that the plight of the one who had no son in the ancient world is serious.[63] Whatever the relation of Eliezer to Abraham, he can never fulfil the function of a son. Even if Abraham were to adopt one of his own slaves, it would solve only the problem of inheritance, not of posterity. In other words Abraham's name will disappear. This is made clear also in Keret's story:

> And Keret saw his portion; he saw that his portion was wealth, that his seat was abundant in power; but at his departure the family would disappear, and someone from his surroundings would inherit (Cassuto 1950: 19; cf. *ANET*, 143).

61. Miller 1994: 71. For other such questions, see Exod. 14.12; 17.4; 32.11; Num. 10.11; 16.22; Josh. 7.7-9; Judg. 6.13; 15.18; 21.3; 1 Kgs 17.20; Jon. 4.2; and numerous examples from the Psalms and prophetic literature. Cf. Broyles 1989: 35-53, 135-36; Miller 1994: 70-78, 100.

62. For a discussion of the problems and the literature, see Westermann 1985: 220; Wenham 1987: 328.

63. The story of Aqhat makes it particularly clear what a son could do for his parents in their old age and death and for the family line to continue. He carried out his parents' funerary rites, which were believed to safeguard the soul's well-being in the after-life. Though no such belief is evident in the biblical stories, child-bearing as social prestige for women is sharply focused (Judg. 13.2-3; 1 Sam. 1.3-8; Isa. 54.1), and children as the continuation of a family line, and in some societies as economic benefit, was widely known in the ancient world. The recurring theme of childlessness in the patriarchal narratives (Gen. 11.30; 15.2; 25.21; 29.31b), which is often attributed to God (16.2; 20.18; 29.31a; 30.2, 22), must be viewed as a social problem in patriarchal society; *ANET*, 150.

The motivation clause in the legend of Aqhat, however, focuses on pious acts of Dan'el as well as the character of El and his relationship to him. Here Baal is the intercessor for Dan'el:

> He gives oblations to the gods to eat,
> Oblations to drink to the holy ones.
> Wilt thou not bless him, O Bull El, my father,
> Beatify him, O Creator of Creatures? (*ANET*, 150).

The motivation is explicit in the description of the devout acts of the petitioner and implicit in the epithets of El as 'my father', and 'creator of creatures', and the epithets are appropriate to the petitions made. The problem of 'inheritance'[64] and the continuation of the family line are certainly considered paramount in Abraham's prayer. Therefore the form and content of the prayer of Abraham and the parallels from Ugarit suggest that such prayers reflect the real life situation of childless fathers in the ancient world and that the biblical editors have probably transmitted fairly accurately what they had received.

Nevertheless, there is a difference in the theology of prayer between the patriarchal narratives and the Ugarit texts. In the former there are neither several gods nor intermediaries. In some sense Abraham's prayer is also unlike prayer among the later Israelites. Most petitioners in the Bible, including Moses, hark back to the relationship of themselves or God to their ancestors, but Abraham does not go beyond himself. Abraham has a unique relation with this God. Thus, as far as his situation is concerned, Abraham fits well with the second-millennium ancient Near East, and with regard to his faith in one God, though this is not explicit, he fits well with the religion of Israel. His relationship with God, however, is unique in the ancient Near East as well as in Israel.

---

64. Cassuto (1950: 19-20) points out that the same stem is used for inheritance both in Ugaritic (*yrt*) and in biblical texts (ירש). Therefore it is not necessary to assume, as Westermann does (1985: 220), that ירש acquired significance during the sedentary period of Israel when a son as 'heir' became important, whereas for the patriarchs, the 'son continues the life of the father; this is what the genealogy expresses'. However, the Ugaritic texts show that 'son' means both 'heir' and 'continuation of family line'. Given the value of Abraham's possessions and of his general characterization as a rich prince, inheritance is as much at stake as family line here. Further, it is doubtful if the idea that genealogy expresses family line comes from the patriarchal time.

It may be appropriate to consider here a similar prayer of Abraham for Ishmael. The context is again posterity, but Abraham has made some progress in this direction by obtaining a son through Hagar. God, however, tells Abraham that he will give him a son through his own wife Sarah (Gen. 17.16). Abraham almost protests at this idea, and asks God to approve Ishmael as his heir: 'And Abraham said to God, "O that Ishmael might live in your sight!"' (Gen. 17.18).

Once again a non-technical word, ויאמר, is employed to introduce Abraham's address to God, suggesting the dialogical nature of his prayer. This lacks both an address and motivational clause because it is part of a longer conversation, even though it is only here that Abraham interrupts a long divine speech.[65] All that we have here is petition for Ishmael, but it is still a prayer. However, it was not premeditated by Abraham, nor did it arise out of any distress as with most petitionary prayers. The petition presupposes God's knowledge of Ishmael, although there seems to have been no contact between God and Abraham (for 13 years, Gen. 16.15; 17.1) since Ishmael was born. Nevertheless, the relationship between God and Abraham continued. Once again there is no cult nor are intermediaries involved. Perhaps prayer was the only means of contact with God for the patriarch and theophany the only means of contact with the patriarch for God. Thus the relationship between God and the patriarch appears to be unique.

Jacob's Lament. The most elaborate personal lament in the patriarchal narratives may be found in the prayer of Jacob (Gen. 32.10-13). It has all the elements of a petitionary prayer and could serve as a paradigm for other such prayers in the Bible. My aim is to focus on its form and theology in order to understand the religion of the patriarch.

address:	God of my father Abraham and God of my father Isaac, O YHWH,
(description):	who said to me, 'Return to your country and to your kindred, and I will do you good',
self-deprecation:	I am not worthy of the least of all the steadfast love and all the faithfulness which thou hast shown to thy servant,
(detail):	for with nothing but my staff I crossed this Jordan; and now I have become two companies.

65. In v. 3 Abraham interrupts, not with words, but with an act of prostration which in itself is a prayer posture of extreme humbling of oneself and a great reverence toward God.

petition:	Deliver me…from the hand of my brother, from the hand of Esau,
description of distress:	for I fear him, lest he come and slay us all, mothers with the children alike.
motivation:	But thou didst say, 'I will do you good, and make your descendants as the sands of the sea, which cannot be numbered' (cf. Greenberg 1983: 11, 12).

This prayer also is introduced by the non-technical word, ויאמר, suggesting its dialogical nature (*pace* Westermann 1985: 508; cf. Wenham 1994: 290-91). The address is significantly different from that of Abraham in 15.2, where Abraham did not need to make contact with God. God himself made contact with Abraham, who only had to seize the opportunity and make his case. Jacob, however, was driven by his distressing situation (32.7) and was desperate to make contact with God. This is made amply clear by his repeated call to God in his address, which is also expanded here to establish a common relationship with the deity. Hence the repetition of the name of God, far from being irrelevant expansions (Westermann 1985: 508-509), has to do with the proper 'protocol' in relation to the deity in most ancient Near Eastern and biblical prayers.[66] Indeed ancient Near Eastern prayers, in contrast to biblical prayers, are replete with such epithets in their address to the deity. The epithets in Jacob's prayer, 'God of my father Abraham and God of my father Isaac', are not titles but are relational,[67] indicating indirectly how he is related to God as a child of God's favourites (cf. Greenberg 1983: 12; the Hittite prayers above). Further, he adds his own experience of that relation with Yahweh, who told him when he was still in Paddan-aram (31.3), 'Return…and I will do you good'. This is indirectly telling God that 'his present predicament is the result of obeying the divine command' (Wenham 1994: 291). This is probably the strongest motivation for God to intervene. Yet Jacob has not quite finished with such motivating language. He adds self-deprecation to it.

66. Greenberg 1983: 11-12; cf. Dalglish 1962: 23; Hallo 1968: 77, 79; Gerstenberger 1980: 97; Miller 1994: 14-15.
67. Cf. Eliezer's address, 'O Yahweh, God of my master', Gen. 24.12, 42.

In his self-deprecation, Jacob acknowledges God's care and fidelity which had increased his family from a single individual, owning nothing but a staff, to two companies. Then he openly declares that he is unworthy of all this. This removes any potential suspicion on God's part that Jacob was ungrateful for God's past kindness. The point is rather that not only would what God had promised come to nothing, but also what God had already done would be immediately nullified. On every count, it is God's reputation that is at stake, and this must be motive enough for God to act (Greenberg 1983: 14).

In the petition, though the ground is well prepared by the address and its elaboration, Jacob leaves nothing to chance. He identifies the problem and verbalizes his petition so well in so few words (Greenberg 1983: 14), 'Rescue me'. Repetition of the cause of the distress, 'my brother...Esau' 'is not a doublet, but an intensification' of the cause of trouble (Westermann 1985: 509).

Finally, in the motivation clause Jacob openly confesses his fears that Esau might come and annihilate him, and acknowledges his utter helplessness. Thus Jacob, as Greenberg notes, 'combines God's promise of making him prosper with the promise of numerous progeny... (and) recapitulates items that have occurred all through the prayer. As the family God, as the author of a promise to deal well with Jacob which, trustworthy as he is, he has already honored, YHWH must be moved by the imminent peril to Jacob and his family—which is ultimately a threat to God's declared plan' (Greenberg 1983: 14).

Nevertheless, it may be pointed out here that Jacob's prayer lacks the important aspect of the confession of guilt despite the fact that Jacob knew that his present trouble was the result of his deceiving his brother twice. In many Mesopotamian and Hittite prayers the cause of the trouble is often traced back to an individual or a community's moral or cultic breaches of conduct, and confession and restitution plays an important role in appeasing the gods. Even in Israel, sickness and misery or defeat in battle were often linked to individual or community lapses, and confession and restitution often formed an important part of prayer. This is understandable in the light of the moral code Israel is said to have received at Sinai. Jacob had realized the cause of his trouble, but the story does not portray him as morally wrong. That Jacob's prayer lacks confession of guilt fits well with the lack of any moral code revealed to the patriarchs. Therefore patriarchal religion appears to antedate Israelite religion. Further, in contrast to Israel, there are no moral demands on the patriarchs. There are only promises and blessing. This suggests that the basis of God's dealings with the patriarchs was different from that of Israel.

Communal Lament (?). We have only an allusion to communal lament in the story of Sodom and Gomorrah (Gen. 18.20-21), but the identity of those who lament is not clear. That this is a lament is clear from the two general words, צעק and זעק, 'outcry of the oppressed', for prayer in the Old Testament employed in this passage (for a detailed analysis of these words, see Boyce 1988). The actual prayers behind these words are rarely recorded, but sometimes it is expressed in just an exclamation, 'violence, חמס!' (cf. Miller 1994: 45). Though these words occur only in the divine speech in the story of Sodom, they nevertheless imply the cries of people subjected to violence, and the story of Sodom amply illustrates that. The form of the 'cry' gives no clue to an understanding of its setting, but there are several hints in the surrounding story, which throw light on the situation, such as the citizens' attitude to aliens and strangers and their right to host strangers (19.4-9), their aberrant sexual norms, their failure to protect the marginalized and, above all, the total failure of their legal system.[68] Consequently, the oppressed had no one to whom to turn. Yet unusually, as Boyce notes, it is not the oppressed who come to the court with their complaint,[69] but it is their 'cry' which as 'negative evidence' comes to God (בא plus על, Gen. 18.20), 'the Judge of the earth' (18.25), and 'becomes great "before" him' (*lipnê*, Gen. 19.23; cf. 2 Kgs 19.28, Jon. 1.2, Lam. 1.22) (Boyce 1988: 51; cf. Gen. 4.10; Exod. 2.23; 3.7-9).

The outcome of the story suggests, however, that the crying ones were probably the family of Lot,[70] and certainly Abraham intercedes for the sake of Lot. However, it is possible that the 'outcry' is used as a personification of the violence itself.[71] This continued to accumulate in

68. For the prophetic commentary on the crime of Sodom and Gomorrah, see Isa. 1.10-17, 23; 3.9, 13; Jer. 23.14; Ezek. 16.49. Boyce 1988: 51.

69. Contrast 2 Sam. 14.1-24; 19.25-31; 1 Kgs 20.35-43; 2 Kgs 6.24-31; 8.1-6; cf. *ANET*, 149, 151, 178; Boyce 1988: 28-45.

70. The New Testament describes Lot as 'righteous' who was 'distressed' and 'tormented' over the lawlessness of Sodom (2 Pet. 2.7-8).

71. Cf. the 'blood of Abel' which itself cried from the ground; and the 'cry of injustice' in Isa. 5.7.

increasing proportions before God who had rescued the innocent and finally overthrew the cities. Thus this is hardly a communal lament.

Prayer for Help. Here we shall consider the prayers in which there is no lament or distress.[72] The petition of Abraham's servant (Gen. 24.12-14 cf. vv. 42-44) on his mission to secure a wife for his master's son may be designated as prayer for help. This incident reveals that not only the patriarchs but also their servants offer prayers to the God of the patriarchs in times of need. The servant's piety is repeatedly emphasized in the story (cf. vv. 12-14, 26-27, 42-44, 48; Wenham 1994: 149). This probably reflects the piety of the master who often offered sacrifices and prayer, since the form and theology of this prayer is compatible with the patriarchal prayers.

The form is identical with Jacob's prayer, discussed above, with address, petition and motivation clause. The address is introduced with an ordinary non-technical word, ויאמר, suggesting the conversational nature of the servant's prayer. Like Jacob, the servant identified the deity by name as Yahweh and established his relationship with him as the 'God of my master Abraham'. Thus he made it clear that he was approaching him entirely on the basis of his relationship with Abraham and probably on the basis of God's earlier mercies shown to his master (cf. 24.27, 34-41).

With no further epithets in the address, he made his petition which in its basic form had two parts: 'please grant me success or make it happen before my eyes today', and 'show steadfast love, חסד, to my master Abraham'. The first part highlights the servant's own concern, that is, his success in this mission. This is important for him, first because of his most responsible position in his master's house, and secondly because of his oath to his master. The second part of his petition focuses on Abraham's situation. For Abraham to realize God's promises of descendants and land, Isaac must stay in the land, a requirement for a claim to land, and he must marry, though not necessarily from his own kinsfolk (see Chapter 7 §4c). Thus, whether the servant had realized it or not, God's promises are shown to be at stake in his petition (cf. Miller 1994: 56). The servant adds detail to his petition by suggesting how God should initiate the way of success by helping him identify the

72. For other similar prayers, see Num. 27.16-17; Judg. 6.36-37, 39; 13.8; 2 Sam. 7.18-29. Miller 1994: 378 n. 4.

girl who will pass the particular test he was about to conduct. Accordingly, God complies with it.

The motivation clause, 'By this I shall know that you have shown steadfast love to my master',[73] once again places God's reputation under test—whether he would continue to be faithful to Abraham or whether he would abandon him. Further, this would also begin the process of success for the servant even before he had met with the kinsfolk of Abraham. He could then confidently proceed knowing that God had already shown the way forward. This prayer of the servant is informal, non-cultic and non-polytheistic and there are no intermediaries involved. Therefore it is compatible with both the lifestyle and the religion of the patriarchs portrayed in the narratives.

c. *Prayer of Thanksgiving*

Abraham's Servant's Prayer. We have an example of thanksgiving prayer in the prayer of Abraham's servant (Gen. 24.26, 27, cf. v. 48). This is a spontaneous response to God's answer to his petition just discussed above. In form it is a blessing, but in content, it is thanksgiving for answered prayer.[74]

Like his petition, the servant's thanksgiving is introduced by the ordinary, non-technical word ויאמר, suggesting the informal nature of this prayer. That this was not an ordinary conversation is indicated by his gestures[75] and attitude: 'the man bowed his head, ויקד, and worshipped, וישתחו, Yahweh'.[76] The address first identifies God by name and the

---

73. Miller's (1994: 130) view that this 'functions as a statement of confidence echoing the petition' is unconvincing, since it seems to reinforce the statement of the petition, 'show steadfast love to my master'.

74. For a discussion of the nature and examples of such prayer, see §3.a above.

75. Other examples of 'bowing one's head in worship': Exod. 4.31; 12.27; 34.8; Num. 22.31; Ps. 35.13(?); Neh. 8.6; 1 Chron. 29.20; 2 Chron. 20.18; 29.30. The gestures assumed during prayer in the Bible are: a less common posture of sitting, Gen. 21.16; 1 Sam. 7.18; the most common posture is standing, 1 Sam. 1.26; 1 Kgs 8.22; 2 Chron. 20.5, 13; kneeling, 1 Kgs 8.54; Dan. 6.10; Ezra 9.5; 2 Chron. 6.13; Cf. Miller 1994: 50-54.

76. These two words are used primarily either in worship to God or to pay homage to a man of rank or to a king, Gen. 43.28; Ruth 2.10; 1 Sam. 24.9; 28.14; 2 Sam. 14.2, 22; 1 Kgs 1.16, 31; 2 Kgs 4.37; Prov. 14.19; Esth. 3.2, 5; etc. The second word שחה is also used for bowing before other gods, Exod. 20.5; 23.24; Num. 25.2; Deut. 8.19; Josh. 23.7; 2 Kgs 5.18; Isa. 2.20; 44.15, 17; 46.6, etc.

petitioner's relationship via his master, just as in his petition above. The form of the address conforms with the Israelite prayers of similar nature, with the consistent form, 'Blessed be Yahweh', followed by a description of God's favours, 'who has not forsaken his steadfast love and his faithfulness toward my master'. We may recall that he had petitioned only for God's 'steadfast love', but he gives thanks also for God's 'faithfulness' which, as Miller observes, is the persistence of that 'grace and kindness, the maintenance of the promise and blessing God offered to Abraham at the beginning' (Miller 1994: 182). This description looks like the epithets in Mesopotamian name prayers in which the very names given to children express thanks and praise for the favours received from the deity, for example, 'Sin has heard my prayer' or 'My God dealt compassionately with me'.[77] As the names in Mesopotamian name prayers can express aspects of the petitionary prayer, so here the title in the praise is a reflection of the servant's earlier petition. Thus the thanksgiving flows naturally out of the petition.

Then follows the body of the thanksgiving in two parts: the expressions of praise and thanksgiving, and the report of God's deliverance to others. The first is declared in the personal testimony of the servant, 'As for me, Yahweh has led me on the way to the house of my master's kin'. Meeting Rebekah at the well was only the initial sign for the servant, but meeting her household for marital negotiations was the main purpose. The second part deals with the report of God's deliverance to others, which takes place most naturally in this episode in the household of Rebekah (24.42-49). This in turn is supposed to evoke the praise of others to the God of deliverance.[78] Interestingly, when the servant relates how God led him to identify Rebekah at the well, Laban and Bethuel respond, 'the thing comes from Yahweh' (v. 50), indicating their implicit acceptance of the servant's testimony to the hand of God in this whole mission.

Once again there is no cultic action, and no intermediaries were involved in the prayer of Abraham's servant. Further, the servant's petition as well as his thanksgiving occurred most naturally and spontaneously in the story, suggesting that prayer was basically a relationship with God who had bound himself to his people. Thus the prayers of

77. Cf. §2a above; and the names given by Jacob's wives to their children in Gen. 30.

78. Cf. Jer. 33.11; Pss. 22.22-23; 40.9-10; 52.9; 66.16; 116.14, 18; 118.21-24.

patriarchs' servants (Hagar included) are also compatible with the patriarchal lifestyle.

Matriarchal Prayers (29.31–30.24). Unfortunately the prayers themselves are not preserved, except in the form of thanksgiving or other expression that explains the names. Rachel's demand for children and her desire to end her life amply illustrate the acute social problem of barrenness, as already noted with Hannah. The desperate struggle to conceive children and the rivalry between the sisters to outdo each other even by magical means suggests the compatability of the traditions with the religious and social ethos of the patriarchs. Further, Jacob's marriage to two sisters concurrently, contrary to the Levitical law (Lev. 18.18), and the lack of any hint that the children would be the eponymous leaders of the future tribes suggest the tradition's antiquity and the author's concern to transmit rather than to rewrite it (Sarna 1989: 205-206; cf. Westermann 1985: 472, 477). Jacob's love for Rachel is set in tension with Leah's fertility right through the narrative. There is a clear evidence of the petitions of the matriarchs in the names they gave to their sons. It was a common custom in the ancient Near East for parents to give their children names which expressed their faith or thanks to the deity who granted them.[79]

The explanations of the first four names of Leah's sons allude one way or other to her previous prayer, though God's help was not acknowledged in the birth of every child (e.g. the children of Leah's maids). The name Reuben was explained as 'Yahweh has seen my affliction', ראה יהוה בעניי. Similarly, Simeon's name is explained as 'Yahweh has heard that I am hated', שמע יהוה כי־שׂנואה, suggesting that he was an answer to Leah's earlier prayer to Yahweh. That Yahweh was one who sees and hears the afflicted is already demonstrated in the story of Hagar (16.11, 13). Whether this was a folk etymology or not, it fits well with the circumstances of Leah who was isolated and longing for her husband's affections.[80] Although no religious reasons are given for the birth of Levi, his name still describes Leah's frustration for failing to attract Jacob's attention, despite being the more fertile sister. By contrast, the name Judah is explained as

---

79. Cf. n. 18 above; biblical examples: Jonathan = 'Yahweh has given (this child)'; Jehoachin = 'Yahweh strengthens us'; Fowler 1988: 17-18.

80. Wenham 1994: 243; cf. Fowler 1988: 167; Sarna 1989: 206-207.

'praise to Yahweh',[81] despite no improvement in her relationship with Jacob as hoped for when she bore Levi. It is possible that by this name she acknowledged God's goodness despite her husband's constant distancing of himself from her. Thus 'as in the psalms, lament turns to praise' (Wenham 1994: 244). The author sees the matriarch as one who believed in Yahweh and prayed to him in her most difficult circumstances.

Similarly, the names of Rachel's legal children allude to her previous prayer. Like Sarah, it is now Rachel's turn to obtain children through her maid Bilhah.[82] Here is the clearest indication of Rachel's petitionary prayer. While the name Dan is explained as 'God's vindication', which it was, Rachel clearly alludes to her previous prayer, שמע בקלי, 'he heard my plea' (cf. Ps. 54.3, 4). Given the circumstance, it is impossible that she did not resort to prayer, especially when her own sister could bear children. She could have all the love of her husband and could even blame him in vain for not giving him children. Jacob's sharp retort, 'Am I in the place of God who denied you fruit of the womb?', probably helped her to turn to God in prayer. Similarly, the name of Naphtali whom Bilhah bore next probably reflects Rachel's 'contest or struggle for God's favour', נפתולי אלהים. While this difficult phrase could mean 'mighty struggles', 'divine struggles', or 'struggles in prayer',[83] the context suggests that it refers to both Rachel's struggle for God's favour and her struggle against her sister, as she explains in the following phrase, עם־אחתי נפתלתי (Wenham 1994: 245-46; cf. Sarna 1989: 208). By now the problem was no longer childlessness but a competition as to who would bear more sons to her husband.

In her bid to outdo Rachel, Leah follows her sister's method and through her own maid Zilpah obtains Gad and Asher. These names contain no immediate relevance to her prayer, though their etymology may be traced to certain Assyrian or Canaanite deities.[84] Similarly, no

---

81. Or 'may God be praised'; Millard 1974: 216-18; Fowler 1988: 165.

82. For an infertile wife to provide her husband with a concubine in order to obtain children is widely attested in the second-millennium sources in the ancient Near East; *ANET*, 160 par. 27; 172 par. 144; 543; for the protection of the concubine's rights, *ANET*, 172 par. 146; 525; cf. Sarna 1989: 119.

83. Cf. Delitzsch 1889: 175; Dillmann 1897: 241; Andersen 1969: 200; Fokkelman 1975: 135-36.

84. *TDOT*, II: 382-84; Strus 1978: 67 n. 29; Fowler 1988: 96, 135; Sarna 1989: 208-209; Wenham 1994: 246.

prayer seems to be involved for the subsequent birth of Leah's own sons, Issachar and Zebulun. The author's comment, 'God hearkened to Leah', probably implies his belief that conception and children are granted by God alone, not by the magic to which both sisters resorted. Thus the author dismisses 'the notion that such superstitions may have any validity. Leah, who gives up the mandrakes, bears three children; Rachel, who possesses them, remains barren for apparently three more years'.[85] However, there is a double allusion to Rachel's prayer for Joseph. Rachel was successful in her struggle against her sister when she obtained children through her maid, but this did not take away her reproach as a barren woman. It is the birth of Joseph that took away that shame. Thus Joseph's name is explained by two Hebrew verbs, אסף and יסף, 'take away' and 'add' (Sarna 1989: 210). While Rachel's prayer for her reproach to be taken away is implied in the name, her prayer wish for another son is made explicit. Thus the name prayers are not peculiar to the matriarchs. They are common in the ancient Near East, as already noted in examples from Mesopotamia.

d. *Intercessory Prayer*

As has been noted above, intercessory prayer may take the form of petition or complaint or even confession depending on the context. There are several instances of intercession by Abraham and Isaac in the patriarchal narratives. I shall deal with each separately.

Abraham's Intercession for Sodom. One of the most familiar intercessions of the Bible is the prayer of Abraham for Sodom and Gomorrah (Gen. 18.23-25 cf. vv. 27-32).

Although this passage is set in the form of dialogue 'its character as intercession is unmistakable' (Miller 1994: 267; cf. Clements 1986: 20). The dialogue is initiated by Yahweh himself, first by stating in his soliloquy (vv. 17-19) that he would not hide from Abraham his intentions about Sodom,[86] and secondly by actually declaring them in Abraham's hearing (vv. 20-21). This sets the dialogue in motion. Abraham

---

85. Sarna 1989: 209; cf. Wenham 1994: 247; contrast Westermann 1985: 476.

86. The author probably did not view Abraham as a prophet in the traditional sense, although another text described him as such when he interceded for Abimelech (21.7). Nevertheless, Abraham's role here reminds one of later prophets who stood in the councils of God (Amos 3.7; Jer. 23.9, 18, 21, 22); cf. Westermann 1985: 286-87.

promptly responds to God's decision but with extreme caution, acknowledging his utter unworthiness to question God's decision. However, his plea for Sodom is less concerned than his pleas for a son or for an heir through Ishmael.

The address, introduced with the non-technical word ויאמר, indicates the informal nature of the intercession. There is, in fact, no address proper, as Abraham's speech begins with not a name or epithet but a question, further highlighting the total dialogical nature of this prayer (cf. Gen. 17.18). In what follows, Abraham's speech accepts God's judgment over Sodom, but questions the destruction of the righteous along with the wicked, since this contradicts God's position as 'the Judge of all the earth'. The speech goes even further to press God, although with humility and caution, to pardon the wicked for the sake of the few righteous who might be in Sodom. While God defers to this request, Abraham makes no further plea and the dialogue breaks off. There is nevertheless no idea of repentance in this story, suggesting that the tradition is ancient and compatible with patriarchal religion. The social and moral situation in Sodom may be comparable with that of the time of Noah, but the description of the latter does not even contain the idea of intercession.

Further, while we have no parallels to Abraham's prayer in the ancient Near East, Moses' prayer for disobedient Israel is similar to it though more passionate, since Moses even wished to forgo his own life for Israel's sake. Abraham's prayer may be one of the moral peaks in the patriarchal narratives, but this is not sufficient justification for ascribing the whole passage to the postexilic period, as some scholars do.

Abraham's Intercession for Abimelech. Here we have only the report of prayer, as the prayer itself is not recorded (Gen. 20.17).

Abraham is introduced by God as a prophet who would intercede for Abimelech (20.7). The two most important characteristics of a traditional prophet—that he stands in the council of God (as pictured in the story of Sodom) and that he prays for others—are probably behind the description of Abraham as prophet (for a prophet's varied role in Israel, see Carroll 1969: 407). But the traditional reason given for the former —that the prophet was called to carry his message to his people—is not given here, though God spoke to him both in dreams and face to face in human form. The reasons for the latter are not clear. The traditional prophet assumed the function of an intercessor either on his own

initiative or at the request of others, but Abraham was given this function. It is not certain how important it is for the narrator to portray
Abraham as a prophet, since traditional reasons for this role do not fit
neatly. Indeed, Abraham is portrayed here not only as cheating and
lying but also as one who could not trust God for his safekeeping,
whereas Abimelech is viewed as innocent and righteous. This is not the
portrait of a prophet in general in the Old Testament. So the word
prophet, נביא, is probably not used in a technical sense (so Westermann
1985: 324), nor can it be conceded that it is used because of the function of Abraham as intercessor (*pace* Dillmann 1897: 120-21; Carroll
1969: 402 n. 4). Therefore the notion that it was the idea of a later
author to portray Abraham as a prophet is not likely. It is probable that
the word is used in the sense of a mediator who simply passes on the
divine blessing despite his own personal moral deficiencies. Or, more
probably, it was simply because of Abraham's relationship with
Yahweh that he was asked to pray for Abimelech. In the ancient Near
East kings were the mediators of blessing who interceded for the healing of their people and for the averting of divine judgment (e.g. the
plague prayers Mursilis).

Further, more than the patriarch, the Canaanite king Abimelech is
portrayed as one aware not only of sin and guilt but also of how to
compensate for his unwitting sins. So anyone intending to portray the
father of the nation would not have included such a story unless his
concern was other than the glory of the patriarch. It appears that more
than prayer or religion of Abraham, the story reveals God's relationship
with and commitment to him. The focus of the passage seems to be, not
the prayer or piety of Abraham, but God's protection of him and Sarah
in order that God might bring about the promises he had made to them.

Isaac's Intercession (Genesis 25.21). Here is another occasion where
the prayer itself is not recorded, only the report of it. This may be
regarded as a prayer of petition, since Isaac's prayer was essentially for
himself. However, the fact that Rebekah is described as barren suggests
that the problem was more Rebekah's than Isaac's, given the social
stigma attached to barrenness. It is not clear why Rebekah herself did
not pray for her problem as did Leah and Rachel later. In this regard
Isaac's prayer may be called intercession.

The word עתר used in this context has no inter-human usage in the
Bible, suggesting that its particular focus is on God's response to

prayer (Miller 1994: 41; see p. 100 above). Its usage elsewhere in Moses' plague aversions (Exod. 8.8-9, 28-30; 9.28; 10.17-18) and in David's entreaty to avoid famine and pestilence on Israel (1 Sam. 21.1-14; 2 Sam. 24.25) suggests that it was more an entreaty on behalf of others than for oneself.[87] In the case of David's entreaty, ritual sacrifices followed the prayer. It is not certain if this was involved with Isaac's intercession. In keeping with the patriarchal practice, Isaac, as the head of the family, interceded for his wife. This not only reflects the patriarchal social and religious background where there was no formal cult or priests, but also reveals Isaac's personal relationship with God (cf. Westermann 1985: 412). This is made clear by his involvement in the formal cult in Gen. 25.25, where he is described as building an altar and calling upon the name of Yahweh. Isaac's piety is also revealed in his blessing of his children which I shall examine below. Thus patriarchal prayer, like their sacrifices, is family oriented and unique in comparison with the prayers of the ancient Near East and Israel.

e. *Prayers of Blessing*

We have several prayers of blessing in the patriarchal narratives which are equally important for our understanding of the religion of the patriarchs. The patriarchal blessings focus particularly on increase, protection and fulfilment of promises previously made to them. I shall examine the marriage blessings of Rebekah and Jacob, Isaac's blessing of his sons, and Jacob's blessing of Joseph, his sons and the other tribes of Israel. However, the blessing of the Canaanite king Melchizedek will not be discussed since it does not proceed from a patriarch.

Marriage Blessings. Genesis 24.60 records the blessing of Rebekah by her family after she had decided to go to Canaan to marry Isaac.

This is probably one of the most ancient forms of blessing, in which the occasions of farewell and marriage are combined together (cf. 28.3) (Westermann 1985: 390). Structurally, the subject of the blessing, God, is missing, probably because Rebekah's family did not worship the same God as Abraham. Thus it was probably left ambiguous. The content focuses entirely on the prospects of marriage, fertility and the

---

87. Cf. Manasseh's entreaty for himself in order that God may restore his kingdom and his former status (2 Chron. 33.12-13, 19).

possession of land. These are particularly appropriate for prospective brides and grooms, though the blessings pronounced on women are especially related to their fertility (cf. Ruth 4.11, 12; 1 Sam. 2.20; Miller 1994: 283). This is confirmed from Ugaritic sources, in that the marriage blessing of fertility pronounced on Keret is ultimately related to his future wife who would bear sons and daughters to Keret (*ANET*, 146). The setting of this blessing is the family and there is no cult involved. Thus it reveals the family-oriented religion which is compatible with the patriarchal society.

Genesis 28.3, 4 records Isaac's blessing of Jacob when the latter was sent to Paddan-aram to secure a wife from the family of Rebekah. The occasion of marriage and farewell and the family setting are similar to that of the blessing of Rebekah noted above. There are, however, a few differences of structure and content. The structure is balanced with the clear invocation of the ancient name of God, אל שׁדי, while regarding content the promise of land in the blessing of Abraham, is passed on to Jacob. The form and setting clearly indicate the antiquity of the blessing. But it is radically different from Isaac's earlier blessing of his sons in which the idea is not of a prayer wish but of a blessing which when uttered is irrevocable and works independently of divine agency.

Isaac's Blessing. Isaac's blessing (Gen. 27.27-29) is different from that of a normal blessing in Israel or the ancient Near East.

Before I discuss the form and content of the blessing, a few general remarks are in order. First, it is not clear why Isaac had to have a meal before the blessing. The view that it was a 'festal meal', 'part of a pre-cultic rite' which is an 'early form of the later cult meal', and that this was to give strength in order to pass on the vital power through blessing, is dubious (contra Westermann 1985: 440). The text says that Isaac was old and about to die and he wanted to bless his beloved son Esau before he died. But before he did so, he wanted to enjoy Esau's game which he loved so much (27.1-4 cf. 25.27-28). Thus the meal serves more to fulfil a desire before death than to give strength for a blessing (cf. Brichto 1963: 205-206). Secondly, besides being a prayer wish, the blessing reflects an apparent magical element which eludes the power of God or the one who blesses once it is uttered, so that neither of them can revoke its effects or duplicate the blessing, not even when the deception of Jacob is taken into account. A similar view operates in regard to the curse in the oracle of Balaam as the story seems to focus on the importance of the prevention of its utterance.[88] A closer look at the blessing, however, suggests that it is not simply a magical formula that operates apart from God's activity. The 'jussive form' clearly indicates its divine origin even as God is clearly invoked in the blessing (Miller 1994: 288). As for its irrevocable nature, Miller plausibly suggests that it is 'a kind of performative and declarative speech', as in our modern-day wedding ceremonies in which the 'declaration itself makes legal and real the marriage of the couple... The notion of effective power in blessing is not far from this kind of performative speech' (Miller 1994: 287). In Deuteronomy, God also makes such performative statements about the land which he had promised the fathers that he would give to Israel, suggesting that these provided a 'religio-legal claim upon the land' (Miller 1994: 287).

The form differs from the usual form of blessing. It begins, not with the usual formula, 'Blessed be so-and-so', but with the exclamation, 'How beautiful is the smell of my son...', just like the blessing of Balaam in Num. 24.5, 'How beautiful are your tents...' Both these blessings not only assume divine agency indirectly but also perceive that God has already blessed the recipient, and they both have to do with the future. So the pronouncement of blessing was only a formality for what has already been blessed by God (cf. Westermann 1985: 440; Sarna 1989: 192). The content of the blessing contains three elements, namely, fertility, dominion and protection, but not posterity or land (Sarna 1989: 192; Wenham 1994: 210). The first of them is more appropriate to Jacob than Esau, for whom the blessing was originally intended. The last of these, dealing with curses, is repeated in identical form in Balaam's oracle and was also given to Abraham. All of them, however, anticipate the future blessing of Israel during the monarchy (cf. Sarna 1989: 192; Wenham 1994: 209-210). The blessing may suggest several points pertinent to the religion of the patriarchs. First, the apparent magical element in it indicates its antiquity and the authenticity of the tradition, while the form and content show the origin of the blessing as being God alone. Secondly, Jacob's deception is highlighted, but there is no remorse or repentance for the act on the part of the one who had deceived. This clearly suggests that the patriarchal

88. Brichto 1963: 5, 208-209 refutes the view that there is a magical element behind these blessings or curses.

traditions are not aware of the Mosaic legislation on sin and guilt. Thirdly, the informal family setting of the blessing further confirms the family-oriented religion of the patriarchs.

Jacob's Blessing. Jacob gives two blessings, one of Joseph and his sons (Gen. 48.14-16, 20) and the other of his twelve sons (Gen. 49.1-27). Both are occasioned by his anticipated death. Only the former, however, contains the usual form of blessing, while the latter, though widely called 'the Blessing of Jacob', contains material of mixed nature, such as blessings and curses, praise for natural abilities and reproof of weaknesses, prophecy and observations of geographical and historical nature. Because of this, several scholars have entitled it 'The Last Words or The Testament of Jacob'.[89] Nevertheless, the final author views the whole section as the blessing of Jacob (v. 28). It contains a clear reference to a formula of curse analogous to the formula of blessing (v. 7), although it lacks the usual formula of blessing. Thus it is not surprising that many scholars see it as a collection of tribal sayings, which arose either independently or together but were expanded with time, and finally was placed in the context of P by a redactor (Westermann 1986: 220-22).

First, I shall deal with Jacob's blessing of Joseph's sons. The context of the blessing has several reminiscences of the blessing that Jacob himself extorted years ago from his father Isaac. Like Isaac, Jacob is on the deathbed and cannot see well. The kiss and embrace are similar to the kiss and the physical contact Isaac made with Jacob. And in both cases the younger receives the elder's blessing. The form is that of a usual blessing, but with an unusual introduction in which the God who is invoked is variously described as the one who led his ancestors Abraham and Isaac and who protected Jacob on his way and delivered him from all evil. The content of the blessing is a prayer wish for the perpetuation of the names of all the lads' ancestors, Abraham, Isaac and Jacob (cf. Mendelsohn 1959: 180-83), and a wish for the increase of the recipients,[90] a wish traditionally granted to all the patriarchs by God. Further, it is added that their names will be used as paradigms of

89. Clements 1986: 36; cf. Gevirtz 1975a: 104-12; Sarna 1989: 331; Wenham 1994: 468.
90. That their numbers were really increased is shown in Num. 26.28-37 cf. 1.32-35; Deut. 33.17; Josh. 17.14-18.

blessing in future Israel.[91] The form and setting is very much at home with the patriarchal lifestyle. The invocation of God and his angel, who were closely watching over Jacob's sojourn in Mesopotamia, clearly relates to Jacob's personal experience and religion oriented as they are to the patriarchal nomadic lifestyle.

Secondly, there is Jacob's blessing of his own sons, the eponymous tribal leaders. It is a farewell address at Jacob's deathbed. The occasion is similar to that of the blessings given by Isaac and Moses (cf. vv. 1-2 with Deut. 33.1-2).[92] The blessing starts with a summons to the sons of Jacob to come and hear 'what shall befall you in days to come'. Jacob is probably viewed as a prophet by the author as the phrase הימים באחרית usually occurs in prophetic eschatology.[93] However, the author in v. 28 states that the blessing concerned not with just the twelve sons of Jacob but with 'the twelve tribes of Israel'.[94] Thus the author thinks that what Jacob said in blessing his sons became true of the tribes in their historical development. The fact that the author was speaking retrospectively has not been concealed, but points to the author's belief that the blessing in its kernel originated with Jacob himself. The blessing actually begins with a curse or more precisely a reproof of the firstborn son Reuben for defiling his father's marriage bed (v. 4, cf. 35.22). This appears to reflect a knowledge of the law of Lev. 20.10, but the latter is more precise about the punishment of death for such a crime. Reuben was deposed from his position and pre-eminence as the firstborn. This was fulfilled as the status of the firstborn in Israel was assumed by the tribe of Levi and the Reubenites themselves became insignificant among the Israelites (cf. Wenham 1994: 472-73). However, the author of Genesis 49 does not seem to be aware of the special privileges assumed later by the tribe of Levi, because 49.5-7 still portrays

91. Cf. similar formulae in which Rachel, Leah and Peres are used as paradigms of blessing (Ruth 4.11-12), and Zedekiah and Ahab as paradigms of curse (Jer. 29.22-23).

92. Deut. 33 may be compared to Gen. 49 in form and setting. But Judg. 5.14-18 is part of a thanksgiving prayer in the form of blessing. Even though this passage reproves or praises certain tribes, it is based on non-participation or participation of them in the battle. Thus it has no clear parallel to Gen. 49, *pace* Westermann 1986: 221.

93. The only other occurrence of this phrase in the Pentateuch is in Num. 24.14; Westermann 1986: 223.

94. This is the first mention of the 12 tribes in the Old Testament; Wenham 1994: 487.

Levi as a secular tribe with no hint of its future sacerdotal status. Further, the lack of territory as a punishment for Levi's conduct conflicts with the special status and the priestly grants conferred later on the tribe. Thus Jacob's words here are based on a very early tradition.[95] Verse 7 clearly uses the curse formula for the anger and wrath of Simeon and Levi in massacring the Shechemites. The form is similar to the form of blessing: 'cursed be so and so'. The word used for curse, ארר, means 'to ban, or to exclude from the company of'. This refers not just to their anger and wrath which are the objects of the verb 'cursed', but also to the later deprivation of the independent status of Simeon and Levi. This is clarified in the next sentence, 'I will divide...I will scatter...' This probably suggests that they would no longer work together and ultimately become powerless. This was what had happened to them by the time of the monarchy, when the tribe of Levi was nearly non-existent as a tribe and Simeon had been assimilated into Judah.[96]

However, Jacob's words about Judah contain no form of a blessing, though the intention is clear. Judah was praised for his lion-hearted courage in battle and blessed with lasting hegemony and fertile territory (vv. 8-12). Since the reasons for these are not immediately apparent, diverse interpretations have been put forth. Some are based entirely on Judah's earlier life in Genesis (Good 1963: 427-32; Carmichael 1969: 435-44), others on the immediate context of Judah being raised to the status of the firstborn since the first three sons were denied it due to misbehaviour or bad temper (cf. Wenham 1994: 473), and still others on the tribe's later history, such as Judah claiming kingship for the tribe (Holzinger 1898: 257-58), or the other tribes recognizing him as lord (cf. Gunkel 1902: 423-24; Skinner 1930: 519). Westermann takes it in two parts in keeping with his traditio-historical approach. The first (vv. 8, 9) is a praise of Judah for his heroic deed in battle in the period of Judges; the second (vv. 10-12) is a promise of a future, not eschatological, leader. While all these views are recounted from the past history of Judah, the final author probably believed that they were the result of Jacob's blessing on his death-bed.

The next son or tribe to receive blessing is Zebulun (v. 13), although he is younger than Issachar according to the birth narratives and

---

95. Cf. Num. 3.12-13; 8.14-18; 16.9-10; 18.20-24; Sarna 1989: 334.
96. Brichto 1963: 88; cf. Jacob 1934: 895-900; Westermann 1986: 226-27; Sarna 1989: 335; Wenham 1994: 475.

generally precedes him in the territorial allocation of the land (Gen. 30.17-20; Num. 34.25-26; Josh. 19.16, 17). That Zebulun was more powerful than his older brother is suggested by the primacy accorded to him in the blessing of Moses and the Song of Deborah (Deut. 33.18, 19 and Judg. 5.14, 18; Sarna 1989: 338). The author probably views the tribe's significance in Israel and its prosperity at sea as the result of Jacob's blessing. By contrast, Issachar (vv. 14, 15) was blamed for his passive submission to the Canaanites. He is described as a strong but lazy ass who sacrificed his freedom for a peaceful livelihood. Contrary to the policy of the infiltrating Israelites, he became a forced labourer or 'corvée', סַמ, to the Canaanites.[97] This word occurs also in the Amarna archives in a letter from the king of Megiddo to the king of Egypt: 'I alone bring men for the corvée from the town of Yapu. They come from Shu[nama]... Sunem lies in the territory of the tribe of Issachar, and it is possible that those here brought into forced labour belong to this tribe.[98]

The blessing once again turns to praise in vv. 16, 17, this time of the tribe of Dan, the first of the concubine tribes. Unlike Issachar, Dan will maintain its independence, despite its failures. The snake metaphor indicates that he was small but capable of surprise attack in the manner of guerrilla warfare. Thus he holds his own in his struggle for survival and will not give in to forced labour. The blessing fits well with the struggles and exploits of Samson, the future Danite.[99] At this point, the patriarch suddenly calls for divine deliverance (v. 18), which is probably a petition for strength to finish the blessing, or possibly a petition for the precarious position of the tribe.[100]

The next three tribes, Gad, Asher and Naphtali, are praised for various reasons. Gad's defence against marauding bands is reflected in its many wars with neighbours.[101] Asher will succeed in foreign trade, though it failed to subdue the most important cities in its territory

---

97. Josh. 16.10; Judg. 1.28, 30, 33 cf. Exod. 1.11; 1 Kgs 9.21; Westermann 1986: 234.

98. Westermann 1986: 234; cf. *ANET*, 485; Rainey 1970b: 194; Alt 1989b: 148-49; Sarna 1989: 340; Wenham 1994: 480.

99. So, Delitzsch, Dillmann, Driver, König; cf. Wenham 1994: 481.

100. Sarna 1989: 341; Wenham 1994: 482; *pace* Westermann.

101. Judg. 11; Mesha inscription, ll. 10-13; 1 Kgs 22.3; 2 Kgs 10.33; cf. Deut. 33.20; Sarna 1989: 341.

(Judg. 1.31-32). The blessing of Naphtali, however, cannot be related to a specific event of its history, except that he will love freedom and mobility (cf. Westermann 1986: 236; Sarna 1989: 342).

Just as the curse formula is used in regard to Simeon and Levi, the blessing formula is used for Joseph (49.22-26). The mood is entirely positive, and the blessing is extravagant. A number of titles, including the ancient name Shaddai by which God revealed himself to the patriarchs, are used to describe the God who was invoked to bless Joseph. The blessing itself contains three elements. First, Joseph is described by a metaphor of an animal or a plant.[102] In either case the metaphor illustrates the increase and freedom of the tribe. Secondly, Joseph's patient endurance in the hands of his hostile enemies is attributed to the help of the God of Jacob,[103] who is described with various titles such as 'the Mighty One of Jacob', 'the Shepherd and the Stone of Israel'[104] and El Shaddai. Thirdly, God's blessing on Joseph will surpass the blessing Jacob himself had received. The blessing includes the fertility of land, humans and mountains, all yielding their best for Joseph, thus making him special among his brothers (Westermann 1986: 240-41; cf. Wenham 1994: 487). Finally, Jacob blesses his youngest son Benjamin, who is described as fierce and aggressive in contrast to defenceless Joseph. The future exploits of Benjaminites are probably in view. The blessing, however, is probably ancient since there is no allusion to Saul's kingship in it.[105]

Thus from the author's point of view Jacob's curse and blessing, although it reflects a knowledge of the historical Israel, was a prayer wish of the dying father. He reprimanded some of his sons for their weaknesses and commended others for their good conduct, and wished God's blessing for many of them, especially Judah and Joseph. Jacob's blessing is compatible with his faith in the God of his fathers and his experience with this God all his life.

---

102. Animal: Gunkel, Speiser, Gevirtz, Sarna and Wenham. Plant: Westermann.

103. Cf. Sarna, Wenham; for Westermann, this refers to the tribe of Joseph.

104. This unusual title, instead of the usual 'Rock of Israel', was probably an earlier title that derived from the traditions about Jacob setting up stone pillars at Bethel (Gen. 28.18, 22; 35.14). The fact that the other titles, 'God of your father' and El Shaddai, also occur in the Bethel episodes (28.13; 35.11) suggests that the blessing is very ancient; Sarna 1989: 344; cf. Wenham 1994: 486.

105. Judg. 3.15-30; 5.14; 19; 20; 1 Sam. 10–14; Sarna 1989: 345; Wenham 1994: 487.

5. *Conclusion*

The form of prayer in patriarchal narratives is similar to the form we observed in the ancient Near East and Israel, although the address, with no laudatory epithets, is even more informal and simpler than could be found in Israel. The range of problems which prompted people to approach the deity is similar in the ancient Near East and Israel, but it is much narrower in the patriarchal narratives. Here there is only one reference to prayer for healing (20.7, 17), and it was not for a patriarch himself.[106] There is no prayer prompted by sin and guilt,[107] oppression by enemies[108] or abandonment by the deity,[109] although patriarchs were said to have experienced all these problems in one way or another. It is unlikely that patriarchs going through such problems would not have turned to their God for help, but to record and preserve people's experiences of divine help in such situations would be a concern for the organized cult and society. The only common factor for which petition was made in the ancient Near East, Israel and the patriarchs is the problem of childlessness. This was a relevant issue for the patriarchs because of its association with the promise of land, which was as much of interest to Israel as to the patriarchs. Therefore, its preservation in the history of the origins of the nation is hardly surprising.

The setting of prayer in the ancient Near East and to a large extent in Israel is the organized cult, whereas with the patriarchs it is entirely the family or other informal situations. The most revealing of all their types of prayer in this regard is the prayer of blessing. While the occasions for the blessing in all the cultures, including patriarchal, were identical, the setting of patriarchal blessing was distinct from others, in that it was never cultic. Further, one of the distinctive aspects of patriarchal blessing is the possession of land. While this is pertinent to their lifestyle, it is not found elsewhere.

---

106. Sickness (Gen. 48.1) was not a matter of concern for prayer or ritual as in the ancient Near East.

107. Although cheating and deceit were acknowledged (Gen. 25.29-34, 27.35, 36; 32.10-13, 21; cf. Gen. 29.25; 31.7, 9, 26 [גנב], 27 [גנב]; 'offence', פשע, and 'sin', חטאת (31.36) refer to a violation of norms.

108. Jacob accuses Laban of having been oppressed, עני (31.42), but there is no confession of sin on the latter's part.

109. Abraham blamed God for his childlessness and waited for a long time, but he did not lament because God deserted him (Gen. 15.3; 16.15; 17.1).

As for the theology, in contrast to the ancient Near East and Israel, prayer or sacrifice is not used as a means to an end in the patriarchal narratives. While prayer is assumed in the context of building altars and offering sacrifices, prayer as petition never occurs in the context of ritual or sacrifice. Thus it is precluded from being manipulative or magical as in the ancient Near East or Israel, although it does occur as an inducement in Jacob's vow. The concepts of worship, קרא בשם, entreaty, אתר, thanksgiving and blessing, ברך (in both cases), most naturally occur in contexts which suggest that there was no standardized meaning behind them as in later Israel. Prayer is entirely preserved as a conversation between the patriarchs and God. The intercession of Abraham is the most telling example of this. Thus the content, setting and theology of prayer in the patriarchal narratives is distinct from the concept of prayer in both the ancient Near East and Israel. This fits well with the practice and concept of sacrifice in the patriarchal narratives discussed above. Having seen the patriarchal response to theophanies and to their attitude to prayer, it is appropriate to consider now Jacob's peculiar action of raising pillars in response to theophanies.

Chapter 4

SACRED PILLARS

1. *Introduction*

Along with building altars and offering prayers, raising pillars[1] forms
part of the patriarchal pattern of worship, although this is attested only
in the Jacob cycle. While Jacob is also known to have built altars in
response to theophanies, raising pillars appears to be his special response to theophanies. However, pillars were strongly proscribed in
later Israelite history as symbols of Canaanite religion and inappropriate in Yahweh's worship. This raises several questions: Why were
the pillars approved in the patriarchal narratives while they were condemned in Israelite worship? What was their nature and function in
cult? Who wrote the patriarchal texts? Were they not familiar with the
Yahwistic ethos? We have little evidence to answer these questions
adequately from the patriarchal stories themselves, and later Israelite
history shows a mixed attitude towards cultic pillars, sometimes approving and at others condemning.

On the other hand, much has been made of Jacob's erecting a stone at
Bethel, and it has been identified with sacred stones and *baetyls* of
Aramaic and Greek texts of later times. *Baetyls* or *baetylia* as meteorite
stones occur on Roman coins and in classical Greek writings from the
first to the fifth centuries CE. An unbroken tradition about the deity
Bethel occurs in vassal treaties and in theophoric personal names from
the early seventh to the late fifth centuries BCE, and again in Greek
writings and inscriptions from the first to the third centuries CE. The
expression בתי אלהיא which occurs in the Sefire texts from the eighth
century BCE has been regarded as a Semitic counterpart to the Greek
baetyls, since the Semitic word sounds like its corresponding Greek
word. Thus it is generally argued that these *baetyls*, as described in

---

1. Pillar and *maṣṣēbāh* are used synonymously in this chapter.

different literature, are evidence for the popular notion that certain stones were indwelt by deities and were therefore 'sacred stones'. In the same way scholars also suspect that the stone pillar, מצבה, erected in Gen. 28.22 by Jacob, who called it בית אלהים, was a *baetyl* too. Scholars think that the deity *Bethel* is also present in certain Old Testament texts including the Jacob narratives. These issues raise serious problems about the religion of the patriarchs, which is described in Genesis as a precursor to, yet distinct from, the later Yahwistic monotheism. In this chapter I re-examine the evidence in both the ancient Near East and the Bible in order to see whether raising pillars was compatible with other activities of patriarchal worship such as building altars and calling upon the name of Yahweh, or if it was a form of stone worship whose original context was removed in order to conform with the general Yahwistic ethos of the patriarchal religion portrayed in the narratives.

I shall first deal with the evidence related to *baetyls* and then with that of the Greek deity *Baitulos* and its Semitic counterpart *Bethel* in extra-biblical literature, and see what these entities have in common with the popular sacred stones. Then I shall examine the evidence in biblical and extra-biblical sources concerning מצבות. Finally I shall note the relationship between these different phenomena, and see how this enhances our knowledge of patriarchal religion in Genesis.

2. Sacred Stones outside the Bible

a. Baetylia *and* Baitulos

Baetyls are meteoric stones with magical qualities and *Baitulos* is the name of a Greek deity. Both of these occur in Philo, but with little connection between them. *Sacred stones* are those which represent certain gods and/or stand at a sacred place and thereby become objects of worship. In this sense certain pillars (*maṣṣēbôth*) can be considered sacred stones, but by no means all. Thus these three entities must be differentiated, although some overlap between them may be admitted. However, generally little distinction has been made between them in scholarly writings. In the early eighteenth century, Bochart identified *baetylia* with the anointed stone pillar of Jacob, describing *baetylia* as 'anointed stones'. In their attempt to imitate Jacob, the Phoenicians 'first worshipped the stone which the patriarch had set up; then they anointed and consecrated other stones, and called them *baetylia*, *baetyli,* in memory of the stone at Bethel'.[2] Bochart's equation was subsequently taken over by lexicons, encyclopaedias and commentaries[3] and became popular with several archaeologists,[4] despite the objections raised by some.[5] Though any original distinction between these entities has been almost completely ignored by scholars, I shall argue from the evidence that a distinction can legitimately be maintained.

Baetylia are mentioned as 'animated' stones in Philo, as meteorite stones with magical powers in Pliny, and as indwelt by demons, animated, magical, and associated with different gods in Damascius. I shall discuss first what the texts say and how scholars understand them.

The earliest mention of *baetylia* is to be found in the Phoenician history of Philo of Byblos (second century CE),[6] preserved mainly in

2.   Bochart 1707: 784, 785; cf. Moore 1903: 206; Zuntz 1945: 182-88.

3.   *DB,* I: 27; *RLA,* I: 392; Gunkel 1902: 282; Skinner 1930: 38; Eliade 1958: 228-30.

4.   Evans (1901: 113, 118, 192-96), for instance, constantly uses *baetylia* in the sense of *maṣṣēbāh* (p. 113); he talks about the 'sanctity of baetylic stones and pillars' (p. 118) and of a *baetylic* temple, but in this there is no evidence of a *baetyl* (pp. 192-96). Moreover, Evans derives the idea of 'baetylic qualities' from the 'meteoric origin' of an object and the idea of meteorites from the name 'Baetylos'. But in Philo, as we know, Baitulos had no such origin; cf. Cooke (1930: 26, 161-67), who equates Zeus stone with a *baelyl* and makes no distinction between pillars and *baetylia* . But see Eissfeldt's (1962: 230 n. 1) refutation of Evans.

The trend continued even much later in Teixidor (1977: 38-39). While distinguishing the god Baitulos from *baetylia,* he confuses the latter with Greek stele and popular cult stones: 'The cult of the steles or *baetyls* was universally accepted in the ancient Near East. Accordingly, it is not surprising to find holy stones of various forms associated with the cult of a particular deity. To the cult of the steles of Astarte or Melqart we may add the cult of the baetyl of Zeus Casius frequently represented on the coins of Seleucia Pieria.' So also Mettinger (1995: 35), who refers to the scholarly convention in which the word *baetyl* is used as a designation for a cultic stone, but he does not go to the origin of the idea. Later he uses the terms *baetyl* and *stele* synonymously (1995: 96).

5.   Dillmann 1897: 337; Smith 1927: 210; Moore 1903: 203, 205, 208; Driver 1948: 268.

6.   Moore 1903: 198; but Zuntz (1945: 180) thinks that the earliest occurrence of *baetyls* in literature is in Sotakos of Karystos, whose comprehensive work on gems is now lost, but whose words are preserved in Pliny, of the early first century CE. This apparent discrepancy is due to the uncertain date of Sanchuniaton, who is usually dated between the late second millennium and the early to mid-first millennium BCE.

the works of Eusebius (about 260–340 CE).[7] Philo claims to have translated it from the original by Sanchuniaton of Phoenicia.[8] The word *baetylia* and *Baitulos,* the name of a god in Sanchuniaton's theogony, occur once each in Eusebius:

> And when Uranus knew it, he sent Eimarmene and Hora with other allies on an expedition against Kronos, and these Kronos won over to his side and kept with him. Further, he says, the god Uranus devised the Baetylia, having contrived to put life into stones (Gifford 1903: 42; cf. Baumgarten 1981: 15, 16).

> And Uranus, having succeeded to his father's rule, takes to himself in marriage his sister Gé, and gets by her four sons, Elus who is also Kronos, and Baetylus [Gk. Baitulos], and Dagon who is Siton, and Atlas. Also by other wives Uranus begat a numerous progeny... (Gifford 1903: 41).

It is plain from the texts above that *baetylia*, the 'animated stones', and *Baitulos*, the son of Uranus, occur quite separately in Philo. Neither the context in which they occur nor the purpose for which *baitylia* were invented suggests that they were related to the god *Baitulos*. The context suggests that Uranus had hoped that *baetylia* would somehow help him in his war against Kronos. Apart from these suggestions, we have no indication in Philo of how *Baitulos* was related to *baetylia*,[9] which are more colourfully described in later Greek and Latin writers.

With the description of Pliny (early first century CE), *baetylia* acquire the quality of meteorites. Pliny treats *baetylia* as a sub-category of ceraunia stones ('thunder-stones'). Pliny claims to have been informed about them from Sotakos of Karystos.

> Sotacus [= Sotakos] distinguishes two other varieties of the stone, a black and a red, resembling axe-heads. According to him, those among them that are black and round are supernatural objects; and he states that thanks to them cities and fleets are attacked and overcome, their name being 'baetuli', while the elongated stones are 'ceraunia' (Eichholz 1962: 273-75).

---

7.   Gifford 1903: 35. Porphyry, who is quoted in Eusebius, dates Sanchuniaton during or before the Trojan war. The works of Sanchuniaton were translated into the Greek by Philo of Byblos.

8.   Barr (1974: 17, 31) and Løkkegaard (1954: 74, 76), however, doubt the authenticity of Philo's tradition as coming from Sanchuniaton.

9.   Cf. Løkkegaard 1954: 68; Barr 1974: 28 n. 1; Baumgarten 1981: 203.

Pliny's description of precious stones in general is more scientific than religious, but it is the information from Sotakos that ascribes magical qualities to *baetylia*. But there is no indication in Pliny as to the origin and nature of *baetylia*, although it is possible that he regarded them as meteorites since he treats them under the category of 'thunder-stones'.

By contrast, Damascius's *Vitae Isidori* (early sixth century CE),[10] describes *baetylia* with religious qualities reminiscent of Sotakos. *Baetylia* are pictured by Damascius as globular objects moving through the air, usually whitish in colour and a hand span in diameter, but sometimes turning purple or changing size. They could be hidden in garments or carried in hands by their attendants (worshippers) but could not be controlled by them. They had lettering and holes on their sides through which they gave oracles. The attendants would make requests and prayers and the *baetylia* would respond in oracles. They were dedicated to one or other of the Greek gods, such as Kronos, Zeus or Helios. The *baetyl*'s attendant regarded it as divine, while Isidorus thought that it was moved by a demon which was neither harmful nor altogether pure (Zintzen 1967: 274, 276; cf. Moore 1903: 199-200). However, the exact connection of the *baetylia* with these particular gods is unclear. Possibly the tradition represented in Damascius knew an association of certain stones with certain gods in earlier writings.

Other evidence for *baetylia* is their depiction on Roman coins from the late third century BCE to the third and fourth centuries CE (Hill 1899: 266, 271, 272). This is often claimed as the best evidence for their being regarded as objects of worship in Phoenicia. The stelae depicted on the Tyrian coins are apparently regarded as *baetyls* by several scholars (Baumgarten 1981: 202; cf. Mettinger 1995: 95, 96). But this interpretation is doubtful, first because they do not resemble the *baetylia* we discovered in Philo or classical Greek literature. Secondly, the epigraphy on the coins says, αμβροσιε παιτρε, 'ambrosial rocks' (Mettinger 1995: 96). The shape and the writing suggests that they are probably cultic stones or altars. Thus strictly speaking none of the extant Phoenician coins depicts a *baetyl*, although Phoenicians and Sidonians had coins at least from the fifth and third centuries BCE respectively. On the other hand, fourth-century Sidonian coins depict a Persian king in a chariot with a goat underneath, and coins of the same period from Tyre depict Melqart holding a bow and riding over the

10. The Neo-Platonist, Damascius, was born in about 480 CE; *EB*, VI: 998.

waves on a sea horse (Head 1909: 40, 41, 61, 93, 109). However, the absence of *baetyls* on Phoenician coins does not prove that the Phoenicians did not regard them as objects of worship.

Nevertheless, the foregoing discussion suggests that a distinction between *baetylia* and *Baitulos* can be maintained since, as Moore notes, 'there is no evidence either from Semitic sources or Greek or Latin authors that the name *baetylus* was ever applied in antiquity to the class of objects which modern archaeologists habitually call "baetyls"; on the contrary it was the distinctive designation of an entirely different thing'.[11] While *baetylia* were magical stones associated with demons or gods, for Philo *Baitulos* was a son of Uranus and Gē. He does not appear in Hesiod's theogony.[12]

b. Baitulos *and Sacred Stones*

In some classical Greek writings, contemporary with the Greek literature which mentions *baetylia*, we have evidence for a different type of stones which can be called 'sacred stones' or a type of cultic *maṣṣēbôth*.[13] These are different because, first, they are not called *baetylia*, and secondly, they are larger and were probably erected by humans, though they are also linked with Kronos and Zeus in Greek mythology. They are mentioned in Philo, Hesiod, and Pausanius. Philo has this account:

> And Astarte set the head of a bull upon her own head as a mark of royalty; and in travelling round the world she found a star (ἀστέρα) that had fallen from the sky, which she took up and consecrated in the holy island Tyre (Gifford 1903: 43).

11. Moore 1903: 208. Moore thinks they were pre-historic stone implements. Cf. Baumgarten 1981: 203.

12. Hesiod's Theogony has no *Baitulos*. It has six sons and six daughters to Ouranos, Kronos being the youngest of all, whereas Philo's Theogony has four sons to Ouranos, Kronos being the first of them. It appears that these are two different traditions of the same myth, one Greek, the other Phoenician, and probably one is worked into the other, and it is not certain which is borrowing from which. Philo probably hellenized the Phoenician myth, as several scholars suspect (e.g. Løkkegaard, Barr).

13. *Maṣṣēbāh*, in contrast to *baetyl*, usually refers to a standing stone erected by humans rather than a natural stone that attracted curiosity or wonder. The stone erected by Jacob in Gen. 28.14 is called a *maṣṣēbāh*.

It may be noted here that the word used for this particular object is *astera*. But Milik interprets it as referring to *baetyls* associated with the cult of the Phoenicians (1967: 575, 572; cf. Teixidor 1977: 38).

> Finally I consider as highly probable the Sidonian origin of the worship of god Betyle. The information of Philo on the meteorite set at Tyre is probably only a fragment of a more developed hagiographic legend. The *betyl* par excellence of Astarte, kept at first in Tyre, would have been then transferred to Sidon; one of the successive epitomists of Sanchouniaton would have transcribed only the beginning of the sacred account.

In Hesiod's theogony[14] we have an explicit mention of a stone associated with Kronos. Being told that one of his sons would overthrow him, he began swallowing his offspring as they were born. But his wife was advised by her parents to hide the last of his sons, and gave Kronos a *large stone* instead of the infant Zeus whom he was about to swallow:

> But to the great prince the son of Heaven, former sovereign of the gods, she gave a huge stone [μέγαν λίθον], having wrapped it in swathes: which he then took in his hands, and stowed away into his belly, wretch as he was… And first he disgorged the stone, since he swallowed it last. This stone Jove (Zeus) fixed down upon the earth with-its-broad-ways, in divine Pytho, beneath the clefts of Parnassus, to be a monument thereafter, a marvel to mortal men.[15]

It is clear that this is a large stone (μέγαν λίθον) and is nothing like a *baetyl*, and it was set up as a sign or monument. The story is probably an aetiological account of a sacred stone. There is an interesting parallel to this in Pausanias's *Description of Greece* (second century CE), in which he describes a stone at Delphi which was believed to be the one that Kronos had vomited.

> Ascending from the tomb [of Neoptolemus] you came to a stone of no large size. Over it every day they pour oil, and at each feast they place on it unworked wool. There is also an opinion about this stone, that it was given to Cronus instead of his child, and that Cronus vomited it up again (Jones 1935: 511).

---

14. Hesiod is dated between the eleventh and fifth centuries BCE, while some parts of Hesiod (e.g. Agon) are thought to be not earlier than the second century CE. Mair 1908: xxv, xxvi, xxxvii; Banks 1873: vv. 8-9.

15. Banks 1873: 26-27. Greek words are from Evelyn-White 1982: 114.

Some scholars doubt that the stone at Delphi was brought from Crete, since direct evidence is lacking. For Moore: 'The probability is that the foreign myth was simply attached to an old Zeus stone at Delphi, just as the scene of the deception of Kronos was located at Chaeronea. In later times the terminus on the Capitol at Rome was identified with the stone which Saturn had swallowed...' (Moore 1903: 202, 203).

Thus it is clear from Philo, Hesiod and Pausanias that *baetylia* and 'sacred stones' were two different types of stones. In Philo and Pliny *baetylia* are not associated with a god, though they were in Damascius. By contrast, a large 'Zeus-stone', unmentioned in Philo, Pliny or Damascius, was associated especially with Zeus in Hesiod and Pausanias. Also the concepts associated with these stones are clearly different. One was an animated and magical stone while the other was a sacred stone, a substitute for Zeus himself, and was openly worshipped and offered sacrifices. This stone was not called pillar or stele, although one may surmise that the idea associated with its 'setting up' might suggest that of a *maṣṣēbāh*. The evidence for the worship of *baetylia*, however, is lacking (cf. Zuntz 1945: 178, 179).

If *baetylia* and 'sacred stones' were different, how were they related to the deity Bethel or *Baitulos*? Is there a real connection as often supposed by scholars, or do the words happen to sound alike? Interestingly, we have some third-century CE Greek inscriptions which could refer either to the animated stones *baetylia* or to the god *Baitulos* mentioned in Philo, while Zeus and certain other gods were associated with a certain Betylos. An inscription on an altar dedicated to Zeus Betylos recovered from Syria at Dura-Europos reads:

> To [his] national god Zeus Betylos, [god] of the dwellers along the Orontes, Aurelius Diphilianus, soldier of the 4th Legion Scythica Antoniniana, has dedicated [this altar].[16]

And at Kafr Nabu an oil mill dedicated to Seimios and Symbetylos has this inscription dated from 224 CE:

16. Seyrig 1933: 68-71. Seyrig mentions that two high-places discovered near Aleppo were dedicated to 'Zeus Bomos' and 'Zeus Madbachos', and that the words appended to Zeus are obviously related to the Semitic terms 'high-place' and 'altar' respectively. One may suggest from these high places that 'Zeus Betylos' was probably another altar.

To Seim(i)os and Symbetylos and Leon, ancestral gods.[17]

There are two inter-related issues here. First, is the word *betylos* appended to Zeus and Sym a mere substantive of *baetylia* or of the deity *Baitulos*, or is it connected to the Semitic word Bethel? Opinions are divided. Eissfeldt is inclined to argue that in Philo of Byblos *baetylia* as 'animated stones' and *Baitulos* as deity were differentiations of the root idea *bait-il*, as 'power' and 'person' just as in Genesis *bêt'ēl* was originally the name of a god and subsequently also that of a stone (1962a: 229-31). It must be observed, however, despite Eissfeldt's ingenious suggestion, that *baetylia* and *Baitulos* occur independently in Philo. Except for the identical form of the word, there is no suggestion that the god was associated with the stones. Nor was he associated with them in the later writings surveyed above. On the other hand, it was Kronos and Zeus and other gods of the Greek pantheon who were associated with *baetylia*, not *Baitulos*. The association between the stone and the god, if *bethel* can be translated as the name of the god, is much more suggestive in the Genesis story than in Philo (I shall return to this subject below).

Similarly Seyrig, following Eissfeldt but especially commenting on the inscription at Dura, argues:

> *Betylos* is a Greek transcription of the Semitic compound *bethel*, that means *house of El*, and was used in ancient Semitic worship to describe the cult-stone in which El was considered as being present. By and by, the central place given to this object in ritual promoted it to the rank of an independent god, known as the god Bethel, who at last took advantage of his prominent function to supersede and to evict the former and less materially present owner of the cult-place. Ultimately the word *betylos* became a Greek substantive, and was applied to any baetyl, any stone that seemed to draw supernatural power from the presence of a deity (1933: 69; so also Teixidor 1977: 87).

Seyrig's suggestion is equally ingenious, but lacks firm evidence to support it. It can be conceded that the ancients believed that certain stones were indwelt by deities or demons, but Seyrig does not give any instance of a cult-stone in Semitic worship in which El was believed to have dwelt and to which worship was directed. Further, it is uncertain whether Seyrig is correct in his theory of the origin of the god Bethel. Seyrig's final sentence quoted above once again confuses *betylos* and

17. Porten 1968: 172; cf. Hyatt 1939: 86. Both Porten and Hyatt identify Symbetylos with Eshembethel of Elephantine.

baetylia, which originally had no connection in Philo or in other Greek or Latin writings (see n. 11 above). The Syrian deities in the above inscriptions, for example, Zeus Betylos and Symbetylos plus Eshembethel of Elephantine, were originally Aramaean deities like the deity Bethel (Porten 1968: 172, 73). Thus *betylos* appended to the names of deities was probably related to the deity Bethel rather than to the 'animated stones' or *baetylia*. The former was a well-known west-Semitic deity known in Phoenicia,[18] Babylon (Hyatt 1939: 86), Elephantine, Erech and Nippur (Porten 1968: Appendix V). It is possible that this deity's name had survived by its identification with popular gods of later times.

The inscribed objects at Dura and Kafr Nabu therefore may be regarded as commemorative rather than representative of the gods themselves. Altars were built to offer sacrifices. They were certainly regarded as sacred and were sometimes deified, but were distinct from 'sacred stones', which by their very nature were considered indwelt by a deity and worshipped. The stones that fall in this latter category are: the 'Kaaba' at Mecca, the 'Linga' of Shiva,[19] the Zeus-stone at Delphi,[20] and so on. The inscription at Kafr Nabu is probably dedicatory, with no sanctity implied for, or worship directed to, the oil mill.[21] The altar and the oil mill were certainly not *baetylia*, nor were they 'sacred stones' in which the representative gods were believed to have dwelt, nor was there any suggestion that worship was directed to them as to the other 'sacred stones'. Therefore *baetylia*, *Baitulos* and 'sacred stones' attested in the classical Greek writings and other inscriptions were distinct from each other.

18. *ANET*, 534. Philo's *Baitulos* was probably the Greek equivalent of the Semitic god Bethel.

19. Shiva is one of the three popular gods (along with Brahma and Vishnu) of the Hindu pantheon. 'Linga' is a cylindrical black stone representing Shiva in most Hindu temples in India. The stone is anointed and offerings are made to it. 'Salagrama' is another black stone found in the river Gandaki in Nepal, and is regarded as the abode of Vishnu; *ERE*, XI: 872.

20. In Roman history two other stones were considered sacred: the stone which was believed to be the abode of the mother goddess Cybele, brought from Asia Minor in 204 BCE as a protection during the war with Hannibal, and the sacred stone believed to be the seat of the Oriental Sun-god at Emesa, introduced by the Emperor Elagabalus in the third century CE; *ERE*, X: 50, 51.

21. In India, however, implements of work are dedicated and worshipped during the Dasharah festival.

But what about the stone pillar, מצבה, erected by Jacob in Genesis 28, and the occurrence of El Bethel along with it? Do these suggest that Jacob believed that the stone was the abode of the deity Bethel? Do Jacob's actions of anointing the stone and pouring a drink offering over it imply that Jacob worshipped the stone or the numen inside it? However, one can note at this point that the connection between the Semitic god Bethel and the stone erected by Jacob in Genesis is tenuous, because in the three instances where the word Bethel occurs (Gen. 28.18-22; 35.1-11, 9-15) the focus is the place, not the commemorative stone. One might interpret the word Bethel here as the name of a god (cf. 31.13), but it does not fit the context. Moreover, there is no suggestion in the stories that the stone served as an abode for a god. The Hebrew imperfect יהיה in 28.22 indicates that the stone monument 'will become', but is not yet, the house of God (*ABD*, I: 709). The separation of God and the stone can be more tellingly seen in 35.13-15 where God is said to have 'gone up' from Jacob from the place where he was speaking with him, after which Jacob erected a pillar and called the 'place' Bethel. For the author, God, the pillar and the place are all distinct from each other in the story. It will be appropriate to discuss the extra-biblical evidence on מצבות before considering the biblical evidence on the מצבה erected by Jacob.

c. Maṣṣēbāh
Certain standing stones, rocks and boulders have been considered sacred in many parts of the world because of their appearance or position, and in many cases they have been identified as deities with sacrifices offered before them.[22] My concern, however, is only with the standing stones or *maṣṣēbôth*. The word מצבה comes from the Hebrew verb נצב, 'to erect, set up',[23] and refers to objects set up by humans, usually stone monuments. Out of 36 occurrences in the Hebrew Bible, מצבה is governed by the verb עשה only once (2 Kgs 3.2). This suggests

22. Stone-worship in East Africa, India and Madagascar has been connected with ancestral spirits. Prayers are offered to them to secure favours, e.g. to protect fields. Oaths are taken before them, and they are used in divination. Cf. 'Lia Fail' (stone of destiny) at Tara in Ireland with which the Coronation Stone is identified. *ERE*, XI: 864-67; 870-76; cf. *ERE*, XI: 50, 51.

23. Other verbs like שים, קום and רום are also used for its setting up. The LXX translates the word as στήλη. Derivatives of the root נצב are found in most Semitic languages with similar or identical meaning; *EnBib*, II: 2975.

that מצבות were usually set up, not made (contra Burrows 1934: 46). The RSV translates this word usually as 'pillar', but also twice as 'stump' (Isa. 6.13), and once as 'obelisk' (Jer. 43.13).[24] Archaeological discoveries shed considerable light on various types of מצבות in biblical texts which would have remained inexplicable otherwise.

It must be conceded, however, that there is no absolute distinction between the cultic stones and some of the other kinds of stones found in archaeological discoveries. Interpretation is based on their shape, posi- tion and physical context (Mettinger 1995: 141-42). The *maṣṣēbôth* found in Palestine, Syria and Phoenicia generally lack inscriptions or carved figures, which makes it even more difficult to interpret their precise meaning, and the few inscribed stones found in Palestine are all of foreign origin or influence, which suggests that inscription on stone was a custom common to imperial cultures (Graesser 1972: 35). Thus we cannot be certain that a particular pillar found in excavation rep- resents a particular stone mentioned in the biblical sources, although several archaeologists suggest near certainty about some of them.[25] Therefore it has been suggested that the architectural and artefactual remains of Iron II Palestine reflect the religion of the united and divided monarchic period largely as aniconic compared with the premonarchic period (Holladay 1987: 249-99). The Israelite personal names found on seals and inscriptions from the eighth century BCE suggest to Tigay that the majority of Israelites worshipped Yahweh rather than other gods (1986: 41; 1987: 157-94). However, this interpretation has been strongly contested by other scholars (Albertz 1994: 64-65, 95-99, 187- 88). Nevertheless, archaeological findings confirm that most of the Egyptian grave stones and some of the Assyrian royal stelae, besides being memorial, also functioned as cultic stones. The bronze gate of Balawat, for instance, depicts sacrifice in front of a royal stele erected

24. Of the 36 times in the Hebrew Bible, the word occurs 11 times in Genesis alone: 28.18, 22; 31.13, 45, 51, 52 (×2); 35.14 (×2), 20 (×2); Other occurrences: Exod. 23.24; 24.4; 34.13; Lev. 26.1; Deut. 7.5; 12.3; 16.22; 2 Sam. 18.18; 1 Kgs 14.23; 2 Kgs 3.2; 10.26, 27; 17.10; 18.4; 23.14; Isa. 6.13; 19.19; Jer. 43.13; Ezek. 26.11; Hos. 3.4; 10.1, 2; Mic. 5.12; 2 Chron. 14.2; 31.1.

25. Excavations at Byblos, Hazor, Shechem, Tirzah, Megiddo, Lachish, Arad and Jerusalem uncovered a number of pillars of various sizes, and scholars suggested parallels between them and a number of מצבות mentioned in the biblical sources. For a survey, see Aharoni 1967: 233-49; Graesser 1972: 50-56; Avner 1993: 166-76; Mettinger 1995: 140-91; for problems of general interpretation, see Dever 1987: 209-47.

beside the god Hirbe.[26] The royal stele itself does not become the focus of worship here, but it points to the sanctity of the place and encourages worshippers to practise the cult of that deity. Thus material evidence becomes useful if used judiciously.

3. מצבות *in Israel*

a. *Types of* מצבות
Having examined evidence from outside Israel, now we shall look at archaeological data from Israel and texts from the Old Testament on מצבות.

Archaeologists divide מצבות into four main categories: legal, memorial, commemorative and cultic.[27] A fifth category of those found in non-cultic contexts is too insignificant to consider here, since there are only two such references in the Old Testament: Isa. 6.13, where a tree stump is referred to as מצבה, and in Ezek. 26.11, where the destruction of מצבות bearing a building structure is referred to. I shall examine each category separately.

Legal Stones. These were erected to remind individuals or groups of treaties or boundaries between them. Examples existed already in the third-millennium Sumerian city-states.[28] The eighth-century Sefire inscriptions and the famous Hammurabi code may also be included in this category (Graesser 1972: 38, 39). From the Hebrew Bible the cairn set up by Jacob and Laban (Gen. 31.45-52), the 12 מצבות erected by Moses (Exod. 24.4), and the covenant stone of Joshua at Shechem (Josh. 24.26-27) may be identified with them. Sometimes these stones served as witnesses to a covenant treaty and as documents on which the terms of the covenant were written (cf. Deut. 27.1-8; Josh. 8.30-35).

26. *ANET*, 277; for other royal stelae erected in sacred precincts, see *ANEP*, 442-44, 447. Graesser (1972: 44-45) thinks that these Assyrian royal stelae served all the four functions noted here. See n. 27 below.

27. Graesser 1972: 34-63; cf. *ERE*, XI: 877-78; Eliade 1958: 217-19; Avner 1984: 115-31; 1993: 166-81; Mettinger 1995: 32-35.

28. King 1916: 126-27; cf. *ANEP*, 298-302; the *kudurru* boundary stones of Babylon depict land deals, royal grants and symbols of deities, *ANEP*, 454, 518-21; cf. Graesser 1972: 37, 38.

Several scholars, however, have argued that the Sefire stelae were 'sacred stones' like the *baetylia* or the מצבות of Jacob.[29] The only reason for this is the description of them as בתי אלהיא, 'houses of gods', in the inscriptions. These scholars, in fact, translate this phrase as *baetylia* or 'sacred stones'.[30]

ומן י[א]	....	...... [whoever]
מר להלדת ספרי[א א] לן מן ב		has it in mind to efface these inscriptions from
תי אלהיא אן זי י[ר]שמן ו		the sacred stones where they were written and...
[י]א מן בתי אלהיא ויאמר ל		from the sacred stones, and says to...
ב[ת]		the sacred
י[א]להיא ובלחץ עלב י[מת הא]...		stones, then by crushing torment [let him]...

Jacob's מצבה was also called בית־אלהים, 'house of God'. Nevertheless, as I have argued above, a distinction must be made between *baetylia*, 'sacred stones' and *maṣṣēbāh*. The Sefire stelae cannot be called *baetylia*, nor can they be called 'sacred stones' like that of the Zeus-stone of Delphi, to which frequent sacrifices were offered. There is no suggestion in the inscriptions that any worship was directed to these stones (so also Gibson, *TSSI*, II: 45). Furthermore, sacred stones usually had neither inscriptions nor image, since it was believed that carving would be disturbing and offensive to the indwelling spirit (*ERE*, XI: 871-72). They were certainly מצבות, but were they cultic מצבות? The fact that they bore the treaty inscriptions suggests that they were legal stones, but they were not regarded as witnesses to the treaty, even though no less than 19 different gods were called by name, besides the gods of the open country and the cultivated land, and gods like heaven, earth, springs, day and night, as witnesses to the treaty sealed in those inscriptions (incidentally, El and Elyon occur together here). It is possible that the stones were viewed as cultic מצבות, in the sense that they marked the sacred area where the treaty had been sealed, and the words בתי אלהיא could refer to the temples where the treaty had been made and where the stones had been preserved.

29. Dupont-Sommer 1958: 119; *KAI*, 259, 262; Fitzmyer 1967: 90; *TSSI*, II: 30; Mettinger 1995: 35.

30. *TSSI*, II: 44. Texts and translations in the following are from Gibson unless indicated otherwise.

Memorial Stones. These were ubiquitous as funerary stelae in Egypt.[31] Besides being memorials, they often marked the grave of the dead and the place where funerary offerings were to be made.[32] Sometimes they were covered with inscriptions and pictures of the dead which both indicated their needs in the other world and memorialized them. Aramaean stones of early first-millennium Syria bore reliefs depicting the deceased sitting at a banquet table, sometimes with a servant in attendance, suggesting the importance of food or offerings for the dead (*ANEP*, 630-33, 635; Woolley, 1939–40: 14, pl. III). Such stones were, however, relatively less common in Assyria and Babylon, though the memorial function of stelae was well known.[33] We have probably two examples of memorial מצבות in the Hebrew Bible. One is the pillar erected by Jacob on Rachel's grave (Gen. 35.20).[34] The other is 'Absalom's monument' that was meant to ensure the continuance of his memory since he had no son to 'cause his name to be remembered' (2 Sam. 18.18). The reason given for erecting the pillar precludes it being a funerary stele (cf. Graesser 1972: 40; cf. Chapter 2 §4d). There is a superb example of a memorial *maṣṣēbāh* from Phoenicia, erected during a man's lifetime (*TNSI*, 62).

Commemorative Stones. These point to significant events or to individuals who played important roles in them. The most obvious examples of such *maṣṣēbôth* are the victory stones erected by kings to extol their exploits to the generations to come. There are examples of such stelae set up by the Egyptian pharaohs Seti I and Ramases II at

31. Graesser 1972: 39; cf. *ERE*, X: 881; Spronk (1986: 94) thinks that the tombs of the Egyptians also functioned as memorials.

32. The purpose of gravestones in central India, however, was to provide a temporary dwelling for the soul and to prevent it from roaming about and becoming dangerous. It is believed that stones thus inhabited by ancestors were instrumental for fertilizing crops and women; Eliade 1958: 217-19.

33. More than 130 stones were found within the city walls at Assur memorializing kings and important officials; Graesser 1972: 40, 41. But direct evidence for the cult of the dead is decisively lacking, although indirect references are found in the ritual texts; the Mari texts are an exception where fuller accounts of royal funerary cult are given; see Bayliss 1973: 115-24.

34. *TNSI*, 60; cf. Procksch (1924: 384), for whom it represents the cult of the dead; for von Rad (1965: 341) and Westermann (1985: 555) it is only a landmark with no religious significance. Cf. Chapter 2 §4d.

Bethshan and by Shishak at Megiddo.[35] Biblical examples can be found in 1 Sam. 7.12 and 15.12, where Samuel and Saul set up stone monuments to commemorate victories over their enemies.[36] Stelae which commemorate a special sacrifice like the *mlk*-sacrifice have been found in the sacred precincts among the first-millennium Phoenician colonies of North Africa and the Mediterranean islands.[37] A number of 'votive stelae' with inscriptions have also been found in sacred precincts, showing that worshippers often promised to offer sacrifices or erect stelae if the deities granted deliverance from natural calamities such as flood (Assur-nadin-apli) (Weidner 1930–31: 14; *RAC*, IX: 1058), impotence (a Hittite),[38] or enemies (Bar-Hadad).[39] Is Jacob's pillar erected at Bethel in Gen. 28.18-22 and 35.14 a votive stele commemorating the appearance of Yahweh in that place? Bar-Hadad's stele was raised in fulfilment of a vow while Jacob's pillars were set up in response to the deity's appearance in a particular place. One of these pillars, however, became a focal point for making vows. I shall return to this subject below when I consider these texts in detail.

Cultic Stones. The most frequent occurrence of pillars in biblical sources is in religious contexts, hence they are called 'cultic stones'. Cultic pillars found in archaeological discoveries usually stood at the entry or boundary of a sanctuary or by the side of an altar, and were thought to 'mark the place where the deity is in some manner immanent, so that worship offered there reaches him or her' (Graesser 1972: 44; Mettinger 1995: 32, 191). In this sense cultic *maṣṣēbôth* occur several times in the patriarchal stories where Jacob erects a מצבה, probably to mark the immanence of the deity, and makes vows before the pillar (Gen. 28.18-22). Later he returns to the same place and erects an altar and a pillar, both to worship God and to commemorate his

35. *ANET*, 253-55; 263, 264; 284; cf. *ANEP*, 320-21. Interestingly, no cultic pillars are found throughout the Bronze Age at Megiddo; Mettinger 1995: 175-78.

36. While the stone set up by Samuel was called אבן, Saul's monument was called מציב.

37. Graesser 1972: 42. These were probably the same as the child sacrifices to Molech in the Bible (2 Kgs 16.3; Jer. 32.35).

38. A worshipper in a Hittite text vows, among other things, to raise a pillar or a statue if the deity granted him children; *ANET*, 350.

39. The Bar-Hadad stele (860 BCE) to Melqart. The same verb נצב, 'to set up', is used here as in the biblical texts; Albright 1942: 23-29; cf. della Vida and Albright 1943: 30-34; *ANET*, 655.

appearance (Gen. 34.7, 9-14). Jacob's pillars are not condemned in these texts, but later Israelite history shows a mixed attitude towards cultic pillars, sometimes approving and at others condemning. Therefore we shall first consider why the pillars in the Israelite cult were approved at times and condemned at others, and then see how such an attitude helps one to understand the positive view of the מצבות in the patriarchal stories.

b. *Cultic* מצבות *in Israel*
As noted earlier, most of the pillars found in Palestine are plain with no pictures or inscriptions carved on them, while those from Egypt and Mesopotamia are covered with images and inscriptions. A notable number of stelae with large figures of deities, mostly without inscriptions, can be found in Syria,[40] indicating a 'fusion' of these two traditions (Graesser 1972: 45, 46). It appears that such stelae found their way into Israel through international alliances by different monarchs. The 'מצבה of Baal' erected in the Baal temple in Samaria (2 Kgs 3.2; 10.26-27 cf. 1 Kgs 16.32, 33) probably came from Syria through the influence of Jezebel, at whose table 450 prophets of Baal and 400 prophets of Asherah used to dine (1 Kgs 18.19). This implies that these cults freely flourished during the reign of Ahab, but it is not clear whether the 'מצבה of Baal' was a figured stone where Baal's image was carved (cf. *TNSI*, 104), or simply a stone pillar erected next to the altar marking the sacred area, or a pillar representing Baal himself. De Moor suggests that, since Baal was a fertility god, the pillar was a symbol of this fertility, just as the cult object Asherah was the symbol of the fertility goddess Asherah (*TDOT*, I: 443). It is possible that the pillar of Baal was both an image of Baal and a witness to the cultic transaction that took place on the altar between the worshippers and the worshipped. However, this is the only instance in the Bible where a מצבה was associated with a particular god as *asherah* had always been with the goddess Asherah.

The pillars, עמדים, not מצבות, before Solomon's temple may well reflect the influence of Solomon's alliance with various foreign nations. Their function may have been legal, as their names Jachin and Boaz

40. The votive stele of Melqart mentioned above, and the stone at Jekke are exceptions since they bear inscriptions as well; *ANEP*, 499, 500; cf. Barnett 1948: 122-37.

suggest,[41] as well as cultic, marking the sacred area (1 Kgs 7.21) (Graesser 1972: 46). Hosea's complaint that Israel 'improved' her מצבות (Hos. 10.1, 2) probably refers to such pillars, and especially to the popular cult where they were openly worshipped as symbols of Yahweh's presence. The prophet may have been cynical about Israel's cult objects, but the fact that he did not openly condemn them suggests a certain degree of acceptability in Yahweh worship (Burrows 1934: 46). Alternatively, מצבות may have formed part of Israel's illegitimate worship which subtly incorporated the calf-worship of popular Baalism into official Yahweh worship (cf. 2.8, 13, 16, 17; 4.17; 8.4-6; 9.10; 10.5-6; 11.2; 13.1-2). The pillar, a standard cultic object in Baal worship, probably continued in Yahweh worship as the former was adapted to the latter.

Hosea, however, appears to refer to מצבות positively in 3.4, where they seem to form part of the official cultic furniture along with sacrifice (which probably stands for altar; so LXX, Syriac, Vulgate), ephod and teraphim, all of which presumably aid in seeking Yahweh (v. 5). Interestingly, ephod and teraphim are never mentioned along with pillars as part of the Canaanite cult that was condemned. The ephod, as part of the sacred vestment of priestly apparel, probably belonged to the official Israelite cult and functioned as a divinatory apparatus (1 Sam. 30.7-8; Judg. 18.5) (Haran 1978: 166-67). But its association with teraphim and its description elsewhere (Judg. 8.27; 17.5; 18.14, 17, 18, 20; 1 Sam. 21.9) suggests that it could be an idol (Harper 1936: 221), or at least an image of the original ephod described in the priestly texts. Yet it is uncertain if by ephod Hosea meant an idol. Teraphim, on the other hand, were images of deity in varying sizes which were used in household shrines and could be consulted (Gen. 30.19, 34; 1 Sam. 19.14-16; cf. Ezek. 21.21; Zech. 10.2). It is possible that Hosea was cynical about Israel's cultic life, since v. 5 says that Israel would 'return and seek' Yahweh their true God and David their true leader after these (privileged?) (McNeile 1908: 145; cf. Driver 1911: 248) cultic symbols had been denied to them for a while. It could also possibly mean that they would seek Yahweh by these very symbols. However, in the light of Israel's harlotry with Baalism referred to above, it is unlikely that the prophet considered these symbols as

41. If these are the first words of dynastic oracles, as Graesser thinks, they can certainly have legal as well as cultic functions. 2 Kgs 11.14 and 23.3 clearly suggest this.

legitimate in Yahweh worship. A close reading of Hosea suggests that it is national idolatry, often called harlotry, which shattered the covenant relationship between Yahweh and Israel. So it is improbable that the prophet considered מצבות as legitimate symbols in Yahweh worship, although it is certain that they constituted part of the official cult at Bethel and symbolized the presence of Yahweh or Yahweh himself.[42] Otherwise it is impossible to account for the strong offence the pillars caused to the loyalist Yahwists of Josiah's time who violently smashed them to pieces and burnt them down along with altars, high places, images, idols and *asherim* of the Canaanite cult (2 Kgs 23.4-20).

Isaiah is probably the first of the prophetic books to give a more positive picture of מצבה in the Israelite cult: 'In that day there will be an altar to Yahweh in the midst of the land of Egypt, and a pillar to Yahweh at its border. It will be a sign and a witness to Yahweh of hosts in the land of Egypt' (19.19, 20a). The altar and the pillar are probably in poetic parallelism, implying worship of Yahweh by both the Israelites and the converted Egyptians following the shaking of Yahweh's hand over the latter. The distinct locations of each, however, suggest distinct functions. The altar in the centre of the land indicates Yahweh's worship among the Egyptians, probably by the exiled Israelites at a later date, as the phrase 'in that day' suggests. The 'pillar to Yahweh at its border' cannot be connected with the altar, firstly because it was probably meant to be a 'border stone' (Gray 1912: 338), and secondly because the pillar, not the altar, would be a sign and a witness to Yahweh in the land of Egypt. If this text was an addition by a later author, as several scholars think (Gray 1912: 332-33; Kaiser 1974: 108-109), it would be impossible for a redactor to associate a pillar with Yahweh's worship as he would have certainly known not only the Deuteronomists' objections to מצבות but also the prophet's own attitude to idols and images, not to mention the contempt of a later Isaianic writer for idols and their makers.[43] It is probable that the author purposely dissociated the pillar from the altar so that it would not be mistaken for an obelisk common to Egyptian temples. The מצבה was not a cultic stone but most probably a memorial stone (cf. Young 1969: 38-39; Kaiser 1974: 108) which commemorated Yahweh's acts on behalf

---

42. 2 Kgs 3.2; 10.26. Cf. Mays 1969a: 58; Stockton 1972: 18-22.
43. Isa. 2.8, 18, 20; 10.10, 11; 19.1, 3; 21.9; 30.22; cf. 44.9-20; 57.13, etc.

of the oppressed Israelites and revealed Yahweh's power to the Egyptians who would acknowledge him in worship.

מצבות are mentioned in Jeremiah only once (43.12, 13), when Jeremiah prophesied that Nebuchadnezzar would destroy Egyptian temples and the pillars/obelisks of Beth-shemesh.[44] The pillars or obelisks, originally symbols of the sun-god Atum Re, were probably plain stones marking the cultic area in the Egyptian temples. The exiled Israelites were probably attracted by this cult and Jeremiah's preaching was directed to them. Jeremiah's own view about pagan worship is obvious from his general contempt for, and ridicule of, idols and idolatry in Israel and Babylon (Jer. 10.2-15; 16.18; 51.17-18, 47, 52; cf. 50.2). It is not certain, however, why מצבות, which were certainly present in Israel's cult during Jeremiah's time, did not feature in his condemnation of Israel's idolatry.

Ezekiel similarly prophesied that Nebuchadnezzar would destroy the city of Tyre and its 'mighty *maṣṣebôth*' (Ezek. 26.11). The reference to pillars, however, is ambiguous as they might refer to the supporting structures of the buildings (*ABD*, IV: 602), but if they refer to the famous pillars of gold and emerald in the temple of Melqart (Zimmerli 1983: 36, 37), it confirms that the prophet held pagan worship in contempt. While Ezekiel's condemnation of Israel's idolatry is obvious,[45] he makes no mention of מצבות, which were probably present in Israel's worship during his time, probably for the same reason as Jeremiah, that they did not specifically represent the deity.

Of all the prophets, Micah was most unambiguous about the illegitimacy of pillars in Yahweh's cult (5.12-14). Pillars were condemned along with sorceries, soothsayers,[46] images[47] and asherim,[48] all of which

44. The Hebrew Beth-shemesh usually refers to a place name in Palestine (so NEB here), but here it probably refers to a locality in Egypt. The LXX translates it as 'Heliopolis', but the normal Old Testament name for this was On (Gen. 41.5). This was an important cult centre from ancient times, and the Egyptian Obelisk, originally a symbol of the sun-god Atum Re, originated here. Jeremiah was probably referring to the sun worship in the 'temple of the sun' at Tahpanes where he was preaching to the exiles; Holladay 1989: 302.

45. Ezek. 6.3-6, 9, 13; 8.3-18; 14.3-11 cf. 18.6, 12, 15; 20.7, 16, 18, 24, 31, 39.

46. Sorceries and soothsayers form part of the abominable practices prevalent in Canaan but condemned by the law. For a full list, see Deut. 18.10-11; Lev. 19.26.

47. The basic tenet of Yahwism is the prohibition of graven images (פסל) and every form of idol: Exod. 20.4; Deut. 5.8; 7.5, 25.

48. Some of the biblical texts suggest that the cult object of the goddess Asher-

formed part of the Israelite cult. The text is generally considered as exilic or postexilic, but proscription of idolatry can be seen already in the first three chapters (for example, 1.7), which are generally taken as authentic. Indeed it was because of idolatry and injustice that Yahweh would punish Judah. This suggests that pillars were as objectionable as any idol, image or asherah. Idols, images and even asherim certainly represented specific deities in the Canaanite cult and they must have had similar functions in the Israelite cult condemned by the prophets, but it is unclear whether a pillar represented Yahweh or simply marked the sacred area as did many such pillars discovered by archaeology.

It appears so far that, except by Micah, pillars were not particularly objectionable in Yahweh's cult during the premonarchic and monarchic periods until the time of the Deuteronomists. In fact there is no mention of them as cult objects, either positive or negative, in Joshua, Judges and Samuel, and there is no direct condemnation of them in Isaiah, Jeremiah and Ezekiel. Micah, however, condemns them along with other symbols of pagan worship.

It is probable from the foregoing discussion that מצבות as cultic symbols marking the sacred area, or possibly representing Yahweh, attracted no negative comment in the cults of Israel and Judah through-out their national existence, nor were they judged improper by the Deuteronomists either in Israel, except during the reigns of Ahab's son Jehoram and Jehu (2 Kgs 3.2; 10.18-27), or in Judah, except during the reigns of Hezekiah (2 Kgs 18.4, cf. 2 Chron. 31.1) and Josiah (2 Kgs 23.14) (cf. Albertz 1994: 65, 173). According to the Chronicler, Asa removed the pillars along with other pagan cult objects (2 Chron. 14.3-5). According to the Deuteronomists, however, the asherim were more objectionable cult symbols than the pillars, but the 'high places' were still objectionable,[49] since the Deuteronomists considered the actions of

---

ah was a graven image, פסל, or an image of an idol (2 Kgs 21.7 cf. 1 Kgs 15.13; 2 Chron. 33.7, 15) which was usually made (1 Kgs 14.15; 16.33; 2 Kgs 17.16; 21.3; 2 Chron. 33.3). But other texts suggest that it was a stylized tree probably made of wood (Deut. 16.21; Judg. 6.26), which could be hewed down (Deut. 14.3; 31.1), cut down (Exod. 34.13; Judg. 6.25-30; 2 Kgs 18.4; 23.14), rooted out (Mic. 5.14), pulled down (2 Chron. 34.7), or burned (Deut. 12.3; Judg. 6.26; 2 Kgs 23.6, 15). Deut. 16.21 suggests that it was a natural tree. So Lemaire 1977: 604-607; cf. *ABD*, I: 486. Others think that Asherah could be a stylized tree driven into the ground as it also appears on a clay model of a cultic scene from Cyprus; so de Moor 1974: 438-44.

49. The phrase 'high place(s)' comes from the Hebrew במה/במות, used 103

good kings of Judah in removing the pagan cult symbols to be qualified by allowing the high places to continue.[50] The high places were found throughout the land and here people carried on Yahweh worship using various pagan cultic symbols. They were condemned not only because of their pagan associations but more importantly because they came directly in conflict with the Deuteronomists' scheme of centralization of worship at Jerusalem. The Deuteronomists add that it was in fact such idolatry that brought the final destruction on the northern kingdom (2 Kgs 17.7-18).

The prohibition of מצבות in the Torah occurs in Exodus, Leviticus and Deuteronomy (Exod. 23.24; 34.13; Lev. 26.1; Deut. 7.5; 12.3; 16.21-22). The background was Israel's settlement in the land of Canaan, where the idolatrous Canaanite cult was also represented by local gods (אלהים), idols (אלילם), graven images (פסלים), figured stones (אבני משכית), asherim (אשרים) and altars (מזבחות). Among these, the only cultic symbol common to both pagan and approved Israelite worship was the altar, but the Canaanite altars were condemned in the law. Why were the Canaanite altars condemned? How were they distinguished from Israelite altars? It is probable that they were always associated with other cult symbols just mentioned. Altars per se were not condemned, but they formed part of the total cultic system that was against Yahwistic worship. The pillars probably did not bear any image, nor represented any idol in the Canaanite/Israelite cult, but simply stood next to the altar marking the sacred area, just as did the cultic מצבות recovered archaeologically (Mettinger 1995: 143-44). Thus a pillar standing next to the altar in Yahweh worship was probably viewed as innocent, since it did not represent a deity or idol. Therefore the command to tear down their altars, break their pillars, burn/hew down their asherim and burn/hew down their graven images may be a

times in the Bible. The Hebrew word is interpreted variously as: part of the body, 'back', 'ridge'; a place, 'high ground', 'mound'; or a 'cult centre'. But the most common usage of this word is for a 'cult place' (about 80 times). The precise meaning, architecture and function of a 'bamah', however, is a subject of considerable dispute among scholars. Albright (1957b: 242-58) held that 'bamah' represented a funerary stele, but this view has been rejected. It is probably a cult-house with or without a raised platform. Cf. Vaughan 1974; Barrick 1975: 565-95; *ABD*, III: 196-200; Witney 1979: 125-47. Fowler (1982b: 203-13) commits himself to no interpretation.

50. E.g. 1 Kgs 15.14; 22.43; 2 Kgs 12.3; 14.4; 15.4, 35. However, the Chronicler disagrees, 2 Chron. 14.3-5; 17.6.

general condemnation of the Canaanite cult in totality, without a specific focus on pillars. Thus the pentateuchal traditions, despite their variable dating,[51] are not to be viewed as concerned with specific prohibitions about pillars. Nevertheless, it may be pointed out that the tolerance of מצבות in the earlier traditions does not necessarily prove their approval in Israelite worship. The Deuteronomic reform was triggered primarily by the discovery of the 'book of the law', suggesting that the people and even the clergy were generally ignorant of the demands of the law. Therefore it is not unreasonable to think that these prohibitions about Canaanite cult in Exodus had remained unnoticed and unimplemented earlier.

Thus the מצבות in general were viewed positively in the Israelite cult, or at least not condemned, except by the Deuteronomic reformers and certain prophets who condemned the Canaanite cult as a whole in which מצבות formed a part. The asherim, idols and high places, however, were special targets of their condemnation as illegitimate in Yahweh's cult, but the pillars were more neutral than other symbols.

What about the pillars in the patriarchal narratives? Were they viewed as innocent, simply marking the sacred area, or did they represent deities? What did the authors think of them?

4. מצבות *in the Patriarchal Narratives*

This study so far suggests that *baetyls*, 'sacred stones' and pillars are different entities, though a degree of overlap in meaning and function may be admitted. Jacob's stone erected at Bethel may belong to the last of these categories. Jacob erects pillars on two occasions in Genesis.[52] The מצבה in Gen. 28.22 was called בית אלהים, while Jacob's actions directed to the מצבות in 28.18 and 35.14 included anointing them with oil and pouring a drink offering over one, actions not attested elsewhere in the Bible. Jacob's expression together with his actions suggest that the מצבות he erected were more than mere cultic stones marking sacred precincts. While Jacob's actions are not condemned, the context in both

51. For the dating of Exod. 23.24; 34.13, see Driver 1911: 202; Noth 1961: 192, 93, 262; Childs 1974: 452-61, 613.

52. Cf. n. 24. מצבה occurs 11 times in Genesis alone, all in the Jacob cycle. While the מצבות in Gen. 31.45, 51, 52(×2) were legal stones, and the מצבה in 35.20(×2) was probably a memorial stone, the מצבות in 28.18, 22; 31.13; 35.14(×2) were clearly cultic stones.

instances suggests that they were part of his response to the theophanies that preceded them. Several scholars, however, see a connection between stone and god, and suggest that Jacob worshipped the god who dwelt in the stone. We need to examine the Bethel stories, especially Gen. 28.10-22 and 35.9-15, in their immediate and broader context of the Jacob-cycle in order to understand both the nature of the pillars and the religion of the patriarch.

a. *Place of Genesis 28.10-22 in the Jacob Cycle*
From Gunkel to von Rad, scholars have largely followed the traditional source division of the Jacob cycle (Gen. 25–36), and explained it as having developed in several stages. There is no consensus, however, about the origin of the first Bethel story within the Jacob cycle. While for Gunkel this was one of the latest layers,[53] for Noth Jacob's association with the sanctuaries of Shechem and Bethel belongs to the earlier strata of the tradition (1972: 55-56, 79-101). For Eissfeldt the Bethel story does not play any significant role in the formation of the Jacob cycle (1962b: 369, 370).

   In recent times, however, several scholars have given special attention to Gen. 28.10-22 as having a central place in the formation of the whole Jacob cycle. First, Richter sees the 'vow' in 28.10-22 as the theological framework of the Jacob tradition. He argues that the vow was connected with other texts in the Jacob cycle: 31.5 gives the partial fulfilment of the vow of Gen. 28.20b, 31.13 finds its parallel in Gen. 28.21b, and 35.3 is linked similarly with 28.20a. Even the geographical framework, the departure from and the return to Bethel, is dependent on the vow. The Elohist saw the importance of different elements for the needs of his audience, and thus brought them together in the Jacob tradition in a theologically contrived scheme (Richter 1967: 50, 52). Secondly, de Pury regards the Jacob cycle as a coherent and unified narrative, and the theophany at Bethel with its promise and vow as central to it (1975: 32-33). Thirdly, Westermann regards the stories of theophany and cult places in the Jacob cycle as originally independent but inserted later with a definite plan. The content of Gen. 28.10-22 and 32.1-2 had an important function in the composition of the Jacob cycle, in that it brought to the fore the theological aspect of the Jacob–Esau story (1985: 408). Westermann is right if the theological aspect was the

---

53. Gunkel 1928: 156-67; cf. de Vaux 1978: 169-70. For de Vaux, the fourth layer is 'Jacob-Israel,' and from here onwards de Vaux follows Eissfeldt and Noth.

chief concern of the author. However, for Westermann the genealogies and the itineraries, not the stories of theophany and cult places, formed the framework of Genesis 26–36. Fourthly, Blum considered 28.10-22 as part of the core of the Jacob tradition since it narrates the founding of the cult place. This story, Blum argued, was combined by the vow (28.20-22) and the theme of fraternal reconciliation with the other core part of the Jacob tradition, namely the Jacob–Esau–Laban story, which had its own independent evolution out of smaller units. The Bethel story was built into the broader context of the Jacob cycle by the itinerary note (v. 10), the divine speech (vv. 13a-15) and the vow (vv. 20-22) (Blum 1984: 202-203, cf. 34-35).

While some source critics incline towards the idea of a possible coherence in the overall Jacob-cycle on account of the Bethel story contained in it, several narrative critics, for different reasons, argue that the Jacob cycle is essentially a coherent unit on its own, and is incomplete without its broader context, namely the book of Genesis, and the book of Genesis in turn has its own context, the Hexateuch.[54] It is clear from the foregoing discussion that there is no consensus as to whether the Bethel story was originally part of the larger Jacob cycle. It is safer to interpret the story from the final author's viewpoint than to read the text from a hypothetical reconstruction of the story. So what about the Bethel story—is it a coherent unit within itself?

b. *Composition of Genesis 28.10-22*
There is a wide diversity of opinion among scholars as to the exact assignment of each verse to individual sources.[55] Most critics assign the text mainly to E (vv. 11, 12, 17, 18, 20-22, the dream proper and the vow), with some Yahwistic insertions (vv. 10, 13-16, 19) and some notes by an unknown redactor.[56] But this is strongly opposed by Westermann and Blum.

Westermann sees the main narrative in vv. 10-12 and 16-19 as essentially a unity, with only v. 15, inserted by J, and vv. 13-14, 20-22 as

---

54. Fokkelman 1975: 46-241; cf. Fishbane 1975: 15-38; Gammie 1979: 117-34.

55. De Pury (1975: 33-35) conveniently summarizes the different analyses of 22 scholars. Westermann and Blum may be further added to his list. Only significant deviations that seriously affect the interpretation will be treated here.

56. Skinner 1930: 376; cf. Driver 1948: 264. Contrast Coats 1983: 208, who regards this unit as part of the Yahwistic narrative expanded at points by the Elohist.

later expansions. He argues that the divine designations, traditionally used to assign the text to different sources, are not required in the context. Elohim 'occurs only in the expansions (vv. 20-22) and in two contexts, vv. 12, 17, where its use is conditioned by the material' (1985: 453, 456, 458). The story developed in three stages: it was originally a 'sanctuary narrative' (vv. 10-12, 16-19) about the origin of a holy place, narrated and preserved at the sanctuary. In the second stage, J took over this existing story and introduced (with v. 15) the context of Jacob who discovered the holy place. To the third stage belong the later expansions (vv. 13b, 14 and 20-22), in which the two most important aspects of Israel's sedentary life in Canaan are reflected, namely the promise of land and descendants and the cultic practice of tithes and vows. He concludes: 'the formation of 28.10-22 can be reduced to a few strands in these three stages which correspond to the three stages of the formation of the patriarchal stories in the context of the formation of the people of Israel. Hence there is no place for complicated and hypothetical constructions (e.g. those of A. de Pury and O.H. Steck)' (Westermann 1985: 452-53).

Westermann's proposals appear plausible, but certain points in his theory remain unclear. He assumes on the basis of excavations that there was a sanctuary at Bethel with its aetiology long before the emergence of the Israelites in Canaan. There is no extra-biblical evidence for these claims, however.[57] Westermann says that the *old story* contained only the dream (v. 12), but he seems to assume that the story around the dream (vv. 10, 11, 16-19) was part of the original story. In any case he argues that this whole is a unity. It is hardly plausible that only the dream (v. 12) was narrated and transmitted at the sanctuary. In this case, the name of Jacob (or someone who erected the stone) must be part of the original story as well as the stone he erected, since they are contained in vv. 10 and 18. Westermann does say, however, that the Yahwist introduced the context of Jacob at v. 15,[58] but he is not clear

57. The claims, that an Early Bronze Age traces with a blood-stained rock high place and that a Middle Bronze Age shrine replaced it, are all found to be dubious; *NBD*, 133; cf. Newlands 1972: 155.

58. A little later in his exposition of vv. 16-18, Westermann says that 'it is possible that v. 16 is an addition by J and belongs more closely with v. 15 abb' (1985; 456).

whether the story of the erection of the pillar originated with the Yahwist or was part of the old story.[59]

Blum, while sympathetic towards the synchronic analysis of Fokkelman and others, rejects source analysis of the passage and argues that Gen. 28.10-22 is an independent and self-contained unit (1984: 25). He thinks that vv. 11-13aα and 16-19 are an independent statement of the foundation of the cult by Jacob, the eponymous father of the nation (Blum 1984: 28-29). This was the first building-block in the history of Jacob's tradition, and was built into the greater narrative context of the Jacob cycle by the itinerary note in v. 10, the speech of God in vv. 13-15 and the oath of Jacob in vv. 20-22.

Thus, while the consensus of literary criticism attributes the dream, *maṣṣēbāh* and vow to the same source (E), some recent scholars reduce the original story to the dream alone. A number of scholars, despite their varied methods, assume that the story of Jacob's dream is much older than J or E. It is not certain, however, whether this story had an antecedent in Canaanite traditions prior to its incorporation into its present context. This lacks firm evidence, and can only be presupposed in the light of the tradition history of the shrine at Bethel. What is certain is that the story in its present context reflects the perspective of the Yahwist, or of the redactor with a conscious dissociation of the previous Canaanite background of the place. Any interpretation of מצבה in this passage has to take these observations into consideration.

c. *Analysis of Genesis 28.10-22*
In the light of the above observations, dividing the passage according to source analysis is not satisfactory. Leaving the expansions (vv. 13-15, 20) aside, it is possible to consider vv. 11-12 and 16-19 as belonging to the old story of Jacob's dream. The final form of vv. 11 and 16 may still be assigned to the final redactor, who deliberately describes the place as obscure, Jacob's stopover as unplanned (due to the impossibility of travel after sunset), and the stone Jacob took as ordinary.[60] Such conscious dissociation of any prior sacredness of the site is further

---

59. Several scholars regard vv. 20-22 as an appendage, since they think these verses have no connection whatsoever with the preceding verses; e.g. Richter 1967: 43-52; Otto 1976: 174; cf. Westermann 1985: 458.

60. Contra Gunkel (1902: 280) and Burrows (1934: 45) who consider the stone as so unusually large that only Jacob, being giant-like, could erect it. Donner (1962: 68-70), Frazer (1969: 191), and Houtman (1977: 345) consider it a *baetyl* or holy

reflected in Jacob's total surprise at the theophany (v. 16). The use of יהוה in Jacob's speech is another indication that the final form of v. 16 comes from a redactor, since we know from elsewhere (Exod. 6.3) that the patriarchs did not know God by this name. Thus we are left with vv. 12, 17, 18 and 19a as the core story of Jacob's dream and his response. Jacob's actions towards the stone are to be explained within the context of these verses.

Jacob's reaction to his dream was fourfold. First, Jacob expressed surprise at the theophany. This was unprecedented since neither Abraham nor Isaac reacted in this manner (Sarna 1989: 199; *pace* Westermann 1985: 457). Jacob's words, 'this is none other than בית אלהים', refer not to the stone but to 'the place' where God had manifested his presence to Jacob (Westermann 1985: 457; Sarna 1989: 199 cf. p. 398). Similarly, the expression 'this is the gate of heaven' refers to the place where angels ascended and descended, or to 'something analogous to the stairway in the dream' (Westermann 1985: 457). The notion that such a gateway existed between heaven and earth was widespread in Babylon, where ziggurats were supposed to connect the earthly shrine with the heavenly sanctuary by their ladder or stairway. In Egypt it was thought that the souls of the dead reach up to the gate of heaven by means of a ladder.[61] But it is doubtful if the author of Genesis had these views in mind, though it is possible that he was aware of them. It is unlikely that the place where Jacob passed the night was the traditional Canaanite shrine. As Sarna notes:

> Superficially, the episode recalls the phenomenon of incubation. It was customary throughout the ancient world, both Near Eastern and classical, for a devotee to sleep in the sacred precincts of a temple in order to induce the deity to reveal its will. However, the present narrative emphatically dissociates Jacob's experience from this pagan practice by stressing the wholly unplanned nature of his stopover, the complete anonymity of 'the place', and the total unexpectedness of the theophany (1989: 197-98).

Keret's camping at a shrine before his campaign for his wife was such an instance (*ANET*, 149). Although Jacob's situation may be compared

stone. Contrast *ABD*, I: 709, for whom the stone used as headrest was commensurate with its purpose. To use a stone as pillow seems to be common among the Arabs living in this area even today; Kelso 1968: 46.

61. De Vaux 1961: 291; cf. Driver 1948: 377-78; Speiser 1964: 219-20; Sarna 1989: 199.

to Keret's, the author implicitly denies that Jacob's camping was at the Canaanite shrine. Excavations at Burg Beitin have revealed the existence of an open-air shrine there from 3500 BCE, a temple from the nineteenth century BC, a stone pillar *in situ* from MBI and II (Kelso 1968: 20, 21, 45, 46, cf. 1-3), and the probability that the settlement of Luz and the shrine of Bethel occupied the same site (Kallai 1986: 130-31; *contra* Westermann 1985: 458). Verse 19 implies that the place of Jacob's theophany lay near Luz (Dillmann 1897: 229; Haran 1978: 52), and the name Bethel which Jacob gave to the place probably extended later to the settlement Luz.[62]

Secondly, Jacob erected a מצבה, unlike Abraham and Isaac who built altars in response to a theophany. It is not clear why Abraham and Isaac were not portrayed as erecting pillars. But it is incorrect to argue that 'the need felt for such signs of the Divine presence belonged...to a later stage of the religious development' (Dillmann 1897: 227-28), since stone worship was one of the oldest practices in the history of religion, and it is impossible that Abraham or Isaac were unaware of these practices. Further, it is not certain whether the story in its original form was about the worship of a numen resident in the stone.[63] If the author consciously denied the Canaanite association of 'the place', why would he leave any traces of a belief that could be misunderstood later by his readers? The author obviously stood in the tradition that viewed pillars positively, and not as abodes of a numen. We have no way of knowing exactly what the stone would have meant to Jacob, but what the author thought it meant is reasonably clear. It was a 'sign' of Jacob's dream and a 'witness' to his vow (Sarna 1989: 199). In the light of other occurrences of מצבות in the Old Testament and of archaeological discovery, the stone could also be a marker of a sacred place (Graesser 1972: 45, 46). Such a meaning is quite fitting given Jacob's awe and surprise following his dream. The meaning of the stone is further elucidated by Jacob's subsequent action. This leads us to my next point.

Thirdly, Jacob anointed the מצבה. If מצבות were unique to the Jacob stories in the patriarchal narratives, their anointing is unique to the

---

62. It is probable that the Israelites took over the pagan shrine during the time of Joshua (Josh. 18.21) or the judges (Judg. 1.22, 26) since Bethel became an important cult centre from then on, especially in the eighth century.

63. So Holzinger 1898: 193; Gunkel 1902: 281-82; Procksch 1924: 340-42; Smith 1927: 204, 205; Westermann 1985: 454.

whole Old Testament. Altars were only anointed for consecration or dedication (Exod. 29.36; Lev. 8.11; Num. 7.1, 10). Various cultic objects were 'consecrated' by means of anointing for the purpose of cultic use.[64] Thus several scholars think that a 'consecration' was meant in Jacob's anointing of the stone.[65] On the other hand, various types of people, namely leaders, kings and priests, were anointed with oil, especially when taking office. Such anointing is variously interpreted: as 'sacral', bringing a special relationship between the anointed and God; as 'secular', indicating the community's authorization; or as a combination of both.[66] However, it is unlikely that Jacob established a special relationship between the stone and God by anointing it. Individuals were anointed for their position either by divine sanction or by popular acclaim, but Jacob had neither. It is possible that Jacob's anointing separated the stone from the common realm and made it a cult-object just as the high priest was set apart for cultic duties by is anointing,[67] or that the stone became a representative of god as in the anointing of leaders and kings. Even this is not certain. While anointing certainly does not refer to offering sacrifices to the indwelling numen (contra Holzinger 1898: 193; Skinner 1930: 380), it is uncertain whether it conveys power to the object (*pace* Bertholet 1930: 226; cf. Westermann 1985: 458).

There is, however, widespread evidence among the ancient Semites of the use of oil as a symbol of peace, friendship and fellowship. Anointing was practised in effecting relationships, transacting business, buying and selling land, contracting marriage and international treaties, and liberating slaves. Anointing by a weaker party signified an obligation.[68] Thus Jacob's anointing was probably a symbolic act of establishing a contractual bond with God, as Mettinger proposes:

64. Exod. 30.22-29; 40.9-11; Lev. 8.10-11; Num. 7.1; Hos. 12.2 (here oil is used probably in an international treaty).

65. Driver 1948: 266; Pedersen 1940: 209; von Rad 1965: 280-81; Kidner 1967: 159.

66. For a detailed survey of Old Testament passages and views of different scholars, see Mettinger 1976: 185-94.

67. Kutsch 1963: 26-27; cf. Blum 1984: 268. Incidentally, Kutsch's view presupposes that the stone was of common origin prior to its anointing.

68. Mettinger 1976: 211-24 cites various texts of the ancient Near East in which oil was used to effectuate a relationship.

the events at Bethel provide a contractual setting for Jacob's anointing of the stone... And that *maṣṣebā* can have a function in a contractual setting appears from Gn 31,45. There is thus reason to conclude that the efficacity of the anointing performed by Jacob was not primarily a sanctification or a consecration of the stone, but was to establish a contractual relation between Jacob and God.[69]

Many commentators have been misled by the view that stone worship lay behind Jacob's מצבה. But firm evidence is lacking, and the parallels proposed (for example, Pausanias's description of the stone at Delphi, and the *baetylia* of Philo Byblos) are too remote and the religious views attached to them too different to be comparable.

Fourthly, Jacob makes a vow. As noted above, vv. 20-22 have been generally considered later expansions. The main problems are that these verses have no syntactical link with the main narrative, the oath is a literary construction and not a reproduction of the oath pronounced by Jacob, and there is verbal contradiction between 'it is none other than the house of God!' (v. 17) and 'this stone shall be a house of God' (v. 22) (Richter 1967: 44, 45, 50; cf. Westermann 1985: 458). It will be argued in Chapter 6 that Richter's contention that Jacob's vow is a literary construction of the Elohist is untenable. It will suffice here to state the conclusions that I reach there. It is unclear whether the author recorded Jacob's vow verbatim. The many parallels both in the Bible and the ancient Near East with similar if not identical form suggest that vow making is a universal religious phenomenon, usually occurring in the context of prayer when the individual or community is in trouble.[70] The similarity of form and structure may suggest a certain amount of standardization in the literary preservation of the vows, but this does not prove that a vow like Jacob's could not have been made. On the other hand, if the anointing of the stone belongs to the context of Jacob, it is not improbable to suppose that the oath in v. 22 is a pronouncement of the obligation implied in that anointing. Further, it fits well with Jacob's modest requests and his situation described between his flight and return (cf. de Pury 1975: 435-38). Therefore, it is more

69. Mettinger 1976: 224-25; cf. Sarna 1989: 200. However, Mettinger seems to have changed his views about Jacob's pillar, since he identifies it with *baetyl* (1995: 140-41).

70. E.g. the vows of Israel (Num. 21.2), Jephthah (Judg. 11.30-31), Hannah (1 Sam. 1.11) and Absalom (2 Sam. 15.8). Cf. Keret's vow in *ANET*, 14.

reasonable to suppose that the oath was part of the episode than that it was a creation of the author.

Finally, Jacob's words, 'this is none other than the house of God', are clearly in parallelism with the following sentence, 'and this is the gate of heaven'. Together they refer to the place and its dangerous link with the divine, not to a physical building. Theophanies in the Bible took place both at sanctuaries and in the open field. Thus Gideon and Manoah made offerings where God appeared to them. Further, if the author is consciously dissociating Jacob's stay from any established cult place, it is unlikely that he imagined that there was a cult place. So the above two phrases may be taken with the previous two phrases, 'surely Yahweh is in this place' and 'how awesome is this place?', to refer to 'the place' in relation to Jacob's experience of the dream. It is not necessary to envisage a literal building, since 'the house of God' could refer to the place of theophany. However, the last sentence, 'and this stone, which I have set up for a pillar, shall be God's house', could refer to a physical building. It cannot mean that the מצבה would become an abode of God, as Westermann observes: 'This is impossible not only because of v. 17 but also because of v. 21b. It can only mean a sanctuary is to arise from this stone, or the stone is to be extended into a sanctuary...'[71] If this interpretation is right, it further strengthens my contention that for the final author there was no shrine already existing at the place of Jacob's dream.

Therefore it is not possible to conclude that Jacob's stone was a *baetyl*, although etymologically and religio-historically *baetyl* and Bethel (as deity) are certainly related. Stone as an abode of deity is one of the oldest human beliefs, but this is impossible to read as the view of the author of the Bethel story. Whether Jacob had such a view is uncertain. On the other hand it is probable that the rite performed in relation to the stone was an ancient custom performed to establish a contractual bond between God and Jacob.

d. *Genesis 35.9-15 and its Relation to 28.10-22*
Most scholars ascribe Gen. 35.9-15 to P but consider v. 14, which describes Jacob's setting up of the pillar, as extraneous, since it disturbs the unity of the passage. Opinion is so varied with regard to the origin and place of Gen. 35.14 in its present context that one is inclined to think that there are no valid controls over the different approaches

---

71. Westermann 1985: 459; cf. Driver 1948: 267. Contra Skinner 1930: 379.

followed by scholars. While some assign it to E, along with vv. 1-5 and 6b-8 (Gunkel 1902: 335; so also Skinner 1930: 423), others regard it as parallel to 28.18 and attribute it to J (Driver 1948: 310). Procksch, von Rad and Westermann, however, assign v. 14 to a redactor who inserted it in P. Von Rad thinks that neither is it related to 28.20-22. nor did it originally belong to Jacob stories, while Westermann thinks it was originally an itinerary report available to a redactor who 'adapted it to his context by the double reference to the preceding revelation'.[72] For de Pury, v. 14 fits the context of P but does not come from it, since P rejects all idea of cultic worship in the patriarchal epoch. Nor can it be from E, since it is separated from E's context by v. 8. Therefore it was added by a redactor (de Pury 1975: 546-47, 553-59). By contrast, Blum finds no sufficient reason to excise v. 14 from the context of vv. 9-15, which for him is a unity. 'The narrator of 35.9-15 deliberately described the Bethel episode freshly in a revised version, emptying all its etiological content. Out of the sacred place, the dwelling of God becomes the place of a unique word of revelation, and the sacred stone becomes the memorial stone' (Blum 1984: 268-69).

It is clear from the context that vv. 14 and 15 belong together, since both describe a direct result of the theophany in vv. 9-13 (Westermann 1985: 554). So there is no reason for separating v. 15 from v. 14 and ascribing it to P, as is usually done.[73] Thus it is plausible to consider, along with Blum, that vv. 9-15 are an independent unit incorporated into Jacob's story by the final redactor, who wanted to show that Jacob erected the pillar a second time in response to a fresh revelation. Thus עוֹד, 'again', in 35.9 is not a gloss, as Westermann explains: 'rather R wants to state expressly that the revelation made to Jacob "when he was fleeing from his brother" (vv. 1,7) has its counterpart at the very place ("when he came from Paddan-aram") where he fulfils the vow then made' (Westermann 1985: 553).

As for the content, there are some similarities between Gen. 28.10-22 and this section, in that they both start with a theophany, proceed to give a revelatory address, and finally describe Jacob's reaction in setting up a מַצֵּבָה and naming the place. The differences, however, are also significant. First, the theophany was undramatic, with no ladder or

---

72. Westermann 1985: 553-54; cf. Procksch 1924: 382; von Rad 1961: 332-33.

73. Cf. Holzinger 1898: 184; Driver (1948: 310) regards v. 15 as P's parallel to 28.19 in J; so also Speiser 1964: 271. Contrast Westermann 1985: 553.

angels, and occasioned no surprise as at the first instance. Jacob's surprise confirms our earlier contention that Bethel was not a holy place
before he had his first experience there. This time, however, it is impossible that Jacob did not expect a theophany, both because of his previous experience, and much more because it was the same God who led
him back to the same place in order that he might worship him. Secondly, while the promise of land and increase are repeated, the promise
of presence, protection and returning are omitted because these have
been fulfilled by Jacob's safe return. However, the naming, or rather
renaming of Jacob is something new in this episode. It does not appear
to cohere with the story (Blum 1984: 267), but it is possible that the
author wants to show that the unknown wrestler who first gave him this
name in 32.28 is none other than El Shaddai, the familiar God of his
fathers. This is probably a reminder to Jacob that he was dealing with
the same God. Thirdly, there is the addition of the drink offering here
compared to the mere anointing in the former episode. Blum's view
that, despite the addition of the ritual of a drink offering, the place and
the מצבה have been totally emptied of any sacredness (1984: 269), is
probably an overstatement. It is probable, as Blum points out, that the
words 'then God went up from him at the place where he had spoken
with him' (v. 13) are a virtual negation of what is said about the place
in 28.16, 17. The explanatory apposition אבן (מצבת) precludes any
understanding of מצבה as a technical term for a cult-stone.[74] It is,
however, improbable that the story of Gen. 28.10-22 holds the place as
sacred, since the focus was on the theophany and the response of Jacob
who felt that the place was 'awesome'. It is possible that for the author
the place derived its sanctity from the experience of the patriarchs, but
for Jacob the place was like any other place. However, the fact that
Jacob not only anointed the מצבה but also offered libation to it suggests
that Jacob viewed the stone as more than a mere memorial.

One can understand the anointing of the stone from its previous
occurrence in 28.18, but the problematic drink offering which Jacob
poured on the pillar is variously interpreted. I have rejected the idea
that it was an offering to the dead (see Chapter 2 §4d above). Some
scholars have related v. 14 to 35.8, and regard the מצבה of v. 14 as a
grave stone and the libation as an offering to the dead (Gunkel 1902:
337; Skinner 1930: 424), but Westermann rightly notes that this is
'possible only if the reason given for setting up the pillar in v. 14 is

74. Blum 1984: 268; cf. Dillmann 1897: 306-307; Procksch 1924: 382.

deleted' (1985: 553). Blum thinks that וַיִּצֹק עָלֶיהָ שֶׁמֶן is not borrowed from Gen. 28.18 but is to be interpreted by the preceding וַיַּסֵּךְ עָלֶיהָ נֶסֶךְ, since there is nothing about the consecration of the pillar, but about a unique libation offering which would be clearly understood here as a response to the appearance of God (1984: 269). The word נֶסֶךְ, used only here in Genesis, usually means a drink offering offered both in legitimate and illegitimate cult. It is usually offered on the altar and almost invariably to a deity.[75] But here it is poured on the pillar, not on an altar. An inscription of Sennacherib's (704–681 BCE) mentions anointing and pouring a libation on an inscribed prism that was to be reinstated, but Sennacherib had his name inscribed on it, and stated, that he who found it should do the anointing and offering (libation) before reinstating it (Luckenbill 1924: 130), whereas in Jacob's story it was a pillar and the actions followed the setting up. It is not certain, however, whether Jacob was 'rehabilitating the original stela...now invested with new meaning' (Sarna 1989: 242). The words, 'when he came from Paddan-aram', indicate that the whole tradition of vv. 9-15 was new for the author, so for him Jacob erected a stele afresh at the same place or thereabouts. It is possible that the author knew the Bethel story in Genesis 28, but he probably assumed that the pillar Jacob had erected some 20 years previously no longer stood there. The pouring of oil on the pillar most probably reflects the same rite as in 28.18 and has the same significance, that is to establish once again a contractual bond between God and Jacob. The drink offering was possibly intended to commemorate God's appearance to Jacob, or more probably offered to God himself, since the text appears to point out that Jacob had localized the God who spoke to him to the place by means of a pillar, and by pouring a libation to it he had thought that it was received by God. This incident probably belonged to the original Jacob stories that the redactor was compelled to include here because it was impossible for the redactor, who was consciously emptying any sanctity of the place or the stone previously, to add a tradition with an extra ritual of drink offering which would give an impression of a Canaanite practice of his own time. The phrase 'the place where he spoke with him', called clumsy and redundant by most exegetes, is probably the remainder of the received tradition. Further, the redactor wants us to know that Jacob resumed his journey from Bethel after this event (in v. 16). In the light

---

75. Exod. 29.40; 2 Kgs 16.13; Isa. 57.6 (offered to smooth stones of the valley); Jer. 7.18; 19.13; 44.18, 19, 25; Ezek. 20.28; Hos. 9.4.

of these observations, therefore, the pillar was a cultic מצבה which not only marked the sacred area of the theophany but also enabled Jacob to renew his contract and worship God by a drink offering.

5. *Conclusion*

This investigation into *baetylia*, 'sacred stones' and *maṣṣēbôth* suggests that these were three different entities at their origin, and that the ideas associated with each of them were different. The *baetylia* were animated stones which later came to be associated with the popular gods of the Greek pantheon. They had magical qualities and they gave oracles and helped those who consulted them. 'Sacred stones' were found in their natural setting and were regarded as inherently sacred. They were venerated, and regular worship and offerings were made to them. The Zeus-stone, the stone of Kaába, the Linga, the obelisk and the like, rank among these venerated sacred stones. *Maṣṣēbôth* were of various types. The cultic *maṣṣēbôth* resembled the 'sacred stones', in that they marked sacred precincts, were sometimes anointed, and in some cases even venerated, but they cannot be described as either *baetylia* or 'sacred stones'. The pillars of Jacob are certainly cultic מצבות which marked the sacred area where God appeared. The anointing of them implies the establishing of a contractual bond between Jacob and God, the libation offered in the second account indicates an offering directed to God, but there is no suggestion in either case that Jacob believed that the stone was indwelt by a numen or that he offered worship to it. Building altars and calling upon the name of Yahweh formed the pattern of worship for Abraham and Isaac, and raising pillars indicated a similar intention for Jacob, while he also used altars for worship. Thus Jacob's pillars are cultic מצבות and are distinct both from *baetylia* and the popular sacred stones of the ancient Near East.

Chapter 5

TITHES

1. *Introduction*

Having seen the patriarchal pattern of worship in building altars, calling upon the name of Yahweh and raising pillars, I shall now explore patriarchal religious practices attested in the form of tithes, vows and purificatory rites. I hope to demonstrate that patriarchal religious practices, like patriarchal patterns of worship, are distinct from both the ancient Near Eastern and Israelite practices. I shall deal with the practice of tithes first, not only because it forms a link with the previous chapter where it appears in Jacob's vow when he raised a pillar at Bethel, but also because it appears in the Abraham cycle when the latter offers a tithe of the booty he acquired in a battle.

It is generally recognized that tithing is a very ancient custom practised in many cultures of the ancient Near East. Ancient Israel is no exception in this regard. There is, however, only scanty evidence about the practice both in the ancient Near East and the Bible.[1] Nevertheless, unlike the texts of the ancient Near East, Israel's traditions not only mention tithing but also give various elements of legislation on the practice, notably concerning sanctity, redemption or exchange and the consequences of lapses. Elaborate instructions are given in later Jewish writings, for instance the Talmud, on redemption and exchange of various items from which a tithe was required. This indicates that the tithe was given a significant place in the religious life of Judaism. The practice, however, occurs only twice in the patriarchal narratives: first, in a politico-religious context, Abraham gave a tithe of the booty to Melchizedek, the king of Salem, and secondly, in a purely religious context, Jacob vowed a tithe of everything to God. By these two instances the

---

1.   Jagersma 1981: 116. The technical word for 'tithe' מַעֲשֵׂר, and the verb עָשַׂר together occur over 40 times in the Hebrew Bible.

author wants to show that the patriarchs were familiar with the practice, although only in Jacob's case did it have clear religious implications. However, the text shows no concern that Abraham paid his tithe to a pagan king, or whether Jacob ever paid his promised tithes at all. Therefore in this chapter I shall first investigate the practice in the ancient Near East, secondly examine its relevance to the religion of Israel portrayed in the Hebrew Bible, and finally compare both with the practice attested in the patriarchal narratives, in order to understand whether it had any religious implications for the patriarchs or the authors of the narratives.

2. *The Tithe in the Ancient Near East*

A helpful survey of the evidence on the practice of tithing in the ancient Near East, particularly in Mesopotamia, has been given by Salonen (1972: 1-62). Ancient Near Eastern evidence comes from the twenty-first to the fourteenth centuries BCE, and again from the sixth to the fourth centuries BCE. There is very little evidence on tithing attested between the fourteenth and the sixth centuries BCE. Perhaps some of the biblical texts fill this gap. In this respect Mendelsohn argued from Alalakh and Ugaritic texts that the idea in 1 Sam. 8.4-17 of taxing the 'tenth' from the general public was 'an authentic description of the semi-feudal Canaanite society as it existed prior to and during the time of Samuel and that its author could conceivably have been the prophet himself or a spokesman of the anti-monarchical movement of that period'.[2] The extant sources of the ancient Near East use four different expressions to designate tithes: *zag* (Sumerian), *ešrētu[m]* (Old Babylonian and Old Assyrian), *m'šr* (Ugaritic, cf. Hebrew) and *ešrû* (Late Babylonian) (Salonen 1972: 9-10). The linguistic affinity between the Akkadian, Ugaritic and the Hebrew terms is so close that it is tempting to think that the practice of tithing in all these cultures was similar. For this reason it is imperative to examine the texts of the ancient Near East to find what light they may throw on the biblical practice of tithing.

---

2.   Mendelsohn 1956: 17-22. Gen. 28.22 (E, eighth century BCE) and Amos 4.4 (eighth/seventh century BCE) also form a link between the two periods. The Elohist's story was probably from a much older period.

a. *Sumerian Sources*

All the relevant Sumerian sources come from the dynasties of Ur III, Isin I and Larsa, dating from the twenty-first to the eighteenth centuries.[3] The word used for tithe in these sources is *zag*. For the sake of convenience I shall discuss only a sample of reasonably datable texts from different dynasties. It will be evident from these texts that the practice of tithing was well known as a religious tax required from almost everyone in early second-millennium Sumer.

First, according to Salonen, the practice of tithing is attested in all four different reigns known in the Ur III dynasty. Two texts from the time of king Šulgi (early twenty-first century) state that a tithe was given to the god Nanna from animals like sheep and goats and objects like mill-stones (Salonen 1972: 17). Similarly a text from the time of king Amarsuena (mid twenty-first century) deals with a presentation of a tenth from oil, timber, reed and aromatic substances to the temple of the goddess Ningal (Salonen 1972: 17). The precise number/portion 'ten/tenth' out of hundreds and tens of animals, objects, oil and spices, and the particular name of the god to whom they were presented, indicate that the tithe was an obligatory tax paid to the temples.

Two texts from the time of the king Šusuena (late twenty-first century) also deal with the tithe. While one of them talks about a stolen tithe, '2 donkeys, tithe of Nanna, Šugul, the man from Urusagrig, has stolen (and this) has to be admitted/given extra', the other talks about tithing to Nanna and Ningal from precious stones and sea-merchandise that was kept in storehouses (Salonen 1972: 17-18). These texts suggest either that tithes were pledged for payment at a future date or that the tithes paid were not used up immediately and were stored in a temple store. Hence their stealing becomes possible. Malachi (3.8, 10), Nehemiah (10.38-39; 12.44; 13.5, 12) and 2 Chronicles (31.5, 6, 12) talk about tithes being stored in storehouses at the temple in Jerusalem, and Deuteronomy (14.22-27) about commuting a tithe to the central sanctuary where it was to be enjoyed by the giver and his guests. The latter also implies an initial storing of tithes and the possibility of their being stolen. However, there is no record of tithes being stolen in the Hebrew Bible, though Malachi accused Israel of robbing God when they failed to pay their tithes.

---

3. Cf. Langdon 1923a: 7, 8, and Salonen 1972: 10, 11, for alternative detailed dating.

Five texts from the time of the king Ibbisuen, also of Ur III (late twenty-first century) note the practice of tithing not only cattle and agricultural produce but also finished products such as garments. Interestingly, a tithe of figs from the garden of a 'lamentation-priest' or 'cultic singer' also appears in these texts (Salonen 1972: 8). Thus implicitly (if not explicitly) even the cult personnel paid tithes. It is also not clear if the kings themselves paid tithes. Certainly the tithes were directed to the gods, especially to Nanna and Ningal in the Ur III dynasty, suggesting that these were the patron gods of the dynasty. The clear mention of the 'tenth' suggests that it was an obligatory tax paid to temples. The restoration or extra payment for a stolen tithe indicates the seriousness of such a crime and the penalty incurred for it. On the other hand, there is no ideology of tithing to indicate whether it was a sign that what they possessed also belonged to the gods, or a gift in expectation of future blessing, or simply an obligation to the temple.

Secondly, the practice of ornament and sceptre tithing is attested in the First dynasty of Isin (late twentieth to early nineteenth centuries). A sceptre tithe could be offered only by kings. There is clear reference to the king Ur-Nirurta who offered a tithe described as a 'sacred gift' (Salonen 1972: 18). With this we have the total social spectrum of kings, priests(?) and commoners offering tithes. It is uncertain, however, whether the tithe was obligatory for the kings. The fact that it was described as a 'sacred gift' suggests that it had religious connotation, although it is unclear what this was. Biblical tithes were certainly considered 'holy' to Yahweh (Lev. 27.32).

Thirdly, from the Sumerian dynasties of Larsa, the custom of tithing is attested from five different places and periods. A text from the time of the king Gungunum (late twentieth century) states that a tithe from copper, ivory, corals, beads, silver and other precious stones was offered to Ningal (Salonen 1972: 19). Similarly, several texts from the time of king Abīsarē (from about the same period) and king Sumuel (early nineteenth century), state that a tithe from gold, silver, copper and precious stones was offered to Ningal following an 'expedition to Tilmun' (Salonen 1972: 19). The gold and precious stones suggest that this was an expedition of trade venture. One may recall here the biblical instances of tithing from an expedition of war by Abraham (Gen. 14) and the Israelites (Num. 31). Both the biblical and the Sumerian tithe following an expedition was probably a religious obligation. Tithes to the goddess Ištar are attested from Nūr-Adad and Rīm-sîn (mid-nineteenth to mid-eighteenth centuries) (Salonen 1972: 20).

b. *Old Assyrian and Old Babylonian Sources*
Both *ešrātu* and *ešrētu* are used in these sources to describe the practice of tithing, and the idea was current in both religious and secular contexts (Salonen dates these sources in the mid to late nineteenth century). While one Old Assyrian text refers to the tithe imposed on garments as 'tax', another refers to the tenth of a business proceeds as 'share' (*CAD*, IV: 368; Salonen 1972: 22, 23). An Old Babylonian text, however, states that the god Šamaš demands the tithe from those who 'borrowed or vowed' (*CAD*, IV: 368; Salonen 1972: 22). The payment of this tithe was linked to the barley harvest, suggesting that the tithe could have been annual or collected from every harvest. An early Babylonian letter from Larsa probably confirms the idea of an annual tithe: 'On account of the dues (?) for this year (?)...delivered to me, like last year, (in payment) of the tithe' (Driver 1924: 54, 55). This suggests that tithing was not only annual but also obligatory. Further, a tithe is mentioned several times in a letter from the First Babylonian dynasty as imposed or required by both the temple and the palace: 'Concerning the grain (which is) the tithe of the temple of the gods— our lord has bidden us impose a tithe of grain... They have taken the workmen of the temple of the gods for the grain (which is) the tithe of the palace' (Driver 1924: 22, 23). There seems to be a conflict between the temple tithe and the palace tithe; it is not clear from the letter whether the temple tithe was obligatory on the palace and vice versa, but it is clear that a tithe was imposed by both temple and palace.

Thus the tenth of the Old Assyrian period, which appears more like a civil tax, and the tenth of the Old Babylonian period, which was required by both the temple and the palace, were obligatory and probably paid by everyone, though the latter is not explicitly stated.

c. *Ugaritic Sources*
The Ugaritic texts designate the tithe as *m'šr*. It can be observed from the few texts where the idea occurs that the tithe at Ugarit was paid not by individuals but by the whole villages as collective bodies, not as a religious obligation but as a civil tax.[4] A peculiar feature of tithe occurs

4. Heltzer (1976: 36-38) collects records of 31 villages of Ugarit which made grain payments as tithes to royal store-houses. Cf. Salonen 1972: 62.

at Ugarit, where the king grants particular towns and all that belonged to them as a permanent gift of tithe to his favoured officials and their families.[5] The almost identical idea of the royal grant of civil tithes described in 1 Sam. 8.15, 17 was probably patterned after the Ugaritic practice (cf. Mendelsohn 1956: 19, 20; Rainey 1976: 96-97). Some have also argued that the tithes and offerings assured to the Levites and the priests (Num. 18.8, 21-22; Lev. 7.19, 34-35) were formulated in the manner of the royal grants at Ugarit and other Near Eastern cultures (Weinfeld 1970: 184-204; 1972a: 1157).

A ritual text from Ugarit describes tithing in a religious context, with the Ugaritians advised to vow various offerings such as a bull, a first-born and tithes, and to seek the help of Baal in the event of an enemy's attack.[6] There is considerable dispute, however, about the doubtful text that may be rendered as 'tithe'. The restored line reads, '*š[r]t [b'l. n']šr*', 'a tenth to Baal we will tithe'. The opening and closing words of the line are taken as coming from the verb '*šr*, 'to tithe', by Margalit and Cartledge, but as 'banquet' by Herdner (Margalit 1986: 62; Cartledge 1992: 117-18; *Ug.*, VII: 36). In other contexts at Ugarit, '*šr* occurs in connection with preparation for eating and drinking, and is variously translated by scholars 'drink' or 'libation',[7] the two elements of a ritual banquet in the legends of Keret and Aqhat. However, the idea of 'a tithe' rather than 'a banquet' fits better in the context of a vow, because the former forms part of the incentives for the deity to act in favour of petitioners. On the other hand there is no evidence elsewhere of a 'banquet' or a 'drinking party' being vowed, although a 'libation' could be vowed. Therefore if the text meant 'tithes' it

5. Rainey 1976: 95-96; cf. *PRU*, III: 146-47, cf. 69, 70, 93; Salonen 1972: 61; Heltzer 1976: 48, 49.

6. We have no evidence that they ever actually did this, but a biblical text (2 Kgs 3.26, 27) probably alludes to a similar event, though it contains no mention of tithes; cf. Margalit 1986: 62, 63.

7. So Cazelles 1951: 132, 133: 'Il ne semble pas en effet dans ces textes qu'il s'agisse d'une redevance régulière, mais d'une sorte de sacrifice fait une fois pour toutes… S'il était question de batailles on eut pu y voir l'offrande d'un dixième du butin, mais ce n'est pas le cas.' He argues further that the Deuteronomic tithe associated with the eating and drinking at the central sanctuary and the 'tithe' in Amos 4.4 have similar character, and can best be understood as a 'libation'. If Cazelles's observation in these contexts is plausible, then the drink and libation of the ritual banquets were probably offerings of tithes. Cf. *ANET*, 147; de Moor 1971: 71; Jagersma 1981: 118.

indicates that sacrifices and offerings are as much a part of cultic obser-
vance as tithes, although the obligatory aspect of the latter still remains
unclear.

Thus the tithe at Ugarit was largely considered as a civil tax, although it is possible that it was considered as religious practice as well.
As a civil tax, it was obligatory, but as a religious practice it was
probably voluntary, an effective means of seeking divine favour in
times of need. More importantly, the tithe at Ugarit was granted in the
form of cities to the king's favoured officials as a permanent possession. As some scholars think, this is possibly reflected in the biblical
accounts of 1 Samuel, and was applied to the priestly grants in Israel.

d. *Late Babylonian Sources*

The frequent mention of tithes and monthly tributes in the clay tablets
and their payment to the temples of Ebabarra and Eanna suggest that
tithes in sixth-century Babylonia were paid not to the royal treasury but
to the temples.[8] The common word used to describe the tithe in these
documents is *ešrû* (*CAD*, IV: 369; Salonen 1972: 23-33). As in Sumerian, Old Assyrian and Old Babylonian sources, the tithe was paid from
all sorts of goods, like wool, sesame, dates, barley, flax, oil, garlic,
clothes, cattle, sheep, birds, fish, timber, metalware and articles of
silver and gold (Dandamajew 1969: 83). But in contrast to earlier
periods, it was clearly imposed on all people,[9] including farmers,
shepherds, gardeners, bakers, smiths, weavers, potters, fishermen, fief-
holders, various officials, governors, priests, temple officials and even
the tithe-collectors.[10] Kings and their family members made propor-
tionately low payment, obviously not a tenth of their fortunes.[11] Further,
the tithe was collected on certain fixed dates, and if anyone failed to
pay at the appointed time interest was charged on each month's delay

8.   Dandamajew 1969: 82-90; cf. Jastrow 1898: 668; Salonen 1972: 23-24;
Milgrom 1976: 58-59.

9.   This was probably assumed in some Sumerian sources, but is unclear in
others.

10. We have an interesting parallel in the Levites, who were in charge of
collecting tithes and yet were required to pay to the priests a tithe of the tithe they
received.

11. Dandamajew 1969: 84, 85; cf. Salonen 1972: 43. The percentage of tithe
varied from 5.5% to 13.3%, although 10% was the norm. The reason for this was
probably consideration of the means of the one who paid, but why anyone would
pay more than 10% is unclear.

(Dandamajew 1969: 86, 87; cf. *CAD*, IV: 369). Sometimes the tithe was described both as a regular payment and as a gift vowed to a deity in crisis or sickness (*CAD*, IV: 369). It is very clear from some texts that some deities possessed tithe lands (lands tithed to temples) which were given on lease and the proceeds were turned over to the temple (Salonen 1972: 28; cf. *CAD*, IV: 370).

Thus according to the late Babylonian sources tithing was obligatory, levied from all kinds of goods and from people of all walks of life. A tithe was also vowed in times of crisis, probably in addition to the obligatory dues. The tithe lands may have been the permanent property of the temple and clergy just as the Levitical cities were for the Levites. The idea of interest accruing on a deferred payment was probably unique to the late Babylonian period.

3. *The Tithe in Israel*

The Hebrew Bible is our only source for an understanding of the tithe in Israel. The Bible makes no attempt to trace the origin and the practice of tithing, but simply assumes the concept and the practice. The verb עשׂר, 'to tithe', and the noun מעשׂר, 'tithe', together occur 41 times in the Bible,[12] 22 times in the Pentateuch alone. Thus much of our information about the Israelite concept of tithe comes from the Pentateuch which sets a complex legislation on the subject, in contrast to the mere description of practice in ancient Near Eastern texts. The texts outside the Pentateuch are largely concerned with the misuse (Amos 4.4), lapses (Mal. 3.8, 10) and restoration (Neh. 10.38, 39; 12.44; 13.5, 12; 2 Chron. 31.5, 6, 12) of the practice in Israel. I shall first consider the sources and then briefly summarize the legislation on tithes in Israel, and finally compare the idea of Israelite tithe with that of the ancient Near East. This will give a basis for subsequent discussion of tithes in the patriarchal narratives.

---

12. עשׂר occurs 9 times (Gen. 28.22 [×2]; Deut. 14.22 [×2]; 26.12; 1 Sam. 8.15, 17; Neh. 10.38, 39), and מעשׂר 32 times (Gen. 14.20; Lev. 27.30, 31, 32; Num. 18.21, 24, 26 [×3], 28; Deut. 12.6, 11, 17; 14.23, 28; 26.12 [×2]; Ezek. 45.11, 14; Amos 4.4; Mal. 3.8, 10; Neh. 10.38, 39 [twice]; 12.44; 13.5, 12; 2 Chron. 31.5, 6 [×2], 12). The references in Ezek. 45.11, 14 are not relevant to tithing, and hence are left out of consideration here. Jagersma's reference (1981: 117 n. 4) to Gen. 28.22 and 2 Sam 8.15, 17 (printed as 18.15, 17), as having a noun form is incorrect.

a. *Sources*

In contrast to the ancient Near Eastern sources which often report individuals (frequently by name) who brought (or failed to bring) tithes from various commodities, there is not a single instance in the Bible (except in Genesis) where a specific individual is reported to have brought (or failed to bring) the tithe to God. Thus all the texts, especially pentateuchal texts (minus Genesis), are concerned more with the legislation about the practice than what was currently happening, suggesting that the legislation arose in order to standardize the pre-existing custom. Thus we will not know what was the practice of tithing in Israel prior to the legislation, although certain traces of it may still be seen in that legislation. The Pentateuchal legislation on tithing has been ascribed chiefly to two sources, namely the Priestly (Lev. 27.30-33; Num. 18.21-28) and the Deuteronomic (Deut. 12.6, 11, 17; 14.22-28; 26.12-15). There is no consensus, however, about the dating of the sources or the nature of the tithe described in them (Herman 1991: 35, 36). While most scholars date the Deuteronomic sources to the pre-exilic period, they differ widely on the Priestly sources.[13] My aim here is not so much to date the sources and investigate the origin and the development of the idea of the tithe in different sources as to approach the sources synchronically in order to see the practice of tithing in Israel in its totality. It appears that a single basic tithe institution is reflected in different ways in the sources, and its essential character was that it was paid as a sacred due to the temple and its personnel (McConville 1984: 74). The Israelite concept of tithes may be summarized as follows: the tithe was from both animals and land produce, paid to the temple, obligatory and annual. However, Israelite law concerning tithes may be summarized in the following five points.

b. *Legislation*

First, Israelite law prescribed that all the tithe, כל־מעשׂר—that is of the animals from herds and flocks, בקר וצאן, and of the farm-produce from

---

13. While Wellhausen, Eissfeldt and Jagersma date P source on the tithe to the postexilic period, Weinfeld dates it to the pre-exilic period. Milgrom dates P and D as roughly contemporaneous and pre-exilic, while McConville (1984: 68-87, 154-56) thinks that precise dating of sources is impossible, but where P and D deal with similar laws such as tithes, the former preceded the latter. Herman (1991: 9-37) follows McConville and rejects all methods of dating the sources. Employing a synchronic approach, he argues that in Israelite tithes a compulsory exchange of livestock and farm-produce was given to the Levites in return for divine blessing.

the field and trees, מזרע העץ מפרי הארץ—belonged to Yahweh and was sacred, קדש (Lev. 27.30-33; cf. 2 Chron. 31.6[14]). Deuteronomic law (Deut. 12.6, 11, 17) limits the tithe to land produce only, but its sanctity was maintained by including it among the sacred gifts along with the burnt-offerings, sacrifices, firstlings, votive offerings and free-will offerings. Similarly, Amos and Malachi mention tithes along with sacrifices, זבחים, and offerings, תרומה, which probably indicates their sacred character (Amos 4.4; Mal. 3.8) (cf. Jagersma 1981: 122). The fact that the tithe was said to be 'holy' and belonged to Yahweh suggests that, like the 'firstlings' (v. 26), it was 'non-dedicatory' and mandatory.[15] Malachi (3.9, 10) not only confirms that the tithes were obligatory, but notes that deferring their payment would be a serious offence of stealing from God himself, and conversely that overflowing blessing awaited those who paid them faithfully.

Secondly, any agricultural tithe may be redeemed by adding a fifth to its value,[16] but under no circumstance may a tithed animal be redeemed or exchanged (Milgrom 1976: 59). If any animal was exchanged, both the animal and that for which it was exchanged became Yahweh's, and could not be redeemed. Interestingly, the land tithe in Babylon was also commutable, while the animal tithe could not be exchanged or redeemed (Milgrom 1976: 59).

Thirdly, the tithe in Israel was granted to the Levites and their families as a permanent inheritance for their service in the sanctuary in lieu of a tribal possession (Num. 18.21, 24, 26, 28). Some scholars think that the whole tithe was given to the priests because the whole tithe was declared 'holy' (Kaufmann, Weinfeld, Milgrom), while others argue that only the animal tithe which was unredeemable and probably holier than the land tithe went to the priests, while the land tithe went to the Levites (cf. Milgrom 1976: 60). The Levites, however, were required to pay a 'tithe of the tithe', מעשר מן־המעשר, as their 'gift' or 'offering', תרומה, to the priests (cf. Neh. 10.39), but there is no law requiring the priests to pay tithes (cf. Milgrom 1976: 60). The Ugaritic parallel of tithe awards to the king's favoured officials and the similar allusions to such practice during the time of Samuel (1 Sam. 8.15, 17) allow us to

14. This is the only other text that explicitly supports the animal tithe prescribed in Leviticus.

15. Milgrom 1976: 56; contra Kaufmann 1961: 190; Weinfeld 1972a: 1158.

16. Interestingly, Deuteronomy allows commuting, but does not require an additional one-fifth.

think of an early origin of this law in Israel,[17] although Israel adapted it entirely to her religious context.[18] Further, Levites, as tithe-collectors and tithe-givers (Neh. 10.38, 39), have their counterparts in Sumerian and late Babylonian sources.[19] The Deuteronomic law (14.22-28), however, does not assign the tithe to the Levites or priests,[20] but allows it to be enjoyed by the worshipper and his guests in a sacred feast at the central sanctuary every year, and the Levites were invited to participate in it along with other needy persons every third year only. It is possible, however, that according to v. 27 the Levites joined the family sacrificial feast every year (Noth 1968: 137; cf. Driver 1902: 167, 170). Further, Deuteronomy seems to assume knowledge of the Levitical tithe in Numbers, since it reminds the Israelites not to forsake the Levite who has 'no portion or inheritance with you' (14.27, 29), and the addition of חלק to נחלה is certainly explanatory since Numbers uses only נחלה and states that the idea of 'no inheritance' to the Levites is to be a perpetual statute.[21]

17. Weinfeld (1972a: 1159-60) thinks that the Levitical tithe arose during the time of David who granted the Levitical cities with their tithes to the Levites, who were loyal functionaries at David's newly occupied cities in the borders. It is possible, however, that David was acting in accordance with a previously known practice.

18. For Milgrom (1976: 57) the distinction between the temple and royal tithe in Israel is sometimes lost, 'since temples were ipso facto royal temples (Amos 7.13) and the kings controlled their treasuries (1 Kgs 15.18, 2 Kgs 12.19; 18.15) and were responsible for their maintenance (2 Kgs 12.7-17; 22.3-7; Ezek. 45.17; 2 Chron. 31.3-10)'.

19. Milgrom 1976: 60 n. 211. The rabbinic tradition supports this view, according to which the Levites were given their tithes on the threshing-floor; Weinfeld 1972a: 1161.

20. It is possible that the whole tithe was not consumed by the worshippers, but payments to the sanctuary were deducted before it was given for a feast; von Rad 1966: 103; Mays 1979: 245-46; Jagersma 1981: 118.

21. There is contradiction between Numbers, which designates the whole tithe to the Levites and priests, and Deuteronomy, which makes it a charity. On the basis of LXX Deut. 26.12, Tob. 1.7-8 and Josephus, *Ant.* 4.22, Jewish legalists made attempts to harmonize this discrepancy by supposing that the tithe in Deuteronomy refers to a *second* tithe in addition to the normal (first) tithe prescribed in Leviticus–Numbers; the first tithe was prescribed for the payment of the clergy while the second tithe was meant for a religious feast. And a '*third tithe*' levied every third year, that is, the year of tithing, was meant for the poor. However, this interpretation was

Fourthly, the tithe in Israel was paid annually, or from every crop. This is not clear from Leviticus or Numbers, which seem to be concerned more with the sanctity and ownership of the tithe rather than its frequency. Deuteronomy, however, makes it clear that the tithe was to be brought to the central sanctuary every year,[22] and it could be given to charity in other towns every third year. It is possible that the Deuteronomic reformers innovated this scheme in conformity with their humanitarian concern evident elsewhere (12.18-19; 16.11), because the local sanctuaries were abolished and the Levites were made redundant (cf. Mays 1979: 246). However, it leaves the question of the support of the Levites serving at the central sanctuary unanswered.[23]

Fifthly, the whole tithe was given the character of a sacrificial feast to be enjoyed every year by the worshipper and his household at the central sanctuary. The tone of the feasting, the conversion of tithe without augmentation and the idea of buying whatever one desired at the sanctuary might suggest that Deuteronomy relieved the tithe from its inherent sanctity conceived in earlier legislation (so Weinfeld 1972b: 215). But Deuteronomy included the tithe among the sacred gifts (12.6, 11), clearly designated it as 'sacred portion' (26.12, 13) and further charged the owner to make a solemn declaration that the tithe was not removed in a state of ritual uncleanness or used for profane purposes. This strongly suggests that Deuteronomy added a social dimension to tithes while affirming their sanctity (cf. Milgrom 1976: 56; contrast Driver 1902: 172-73). A number of late Babylonian texts also consider tithe as an offering or sacrificial meal (Salonen 1972: 38).

not universally held even among the Jews, and most modern critics generally regard as implausible; Driver 1902: 170.

22. The unusual text in Amos 4.4 mentions a practice of sacrifices every morning, and tithes every three days. While the former was a usual practice, the latter was unusual. Some scholars suggest that this was probably a reference to the practice during some festive season when the worshipper offered his זבח on the first morning and his מעשר on the third day; Harper 1936: 91; Mays 1969b: 75; Rudolph 1971: 176.

23. It is probable that the Jerusalem temple could support its clergy and cultic activities with the voluntary offerings of the people (Deut. 12.6, 11, 17-18, 26-27) and with the king's subsidies (1 Kgs 9.25; Ezek. 45.17; 2 Chron. 8.12-13; 31.3-10); Milgrom 1976: 57.

c. *Comparative Analysis*
Israel's idea of tithe reflects almost every view that was already present
one way or the other in the ancient Near East. The tithe in Israel was
collected from animals and farm-produce, from laity and clergy (cf.
Sumer); it was paid as civil tax as well as religious levy (cf. Old Assyrian and Old Babylonian periods); it was granted to the king's officials
as well as to the Levites and priests (cf. Ugarit, Late Babylonian
period); it was paid by all except kings and priests, and collected by
temple personnel and stored at the temple (cf. Late Babylonian
practice). Nevertheless, none of the sources of the ancient Near East
makes explicitly religious sanctions on the practice of tithing as we find
them in the Bible. This suggests that Israel consciously adapted the
practice known from her neighbours to her own religious context. The
idea of the tithe as divine grants to the Levites who had no inheritance
in Israel gives a rationale for tithes to be paid to them, and an obligation
on Israel because the Levites also served at the temple. This is probably
unique to Israel.

4. *The Tithe in the Patriarchal Narratives*

The concept of the tithe occurs only in two contexts in the patriarchal
narratives, once with Abraham following a successful expedition, and
once with Jacob's vow to God where Jacob promised to give a tenth if
God looked after him. We note at the outset that neither context is
unique to the patriarchs. As I have observed above, several texts from
the Sumerian period from the dynasty of Larsa describe tithing
following an expedition as common, and tithing as part of a vow was
known from Old Babylonian and Ugaritic sources. Similarly, Israel
appears to have known the practice of tithing in the context of an expedition, as a secular tax, and more importantly, as a religious obligation.
I shall examine patriarchal practices in the light of these parallels.

a. *Abraham's Tithe to Melchizedek*
According to Genesis 14, Abraham gave a tenth of all his booty to the
Canaanite king Melchizedek when he returned from a war expedition
against the kings of the East. As a whole, Genesis 14 poses many
difficult problems, with some scholars describing it as an 'isolated boul-
der' unrelated either to the preceding or the following texts, but others

argue its essential coherence in its present context.[24] My main concern is with vv. 18-20, in which the encounter between Melchizedek and Abraham and the exchange of gifts took place. There is no consensus over whether this episode is integral to Genesis 14.[25] The chief problems in this passage have been the identities of Melchizedek, king of Salem, and of the God El Elyon, in whose name he pronounced a blessing on Abraham. If Salem was in any way related to Jerusalem,[26] Melchizedek[27] probably ruled over the city during the time of Abraham,

24. It has apparent reminiscences of only three words from J and another three from P. While one-third of the chapter contains proper names, a high percentage of the remaining words and expressions are either rare or unattested elsewhere in the Old Testament. Further, two or three different genres seem to have been put together: while the first part of the chapter (vv. 1-12) resembles an annalistic report, the second part (vv. 13-17, 21-24) the hero stories of Judges. The Melchizedek incident seems to be an altogether different element which strangely intrudes a post-war settlement between Abraham and the king of Sodom. Cf. Emerton 1971a: 24-47; 1971b: 407-39; McConville 1993: 112-18.

25. Skinner (1930: 156, 269), Speiser (1964: 105-106) and Wenham (1987: 307) think that it is integral to Gen. 14, while von Rad (1965b: 174) Emerton (1971: 431-32) Van Seters (1975: 299) and Westermann (1985: 191-92) see it as an insertion.

26. The only other occurrence of this name is in Ps. 76.3, where it is equated with Zion; so also *Genesis Apocryphon*, *Targum Onqelos*, *Targum Jonathan* and Josephus, *Ant.* 1.2 (cf. LXX Jer. 48.5 [MT 41.5]; Jdt. 4.4). Ur-Salim (cf. Jn 3.23) is well attested in the Tel Amarna letters, although the shortened form Salem is still unattested outside the Bible. For various suggestions, see Albright 1961: 52; Haran 1965: 45 n. 14; Smith 1965: 141-45. Salem as a place name is most appropriate in the context, since מלך־סדם is used several times in the same way. For examples where the first element of the compound name was dropped from place names, see Josh. 19.6 and 15.32; Josh. 15.30 and 1 Chron. 4.29; Josh. 13.17 and Num. 32.38; cf. Aharoni 1979: 115-16; Emerton 1990a: 57. The Salem tradition probably concerned a different place, and came to be identified with Jerusalem later; so Emerton 1971b: 413; Jagersma 1981: 120.

27. Attempts to unravel the origin and background of this figure through etymological study have produced no satisfactory results; Noth 1928: 161 n. 4; Fisher 1962: 265; Rosenberg 1965: 162-65. Ps. 110.4, the only other place where Melchizedek occurs in the Hebrew Bible, describes Yahweh's promise to a Davidic king of an eternal office of priesthood like that of Melchizedek's. The text assumes that Melchizedek's office of priesthood is an established tradition of antiquity, 'to which the ideal king of Israel, ruling on the same spot, must conform'; Driver 1948: 167. Some scholars think that this text is a scribal note, and the Psalm comes from postexilic times, but this view is refuted by Emerton 1971b: 415. Gunkel (1902: 252) had already observed the improbability of the postexilic community, which

like Adonizedek did later (Judg. 10.1, 3). It is difficult to associate the compound name El Elyon[28] and the compound title 'the creator of heavens and the earth' with any known deity in the Canaanite or other pantheon, because neither the name nor the title are attested outside the Bible (Rendtorff 1966: 284). On the other hand, since Elyon in the present context is in apposition with both El and Yahweh (v. 22), and the only other occurrence of the compound El Elyon (Ps. 78.35) parallels Elohim,[29] it is probable that the Genesis author adapted 'El Elyon' as a designation for the God of Israel, who was most frequently referred to as either Yahweh or Elohim, but it is still possible that the author or his sources know that El Elyon was the god of Melchizedek, because the

was prejudiced against all sorts of paganism, especially Canaanite, searching for a Canaanite model of high-priesthood.

28. While El occurs at Ugarit as a personal name and as an appellation, Elyon does not appear at all. El and Elyon occur as distinct deities in the eighth-century Sefire texts (cf. p. 148 above). According to Hittite and Philonic sources, Elyon, a celestial deity, was older than El by two 'divine generations', and the grandfather of El; cf. della Vida 1944: 8, 9; Pope 1951: 52, 55. Further, the title קנה שמים וארץ attached to El Elyon in this context is not found with El in Ugarit; Pope 1955: 52-54; Rendtorff 1966: 286-87. A thirteenth-century BCE Hittite version of a Canaanite myth, the eighth-century BCE Phoenician, and the first-century CE Neo-Punic inscriptions, however, describe El as the 'creator of the earth', but not 'creator of heaven and the earth'; cf. *ANET*, 519-20; Hoffner 1965: 5-16; O'Callaghan 1949: 203-205. Given this, the interpretation of El Elyon in Melchizedek's blessing is widely varied. For some scholars, El Elyon was an artificial combination of El, the lord of the earth, and Elyon, the lord of heavens, a theological speculation of the Genesis author; so della Vida 1944: 9; Cross 1962: 241-42. However, if this was the theological achievement of the author of Genesis, he might be expected to have used this title more consistently in Genesis, especially in the first chapter where creation of heavens and earth is the main theme, but is conspicuously absent. While only אלהים is used in Gen. 1 and 2, both אלהים and אל are used separately and together throughout Genesis.

29. Besides this, עליון occurs both alone, though not entirely in isolation from other divine names (Deut. 32.8; Ps. 9.3; Isa. 14.14; Lam. 3.35), and in apposition with Yahweh (Ps. 47.3), Elohim and El (Pss. 57.3; 78.56). Elyon also occurs in parallelism with El (Num. 24.16; Pss. 73.11; 77.10-11; 78.17; 107.11), with Elohim (Pss. 46.5; 50.14; 73.11; 82.6) and with Yahweh (2 Sam. 22.14; Pss. 7.18; 9.2-3; 18.14; 21.8; 83.18; 87.5-6; 89.1-2, 9; 92.2; Lam. 3.37-38 with אדני). In the Aramaic Daniel the plural עליונין is used to describe '(the saints of) the Most High', קדישי עליונין (7.25, 27).

latter is explicitly described as עליון כהן. However, other biblical references probably reflect no pre-Israelite view of El Elyon (contra Eissfeldt 1956: 29-30; cf. della Vida 1944: 2). What then is the significance of this to the patriarchal religion? Since this name does not appear again in the narratives it is reasonable to think that it was not one of the names of the God of the fathers. This name with the blessing of Melchizedek probably survived in the sources of the Genesis author, who tried to identify El Elyon with Yahweh in Abraham's response to the blessing because he did not appreciate Abraham being blessed by El Elyon alone. Therefore El Elyon was a Canaanite god whom Abraham probably did not know but whom later Israelite authors assimilated into the Yahwistic religious ethos.

We are not told why Melchizedek did not join the coalition against the Eastern kings, but on hearing of Abraham's victorious return he came to greet Abraham and his exhausted troops and offer them refreshments, probably on behalf of the coalition (cf. Skinner 1930: 270). The text clearly describes Melchizedek both as king and priest, and it is not uncommon in the ancient Near East for a king to assume the priestly office as well.[30] The context of meeting suggests either diplomatic or religious reasons, even as the whole account is loaded with cultic language of priesthood, blessing and tithes suggesting that 'cultic exchange' took place between Melchizedek and Abraham (Westermann 1985: 203). Was Melchizedek pronouncing a priestly blessing on Abraham? Was Abraham paying a tithe as a religious obligation at a Canaanite shrine? Was there any cult or ritual involved? We need to examine the passage closely in order to establish the nature of the exchange and its bearing, if any, upon the religion of the patriarch.

In the exchange that took place in vv. 18-20, Melchizedek brought bread and wine for Abraham and his men and bestowed a blessing on him, while Abraham gave him a tenth of the booty. It is probable, as many have observed, that the bread and wine were refreshments for the exhausted troops of Abraham. A clear gesture of friendship and welcome was implicit in this act, but was Melchizedek's blessing a cultic blessing? It is hardly unlikely that the blessing of a priest-king would have no religious overtones. First, Abraham's encampment was in the King's Valley, probably in the vicinity of Salem, on the way to

---

30. Skinner 1930: 268; van Selms 1958: 210. Cf. the biblical examples of kings (David and Solomon) and judges (Samuel) who sometimes also assumed the priestly office; but see Wenham 1985: 79-82.

Abraham's home in Hebron. The author says that Melchizedek brought out, הוֹצִיא, his gifts to meet Abraham in the valley, suggesting that the exchange took place in the open country. Thus there was probably no organized cult involved in the pronouncement of Melchizedek's blessing (cf. Towner 1968: 388-89). Secondly, whether cultic or non-cultic, blessing had a fixed form in the ancient Near East and Israel (see Chapter 3 for form and setting of 'blessing'). It was often pronounced both as a thanksgiving to God for his saving actions and as a prayer-wish for the protection and prosperity of the one being blessed. It appears that these intentions were combined in Melchizedek's blessing. Abraham is the subject of בָּרוּךְ in the first sentence, 'Blessed be Abram by El Elyon...', suggesting a prayer-wish for the safekeeping of Abraham. In the second sentence, El Elyon is the subject and his deliverance of Abraham is then noted, suggesting a thanksgiving. This kind of spontaneous and non-cultic blessing was frequently used in conversations between persons.[31] This probably means that Abraham received a spontaneous blessing in the name of the god of Melchizedek, who was later identified with Yahweh by the Genesis author. If the blessing was non-cultic, and the context of meeting between Abraham and Melchizedek was friendly, why then did Abraham give a tithe of the booty to Melchizedek?

Most versions render Gen. 14.20b as 'And Abram gave him a tenth of everything', but the subject of the sentence in Hebrew is the personal pronoun 'he', not 'Abram'. Some scholars take Melchizedek as the subject of this sentence, since he was the subject of the author's report in v. 18 and of the speech in vv. 19 and 20a. Having seen the ominous presence of Abraham the aggressor, Melchizedek gave a tithe to prevent him from attacking his city (Smith 1965: 134). However, the mood of the story appears no longer to be aggression but peace and a post-war settlement, in which Abraham was willing to give up the booty which was rightfully his. It seems rather that it was Abraham's natural response to share a tenth of the booty with the local priest-king who had received him with refreshments and blessed him by the name of El Elyon 'who delivered your enemies into your hand' (cf. Westermann 1985: 203-204). Therefore it is probable that it was Abraham who gave the tenth to Melchizedek, not vice versa.

31. Cf. Exod. 18.10; Ruth 4.14; 1 Sam. 25.32, 39; 2 Sam. 18.28; 1 Kgs 1.48, etc.

If my reading of the text so far is correct, it is improbable that Abraham was employed by Melchizedek to fight his battles (so Fisher 1962: 269). Others have suggested that Abraham was following the ancient laws of 'booty-restoration', which required equal distribution of booty with those who did not actively participate in the battle (Muffs 1982: 88-96). This would be plausible if we accepted Albright's suggestion that *melek šelōmōh* meant 'a king allied to him (Abraham)', but this is unlikely (see Albright in n. 26). Moreover, the story mentions Aner, Eshcol and Mamre as his allies, but no other king. In Numbers 31 the Israelite army shared a huge spoil recovered from the Midianites with the non-combatant rest of the congregation in some form of 'booty-restoration', yet what was shared was not a tenth but half the spoil (v. 27). Abraham's situation does not appear to be similar. The Israelite incident involved an offering to Yahweh from the booty, and even this was not a tenth: it was a five-hundredth from the soldiers' half and a fiftieth from the congregation's half (vv. 28-30). Further, the commanders of the Israelite army made offerings from gold and jewellery for their atonement (vv. 50-52). Prior to their offering, they were ritually purified (vv. 22, 23), and the soldiers themselves ritually cleansed before they entered the camp (vv. 19, 20, 24). The whole postwar operation appears to be highly religious and highly significant both for the community and for the soldiers. Thus this Israelite practice was entirely different from Abraham's action.

As already noted, the practice of offering the deity a portion of the booty was an established norm in the ancient Near East (cf. §2 above), although it was not necessarily ten percent. In the Sumerian dynasty of Larsa a tithe was paid following an 'expedition' of trade venture (Salonen 1972: 19, 20). In paying a tenth, Abraham was probably following the Mesopotamian practice. It is not certain, however, whether he was pledging his allegiance to the deity of Melchizedek. The present context certainly represents the deity as Canaanite in Melchizedek's understanding and Israelite in Abraham's understanding, but the author meant that Abraham paid a tenth to the Canaanite priest-king. The author did not mean that Abraham paid the tenth to Yahweh because he knew that there were no priests or sanctuaries involved in the patriarchal religious activities and no Israelite tithing laws applied to the patriarchs. The idea of paying a tenth may have been motivated by Melchizedek's hospitality and blessing; it had not been Abraham's usual practice, which was rather to build an altar and call upon the name of God.

Further, neither priests nor the name El Elyon appear again in the patriarchal narratives. Thus this appears to be a unique action of Abraham. Further, Abraham is portrayed as the officiant in all the cultic activities he undertook, and it does not appear that he paid tithes anywhere, although his frequent action of building altars implies offering sacrifices to God. Therefore Abraham's tithe to Melchizedek was not part of his own normal religious practice, but, being a deeply religious person, he did not hesitate to pay a tenth to the Canaanite priest-king who extended hospitality and blessing. The author did not mean that Abraham offered worship to the god of Melchizedek nor did he reject his blessing. This is quite in conformity with the nature of the patriarchal religion which is neither polemic nor exclusivistic. The issue that 'you shall have no other god before me' did not exist for the patriarchs, neither did they really engage in worshipping other gods. Abraham's religion is portrayed as family oriented and his God as personal and family bound. To this end Abraham is portrayed as being faithful to this God who is portrayed as making no demands of sacrifices, offerings or tithes as he did with later Israel.

b. *Jacob's Tithe*

Jacob's promise of tithes is part of a larger vow (Gen. 28.20-22) in which Jacob promised that he would make Yahweh his God and build a sanctuary for him. The vow concludes: וכל אשר תתן־לי עשר אעשרנו לך, 'and of all that you give me I will surely give a tenth to you' (v. 22b). As will be argued in Chapter 6 below, the vow was not a secondary insertion but a logical conclusion of the Bethel narrative (28.10-22) (see Chapter 6 §4; cf. de Pury 1975: 436-38; Wenham 1994: 224). The tithe being one of the things vowed, it is reasonable to think that it formed part of Jacob's religious obligation. Nevertheless, when decades later Jacob finally returned safely to Bethel, the condition stipulated in his vow, he only built an altar and did not present a tithe. Therefore several scholars suggest that the story simply reflects the author's desire to justify bringing tithes to the busy sedentary cult centre Bethel (de Pury 1975: 444-46; Westermann 1985: 460).

However, if the passage is from the Yahwist, there is no reason why he should press people to bring tithes to Bethel, since Jerusalem would have been more appropriate for his concern. Moreover, Bethel was already an established cult centre since pre-monarchic times (Judg. 20.18; 1 Sam. 10.4) (cf. Amos 4.4; LXX 1 Sam. 1.21), and those who worshipped there all along would have continued to do so. The author could hardly have come from the time of the divided monarchy, since such advice would not have been acceptable to the official Yahwist, who thought Bethel an illegitimate cult centre, and would not have been accepted into the official tradition. Further, if the author was so concerned to show that the patriarch vowed a tithe at Bethel, he would surely have added that he also paid it there. This would have not only strengthened his case but also portrayed the patriarch in a better light.

Therefore the author was not legitimizing the place. Nor was he legitimizing tithes. There is no reason to think that tithes were novel to the Israelites, who were aware of them since the pre-monarchic times, at least as secular tax (cf. 1 Sam. 8.15, 17). The pentateuchal tithe laws, whatever their date, reflect only the time of the standardization of tithing in Israel, not the origin of the practice. The evidence from the ancient Near East clearly suggests that the practice, as both secular and sacred tax, was very ancient. Therefore there is no reason to think that the author was legitimizing the tithe by the example of the patriarch, especially when the patriarch did not actually pay it. So this was an anomaly in the traditions received by the Yahwist who had to put up with his traditions at hand. Contrary to his own beliefs the Genesis author had no difficulty in portraying patriarchs as building altars and offering sacrifices without the assistance of official priests, or as having direct access to Yahweh through dreams and visions and interceding on behalf of others. Thus the author here was simply reporting a received tradition.

It is probable that Jacob vowed tithes to God following the popular custom in the ancient Near East where things such as a sanctuary, tithes, sacrifices and offerings were promised by worshippers.[32] There is no reason to think that vowing a tithe fits only with a sedentary lifestyle, not with Jacob's nomadic lifestyle, though the parallels from the ancient Near East imply established cult centres. The latter also imply regular annual tithes, while Jacob's vow was a single obligation (cf. Sarna 1989: 201) to be fulfilled when God on his part fulfilled the condition stipulated. The other two obligations—that he would make Yahweh his God and raise the pillar as a sanctuary—also seem to be single actions, although Jacob managed to fulfil only the first of them. This may mean that the place had not yet become a fully-fledged cult-

32. Cf. Sumerian, Old Babylonian and Ugaritic parallels above; also see *ANET*, 349, 350; Margalit 1986: 62-63; Cartledge 1992: 75, 82.

centre, with no clergy to receive tithes. If, as I argued in Chapter 4, it was an obscure place, the promise to raise a shrine and pay tithes could not have been fulfilled, since these involved a community and a clergy. Alternatively, it is possible that Jacob, and probably other patriarchs, normally used the tithes and offerings for the sacrifices and the subsequent cultic feast. The Deuteronomic law, in which the tithes were allowed to be used for the sacrifices and the cultic feast, probably goes back to the patriarchal practice.

5. *Conclusion*

The tithe in the patriarchal narratives occurs only in two contexts: first with Abraham, who paid from his booty to the priest-king Melchizedek, and secondly with Jacob, who vowed a tithe in a crisis situation but did not pay it. In contrast to the tithe practices in the ancient Near East and Israel, tithing in these two instances was not a regular annual tithe, but a single voluntary payment. It is not clear whether Abraham's tithe was a religious obligation, although it is possible that, by paying a tenth to a priest, he was following a common practice of the ancient Near East where a portion of the booty was paid to the deity. But this was not part of his regular religious activity, which normally involved building altars and calling upon the name of God with neither priests nor established cult involved. The practice of paying a portion from the booty was also followed by the Israelites who recovered booty from the Midianites, but here it was clearly associated with religious sanctions and appropriate ceremonies. Jacob's tithe was part of his vow, and thus certainly a religious obligation. He probably paid it in the form of sacrifices and offering during the religious feast he observed in fulfilment of his vow to God. Unlike in the ancient Near East and Israel, Jacob's tithe was not paid to a temple or clergy. Thus the patriarchs' tithes, while resembling ancient Near Eastern and Israelite practices, were distinct from them and were compatible with their own lifestyle and religion which fitted with the lack of an established, organized cult.

Chapter 6

Vows

1. *Introduction*

The concept of vow-making is the second of the patriarchal religious practices that concerns us here. It occurs only in the Jacob cycle in the same context where Jacob raised a pillar at Bethel (Gen. 28.20-22). However, the fulfilment of Jacob's vow is only alluded to but not clearly stated (Gen. 35.1-4), though this is an important, if not indispensable, aspect of vow-making in both the ancient Near East and Israel. The ambiguity around the fulfilment and the non-cultic context of Jacob's vow contribute to the distinctive nature of vow-making in patriarchal narratives. As in previous chapters, I shall show how vow-making forms part of Jacob's religion and yet remains distinctive to his own lifestyle and religion.

It is widely recognized that vow-making was a universal custom in ancient religions (*DB*, I: 872), and 'as old as the feeling for God and the experience of distress' (*ERE*, XII: 654). Distress and 'feeling for God' are especially linked with making vows, since almost all the vows that we know of, whether from the Bible or from the ancient Near East, arose out of some kind of human predicament in which the individual or the group sought divine help (Nazirite vows of the Bible are an exception). Jacob's vow is no exception in this regard. Nevertheless, since this is the only instance of a vow in the patriarchal narratives, and since most religious activities of the patriarchs lack religious sanction or precedent, it is difficult to interpret it precisely. Hence we need to examine, as in previous chapters, the broader context of the life and setting of people who were engaged in vow-making in the ancient Near East and Israel in order to elucidate the patriarchal texts. I shall deal first with the evidence in the ancient Near East and Israel and then with the vow text in the Jacob cycle of the patriarchal narratives.

2. *Vows in the Ancient Near East*

In this section, I shall explore the evidence from the traditions of Israel's neighbours, especially from Mesopotamian, Egyptian, Hittite and Ugaritic sources, most of which belong to the second and first millennium BCE. It would be impossible to deal in detail with the date, composition and structure of each vow in these sources; this would require a separate study on its own and would not be relevant to my purpose here (cf. Cartledge's [1992] excellent work in this regard). My aim is to know when people in the patriarchal world made vows, why they did so, what they promised and how they fulfilled them.

The evidence suggests that vow-making as a religious practice was widely known in all the cultures of the ancient Near East. Vows were usually made in times of crisis and it was expected that vows once made would be fulfilled, since otherwise the gods would be angry and cause disaster on those who failed to fulfil them.

a. *Mesopotamian Vows*
Though there is no specific word for vow in Sumerian, the idea of a conditional promise to a deity in return for a favour is clearly present. Vows in Sumer, as elsewhere, were usually made in a situation of crisis. As in biblical vows, not only concrete gifts but also abstract praise was promised to the gods, since praise was considered as much a food to the deity as was sacrifice (Westermann 1981: 7). The Sumerian letter prayer (from the Neo-Sumerian period, prior to and during the Old Babylonian period) which was considered above (Chapter 3 §1), also illustrates the Sumerian idea of vow. To a lengthy prayer is attached an equally lengthy vow of praise in which Sin-šamuh the scribe, apparently confined to bed or isolated from the general public by deadly sickness, promised the deity that he would dwell in his gates, sing his praises, proclaim his exaltation, and appear to the public as a witness if the deity removed his sin and guilt and rescued him from the grave (Hallo 1968: 86; cf. Cartledge 1992: 75). Similarly, in another letter prayer, a woman worshipper who was haunted by a demon promised to the deity a house, worship, allegiance and the title, 'The one who helps the haunted!'[1] Though these are not psalms, the promise of praise and the motivation for it have clear parallels in Israelite psalms of petition

1.   Falkenstein and von Soden 1953: 218, 219; cf. Cartledge 1992: 75.

where the vow of praise is a constant component. In other psalms where the vow is lacking, it appears in various different forms.[2] Both in Israel and among her neighbours, the vow of praise usually appears at the end of the petition, indicating that the vow is conditional. As Westermann observes: 'The praise of God in Israel is essentially praise after the petition has been answered' (1981: 152 cf. 36-39). The Sumerian woman's promise, however, resembles Jacob's vow, though the situation and the motivation are different.

Vows appear extensively in Assyrian and Babylonian literature: in temple records, building inscriptions, letters, omen literature and formal prayers. However, the vocabulary is distinctive. The Akkadian *nadāru* means 'to rage' or 'to be wild', and is not related to the Northwest Semitic root *ndr*, which means 'vow' in Hebrew, Phoenician and Ugaritic. The Akkadian noun *ikribū* and its cognate verb *karābu*, however, belong to the general vocabulary of prayer and benediction, and could be used specifically to mean 'vow' just as *qārab* was so used in biblical Hebrew (*CAD*, VII: 62-66; cf. Hebrew קָרֵב in Lev. 27.9).

Several examples from the Old Babylonian period illustrate conditional vows in the Akkadian sources. In one, from temple records, Adad-shar-ili vowed one-sixth of a grain of silver for the healing of Awil-Adad. Apparently a third person would pay the dues when Awil-Adad was healed: 'When (he is) healthy and whole, Idyatum will pay his vow to Sin...' (*CAD*, VII: 64; Cartledge 1992: 77). In another, from 'temple loans' (Harris 1960: 128-29), a deity appears as creditor. Individuals with various troubles or sickness could turn to deities and make vows which were considered as loans to the temple; the payment was not expected until the individual was delivered from trouble. The relevant texts are called *shalmu baltu* texts because the clause *ina baltu u shalmu*, 'when he is physically well or solvent', often occurs. But the fact that *ikribu* occurred together with loans has led scholars to think that some loans were basically vows made to the deity (cf. Harris 1960: 136). In a third example, taken from the twelfth-century Assyrian building inscriptions, the king Assur-nadin-apli made a vow when the floods of Tigris threatened his crops and city. He promised to Assur and Šamaš

2.   E.g. report (Ps. 73.28), exhortation (Pss. 27.14; 31.24), future condition (Pss. 43.4 cf. 6.5; 88.10, 12; Isa. 38.18), or praise itself (Pss. 6.8-9; 10.16, 17, 18; 12.6; 102.24b-27); Westermann 1981: 75 n. 24.

that he would make and erect images of them if they returned the course of the Tigris to its place.[3]

As at Sumer and in biblical psalms, the vow of praise occurs in Akkadian, in hymns of prayer and incantation called *Shu-illa*, 'prayer of the lifting of the hand', and *Ki'utukam*, 'prayer to the rising sun' (from about 1400–1300 BCE; Dalglish 1962: 19). The vow of praise may be related to the absolution of sins,[4] or to favours received, and the things vowed include not only praise and proclamation but also concrete things, such as providing and furnishing a house for the deity (Cartledge 1992: 82; cf. Jacob's vow). Similarly, promises of thanksgiving and praise are routinely accorded for expected favours and ritual purity from the deity in a group of incantations called *dingir-šá-dib-ba* ('appeasing the wrath of a god') (Lambert 1974: 275, 277; cf. Ps. 51.7, 8).

A number of Assyrian and Babylonian texts speak of the gods being angry with unpaid or delayed vows. Prompt payment of vows was expected: 'do not by any means neglect the votive offering which you pledged to DN, the goddess is angry' (*CAD*, VII: 64, 65); and worshippers were commanded not to 'alter their words', implying that any exchange was unacceptable.[5] Several letters of the Old Assyrian period reveal that sickness was sometimes attributed to the gods who were angered by unpaid vows. A child's restlessness at its mother's breast, for instance, was believed to have been caused by a deity whose votive gifts were unpaid. Similarly two women, Tariš-matum and Belatum, came to realize through diviners that their father's house was devastated by sickness because the gods were angry about their unpaid vows, and they made arrangements for the vow to be paid immediately (Oppenheim 1956: 221, 222; Cartledge 1992: 88, 89).

These examples demonstrate that vow-making and votive offerings were well known among kings and common people, and were an important part of private and public religious life in ancient Mesopotamia. Cartledge comments appropriately: 'Although the *ikribu* does not always function in the same way as the Hebrew vow, it often has much in common with its Hebrew counterpart, including similar life situations

---

3. Weidner 1930–31: 14; *RAC*, 9, 1058; Grayson 1987: 300-301; Cartledge 1992: 90.

4. Dalglish 1962: 31, 41, 47; Cartledge 1992: 81; cf. Pss. 13.6; 51.14; 54.7.

5. *CAD*, VII: 65. Cf. Mal. 1.14 ('Cursed be the cheat who…vows…to the Lord what is blemished'); Deut. 23.21-23; Num. 30.2; Eccl. 5.4, 5.

(distress), locations (the sanctuary), literary forms (prayer, especially lament), contents (temple offerings, public praise), and regulations (vows are sacred and must not be withheld)' (1992: 91).

b. *Egyptian Vows*

There are no clear examples of vows in the literature of the Old Kingdom (c. 2650–2135 BCE),[6] and examples cited from the Middle Kingdom (c. 2040–1650 BCE) are dubious. The promise of the 'ship-wrecked sailor' is sometimes regarded as a vow, but wrongly, since the sailor promises to offer gifts and offerings for protection and kindness already received, and it is not certain whether he regards the snake to whom he makes promises as a god (Lichtheim 1975: 214). Similarly, the 'eloquent peasant' makes a promise when he was robbed and beaten on his way to Egypt (Lichtheim 1975: 171). Cartledge considers this a vow (1992: 92-93), but this is hardly appropriate, since there is no specific promise to the deity, and the promise is for the peasant himself. This is more a distress call than a vow.

Evidence of specific vows is found on the votive stelae of the New Kingdom (c. 1550–1080 BCE). The relevant stelae were recovered at the modern village of Deir el-Medina in the area of Thebes. A draftsman, Nebre, made the votive stele in accordance with the promise he made to Amun-Re for saving his son Nakhtamun.[7] As in Mesopotamia, the view that the vow must be fulfilled without alteration comes out clearly in this inscription: 'So I said to you and you listened to me. Now behold, I do what I have said' (Lichtheim 1976: 107).

As in Mesopotamia, a number of Egyptian prayers and laments from c. 1350–1250 BCE contain specific promises of praise (Assman 1975: 363; cf. Cartledge 1992: 97). Egyptian literature from later periods also contains conditional promises to deities, which suggests that the practice of vow-making was common to all periods of its history.

c. *Hittite Vows*

Vow-making is frequently attested in the Hittite literature, but it appears to be more common among the royalty than the ordinary

---

6.   Wilson's (1948: 129, 131) claim that some of the promissory oaths of this period can be regarded as vows is dubious; cf. Cartledge 1992: 91.

7.   I have considered this example in connection with 'thanksgiving prayer' in Chapter 3 §2.

people.[8] A vow of common people is found in an elaborate ritual text called the 'Ritual against Impotence', where the priestess performed a ritual on behalf of the impotent person. She promised that the patient, if healed, would give the deity a shrine, cattle, his sons and daughters as male and female servants to provide continually for his sacrifices (cf. Hannah's vow and Samuel's vocation), total allegiance,[9] worship, sacrificial vessels and a stone pillar (cf. Jacob's vow) or a statue (*ANET*, 349, 350). One can see both Jacob's and Hannah's vows paralleled in this vow.

The best known example among the royal Hittite vows is the vow of Puduhepas, a Hurrian queen, who makes a vow on behalf of her husband Hattusilis III (c. 1275–1250 BCE) who was critically ill. The prayer and vow are directed to a number of deities, but especially to Lelwanis, the patron deity of Hattusilis.[10] She promised to the deities life-size silver statues of the king, ornaments and golden shields (*ANET*, 394; cf. Cartledge 1992: 102, 103). In both these examples the conditional nature of the promise is as clear as in biblical vows.

d. *Ugaritic Vows*

The best known example of vow-making in Ugaritic is preserved in the epic of Keret (*KTU*, 1.14.iv, 34-43). This vow has many similarities with both the ancient Near Eastern and the Hebrew practice of making vows. According to Parker, the vow's structure and content bear many parallels with the narrative vows in the Hebrew Bible (Parker 1979: 693-700). The conditional protasis is introduced by *hm* (cf. *'im* in Hebrew) and contains imperfect verbs (cf. imperfect or perfect consecutive in Hebrew), and is followed by an apodosis stating the promise, in which the first person singular imperfect is used (cf. imperfect in Hebrew) (Parker 1979: 693-96; cf. Cartledge 1992: 111, 115). The vow reads (*CML*, 87-88; cf. *ANET*, 145; *UL*, 72):

---

8.   Cartledge (1992: 100) thinks that this was because the royalty had both the means of commissioning inscriptions and the desire to publish their piety.

9.   The text mentions elsewhere that this individual did not know this god before, which in itself was an incentive to the deity to grant his request.

10.   I have considered this prayer in connection with the 'intercessory prayer' in Chapter 3 §2. For a comprehensive discussion of the background and history of queen Puduhepas, see Fontaine 1987: 95-126.

> He came to the sanctuary of Athirat of the two Tyres
> and to (the sanctuary of) Elat of the Sidonians.
> There the noble Keret vowed, (saying):
> 'As surely as Athirat of the two Tyres
> and Elat of the Sidonians exists,[11]
> if I may take Huray (into) my house,
> introduce the lass to my court,
> I will give twice her (weight) in silver
> and thrice her (weight) in gold'.

The most significant difference from the biblical vows is that the word *ndr* occurs here for the promise of the deity Athirat. As Cartledge notes, 'In the Hebrew Bible, Yahweh makes conditional promises to Israel in the form of a vow, but *ndr* is never used' (1992: 113; cf. 109-15). As in Mesopotamia and Egypt, the gods expect that vows made must be fulfilled. It appears that Keret forgot his vow and was afflicted with sickness. Athirat says, 'Has Keret...broken his vow? Then I shall break...' (*KTU*, 1.15.iii, 28-29). The text is broken here, but the context suggests that some revenge was in view.[12] This is also reflected in a ritual text where the Ugaritians were advised to make vows to Baal when they were in danger of enemy attack. The text records both the vow of worship, sacrifices and tithes, and also a promise of fulfilment (for full text see Chapter 2 n. 28; Cartledge 1992: 117, 118). Apparently, magical results were expected in this ritual (Margalit [1986: 62, 63] sees a similar allusion in 2 Kgs 3.27). These two texts indicate not only that *ndr* is used for a conditional promise in Ugaritic but also that making vows is important in the religion at Ugarit.

e. *Other Ancient Near Eastern Vows*
Examples of vow-making also occur in Aramaic, Phoenician and Punic inscriptions, and the epigraphic evidence goes well into the Greek

11. Fisher (1975: 147, 152) insists that the original should read here *itt*, 'gift' and not 'exist' or 'live'. It is a noun that goes with the verb 'to vow', thus the translation is 'there the noble Keret vowed a gift...'; so also Cartledge 1992: 109, 110.

12. Keret did fall sick later, but since the story directs attention to his healing, and since the vow does not occur in the story again, some scholars think that the vow was a later insertion to account for Keret's illness, and the vow's absence in the later part of the story was because the narrator did not want to show that El was the cause of Keret's sickness; Parker 1977: 163-67; but Cartledge (1992: 109) thinks that the vow was integral to the narrative.

period (Cartledge 1992: 122, 133), which suggests that the concept was known in other Semitic cultures as well. It will suffice to take a single example from the inscriptions to make my point here. An Aramaic inscription (ninth/eighth century BCE)[13] states that Bar-Hadad, king of Aram, erected a stele he vowed for his lord Melqart because the latter heard his prayer (Albright 1942: 23, 24; *TSSI*, 2.3).

3. *Vows in Israel*

The most common term used to designate a 'vow' or 'votive offering' in the Hebrew Bible is the root נדר, which occurs 91 times, 49 times in the Pentateuch alone (the nominal form occurs 60 times, 34 times in the Pentateuch). However, no text attempts to define vow-making and there are only five recorded vows. Nevertheless, the pentateuchal legislation on vows, the different contexts in which the concept occurs and the actual recorded vows give sufficient information to understand their nature and religious ethos in Israel.

a. *Nature of Biblical Vows*

As in the ancient Near East, vows in the Bible always took place in the context of prayer but not necessarily of the cult. Thus vows, like prayer, could be made informally, but their fulfilment always involved cultic rituals. Of the five recorded vows in the Bible,[14] only Hannah's was made at a cult centre. While Jonah made his vow in the fish's belly, the sailors made theirs while aboard ship, and the exiled Israelites in Egypt probably in their homes (Jer. 44.25). Most Israelites made their vows at home (Num. 30.1-17).

Vows in Israel generally arose in times of distress just as in the ancient Near East. For instance, Absalom made his during his self-imposed exile in Geshur (2 Sam. 13.38). Many unspectacular vows were probably made in ordinary life and fulfilled during annual feasts (Lev. 23.38; 1 Sam. 1.21; Nah. 2.1) (cf. Cartledge 1992: 12, 13).

13. For varied views on date and identify the individual in the inscription, see Cartledge 1992: 123-27.

14. Jacob's vow is the most elaborate. Israel's vow (Num. 21.2), the shortest, deals with the things 'devoted' (חרם) to Yahweh, and Jephthah's (Judg. 11.30, 39) with an unspecified votive object. Hannah's vow (1 Sam. 1.11) is related to the Nazirite vows and Absalom's (2 Sam. 15.7, 8) reflects a past crisis.

As in the ancient Near East, vows in Israel were usually conditional promises to God, even if many psalms do not state conditions explicitly.[15] The promise was the basic element of both vows and oaths. It strengthened an earlier petition to the deity in the former and was reinforced by the addition of a curse, usually in conjunction with an appeal to a deity (e.g. 1 Sam. 3.17; 2 Kgs 6.31), in the latter (Cartledge 1992: 16, 17). It is uncertain, however, whether a clear distinction existed between vows, oaths and promises in Israel. Sometimes what were clearly declarative statements or promises of Yahweh were later regarded as sure oaths (e.g. 2 Sam. 7.11, 12, 16; cf. Pss. 89.4, 5; 132.11), and what may have been an oath was later described as a vow (Ps. 132.1-5) (Cartledge [1992: 15] considers this as an oath). Similarly, the distinction between vows and oaths is blurred in Numbers 30, where both are described as 'binding obligations' to be meticulously fulfilled or to be cancelled by father/husband. Thus some scholars propose that at one time they were regarded as the same thing (Noth 1968: 225), while others differentiate between an earlier and a later usage of *ndr*, a positive oath (e.g. Jephthah's), and *'sr*, a negative oath (e.g. a Nazirite's) (Snaith 1967: 321). The former view is possible, but the latter is unlikely. In Numbers 6, the idea of 'binding oneself', *'issār*, is not used, and restrictions are imposed on the Nazirite not by himself but by law. On the other hand, in Numbers 30 where *'issār* is used (only here in the Old Testament), a Nazirite vow does not seem to be the issue and the restrictions imposed are not by law but by the vow-maker.

However, the majority of scholars view vows as conditional promises. This is confirmed by the form and content of the five recorded vows of the Bible. They portray a similar structure, consisting of introduction, condition (protasis) and promise (apodosis).[16] Some are elaborate, others simple. Hannah's vow (1 Sam. 1.11), which also includes an address to the deity, may be taken to illustrate the structure of a biblical vow:

15. Pss. 50.14; 76.11; *THAT*, II: 41, 42; contrast *ThWAT*, V: 264-66; Cartledge 1992: 64, 65.

16. Cf. Richter 1967: 22-23; Fisher 1975: 149-50; Parker 1979: 694.

Introduction:	And she vowed a vow and she said,
(Address to the deity):	O [Yahweh] of hosts,
Condition (protasis):	If thou wilt indeed look on the affliction of thy maidservant, and remember me, and not forget thy maidservant, but wilt give to thy maidservant a son,
Promise (apodosis):	then I will give him to [Yahweh] all the days of his life, and no razor shall touch his head.

The condition is the heart of the vow. Some scholars think that vows are bargains with deity and are of inferior religious quality (Heiler 1923: 145; cf. Cartledge 1992: 47). Others argue that conditional vows gradually gave way to unconditional vows and eventually lost all religious content, becoming simple solemn promises, the equivalent of oaths (Wendel 1931: 13-14; Davies 1962: 792-93). Though certainty is difficult, the different form of several vows in poetry relieves the tension between the condition and promise, leaving the vow account in mere imperative and indicative statements as in Job 22.27 and Ps. 61.9. Sometimes the vow is unmentioned but the concept is quite explicit, as in Ps. 22.21, 22. Interestingly, Keret's vow considered above has a similar structure with the condition made explicit. Therefore the vows in the psalms lack a conditional protasis probably because of their genre, not development of concept. However, the Nazirite vow in Numbers 6 is a special vow with no conditions, except separation to Yahweh, לנדר נדר נזיר לחזיר ליהוה (contra Cartledge 1992: 23). In this sense it looks more like an oath than a vow. In the cases of Samson and Samuel, the vows were made not by themselves but by God or parents. The Nazirite law probably arose in later times when individuals wanted to emulate such persons.

b. *Legislation on Vows*
Legislation on various kinds of vows occurs 11 times in the Hebrew Bible, only in the Pentateuch.[17] This attention suggests not only a cultic interest in systematizing vows but also the importance of vow-making in the religious life of Israel.

First, as in the ancient Near East, vows had to be promptly fulfilled, especially since they were voluntary (Deut. 18.22-24; Eccl. 5.4-5; cf.

---

17. Lev. 7.16; 22.18-23; 23.38; 27.2, 8; Num. 6.2, 5, 21; 15.3, 8; 21.2; 29.39; 30.3-15; Deut. 12.6, 11, 17, 26; 23.18-23. Eccl 5.3, 4 is a reiteration of Deut. 23.22, 23 and not a new law.

Num. 30.3). However, a woman's vow not approved by her father or husband was annulled (Num. 30.4-17).

Secondly, objects vowed in Israel were both general and specific. The former includes free-will offerings (נדב, Lev. 22.18), peace offerings or burnt offerings (עלה, זבח שלמים, Lev. 22.21), votive offerings (נדרים, Lev. 22.23, 38; Num. 29.39; Deut. 12.6, 11, 17, 26; cf. Jephthah's vow), sacrifices (זבח, Jon. 2.9) and libations (נסך, Jer. 44.25).[18] The latter includes persons, sacrificial and non-sacrificial animals, houses, lands and fields, and they became 'holy' to Yahweh (Lev. 27.1-29). Although קרב hiphil (vv. 9-13) and קדש (vv. 14-27) cannot be translated as 'vow-making' or 'vow',[19] they seem to be used here synonymously and in some way related to the objects vowed. As in the ancient Near East, abstract praise and even thanksgiving (תודה, Ps. 50.14) could also be vowed to Yahweh, as the parallelism between vows and prayers (Job 22.27), praise (Pss. 22.26; 61.9; 65.2), thanksgiving (Pss. 50.14; 56.13; 116.17, 18) and even the 'cup of salvation' (Ps. 116.13, 14) suggests.

Thirdly, animals vowed could not be exchanged, but anything vowed could be redeemed by adding a fifth to their value, especially persons who could not be sacrificed (Lev. 27.2-8). However, cities, humans, animals or inherited land-holdings (Lev. 27.28-29) vowed for 'utter destruction' (חרם, Num. 21.2), being 'most holy' to Yahweh, could not be redeemed. While no regulation in the ancient Near East prohibited objects from vows, Israel prohibits the 'hire of a harlot or a dog' (Deut. 23.19), probably the gains of male and female prostitutes which were often dedicated to deities in non-Israelite worship.[20] Firstlings also could not be vowed because they already belonged to Yahweh.

Fourthly, the Nazirite vows involved special regulations: abstention from wine, cutting hair and corpse pollution, even following the death

18. Cf. the exiled Egyptians who vowed 'incense', קטר, to the Queen of Heaven.

19. So Cartledge 1992: 137-38. It is interesting to note that the Akkadian *ikribu* that I discussed above has similar meaning to קרב hiphil. Further, קדש appears to be equivalent to a 'vow' in Prov. 20.25. In the Jerusalem Talmud this verse is quoted as valid vow (*Ned.* 1.10). Similarly words of swearing, שבע, and oath-taking, אסר, are associated with נדר in Num. 21 and 30, and שבע and נדר are paired together in Ps. 132.2.

20. Driver 1902: 264-65; Wendel 1931: 21; Thomas 1960: 424-26; cf. von Rad 1966: 148; Mays 1979: 320.

of the nearest of kin (Num. 6.1-21). Nazirites are comparable only to the high priest in this regard.

Fifthly, the law gave equal opportunities for women worshippers in making vows. But it also made concessions if they could not fulfil vows immediately disowned by their father/husband (Num. 30.6, 9, 13). However, men who attempted to annul such vows later would bear their guilt.

c. *Comparative Analysis*

First, it is abundantly clear that vow-making was not peculiar to Israel, but was very common among her neighbours long before Israel ever became a nation.

Secondly, both in Israel and the ancient Near East vows were made in the context of prayer, and in situations of distress, such as sickness, childlessness and danger from natural calamity or enemy attack. Occasionally the problem was individual guilt, as especially in the Babylonian hymns. In Israel, however, there was no instance of a vow or any other promise for an absolution of guilt.

Thirdly, objects vowed in the ancient Near East and in Israel were both material gifts and abstract praise or thanksgiving. However, silver and gold, ornaments, statues, pillars, sun-disks and stelae, which either represent or decorate the images of the gods, were common in the former but not found in the latter. This probably indicates the aniconic nature of Israel's religion.

Fourthly, the only specific law on vows in the ancient Near East concerned prompt fulfilment. The Pentateuch maintains this and also gives various other laws, such as the objects which could not be vowed, the Nazirite vows, the non-exchange of vowed animals and the redemption of persons and objects vowed.

Fifthly, the semantic root used for vow-making is general in Akkadian (*krb*) but more specific in Ugaritic (*ndr*). In one Ugaritic text a deity is the subject of *ndr*; in Israel only humans made vows.

4. *Jacob's Vow in the Patriarchal Narratives*

The longest of the five recorded vows in the Bible occurs in the patriarchal narratives, in the Jacob cycle. Since there are no other examples of vows in the patriarchal narratives, it becomes imperative to compare Jacob's vow with others in the Bible and the ancient Near East. My aim is to analyse Jacob's vow (Gen. 28.20-22) in order not only to understand the religious ethos behind it but also to see the similarities and dissimilarities between Jacob's religion and the Israelite and ancient Near Eastern religions.

a. *Form and Structure*

With minor variations critics acknowledge that all the narrative accounts of vows in the Hebrew Bible consist of the same basic form and structure: (1) narrative introduction, (2) address to the deity, (3) condition (protasis, introduced by *'im* + imperfect verb), and (4) promise (apodosis, introduced by *waw*-consecutive + perfect verb).[21] However, the second element is present only in Hannah's vow and possibly also in Keret's (Keret's vow follows a similar structure, see §2d above). Thus Jacob's vow may be analysed as follows:

(1)	וידר יעקב נדר לאמר	Then Jacob made a vow, saying,
(2)	—	—
(3)	אם־יהיה אלהים עמדי	'If God will be with me,
	ושמרני בדרך הזה אשר אנכי הולך	and will keep me in this way that I go,
	ונתן־לי לחם לאכל ובגד ללבש	and will give me bread to eat and clothing to wear,
	ושבתי בשלום אל־בית אבי	so that I come again to my father's house in peace,
(4)	והיה יהוה לי לאלהים	then Yahweh shall be my God,
	והאבן הזאת אשר־שמתי מצבה יהיה	and this stone, which I have set up for a pillar shall
	בית אלהים	be God's house;
	וכל אשר תתן־לי עשר אעשרנו לך	and of all that you givest me I will give the tenth to thee.'

The first element appears to be more a matter of choice than a fixed form even though it is relatively uniform in all other vows. A report of a vow must introduce it in the third person, though with Absalom's vow the author chooses to report it in Absalom's words (2 Sam. 15.8). Thus, this was not necessarily a fixed introductory formula. Similarly, the second point, address to the deity, does not occur in Jacob's vow, though it does in Hannah's and in Keret's vows. While the protasis is common to all narrative vows, there are real differences among them.

21. Cartledge 1992: 160; cf. Richter 1967: 22-23; Fisher 1975: 149-50; de Pury 1975: 436-37; Parker 1979: 693-96. For discussion of the structure of other narrative vows in the Bible, see Cartledge 1992: 143-50.

Jacob's vow uses the third person, 'If God...', while Israel's, Jephthah's and Hannah's vow use the second person, 'If you...' and Keret's
vow uses the first person, 'If I...' Parker's suggestion (1979: 392-96)
that the first person form in Keret's vow is influenced by marriage language may apply also to the biblical vows, especially Hannah's, where
the protasis is long and the repetition of 'your maid' emphasizes her
humble situation. Similar language is used in the protasis of Puduhepas' vow. Similarly, the precise conditions presented in the protasis of
Jacob's vow were probably due partly to his insecurity and uncertain
future and partly to his character as 'trickster' as portrayed by the
narrator (cf. Cartledge 1992: 149-50). Since this leads us into the larger
structure of Jacob's vow, it is instructive to note that no vow can be
studied in isolation. The larger structure of the story plays its part.[22] The
structure is not uniform in the apodosis either. Keret's vow, like
Israel's, does not mention a divine name but only the promised gift,
while all others mention in the third person the deity to whom the
promise was made. Here again Jacob's vow is different, in that it starts
with the third person and then changes to the second person.

Thus we cannot lay out a neat structure into which every form can be
fitted. The first two elements are more erratic than the last two. While
the former are more a matter of authorial choice, the latter probably
arose from the language of social bargain in which condition and promise play an important role—bargainers exchange what they have for
what they want. Cartledge rightly points out that 'any person who knew
how to make a bargain could also make a vow without consulting a
common repository of vow-forms for the most appropriate type' (Cartledge 1992: 150). Thus it is unlikely that the relative consistency in the
form of the vows necessarily suggests, as Richter argued, that there
were 'fixed forms' of vows in stock available at certain cult places for
the worshippers to use in times of need (contra Richter 1967: 26-30, 31;
Westermann 1985: 459). However, this form is relevant only for narrative vows. The vows that appear in poetic parts of the Bible and in a
Ugaritic ritual text have no conditional protasis or apodosis, but only
imperative and indicative statements (see §3a above). Sometimes the
vow is not even mentioned, yet conditionality is explicit (cf. Cartledge
1992: 150-61). Thus the present form of Jacob's vow is more a 'literary
adaptation' than a 'transcript' of the actual vow (Cartledge 1992: 144),
and not necessarily more distorted in form than other narrative vows

22. De Pury 1975: 435-36; cf. Richter 1967: 47-50; Cartledge 1992: 166-74.

(contra Parker 1979: 698). This does not mean, however, that the vow is secondary to its present context (de Pury 1975: 435-37; contra Richter 1967: 44-49).

b. *Content*
The biblical narrative vows deal with repatriation (Jacob, Absalom), military victory (Israel, Jephthah, cf. the Ugaritic community) and childlessness (Hannah, cf. Keret) (Parker 1979: 699). Fisher thinks that the purpose of Jacob's and Keret's vows was to obtain a wife (1975: 149-50), but this is not explicit in Jacob's vow, and is only a secondary interest in Keret's. Parker's view that Hannah's and Keret's vows have closer parallels than Jacob's and Keret's is plausible, since both were concerned with children, and the promise made in return was an offer of persons, although in Keret's case the silver and gold of the person's weight was probably a redemption of the person vowed. In this sense the vow of Puduhepas was similar since her promised gift was also a substitute for the person.[23] On the other hand Jacob's vow is similar to Absalom's because the concern in both was a safe return from abroad, and the promise made was of worship (cf. Parker 1979: 699).

However, we are bound to be disappointed if we expect exact parallels between these vows, since each situation is different. Hannah's desire for a son was not so much to continue her clan as to relieve her from the shame of barrenness, whereas Keret's concern was only posterity, so they are not strictly the same. The only real parallel of content is the promise of persons, if we take the silver and gold of a person's weight as substitute for the person. But we cannot be certain that Keret and Puduhepas meant it in this way. Instead, it could indicate that they valued the person so much that they would rather part with silver and gold than with the person. Some of the things promised in Jacob's vow can be seen in other ancient Near Eastern vows. In a vow from the Neo-Sumerian period a woman promised to build a house to the goddess and serve before her. In Akkadian vows from the Old Babylonian period vow-makers promised to provide for the deity's house and furnish its enclosures. In a Hittite vow the 'Arzawa woman' promised on behalf of the impotent man a place and a house for the deity and to set up a stone pillar or a statue. In Ugaritic vows, apart from Keret's, promises

23. Cf. Parker (1979: 694-95) who also cites an example from the Mishnah where a woman vows a gift equal in value to her sick daughter if she recovers.

included tithes to Baal (see examples in Chapter 5 §2c above). Shrine and money seem to be the commonest things vowed to gods.

Jacob's vow, however, is concerned as much with the condition as with the promise. Jacob sought God's protection, provision and safe return, all of which may be summed up in the first sentence of the protasis, 'If God will be with me'. In return, he offered to raise a sanctuary and pay tithes for the deity's patronage, all of which may be summed up in the first sentence of the apodosis, 'then Yahweh will be my God' (cf. Cartledge 1992: 149). The parallels suggest that Jacob was no different from any worshipper in the ancient Near East in offering a shrine, a pillar and a tithe. It appears that Jacob was more aware of the general religious customs in Mesopotamia and Canaan than were his forebears. Abraham encountered childlessness, war and famine resulting in travel to Egypt and back, but in none of these occasions did he make a vow, although he did pray for an heir. He paid tithes from the booty to Melchizedek, but there is no indication that he had vowed to do this. Similarly, there is no mention of tithes or vows in the Isaac cycle, although he also was childless and prayed for his barren wife, and was forced out of Canaan by famine.

c. *Function*
Richter's view, that all the biblical narrative vows except Jacob's reflect the form of personal piety attested in early and later monarchical times (1967: 26), is possible. But this need not mean that such pious practice was unknown in pre-monarchic or patriarchal times. The parallels from the ancient Near East clearly prove it was. The final authors of Israel's and Jephthah's vows assume this, despite the uncertainty of the time of the origin of these texts. Further, neither the situation in which they vowed (e.g. battle) nor the things they vowed (e.g. humans, livestock) were uncommon in the ancient Near East (cf. Ugaritic community). One cannot prove this, but neither can one deny such a possibility. Richter's second premise is that Jacob's vow, unlike other narrative vows, has an overarching theological function in its present context. It is part of the 'vow-scheme' along with Gen. 31.2, 4-16, which echoes the granting, and 35.1-5, 7, which echoes the fulfilling of the vow, though neither of these is a unified narrative (1967: 44-49). However, this appears a circular argument. Richter's assumption that the vow was a secondary insertion in its present context

necessitates similar assumptions about the other passages. Moreover, as de Pury notes:

> The fact that the significance of the vow transcends its immediate narrative context is insufficient to establish the secondary character of the vow. The presence of the vow, just like that of promise, simply shows that the account of Gen. 28 does not subsist as an isolated 'story' which unfolded entirely outside of time and space. As for the 'structuring' function of the vow, it shows us that the account of Jacob's dream could only be understood in the framework of a more extended cycle of account (de Pury 1975: 435-36).

Further, the vow may not necessarily be the overarching theme of the Jacob cycle. For Fishbane it is 'birth', 'blessing' and 'land', set in tension with their opposites, 'barrenness', 'curse' and 'exile', that charge the whole of the Jacob cycle. These themes are of fundamental significance to each of the narrative cycles of Abraham, Isaac and Jacob (Fishbane 1979: 60-61). For Westermann, genealogies and itineraries form the framework not only for the whole of the Jacob cycle but also for the Abraham cycle, and the Jacob cycle is especially characterized by the familiar structure of 'flight-return' (1985: 406-407). Thus the overarching theme could be 'blessing', 'promise' or 'land'. It is tempting to see it as 'promise', since God's promises to be with Jacob and to bring him back to his father's land, the conditions of Jacob's vow (vv. 20, 21), were already stated in the dream (v. 15), and they are echoed in the same passages in which the vow is echoed (31.3, 5; 35.3). So Richter's contention, that vow must form the overarching structure of the Jacob cycle because it is echoed in these passages, loses its force.

d. *Fulfilment*

Genesis 35.1-7, which belongs to E according to traditional source analysis, describes the fulfilment of Jacob's vow. Richter and Cartledge argue that these verses, along with 31.2, 4-16, are connected with 28.20-22 and cannot be regarded as an independent unit of tradition. The chief reason for their contention is that the making (28.20-22), granting (31.2, 4-16) and fulfilment (35.1-7) of the vow do not occur in the same narrative, as is usual with other vows (Richter 1967: 26-31; Cartledge 1992: 172-73). Hannah's and Absalom's vows, which also have deferred fulfilment, are allowed as exceptions.

There are several important observations. First, as has been noted above, the making of the vow in 28.20-22 was not an insertion in the narrative. As de Pury has argued, the vow fits well with the situation of Jacob, who was in distress and running away from his brother who intended to kill him because of his double deception. On his way he received an unexpected revelation in which the deity promised land, offspring, increase and blessing, in reiteration of earlier promises to Abraham and Isaac, besides protection and safe return, of particular relevance to Jacob. Jacob takes up only the last two aspects of the promise and adds another condition, that of food and clothes, and then binds the deity with a vow. This fits well with the uncertain future that Jacob was to face. So there is nothing illogical about the vow's occurrence in the dream story (cf. de Pury 1975: 438). Interestingly, de Pury's explanation is clearly also the perspective of the final author.

Secondly, 'the granting of the vow' in 31.2, 4-16, in contrast to that of other biblical narrative vows, is not as clear as Richter and Cartledge think. Elsewhere the conditions were often straightforward, such as victory (Israel, Jephthah), children (Hannah) and safe return (Absalom). All except Absalom's are specific and time-bound. Their situation required one event before their fulfilment followed. Similarly, the vows of the ancient Near East, considered above, were all concerned with immediate circumstances, such as sickness, childlessness, flood or attack of the enemy. Thus it becomes easier to assess their divine fulfilment than it is with Jacob's vow. In contrast, Jacob's vow, even though concerned with specific conditions such as safe-keeping, food and clothing and safe return, neither is time-bound nor anticipates a single event. Strictly speaking, the content of its protasis cannot be compared with other biblical or ancient Near Eastern vows, although it shares with them several elements of its apodosis such as pillar, house for God and tithes. Further, Genesis 31 seems to be concerned also with Jacob's providing for his own family (30.30), which was not part of the conditions of his vow. It appears that Jacob wanted to return home at this point of the narrative (30.26), and the conditions he laid in his vow would still have been fulfilled if he had done so. Jacob had promised a tithe from what God would give him. So it is not necessary to suppose that tithing was inserted in the vow in order to account for the possessions he acquired in Paddan-aram, or vice versa. Jacob's unscrupulous methods to achieve his ends during his employment by Laban led to the accusation of his brothers-in-law that he took away all their property (31.1). In 31.10-16 it appears that Jacob was trying to justify his actions before his wives by claiming divine sanction. The indirect and direct references to the vow (31.12, 13) appear to blend well with the narrative, with no suggestion that these passages are secondary to the narrative. Therefore the assumption that this passage reflects 'the granting of the vow' in the overarching function of the vow in the Jacob cycle, is unconvincing. Moreover, there is no consensus over whether 35.1-7 belongs to the same author as 28.20-22 and 31.2, 4-16, as Richter and Cartledge claim, since most modern authors find no E material there (cf. Westermann 1985: 548-49; Wenham 1994: 323). In any case, it is impossible to be certain about the intention of the Elohist just as it is impossible to be certain about the extent of his material. So it is safer to look for the intention of the final redactor, despite the obvious seams between the traditions.

This leads me to the third point against Richter's contention that Gen. 35.1-7 is part of the overarching vow structure anticipated in 28.20-22. This is not convincing because the vow is only vaguely reflected here. If it was the author's intention to show that this was the decisive point in Jacob's story where the vow needs to be fulfilled, he would have stated it clearly. The place in the narrative where one would expect the fulfilment of the vow to be related is after 33.18, where Jacob's safe arrival at Shechem is described. Bethel could easily have been substituted for Shechem and the theme of fulfilment would have fitted well, since Jacob had now safely returned and had been delivered particularly from the feared revenge of his brother from whom he originally fled to Paddan-aram. However, the final author did not rearrange the received traditions in this way. According to him, Jacob settled down at Shechem on his arrival from Paddan-aram. Having acquired some land, Jacob probably stayed for a long period at Shechem until he was forced to leave after the massacre of the Shechemites.[24] At this crucial point God commands Jacob to move to Bethel specifically to worship the God who had appeared to him there when he fled from his brother. It was not explicitly in order to fulfil his vow, although it is possible that Jacob did fulfil it along with the sacrifices on the altar he built there, but neither this nor the payment of his tithes is clearly stated. This was probably because there was no sanctuary or priests to appropriate these things in a manner fitting to the rituals.

Furthermore, the fact that the fulfilment of Jacob's vow does not occur in the same narrative is not sufficient to prove that 35.1-7 is a

---

24. Jacob's children were relatively young when they arrived, but were adults when they left Shechem; cf. 33.23, 24 and 34.25, 27.

later insertion. There are many examples in the ancient Near East where the fulfilment of vows was deferred or delayed and the gods were then angered. Sometimes particular sicknesses were attributed to this. Certainly the fulfilment of Keret's vow does not occur in the immediate narrative (cf. *ANET*, 145, 146; *CML*, 82-94). In fact, Keret had completely forgotten about it. We do not know if he honoured his vow at all, since the text where this occurs is irretrievably broken. It is clear from the story that the goddess to whom he vowed waited for at least seven years, during which Keret's wife bore sons and daughters to him, before taking revenge by afflicting him with serious illness, but the story's attention thereafter diverts to the healing of the hero rather than the fulfilment of the vow (cf. Cartledge 1992: 112-14). In any case, it is clear that we have at least one extra-biblical example where the fulfilment of the vow was not part of the same narrative.

Therefore, apart from the fact that the fulfilment of the vow is not stated in 35.1-7, the passage follows a logical sequence of events in the narrative. It is possible that the author intended to show that Jacob's return to Bethel was to fulfil his vow. But it is strange that he does not make this explicit. Neither is there an allusion to the vow. Instead, the situation of Jacob's flight from home and his encounter with God at Bethel are mentioned twice in this passage with a command to make an altar, and Jacob's implicit obedience to it: 'make there an altar to the God who appeared to you when you fled from your brother Esau...and there he built an altar...because there God had revealed himself to him when he fled from his brother' (vv. 1, 7). Mention of Jacob's flight from his brother is probably appropriate here because Jacob now faces a similar danger to his life from the neighbourhood of Shechem. The author is more concerned to show how Jacob escaped from his near annihilation than to state whether he fulfilled his vow. Another possibility is that the author believed that the patriarchs lived in a society in which they had no priests or sanctuaries. The author of the Bethel story (28.10-22) certainly denies any sacred associations to the place prior to Jacob's encounter with God there. Therefore it is only logical for him not to mention the vow's fulfilment which involved erecting a shrine and paying tithes, both of which envisage an established cult. Instead, the author records that Jacob built an altar and worshipped God in the same way his fathers had done. I have already discussed the reasons and the purpose of patriarchal altars in Chapter 2 §4. Accordingly, Jacob's situation at Bethel suggests once again that there were no altars existing at the place where he built his altar, and the purpose was probably that of offering thanksgiving or votive sacrifices. Thus Jacob's vow, while sharing some common elements in form and content with ancient Near Eastern and Israelite vows, is distinct in the aspect of its fulfilment, but it is compatible with the patriarchal nomadic lifestyle and family-oriented religion.

5. *Conclusion*

It is clear from the second- and first-millennium ancient Near Eastern and Israelite sources that the practice of vow-making was very ancient and continued through the ages with little or no change in form, setting, content or function. Though the basic form of vows is the same in all these cultures, there is a rich variety in the choice of words both for the vow-maker and the narrator. The vow language was probably borrowed from the social and business transaction of the bargain, and anyone who could bargain could also make vows without looking for an appropriate form. Vows were usually made in times of crisis, at home or at a sanctuary, and were expected to be fulfilled at the sanctuary. Deferred or delayed vows attracted the anger or displeasure of the deity, and sometimes the god sent disease. However, the elaborate legislation on vows in Israel was unique in the ancient Near East where there was hardly any legislation, except for the common expectation that vows once made must be fulfilled.

In the light of this evidence, it is reasonable to assume that the patriarchs were aware of the practice of vow-making. Their nomadic lifestyle does not necessarily deny them the knowledge of such a practice among the sedentary people with whom they often came in contact. The fact that vows are not recorded for Abraham or Isaac suggests that they did not use the practice, although they encountered crises such as childlessness, enforced travel and war. Abraham and Isaac repeatedly prayed concerning their childlessness, and when abroad used other ploys, such as passing off their wives as sisters. By contrast, Jacob does not pray when his beloved wife Rachel was found to be barren (29.31), although he knew that it was God who 'withheld the fruit of the womb' (30.3). However, he chose to bargain with God when he faced an uncertain future. This kind of piety suited his character well and Jacob used the conditional promises in vows to his own advantage, although they are perfectly normal in vows among all cultures. The narrative had previously recorded that Jacob was a trickster and bargained his brother's birthright for lentil stew (25.33). Despite Esau's willingness to part with his birthright, Jacob wanted to make sure that Esau would not go back on his word, so he made him swear before giving him the food. Similarly Jacob binds God with a vow, although God had already promised more than Jacob required in the vow. Therefore Jacob's vow was a matter of his choice, in conformity with his character portrayed in the narrative. However, the narrator was more concerned with Jacob's escape from Shechem than his fulfilment of the vow. Or he was deliberately vague, if not silent, about the fulfilment of his vow, probably because it involved an established cult and priests which are incompatible with the patriarchal religion and lifestyle that he had portrayed thus far. Therefore Jacob's vow was only partially fulfilled, in that he offered worship and pledged his loyalty to the God who had been with him, but he did not pay tithes or raise a sanctuary.

Chapter 7

POLLUTION AND PURITY

1. *Introduction*

The last of the patriarchal religious practices that I am concerned with
is the idea of purification. Like vow-making, the concept of ritual purity
occurs only in the Jacob cycle, and like tithes and vows, it is a voluntary action of the patriarch. Neither cult nor cultic regulations were
involved in the patriarch's action. This is further suggested by the patriarch's assumption as the sole officiant in the ritual. Thus I hope to show
that, like tithes and vows, the idea of patriarchal ritual purity is distinct
from that of the ancient Near East and Israel and compatible only with
the religion and lifestyle of the patriarch.

We have only one clear instance of purification in the patriarchal
stories, in Gen. 35.1-5. Jacob exhorts his family members to put away
the foreign gods that were with them, purify themselves and change
their clothes before they go to worship the God who has been guiding
Jacob in his journeys thus far. Jacob's exhortation presupposes that he
and his family members have been in a state of defilement or uncleanness, and that it is inappropriate to meet with this God in that state. The
consequent actions of his family members imply that they were following a custom or a religious ritual familiar in Mesopotamia and probably
also in Canaan, and that a belief system or a world-view lay behind that
custom or ritual in which a state of uncleanness and cleanness, purity
and acceptance were more or less defined. But it is equally possible that
this belief system or world-view partly reflects the ideas of the Genesis
author(s),[1] who wanted to characterize Jacob as contaminated by the

---

1. According to traditional source analysis portions of Genesis (including Gen.
35.2-4), Exodus and Numbers, all of Leviticus and a small part of Deuteronomy
belong to P; cf. Eissfeldt 1965: 155-241; Fohrer 1970: 103-92; Rendtorff 1985:
131-64.

idolatry of Mesopotamia. A purification ritual was thus in order before he entered the promised land.

Apart from this, we have a number of references to death and mourning in the patriarchal stories (cf. §4a below). Although there are no explicit statements about purification following death, it is possible that some of these instances involved such rites. The aim of this chapter is to investigate the ancient Near Eastern and the Priestly backgrounds for the ideas of purity and impurity, and thereby see how these backgrounds enlighten our knowledge of the religion of the patriarchs.

2. *Pollution and Purity in the Ancient Near East*

The idea of purity in the ancient Near East is hard to define. Though this is the fundamental concept in many ancient religions, no one knows how far this goes back into a non-literate culture (Douglas 1966: 4). Sometimes it is argued that primitive peoples make little distinction between sacredness and uncleanness so that 'the sacred is at once "sacred" and "defiled"' (Eliade 1958: 14-15). This apparent contradiction will be resolved when we examine the various ideas about purity and defilement in the ancient Near East (cf. van der Toorn 1985: 27).

a. *Assyrian and Babylonian Sources*
The various words associated with purity also occur in texts of healing rituals, exorcisms and even legal freedom. Four Akkadian words, *ellu*, *ebbu*, *namru* and *zakû*, denote different aspects of purity. *Ellu* primarily denotes cleanliness in the sense of brilliance, luminosity or absence from dirt. It is used of both secular and cultic objects (*CAD*, IV: 102-106), and in legal contexts of freedom of slaves, and of real estates (*CAD*, IV: 105-106), but never physical cleanliness (*CAD*, IV: 4; cf. van der Toorn 1985: 27, 28). Similarly, *ebbu* describes glittering precious stones, lustrous surface quality of metals, stones and wood (*CAD*, IV: 1, 2, 4). It also refers to trustworthy people, but mostly to deities, ritual animals and objects in a cultic sense.[2]

While *namru* describes materials, artefacts, stars and gods as 'bright' and 'shiny', and of humans as 'healthy' and 'whole' (*CAD*, XI: 1, 239-44), *zakû* refers to liquids and sky as 'clear', and to garments and

---

2. An exception to this is non-cultic garments, which are referred to as 'clean', but only in a sense; *CAD*, IV: 3; cf. van der Toorn 1985: 28.

humans as 'clean' and 'in good order' (*CAD*, XXI: 23-24). *Zakû* also
refers to the freedom of persons and merchandise in legal contexts
(*CAD*, XXI: 23-24). Sometimes the verbal form, *zukkû*, refers to ritual
cleaning or washing of impurities (*CAD*, XXI: 28-29, 32). Both *namru*
and *zakû* are contrasted with *ešû*, 'gloomy, dull', and *dalḫu*, 'blurred',
'muddy'.[3] Some of these words are also used in various exorcisms and
healing rituals. The variety of ways these words are used suggest that
there is enough flexibility with the words to apply to any kind of ail-
ment, physical, psychological or spiritual, that hinders a person's happy
life (van der Toorn 1985: 28). In fact the purification often mentioned
in the various incantations is, strictly speaking, not ritual purification
but healing of various kinds. This will become clear as we look at some
examples.

Purity of the Gods. Gods, kings, priests, their bodies and their activities
are often described as sacred in Old Babylonian and Old Assyrian
literature. The deities especially are described as pure, with shining
light and brilliant face (e.g. Ištar, *elletum* and Ninurta, *ellu*) (*CAD*, IV:
104, 105). This is probably because of the anointing oil that was often
poured on their images, not to purify them (contra Kutsch 1963: 6) but
to give them a shining glow which represented both their happy mood
and their strength and vitality.[4] Sometimes the name of the deity is
described as holy (Langdon 1927: 16). However, even the gods could
be defiled by the evil spirits just like humans, hence they resort to
carrying amulets to ward off the demons (Saggs 1962: 303; cf. Toombs
1962: 643). This evidence suggests that a certain idea of purity was
ascribed to the gods and the objects associated with them in the ancient
Near East, but it is not clear what this purity meant for worshippers in
their relationship with the gods or in their daily living.

Purity of the Ritual Materials. The idea of clean and unclean occurs in
relation to not only the abodes and furnishings of the gods but also the
cultic objects, materials and animals in cultic use from the Old Assyrian and Old Babylonian periods.[5]

---

3. Van der Toorn 1985: 28; in *CAD*, XXI: 26, *zakû* and *dalḫu* are contrasted.
4. Cf. Meier 1937: 31, 32; Veenhof 1966: 309; *ANET*, 97; van der Toorn 1985:
28.
5. Occasional references to such ideas can be found from an even earlier period,

The purification of the temple forms an important part of the ritual on the fifth day of the New Year Akitu Festival in Babylonia, in which the *mašmašu*-priest performs a purification ritual. The ritual affirms that god Marduk purifies the temple.[6] Such an idea of purification presupposes that the sanctuaries were inherently holy because the gods dwelt there, and that for some reason they became defiled. This is clearly evident in the Sumerian hymns to Enlil and Šamaš (*ANET*, 574; cf. Langdon 1927: 50).

Purity of Individuals. The cultic status of individuals is described as clean or unclean depending on their status as priests or laymen. The priests could not serve the gods if deformed in limb, face, eyes, teeth or finger, or if he had a sickly look or pimpled face (Contenau 1959: 281, 287; cf. *CAD*, IV: 106). If a man has continual ejaculations, he is described as both impure and carrying a weighty sin, but he could be purified through rituals.[7] Similarly, a menstruating woman is described as unclean (*CAD*, IV: 106). The sacrifices are taboo for an unclean person (*CAD*, IV: 106; cf. Milgrom 1970: 35). Such ritual language is also used in the Epic of Gilgamesh when Utnapishtim advised the boatman, Urshanabi, to lead Gilgamesh to the place of washing before he was given the plant of life (*ANET*, 96; cf. *CAD*, I: 106). As in the Bible, higher standards are required with regard to those serving in the temple, but unlike the Bible, sin is attached to semen ejaculation in Babylon.

Purity and Healing. A large number of Akkadian texts refer to healing from various diseases as purification or cleansing. Nearly all of these diseases were believed to stem from evil spirits or sorcery, although they were sometimes attributed to the individual's negligence with regard to certain ritual taboos, for example, eating taboo food, eating or drinking from an accursed man or sinner, treading in libation or unclean water, or nail-parings, or shavings from the armpit, or shoes with holes in them, or a tattered belt, or a leather bag with black magic, or scales of a leper (Reiner 1956: 137-43; Saggs 1962: 318-20); casting eye on the water of unwashed hands or touching an accursed man,

e.g. in a Sumerian hymn to Enlil-bani dating from about 1850 BCE; cf. Langdon 1923a: 15. For examples, see Langdon 1927: 27; *CAD*, IV: 3-4, 103-105.

6. *ANET*, 337-80; cf. Weinfeld 1983: 111-13; Wright 1987: 62-65.

7. *CAD*, IV: 104; cf. XXI: 24. It is probable that this refers to the chronic discharge mentioned in Leviticus.

coming into contact with an unclean or bewitched person.[8] A series of texts called *utukki limnuti*,[9] the pure 'water of Ea' and the magic power of the tamarisk, the powerful weapon of Anu, were often used in exorcising these evil spirits.[10] Besides, the burning rituals called *Šurpu* (for unknown evils)[11] and *Maqlû* (for known evils of witchcraft)[12] are performed. The objects given over to fire in these rituals are viewed as carriers of the patient's sins and diseases.[13] While the Old Babylonian *lipšur litanies* are used for moral sins such as murder, adultery and false oaths,[14] the Late Assyrian and Late Babylonian *Dingir-ša-dib-ba* incantations (literally 'incantation for appeasing an angry god') are used for evils thought to have come from a deity. Although the Akkadian *Namburbi* texts (eighth–sixth centuries BCE) are concerned with the rituals against unsolicited portents (e.g. the presence or actions of a threatened man, strangers, domestic and wild animals, household objects and a limited range of natural phenomena, especially light and fire),[15] and the Babylonian 'Prophylactic figures' (eighth century BCE) with rituals against the attacks of the demons on houses, the idea of purification often features in the rituals (Gurney 1935: 31-96). Thus, by implication, ritual/moral sins, evil spirits/gods and evil portents caused disease which in turn resulted in uncleanness, and exorcism and rituals brought healing which in turn resulted in purification. However, the sufferer often did not know by what acts or omissions he offended the gods.

8.   Thompson 1903: 39-49, 51-63; 1904: 137-39; for Sumerian examples, see Langdon 1927: 54.

9.   Thompson (1903: xi-xii) dates the ritual texts to the fourth millennium BCE, Saggs (1962: 308) to the late third millennium.

10.   Thompson 1903: xlviii, xlix, 19-23. The tamarisk tree appears again and again in the process of cleansing from the evil spirits, see especially pp. 103, 119, 173 and 197; cf. on Ea's magic, Thompson 1904: 21, 107-111; on the tamarisk tree, p. 63; Saggs 1962: 305.

11.   'Burning' rituals, used mainly to get rid of sins. The sufferer's sins, ritual offences or taboos that were thought to have offended the gods were made over to some object which was then burned; Saggs 1962: 308; Reiner 1958: 1-3.

12.   Saggs 1962: 308; Abusch 1974: 251-62; cf. Gurney 1960: 221-27.

13.   Reiner 1958: I, ll. 1-24; V–VI, ll. 164-69; VII, ll. 69-83; VIII, ll. 79-84; cf. Reiner 1956: 139; *CAD*, IV: 5.

14.   The root *ellu* is used to refer to purification in these rituals. But the most common word is 'Lipšur', which means 'to absolve' or 'to undo' evil.

15.   Caplice 1965: 105-31; cf. 1967: 5-36; 1970: 137-39, 142, 146, 149.

Sometimes he simply confesses his many sins in the hope that confession alone will appease the gods. At others he denies any consciousness of sins, though admitting that they must have taken place since man is naturally sinful.[16] Hence the priest enumerates all possible offences—religious, ritual and moral. It appears from the priest's enumeration of a large number of deities and the possible moral and ritual sins that the precise requirements of particular deities are unclear. In any case, no deity is described as claiming a particular kind of purity, or prohibiting a certain defilement. Therefore it is not certain whether the texts are concerned with the individual's ritual purity and defilement, and whether these were ultimate concerns for the individual to be permitted or banned from the presence of the deity.

b. *Hittite Sources*

In contrast to Babylonian rituals, in which evil and disease are almost always seen as the result of evil spirits who need to be exorcised, the Hittite rituals treat evil and disease largely as the result of physical contamination or the anger of a god who needs to be appeased (cf. Wright 1987: 262). 'Only where a god was thought to be involved was it necessary to combine them [exorcism and appeasement] with methods proper to religion, such as prayer and sacrifice' (Gurney 1977: 46, 47; cf. Wright 1987: 31-60, 261-71). However, most of these rituals are still concerned chiefly with disease, infirmity or portended evil with which a person has been afflicted, and not ritual purity which is expected from, or desired by, a deity or devotee.[17]

The basic idea of purity and defilement apparently derives from the idea of cleanness and dirt in daily experience. Thus the bakers who make daily loaves for the gods and the place where they make them must be ritually clean (Furlani 1938: 355-56). No pig or dog was allowed to 'stay at the door of the place where the loaves were broken' (*ANET*, 207). Sometimes even abstract words of evil, curse, oath or blasphemy were thought to defile the gods and the priests, and certain

16. Lambert 1974: 274-75, 283, 285. Interestingly the patient relates that he entered the temple in a 'state of impurity', *la elluti* (the same root as seen above), and transgressed the 'rules of the gods', though it is not made clear what these rules were.

17. It is healing or relief from certain evil that is sought in most of the rituals, rather than purity (*pace* Wright).

rituals were performed to remove their evil effects (*ANET*, 346). However, the concern of these rituals often appears to be the fear of the evil effects that might follow the curse, not ritual purity itself. Similar beliefs of fear are expressed in the Hittite ritual of *Tunnawi*.[18] The uncleanness is not specified, except in terms of disability, impotence and barrenness (Goetze and Sturtevant 1938: 5), and the possible influences, such as evil, uncleanness, witchcraft, and so on (Goetze and Sturtevant 1938: 13, 15, 17, 19, 21). Elaborate rituals were then performed with the aid of sacrifices (cf. Gurney 1952: 151). Thus uncleanness in this context actually means sickness, and purification means healing. It is not certain if there is any idea of ritual impurity that banned a layman from approaching a deity.

Ritual Purity of the Priests. The priests must not approach the gods without being ritually pure (*ANET*, 209; Gurney 1952: 150). Sexual intercourse defiles the priests and the penalty for those who fail to observe purification rites before resuming their duties is capital punishment. Deformed and mutilated persons are taboo in and around temple precincts, and a ritual purification must be performed if they happen to walk about the temple (*ANET*, 497). This suggests deformed people cannot even worship at the temple, which clearly excludes them from temple service.

Purity of Sacrificial Materials. Animals for offerings must be without blemish (Gurney 1952: 151), and everything that was presented to the gods must be holy and pure. The utensils and the vessels by which offerings are made to gods must be kept ritually pure. No common person may draw near to them (*ANET*, 397, 399). If a dog or pig approaches the temple vessels, or the food table, or eats the sacrificial loaves, all of them must be discarded.[19]

c. *Egyptian and Ugaritic Sources*
Due to constraints on space, I will not be able to treat in detail the concept of purity in these sources. The common phrase, 'pure hands', w'b 'wy, is used to describe priests in the presence of the gods or

18. This probably refers to the 'Old Woman' who performs the ritual on behalf of the afflicted; Goetze and Sturtevant 1938: 5.
19. *ANET*, 209, 497. Similar instructions are found to keep the king pure, but they may be aimed more at personal safety than purity.

servants before kings, and the idea of purification plays an important role in the cult of the dead (*TDOT*, 288; cf. Chapter 2 §26). However, the concept of purity appears to have little significance in the Ugaritic literature.[20] The contrast between the extent of ancient Near Eastern sources on purity and the biblical texts may not necessarily be due to lack of interest in it but partly due to the survival of different kinds of texts. Nevertheless, the frequent references to purity and rituals for purification suggest that it was very important in Babylonia.

3. *Pollution and Purity in Israel*

In contrast to the ancient Near Eastern literature where the concept of purity and impurity was only a secondary interest, the Israelite sources, especially the Priestly texts, present a highly developed system of purity and impurity in relation to the sanctuary where God was believed to be present. Everything was graded according to its proximity to, or function in, that sanctuary. Areas, cultic furniture and the ministrants within the sanctuary were graded according to their closeness to the 'most holy place' within the sanctuary where God's presence is epitomized.

The range of words and concepts used to identify and to deal with the impurity in different contexts (personal, social, religious) and in different respects (food, sex, relationships) suggests that Israel is more sensitive toward impurity than any other culture in the ancient Near East.[21] I shall study these Hebrew terms in their important contexts, especially in the Priestly texts, to obtain a comprehensive picture of their meaning in relation to purity and defilement in Israel, and then compare the findings with the patriarchal idea of pollution and purity.

a. *Purity and Defilement in the Priestly System*
As noted above, everything in the Priestly system is graded according to its relation to God, who is thought of as dwelling in the sanctuary in the midst of the Israelite camp. Meanings are given to people, places

---

20. *UM*, 269, 270; *TDOT*, V: 288.

21. Four main words are used to signify the idea of purity and defilement: קדשׁ, 'holy', חלל, 'profane', 'common', טהר, 'clean', and טמא, 'unclean'. Other less common words convey similar ideas. For a complete list of words and references, see Jenson 1992: 40; *ABD*, VI: 729.

and objects according to their closeness to, or function in, the sanctuary, which is the heart of the priestly hierocracy, the high priest being the head and the clergy the skeleton (Wellhausen 1885: 127). So we shall begin with the heart of the Israelite hierocracy, the tabernacle/sanctuary of God.

The Tabernacle. According to P the tabernacle constitutes two parts (Exod. 25.9, 40; 26.30; 27.8). The inner sanctum is the holy of the holies, קֹדֶשׁ הַקֳּדָשִׁים[22] (Exod. 26.33).[23] Everything is graded according to its proximity to this space. Next to this is the outer sanctum, the holy place, קֹדֶשׁ (Exod. 26.33; 29.30; Lev. 6.30; Num. 28.7). The two sancta are separated by a curtain. Another curtain separates the outer sanctum from the court, a rectangular enclosure.[24] The court is graded as a holy place, מְקוֹם קֹדֶשׁ (Exod. 29.31; Lev. 6.9, 19), and the camp around is a clean place, מְקוֹם טָהוֹר (Lev. 10.14; 4.12; 6.11; Num. 19.9). The materials used in each area of the tabernacle are also graded according to their closeness to the holy of the holies.

Nevertheless, the tabernacle built in this manner does not automatically become holy. The ritual status of the materials of the tabernacle can be viewed only as pure (Jenson 1992: 93), and it must be elevated by a 'founding ritual' (Gorman 1990: 54) of consecration (Exod. 40.9-11; Lev. 8.10-11), by which God will sanctify the tabernacle through the real presence of his glory (29.43-45).[25]

The People of Israel. As noted above, Israelite society constitutes a clear hierarchy of priests, Levites and the people in general. The purity of the group depends on its closeness to the sanctuary. Aaron being the high priest heads the hierarchy and all priests must come only from his line. The initiation of the priesthood, described in great detail (Exod. 28–29; Lev. 8–9), takes place along with the founding ritual of the tabernacle with the appropriate rituals. From this moment the priests

22. Baudissin (1878: 20) first proposed the fundamental idea of the root as 'separation', and argued that קֹדֶשׁ is synonymous with טָהוֹר. But this view is strongly disputed by Costecalde (1985: 1391-93), who sees its root meaning as 'consecration'.

23. The Priestly system does not envisage a shrine for a form of God.

24. The position of the tent in the court is adapted from Haran 1978: 149-56.

25. Wilson 1992: 137, 185. Cf. the idea of Marduk purifying the temple, as we have seen above, but it is not integrated in a context like the biblical ritual.

are permanently set apart from the community and elevated to a holiness equivalent to that of the sanctuary where they minister. However, no member of the priestly family with any physical defect or deformity may officiate in the cult, although he may partake of any of the offerings that are permissible to any priest (Lev. 21.16-24).[26]

The priesthood is given a unique grade of holiness with corresponding special rules of ritual, personal, family and social life. The high priest ministers in the inner sanctum, implying a special degree of holiness to him (Exod. 28.5-43) (his garments possess communicable holiness; Jenson 1992: 127), while the priests officiate in the holy place, the outer sanctum (Num. 4.16, 28, 33). The high priest must marry only a virgin from his own clan, while ordinary priests may marry any virgin from Israel or a priestly widow (Lev. 21.1-15; cf. Ezek. 44.22).[27] The high priest cannot defile himself with a corpse or mourn for anyone, even his own wife, while the priests may defile themselves for close relatives, such as father, mother, brother or virgin sister.

The Levites stand next in the hierarchy. They are never described as holy (Jenson 1992: 131), but were consecrated to God in place of the first born of Israel, and they have no access to the holy things on pain of death (Num. 4.15). They are responsible for guarding the tabernacle from defilement from the outside while the priests protect the holy items inside. They probably acted as a buffer zone between the Israelites and the cult to protect the purity of the sanctuary. However, their ritual status is probably clean like other Israelites.

The people in general are next in line in order of purity. The normal Israelite is pure, טהור,[28] for most of his life, and purity is a necessary precondition for anyone to approach the sanctuary and offer sacrifices. From here on the grading of people and objects is that of 'unclean', that is, those outside the camp, certain foods, and the gentiles. The 'very unclean' are those contaminated by the major impurities, such as scale disease, abnormal discharge and corpse contamination. Some scholars term this grading scale a 'holiness spectrum' (cf. Jenson 1992: 36-37). So the ordinary Israelites, and even the priests when they are off duty, are clean and stand in the centre of the grading scale dividing the holy

---

26. The ban on deformed persons in and around the temple precincts in Hittite religion seems to be more severe than it is in the Priestly system, see §2b above.

27. An ordinary Israelite can also marry a divorcee or a non-priestly widow.

28. This root with its nominal and adjectival form occurs over 200 times in the Hebrew Bible. Its most common occurrence is in the cultic contexts; *THAT*, 647.

and the very holy on the one hand and the unclean and the very unclean on the other.

However, the normal ritual status of priests or laity can be defiled and the unclean cannot partake in the cult, especially the flesh of the peace offering.[29] But anyone can be purified with an appropriate ritual and be brought back to his normal status. I shall now turn to this various ritual defilement and its remedy in the Priestly system.

b. *Ritual Defilement*

The causes of impurity stem from some of the most mundane and common aspects of daily life, such as food, genital discharge, illegal sex, murder, disease and death.[30] Among these, scale disease, abnormal discharge and corpse-contamination are viewed as major impurities. People affected with them are to be put out of the camp because their very presence in the camp would defile the tabernacle. But they can be allowed back into the camp after appropriate rituals. There is no sin or guilt attached to their impurities unless they fail to follow the stipulated purification rituals.[31] I shall summarize the priestly views about these issues and their relevance to the idea of purity in Israel beginning with the dietary laws. Leviticus 11 forms the first section of a series of instructions given on ritual purification from various impurities, including childbirth (ch. 12), skin and fungus diseases (chs. 13, 14) and bodily discharges (ch. 15) affecting the people of Israel.

Food Laws. Leviticus 11, 20.25-26 and Deut. 14.3-21 are the most important texts dealing with the food laws of Israel.[32] The thrust of Leviticus 11 is to identify the *unclean*, טמא, and the *abominable*, שקץ, animals which communicate degrees of impurity, and to give procedures of purification in the event of pollution contracted by them. However, I cannot discuss here the issue of why certain foods are טמא and

29. Lev. 7.19-21; Num. 9.13; 2 Chron. 30.17-19; Ezra 6.19-22; cf. Num. 18.11, 13; Lev. 10.14; 22.4.

30. Wright helpfully distinguishes between necessary and avoidable impurities; *ABD*, VI: 730.

31. Jenson's (1992: 139) view that the restrictions are only precautionary, not punitive, is an understatement. Cf. Mesopotamian evidence that people with abnormal discharge are guilty of a weighty sin and Hittite evidence that those who fail to purify themselves after intercourse are liable to capital punishment.

32. Deut. 14.3-21 is almost exactly parallel to Lev. 11, with the ideas of clean and unclean described by the same words. טמא is used thrice (vv. 8, 10, 19) and

others are not, or which came first, criteria or taboos.[33] The author's reasons in vv. 44-45 seem to be theological, implied in v. 44: אני יהוה כי, 'for I am Yawheh' and כי קדוש אני, 'for I am holy'. As Milgrom notes, a phrase with כי 'always provides the rationale for the previous statement' (1991: 686). Thus the reason Israel must avoid certain animals[34] in their diet is that, first, Yahweh their God is holy. Secondly, the people who follow him likewise must be holy (Feldman 1977: 52; Houston 1993: 54). This is reinforced by the idea of Yahweh's legal ownership of Israel in v. 45 (cf. Lev. 19.2; 20.7, 26) (Milgrom 1991: 688; Houston 1993: 54).

Similarly a distinction is placed upon the animal kingdom in relation to Israel that some are טהור while others are טמא, although there is nothing intrinsically bad in the forbidden animals themselves. Yet since they are forbidden they are 'desacralized, undivine and sacrally unfit' (Feldman 1977: 51). While the food regulations mark Israel's separateness from other nations, the bodily discharge, various kinds of scale disease and death pollution separate the individual from other Israelites as unclean.

Genital Discharges. Five major types of bodily discharges, varying in their duration and intensity and accordingly in their procedures of purification, have been identified in the Priestly system. All of them are described as unclean, טמא, and they exclude individuals from normal social intercourse and from worship.

First is a woman's discharge after childbirth (Lev. 12). The impurity involved here is compared to that of menstruation (vv. 2, 5). The second is the woman's normal discharge or menstruation, נדה (Lev. 15.19-24). The third, the woman's abnormal discharge, זבה (Lev. 15.25-30), is different from menstruation. She will be unclean, טמא, for all these impurities for varying periods. However, there is no moral guilt or

---

טהור twice (vv. 11, 20) in the same sense as in Lev. 11. Cf. Gen. 7.2, 8, where טהור is used both positively and negatively to designate 'clean' and 'not clean' animals. For a recent and detailed analysis of these texts and a comprehensive bibliography on dietary laws, see Firmage 1990: 184; Milgrom 1991: 643-742; Houston 1993.

33. For a critique of different views, see Feldman 1977: 49-53; Wenham 1981: 6-11; Milgrom 1990: 176-91; Firmage 1990: 177-82; Jenson 1992: 76-79; Houston 1993: 69-78; 93-114.

34. The immediate context may refer only to swarming creatures of v. 43 but the verb רמש also in v. 46 can apply to all animals; cf. Gen. 7.21; 9.3 for land animals, and Gen. 1.21, Ps. 69.35 for sea creatures; Milgrom 1991: 687.

social stigma attached to her impurity (Milgrom 1991: 760), nor is there any hint of apotropaic or medicinal functions to the sacrifice as in other ancient Near Eastern cultures (cf. Egyptian and Hittite customs, *ERE*, X: 47; Milgrom 1991: 750).

The fourth, the abnormal male discharge, זב (Lev. 15.2-15), is probably due to a type of gonorrhoeal disease (Milgrom 1991: 907). This person is unclean, טמא, and becomes a primary source of uncleanness. His bed, saddle and seat, as also his body and spittle,[35] become potential secondary sources of pollution. When he is 'healed', טהר,[36] of his discharge he must bring an offering of two turtle doves or two young pigeons to the priest who 'offers'[37] them 'for his discharge', which implies that the person with the impurities is not accused of sin as in Mesopotamia.[38]

The fifth, the normal male discharge with no intercourse involved, is ritually unclean, טמא.[39] As in the ancient Near East, the discharge during normal intercourse defiles both men and women. That sexual intercourse pollutes and must be followed by a bath is attested among Hittites,[40] Sabaeans, ancient Persians (Milgrom 1991: 932), Hindus (Manu [2.181; 5.63, 144; 11.121-23] cited in Milgrom 1991: 932) and Greeks (Burkert 1985: 87; cf. Milgrom 1991: 932). But only among the Hebrews does pollution remain until evening.[41]

---

35. Among the Hittites, saliva was considered a source of impurity, and in Mesopotamia, a symptom of certain diseases or poisonous in the form of foam. But in Israel, spitting was just an expression of disdain (Num. 12.14; Deut. 25.9), not a source of impurity (Milgrom 1991: 915).

36. טהר in v. 13 is used in this sense and not in ritual sense (Milgrom 1991: 921). Interestingly, this is probably the only place where the idea of 'purity' or 'clean' is used of healing disease. In the ancient Near East, however, the most common terms used for healing indicate 'to clean, purify'.

37. The verb used here is עשה which 'in cultic context connotes the entire sacrificial ritual (e.g. 15.30; 9.7; 14.30)' (Milgrom 1991: 925). Cf. Chapter 2 n. 35.

38. A man with continual ejaculations carries a weighty sin, see above; cf. Milgrom 1991: 926.

39. In Egypt, one had to abstain from sex for at least a whole day, nine days for a priest, before entering a temple; Sauneron 1960: 39, 40; cf. Milgrom 1991: 932.

40. See the section on Hittite rituals above. An interesting example of affliction of loss of speech on king Mursili because of his neglect of purification after sexual intercourse is cited in Goetze and Pedersen (1934: ll. 18-21) cited in Milgrom 1991: 933.

41. That semen defiles because it involves loss of life was first suggested by Ramban; Milgrom 1991: 934; 1001-1003; cf. Wenham 1983: 433-34; *ANET*, 665.

Disease. Leviticus 13 and 14 deal with the identification and purification of a kind of disease called צרעת, which affects people (13.2-46;
14.1-32), clothes (13.47-58) and houses (14.33-53). צרעת in its various
forms occurs no less than 33 times in these two chapters, and another
22 times elsewhere.[42] It is not a leprosy as has been traditionally translated, but probably a type of scale disease which may not be infectious,
or dangerous. It is ritually unclean, טמא (used 30 times in this context),
like other impurities discussed above (cf. Milgrom 1991: 817-18). In
each of the cases symptoms, priestly inspection, diagnosis and prescription are described. Elaborate rituals, including a bird-blood ritual, are
performed for people and houses (cf. Wright 1987: 78; Chapter 2 n. 54).

Death. The priestly system reckons corpse contamination as the highest
form of pollution.[43] The law of corpse-contamination (Num. 19) states
that persons contaminated by corpse pollution (Num. 19.11, 14-16) can
be purified by the sprinkling of 'the water of impurity' מי נדה, on the
third and the seventh day of their impurity followed by washing their
clothes and bathing and waiting till evening on the seventh day. Similarly, inanimate things are to be purified by the sprinkling of the water
of impurity on the third and seventh day. But metal articles, besides
sprinkling, must be purified by fire while non-metal objects must be
washed with water (vv. 17-19; cf. Num. 31.19-24). Anyone who fails to
purify himself from such a defilement pollutes the tabernacle/sanctuary
of Yahweh and consequently risks the extirpation of himself from the
people of God (19.13, 20). The priest must be kept apart from corpse
contamination[44] at all costs[45] since he deals with the holy things of God
(Lev. 21.1-4, 10-12, cf. Lev. 10.4-7).[46]

42. Exod. 4.6; Lev. 22.4; Num. 5.2; 12.10 (×2); Deut. 24.8; 2 Sam. 3.29; 2 Kgs
5.1, 3, 6, 7, 11, 27 (×2); 7.3, 8; 15.5; 2 Chron. 26.19, 20, 21 (×2), 23.
43. The author of 2 Kgs 23.14, 16, 20 probably had this view; cf. Levine 1993:
469, 477.
44. Corpse-contaminated persons and objects carry a secondary pollution, v. 22,
cf. Lev. 22.4-6.
45. The only instance in priestly legislation where a priest is explicitly stated to
be defiled is when he officiates in the red cow preparation.
46. It is interesting to note that a Nazirite during his vow is set on a par with a
ministering high priest in relation to death pollution (Num. 6.6-9), and in some
cases, such as wine, he is under stricter laws than a high priest (Num. 6.4 cf. Lev.
10.8).

If we go backwards from death pollution on the scale of impurity we come across death at work or symbolized in various degrees in those affected by various kinds of impurities. The scale-diseased experience a kind of living death (cf. Num. 12.12), being excluded from the community and the cult (Jenson 1992: 84). So also the זב, זבה, the parturient and the menstruant are excluded for declining periods of time from the social and cultic access. Then come those polluted by semen discharge, intercourse, carcase-contamination, and so on. Not only the results (denial of social and cultic access), but also the cause (loss of semen, blood, infection) of impurities are to be seen as a form of death at work in those who are affected by them. Thus anything related to death or loss of life, either real or symbolic, pollutes in the Priestly system. But appropriate rituals can restore the unclean to their normal status, that is, clean. The range of sacrifices such as עלה, חטאת, אשם and מנחה offered in these rituals suggest that they deal with any sacrilege against Yahweh or inadvertent sin related to God's moral and ritual law.

c. *Comparative Analysis*
First, in all the extra-biblical examples of ritual cleansing the parallel with biblical ritual exists only in the release of the birds. Thereafter the analogy breaks down. As Wright correctly notes, the biblical rite is intended to remove the residual impurity after the healing, whereas in Mesopotamian ritual it is not a disease but an evil, or sometimes a suspected evil. And the bird in the ritual is concretized as the evil itself and the evil is removed as the bird is dismissed. But no biblical ritual is meant for healing, and the released bird in this case does not take away the disease but only the ritual impurities.[47] Only in one case, the scapegoat ritual, is it assumed that the dismissed animal takes away the sins of the community confessed over it by the high priest. However, this ritual has nothing to do with the particular evils stemming from sins of the individual.

Secondly, the cultic law implies, but does not explicitly state, that the disease could be a result of moral failures on the part of the afflicted. The various sacrifices prescribed for the healed person point in this direction (e.g. the אשם covers the sins related to sacrilege against Yahweh

47. Wright (1987: 84 n. 37; 85), though correct in his argument, is still vague in his definition of evil as he confuses it with impurity, which the priestly writer is at pains to avoid.

[Milgrom 1976: 80-82], while the חטאת, עלה and מנחה which serve an expiatory function, cover a person's inadvertent sins related to God's moral as well as ritual law) (Milgrom 1991: 822). Other non-priestly texts confirm this view (Miriam, Num. 12.9; Gehazi, 2 Kgs 5.27; Uzziah, 2 Chron. 26.18-21; cf. 2 Kgs 5; 2 Sam. 3.29; Deut. 28.27). In other words, as the disease proceeds from God, so also does the healing (cf. Lev. 14.34). This is particularly important for the priestly editor because all over the ancient Near East such things are taken as signs of the portended evil caused by either evil spirits or a sorcerer.

Thirdly, the sole concern of the biblical rite is impurity and its implications for the community and the sancta, whereas the sole concern of the non-biblical rites is the evil in its various manifestations—various kinds of disease, fear, misfortune, failure, defeat and even death—but never the impurity. Ritual impurity or breaking ritual taboos could be the cause of the evil, but its removal or restoring of purity is never the object of the rituals. This is the fundamental difference with which one must reckon. There is the idea of purity in the ancient Near East, but it is often identified with healing and wholeness. There is no rationale for purity, and logically there could be no demand for it. This is probably the unique contribution of the Priestly writer.

4. Pollution and Purity in the Patriarchal Narratives

As noted in my introduction, there are a number of allusions to death and burial mourning customs in the patriarchal narratives. I shall first examine these instances to see whether they reflect a belief of pollution contracted by a corpse or tombs such as was common in Israel and the ancient Near East. Then I shall examine the one clear incidence of purification in the Jacob cycle to discern its implications for the religion of the patriarch.

a. Pollution in Relation to Death and Burial
It is not certain whether the patriarchal stories show any concern for defilement contracted through contact with the dead. Several times death, burial and even mourning are recorded but the texts seem to be interested more in the grief caused by the death of the loved ones and their proper burial than in any pollution caused by the dead.[48] For

---

48. Gen. 23 cf. 24.67; 25.7-10; 35.18,19; 35.29; 47.29-30; 49.29-32; 50.5, 13,

instance, there is no mourning recorded at the death and burial of Abraham, Isaac or Rachel, while it is recorded for Sarah and for Joseph's assumed death, and it is alluded to in the case of minor characters like Deborah, Rebekah's nurse and Judah's unnamed wife (Gen. 37.34, 35; 35.8; 38.12). The concept of pollution caused by death is more likely to occur where mourning rituals are described. So I shall examine Genesis 23 and 50, where mourning for Sarah and Jacob are recorded.

Genesis 23. As I have argued in Chapter 2 §4d, the exclusive use of ספד for mourning for the dead and בכה both for weeping in general and for mourning for the dead (v. 2) suggests that ritual mourning was involved in Genesis 23, although this chapter is mainly concerned with Abraham's purchase of the cave of Machpelah for Sarah's burial. This might involve other traditional mourning customs (cf. Chapter 2 n. 115). But is there an idea of pollution by death here? Westermann says: 'Das מלפני [in Gen. 23.4] bringt zum Ausdruck, daß ein Toter unrein ist'.[49] מלפני, literally 'from before me' or 'out of my sight', probably a fixed phrase, is also used in v. 8. The noun פני is variously used with the preposition מן to indicate removal from before a person, place or object, but there is no suggestion in any of the instances that the ritual status of the latter is in view.[50] Therefore Westermann's suggestion that Abraham's expression 'out of my sight', מלפני, indicates the uncleanness of the corpse is unlikely (no other commentator so far has suggested this). Nevertheless, the idea that death causes pollution is taken for granted in many ancient cultures, although it is not explicitly stated here.

Genesis 50.1-14. Jacob's death, burial and mourning involving both Egyptian and Israelite customs are elaborately described in this passage. There is an allusion to uncleanness caused by death in v. 4 where Joseph does not present himself before Pharaoh to request leave in

25. For a discussion on the concern for proper burial in Israel, see Chapter 2 §4d; cf. Sarna 1989: 156.

49. 'The expression מלפני [in Gen. 23.4] shows that a dead person is unclean', Westermann 1981: 457 = 1985: 373. The English translation misquotes the Hebrew as מעלפני.

50. Cf. Gen. 41.46; 47.10; Lev. 9.24; 10.2; Deut. 17.18; 1 Kgs 8.54; 2 Kgs 5.27; 6.32; Jon. 1.3, 10; Est. 1.19 Eccl. 10.5, etc.; BDB, 817-18. Only in 2 Kgs 5.27 is the person removed unclean, but this is not indicated by מלפני.

order to go to Canaan to bury Jacob. This is probably because a person in mourning clothes is not allowed in the presence of a king (Est. 4.2; Sarna 1989: 348; cf. Westermann 1986: 199).

b. *Pollution and Purification in the Jacob Cycle*
Genesis 35.1-4 in Recent Discussion. We have a clear example of purification in Gen. 35.1-4, where Jacob exhorts his family members to purify themselves before they appear before the God of Bethel. Jacob's call to purification of his family is summed up in three imperatives and an action in vv. 2b and 4:

הסרו את־אלהי הנכר אשר בתככם	Put away the foreign gods that are among you
[51]והטהרו והחליפו שמלתיכם	and purify yourselves, and change your garments;
ויתנו אל־יעקב את כל־אלהי הנכר אשר בידם	So they gave to Jacob all the foreign gods that they had,
ואת־הנזמים אשר באזניהם	and the rings that were in their ears;
ויטמן אתם יעקב תחת האלה אשר עם־שכם	and Jacob hid them under the oak which was near Shechem.

The call to purification and the renunciation and burial of foreign gods raise serious issues with regard to their origin and setting, and many scholars have interpreted them assuming different situations behind vv. 2b and 4. Alt, Nielsen and Schmitt focus chiefly on Jacob's command to part with foreign gods and his subsequent action of burying them. For Alt 'the renunciation of foreign gods' was originally a Canaanite/Shechemite rite adopted by the Israelites who reduced it to a preparatory ritual for pilgrimage from Shechem to Bethel. Its origin lies in the exclusiveness of Yahwism and is closer to Josh. 24.14, 23 than to Gen. 35.2, 4. Thus in Gen. 35.1-4, 7 the Elohist projected on Jacob a custom practised in his time (Alt 1953: 79-88; cf. de Pury 1975: 573). Nielsen agrees with Alt that the ritual was of Canaanite origin, but thinks that it was a magical ritual analogous to those attested in the Egyptian execration texts and certain magical texts of Mesopotamia where it was

---

51. We may recall טהור, the common technical word, for purification in the Priestly writings.

used against enemies.[52] When the Israelites adopted it from the Canaanites, they also used it for a similar purpose, and only later did it take on
the new meaning of renunciation of foreign gods as in Josh. 24.14, 23
(Nielsen 1954–55: 103-22; 1955: 234-40).

Schmitt, on the other hand, rejects the views of both Alt and Nielsen.
He thinks that the burial of 'foreign gods' in Gen. 35.2, 4 could hardly
have its origin in the exclusivism of Yahwism. Nor do the foreign gods
represent the enemy figurines that were destroyed or abused as was the
practice in the execration texts and the Mesopotamian texts, but were
kept in the holy *temenos*. For Schmitt, the foreign gods were simple
'talismans' or 'guardian gods' analogous to teraphim (Gen. 31.19, 30-
35), and the burial of these statues was a once-for-all act which ought to
be compared to the foundation-deposit that guards the sanctuary against
its possible enemies. Thus Gen. 35.2, 4 belongs not to the 'pilgrimage
from Shechem to Bethel' but to the 'foundation legend' of the sanctuary of Shechem, and the burial of these statues would have been interpreted later as a 'renunciation' of the 'foreign gods' (Schmitt 1964: 48-
54, cited in de Pury 1975: 574-75).

Garcia-Treto focuses on Jacob's exhortation to purify and change
garments and the aspect of the renunciation of earrings, aspects largely
ignored by the previous scholars. He thinks that the ritual behind 35.1-4
was a 'transition rite' or a 'separation rite', analogous to that performed
by Muslim pilgrims before entering the sacred area of Mecca, in which
devotees not only put aside foreign gods (which he considers as fetishes
or guardian gods analogous to the teraphim) but also earrings (which
for him are charms), and purify themselves and change their clothes at
one holy place with a view to leaving for another.[53] He argues that the
text does not specify that Jacob 'buried' or 'destroyed' the figurines; it
simply states that Jacob 'hid' (ויטמן) them under the tree (cf. Keel 1973:
307-308), probably with a view to recovering them after the pilgrimage. The rite was later interpreted as a 'renunciation of foreign gods'.
Further, he identifies Bethel with Mount Gerizim, because it does not
make sense for pilgrims to perform the preparatory rite a good day's
journey before they enter the מקום area at Bethel. Thus 35.1-4, 7 does
not indicate Jacob's going up to Bethel, but rather explains the preparatory rite of Jacob and his clan at the sacred tree of Shechem (12.6),

52. It may be added here that the enemy figurines in the Mesopotamian rituals
were usually made for the purpose, not surrendered by the devotees.
53. Garcia-Treto 1967: 195-200, cited in de Pury 1975: 575-77; *ANET*, 144.

before they climb in procession up to the מקום of Bethel on Mount Gerizim, the traditional spot of Jacob's dream, where the main cultic act
unfolds (35.7, 14) (Garcia-Treto 1967: 202-204, cited in de Pury 1975:
575-77). De Pury rightly points out that this interpretation does not present the rite as a total reversal of its primitive sense but simply as a
'radicalisation' of its initial scope (de Pury 1975: 577).

However, de Pury rejects Garcia-Treto's hypothesis identifying the
Bethel of 35.1-4 with Mount Gerizim. For him Jacob's מקום should be
looked for between Bethel and Ai (12.8; 13.3-4). He agrees that the
rites of purification, if preparatory, could hardly begin at Shechem, but
he argues that they were performed in the vicinity of Bethel, probably
under the 'oak of weeping' where Deborah, Rachel's nurse, was buried.
He suggests that the 'oak of weeping' in the present tradition is a confusion for the 'palm of Deborah' (Judg. 4.5) probably situated in the
same region, because Deborah, Rachel's nurse, was unknown, and
burial under a tree is unattested elsewhere in the Old Testament. Thus
the burial associated with the 'oak of weeping' originally was concerned not with the death of Deborah but with the figurines and the
charms of the pilgrims who carried them to Bethel. If the tree bore the
name 'oak of weeping', it signified the ritual lamentation as part of the
'rites of passage' (cf. Hos. 12.5). Thus the rites of purification were not
'preparatory', as Garcia-Treto assumed, but the rite of renunciation of
foreign gods in vv. 2, 4 is the result of a later reinterpretation of the
primitive nomadic rite whose original establishment is attested in Josh.
24.23. These two rites were placed together when the two cycles of
Jacob (35.1-4 E) and Israel (33.18-20; 34 J), were joined by a redactor,
and the phrase in v. 4bβ אשר עם־שכם was introduced when these rites
of passage were transferred to Shechem (de Pury 1975: 578-83). However, de Pury gives no clear indication about when the rites were
transferred to Shechem and when the two cycles were joined together.
Garcia-Treto and de Pury differ only over the location where the purification rituals were performed, and they generally agree that the rituals
were preparatory to or part of the 'rites of passage' before entering into
the holy place.

Keel, by contrast, rejects the views of Garcia-Treto.[54] In his view,
removing foreign gods belonged to the Deuteronomic-Deuteronomistic

---

54. Keel (1973: 305-36, 326) shows on the basis of several close parallels from
the ancient Near East that the burial or hiding of idols, votive figurines, cult-
furniture and other articles considered sacred is relatively common in the ancient

layer, while burying idols was inserted by the Elohist. These two cannot come from same author because there is a tension between the two.
The demand to remove foreign gods in the Deuteronomic-Deuteronomistic literature was usually followed by a violent destruction of them
(Deut. 7.5, 25; 12.3; 2 Kgs 23.4-20), but in Jacob's story they were
carefully buried, as was common in the ancient Near East (Keel 1973:
331-32). Thus these statements have different origins and purposes.
The former usually occurs in the context of 'Yahweh war',[55] thus the
demand to purify themselves was not a preparation for a cultic act but
a preparation for 'divine horror'.[56] By inserting 35.2b, the glossator
intended to show how God intervened on behalf of Jacob when he
departed from Shechem. The Elohistic gloss (35.4), on the other hand,
understood the idols as the teraphim of Rachel and their burial as some
obsolete cult objects.

Westermann rejects the idea that the burial of the foreign gods could
be explained by parallels from archaeology (1985: 551), but accepts
that vv. 2b and 4 are later insertions. The ideas of renunciation of foreign gods in v. 2b and purification in v. 4 are combined here by the
redactor. They occur separately in Josh. 24.14 and Exod. 19.10-11, but
nowhere else together. They are out of place here as they presuppose
priests and a fixed cult. This was the context of the redactor who was
concerned with the purity of his time, according to which the patriarch
must renounce all that hinders Yahweh's worship before entering
Yahweh's land and sanctuaries (Westermann 1985: 549-51).

By contrast, Sarna interprets the renunciation of idols and the command for purification in the light of ch. 34 and the rest of the Old Testament. He thinks that the idols of vv. 2b and 4 were most likely
derived from the looting of Shechem. Like Keel, he notes that the usual
procedure of disposing of idols in the Old Testament, including Moses'
handling of the golden calf, was utter destruction, and that Jacob's
burial of them is unparalleled. It was probably intended to neutralize

Near East. Out of respect for their sanctity they were not thrown away but were
buried at a holy place when they become unusable due to lack of space or damage
or change of religious ideas.

    55. Josh. 24.14, 23; Judg. 10.16; 1 Sam. 7.3. Keel 1973: 327-28.
    56. The words used in the present context for purification, טהר, and fear, חטא
are (post)exilic; earlier קדש and פחד were used respectively (Exod. 19.14, 22; Josh.
7.13; 2 Sam. 11.4; Exod. 15.16; 1 Sam. 11.7; Isa. 2.10, 19, 21); Keel 1973: 329-30.

the veneration of the oak.[57] Similarly the subject of purification alludes to the theme of defilement dominant in ch. 34. Jacob's family was defiled both by the polluting effect of the idols carried by them or their captives and by corpse contamination at Shechem. Thus the command to purify themselves was to effect their passage 'from profane to sacred space', or to prepare them 'for an experience with God' (Sarna 1989: 240; cf. Wenham 1994: 324).

As can be observed from the above discussion, there is no consensus among scholars about the origin of either the burial of the foreign idols or the call to purification recounted in 35.2b, 4. The fact that 'burial of idols' is unattested elsewhere in the Old Testament suggests that the author was faithful to his sources. While Westermann acknowledges the patriarch's unique action of the burial of idols, and similar burial and purification in other religions in the ancient Near East, he still insists that these were a projection of the redactor's own situation onto the patriarch. But if the redactor was so concerned with the purity of his own day, why did he allow the patriarch to erect a pillar which was certainly unacceptable in his day?[58] Similarly, Keel accepts that the patriarch's action of burying idols is unique in the Bible and hints at the possible reflection of such a practice in the ancient Near East, but he tries to explain it entirely from the context of 'Yahweh war' in the Old Testament. While this is possible, the idea that the idols were always destroyed violently in the Deuteronomistic tradition is not true. The tradition in Joshua 24, for instance, does not recount what was done with the idols. Therefore, while the call for purification may be explained to some extent from the traditions of later Israel, the burial of idols cannot be explained. Similarly, de Pury's view that the burial of idols was a reinterpretation of the primitive nomadic rite such as attested in Josh. 24.23, or Garcia-Treto's idea that the idols were hidden for safe-keeping with a view to recovering them later, are not convincing. All these authors work on the basis of supposed tradition behind the present text, with varied hypotheses, none of which fits well with the plain reading of the text, especially in regard to the burial of the idols. Sarna, however, takes the final author's viewpoint and tries to establish links between Genesis 35 and 34 on the one hand and Genesis

57. Sarna 1989: 239-40; Keel (1973: 333) thinks that it was to desecrate the place.

58. Westermann (1985: 548-49) argues that the redactor is responsible for bringing together J and E materials and adding his own in ch. 35.

35 and the rest of the Old Testament on the other, and he reaches a similar conclusion as de Pury and Garcia-Treto. He strongly suggests that
the 'foreign gods' to be renounced probably came from the booty taken
from Shechem by the members of Jacob's family or their captives.
Besides flocks and people, Jacob's sons took 'all that was in the
houses' (34.29). Although this expression is hyperbolic, it can hardly
exclude whatever gold and silver was decked on their idols. Further, the
call for purification alludes to the corpse contamination involved in the
massacre of the Shechemites. This is probable in the light of the emphasis on defilement in ch. 34,[59] although this would mean that the author
who consistently portrayed the patriarchal religion thus far as one without priests or fixed sanctuary or laws of sacrifices and offerings, has
now attributed the knowledge of the law of corpse contamination or
pollution by idols to a patriarch who had no knowledge of Mosaic law.
As I have noted above, pollution or purity of an individual or community in Israel was mostly in relation to the sanctuary (see 'purification
offering' in Chapter 2 §3). It is unlikely that the author expected Jacob
to engage in rituals attendant at an Israelite sanctuary. On the other
hand, the patriarch's rituals involved the physical cleanliness of bathing
and washing clothes, as is attested in the ancient Near East and Israel,
and a burial of foreign gods, as is attested only in the ancient Near East.
Therefore, ch. 34 forms only part of the background, in that it explains
the patriarch's actions in relation to the idols. In his call for purification, however, the patriarch was probably following popular custom of
purification before approaching a holy place. Further, both the burial
of the idols and the call for purification can be explained in the light
of Jacob's experience at Bethel, the author's belief that the idols of
Laban's household had invaded Jacob's family, Jacob's long stay at
Shechem and finally Jacob's intention to rally his family's allegiance to
the God of Bethel. Thus all these can be explained from within the
Jacob cycle.

c. *A Synthesis*
The present form of Genesis 35 appears to be a carefully conceived unit
as it presupposes most, if not all, of the other Jacob stories contained in
Genesis (Westermann 1985: 549; Wenham 1994: 322). The links of the

---

59. טמא is used in vv. 5, 13, 27, probably in a moral sense, cf. חלל in 49.4;
Sarna 1989: 234, 333; *pace* Wright, *ABD*, VI: 73. Elsewhere P uses תועבה for
idolatry and intermarriage with idolaters.

story are obvious as the final author brings Jacob safely back from
Paddan-aram to Shechem (33.18-20). Following Dinah's rape (ch. 34),
he was forced to move to Bethel, but not without Yahweh's direction,
since Jacob had vowed to Yahweh to build him a sanctuary there if
Yahweh brought him safely back to his father's home (28.15; 31.13;
35.1; cf. 37.1). For the final author, vv. 1-7, with which we are concerned here, are a unit[60] which follows ch. 34 well. Jacob was preoccupied with, if not dismayed by, the consequences of his sons' violent
actions at Shechem. Genesis 35.1-7 not only shows God's way out of
Shechem but also links it up with Jacob's first journey (ch. 28). Jacob's
response in v. 3 not only picks up the ideas of v. 1 but also refers to his
troublesome life all along.[61] Verses 5-6 refer to the safe passage from
Shechem to Bethel, and v. 7 refers back to Jacob's vow in 28.20-22.

However, the new elements such as the call to purification and the
renunciation of foreign gods and other tokens of idolatry introduced in
vv. 2b and 4 are unique to the Jacob story. At least four reasons, as
mentioned above, may be given from the overall Jacob cycle to show
that these not only cohere with the total Jacob story but also explain the
author's view of the religion of the patriarch.

First, Jacob called for the ritual of purification and renunciation of
idols at Bethel because it was there he first felt the awesome presence
of God. He believed that the God of Bethel dwelt there in a special
way, hence he made a vow to raise a sanctuary there. That this experience and belief of Jacob has been reinforced all along his life in
Paddan-aram is acknowledged in v. 3, which probably recalls God's
promise of presence and the corresponding condition in Jacob's vow
(28.13-16, 20-22). Further, Jacob's wives clearly acknowledged that it
was the same God who gave them children (29.31–30.24), despite their
rivalry and magical means of obtaining children. Besides, Jacob himself acknowledged that it was the God of Bethel, the 'God of my father'
who helped him through his hard service to Laban (30.30; 31.5, 9, 10-
13, 42), and then from the danger of Esau on his return to the land of
Canaan (chs. 32, 33). Thus the place and the God associated with the
place became special in the experience of Jacob. Once the place is
reckoned as sacred on account of a theophany, the worshipper cannot

---

60. Gunkel 1902: 335; cf. Westermann 1985: 549; Wenham 1994: 323-24.

61. This may refer first to his flight from and return to his brother Esau (28.15;
32.9-12), then to his troubles with Laban (31.24, 29, 42), and also to his recent
trouble at Shechem (34.30, 31).

approach it without proper preparation, since he believes that God dwells there. Further, the naming of the place thrice (28.19; 35.7, 15) indicates its special significance for the author.

Therefore Jacob's call for a special preparation of his household to meet with the God of Bethel is not out of place in the present context, although preparation of this sort was not called for elsewhere in the patriarchal narratives (*pace* Westermann 1985: 550). It is not necessary to suppose that the religious situation was the same with all the patriarchs. Jacob's first encounter with God at Bethel and his reaction to it in raising a pillar instead of the usual altar by Abraham and Isaac suggests that his situation was different from other patriarchs. It may be pointed out that nowhere else was a patriarch commanded to build an altar (cf. Wenham 1994: 323). Abraham and Isaac, even Jacob at times, built altars on their own, either in response to a theophany or on arriving at a new place. No preparation of any sort is reported, but it would be unlikely that the ancients performed worship without proper ritual preparations.[62] Preparation of some sort, moral or physical, before meeting with a deity or appearing at a sanctuary is almost universal, as we have seen in the Mesopotamian and Hittite literature. Although there was no sanctuary for Jacob at Bethel, the place was reckoned by him as God's abode, בית אלהים.

Secondly, Jacob called for purification because he (or the editor) realized that אלהי הנכר, literally 'foreign gods',[63] had invaded his household through his association with Laban's household. Jacob would have known this by his long association with the house of Laban, or at least by his last encounter with Laban who charged him with stealing his household gods. Several texts make clear that both Jacob and Laban were aware of the distinction between the God of Jacob's father and the gods of Laban. As I have already noted, Jacob was constantly aware of the presence of the 'God of my father', while Laban admits that Yahweh blessed him on account of Jacob (30.27), and that he could not harm Jacob because he was warned by Elohim, the 'God of your father' (31.24, 29).

---

62. Cf. Garcia-Treto 1967: 178-208; de Pury 1975: 575-77; Exod. 19.10, 14; Josh. 24.14, 23; cf. 1 Sam. 16.5. Similar preparations are also required in Hittite rituals. See above.

63. This phrase 'invariably connotes non-Israelite' gods, cf. Isa. 56.3, 6; Sarna 1989: 240.

The distinction between the gods of Laban and Jacob is nowhere clearer than in the episode of Jacob's flight from Laban and in the subsequent covenant between them. Laban charged Jacob directly with stealing *his* gods: 'why did you steal *my* gods?' (31.30).[64] Jacob's reply makes this distinction equally clear: 'Anyone with whom you find *your* gods shall not live' (31.32); 'If the God of *my* father, the god of Abraham and the Fear of Isaac, had not been on my side, surely now you would have sent me away empty-handed' (31.42, italics added; cf. 29, 30, 32). Then in the covenant between them each swears by his own god, while Laban also says, 'The God of Abraham and the God of Nahor, the God of their father (אלהי אביהם), judge (ישפטו) between us' (31.53). If this treaty is analogous to boundary treaties of the ancient Near East, it is not difficult to see that Laban invoked two (or more?) different deities, the God of Abraham and the God of Nahor, 'the ancestor of the Aramaeans' (22.20-23) (Sarna 1989: 222). The plural verb indicates that Laban saw the distinction between the god of Nahor and the God of Abraham.[65] The different deities invoked in the Sefire texts similarly indicate 'the ethnic diversity of the parties involved' (Sarna 1989: 222; cf. *TSSI*, 2, iA, 8-12). The term אביהם probably refers to Terah, the father of Abraham and Nahor. Elsewhere he is described as a polytheist (Josh. 24.2). So Laban probably also invoked the gods of their common ancestor. In response, however, 'Jacob ignores Laban's formula and invokes only the 'Fear of his father Isaac'.[66] Thus it is plausible to think that Jacob also knew the distinction between them. Therefore Jacob's command to renounce 'foreign gods' probably alludes to the gods of Laban, although he is portrayed as ignorant of Rachel's stolen teraphim.[67]

Thirdly, Jacob's long stay at Shechem (33.18–34.31) would have made it possible for foreign idols to enter Jacob's household (cf. Procksch 1924: 381-82). This may be a reasonable inference as Jacob

64. Rachel's תרפים are equated here and in v. 32 with Laban's אלהים.

65. LXX and *Sam. Pent.* have a singular verb. The treaty was meant to be between the clans of Nahor and the clans of Abraham; cf. Skinner 1930: 398; Driver 1948: 289.

66. Sarna 1989: 222. 'Fear of Isaac', פחד יצחק, is found only here. Its exact meaning is uncertain, although the context suggests that this is another name or expression for the 'God of the father'. For various suggestions, see Albright 1957a: 248-49; Hillers 1972: 90-92; Westermann 1985: 497.

67. Images and tokens of foreign gods, like Rachel's teraphim, were presumed to belong to women, servants and maids from Aram; Westermann 1985: 551.

came very close to integration with the Shechemites in every way, except for circumcision, which in ch. 34 is shown as the feature distinguishing his family from the Canaanites.[68] The Shechemites see marriage as the link by which they become one with the family of Jacob, while the latter sees circumcision as a prerequisite for such a link (34.15, 16). The view that marriage forms an irrevocable bond between two different groups is illustrated by the strong law in Israel against intermarriage, which is described as תועבה, an abominable or ritually unclean thing (Deut. 7.1-4; Ezra. 9.1-2, 11-12, 14). However, the patriarchal narratives do not view marriage alliance with other nations as a religious issue, much less as impure. Their reason for marrying within their own clan was not religion or race, but tradition. Isaac and Rebekah give no religious reason for wanting Jacob to marry someone from their own family (27.46–28.2). Esau's Hittite wives were disliked for making life bitter for Isaac and Rebekah, not for their religious affiliation (26.34, 35). Joseph's marriage with the daughter of the Egyptian priest passes off without religious or racial comment (41.45). It is possible that for P, to whom these texts are usually ascribed, marriage within one's own people became a 'critical command' during the exilic period when, after the dissolution of the Israelite state, the family became 'the form of community that preserved the continuity of Israel and its religion' (Westermann 1985: 448). However, if P altered the Jacob narrative to provide a basis for his views in the patriarchal stories, as Westermann thinks, why did he not also do the same with the Joseph story? Conversely, why did J (and E, or a J variant), who must be ignorant of Israel's exilic situation, prohibit marrying foreigners in Genesis 24? Did J think of the purity of stock, as Skinner assumes?[69]

---

68. 'Circumcision', מולה (including 'uncircumcised', ערל, ערלה, literally, 'with foreskin') occurs 24 times in the patriarchal narratives, all on three occasions (Gen. 17, 34 and 21.4). For many scholars circumcision in Gen. 17 is closely related to God's covenant with Abraham; Isaac 1964: 444-56; Kline 1968; Alexander 1983: 17-22. Hoenig (1962–63: 322), however, points out that the biblical passage does not define the circumcision itself as covenant. For ancient Near Eastern background, see Sasson 1966: 473-76. Rabbinic terminology, in which the rite of circumcision designated as ברית, is based on this text, Hoenig 1962–63: 322-34. However, it is not clear how important circumcision was for the religion of the patriarchs. Since circumcision does not form part of patriarchal religious or cultic practices, as noted above in Chapter 1 §3, it will not occupy us here.

69. Most scholars attribute Gen. 24 to J, though some assign it to J, E and a J variant; Gunkel 1902: 215-21; Procksch 1924: 4-6; Skinner 1930: 340.

On the contrary, the patriarchs seem to have no concept of purity of either race or religion comparable to that of later authors of exilic/postexilic times. Their practice of marriage does not suggest that they saw themselves as a specially chosen people by God who must remain distinct by marrying only among themselves. Neither did they conceive their religion or God as unique among other nations. They seem to have accepted their religion as one among others, or more precisely, they conceived of it as a family religion, and seemed to have no concern whether others knew, or should know their God. Neither did they seek after other gods.

Fourthly, besides realizing that foreign gods or ritual contamination clings to his family, Jacob's call to purification and a renunciation of idols was meant to rally his family's allegiance to his God in order that he might be delivered from the possible retaliation of the neighbouring towns of Shechem. Jacob was seized with panic when his sons massacred the Shechemites. He realized that his family was isolated and few in number and could easily be annihilated by the people of the land. He was desperate for help, and wanted to ensure by every possible means that this God was favourable to him once more, as he had been in the encounter with Esau. Miraculously, what could have been a nightmare became a dignified pilgrimage to Bethel (Sarna 1989: 239). Therefore the author of Genesis assumes by Jacob's call for purification that Jacob knew the basic notion that a ritual preparation was in order before meeting a god in worship. The details of Jacob's command to part with the foreign gods and their subsequent burial along with the earrings[70] are the result of Jacob's awareness of their presence among his family members. The fact that they were carefully buried suggests that Jacob was not antagonistic toward them, but it was to give his total allegiance to the God of Bethel according to the promise he made in his vow that he buried them.

5. Conclusion

In contrast to the enormous attention given to ritual and moral taboos in the ancient Near East and Israel, the concepts of purity and defilement are rarely mentioned in the patriarchal stories. The taboos of the ancient

---

70. *Sam. Pent.*; Keel (1973: 306) thinks that earrings never have the meaning of amulets in the Old Testament.

Near East are preoccupied more with the threat of danger and disease to the individuals than with ritual purity, and there is no clear idea of what the latter meant and what a particular deity expected of his devotees. By contrast, Israelite sources provide a clear legislation and rationale on purity and defilement, and the legislation is concerned with the individual's participation in cult and social life. However, the patriarchal narratives contain neither legislation nor any concern for ritual or moral taboos; rather they contain frequent unconditional promises of posterity, land and protection. Death, burial and mourning customs are frequently attested indicating a belief in afterlife that is common to other cultures in the ancient Near East. There is only one allusion to an idea of pollution by contact with the dead in the Joseph cycle, but there is no record of purification from it. It is not certain if the author was alluding to the Egyptian or patriarchal customs. The idea of defilement occurs several times in connection with illicit sex, but it seems to have no implications for ritual purity. The only time the concepts occur with any religious importance is in the Jacob stories. But even here they do not have the same import as they have in the Priestly texts. Jacob's call for purification was a preparation before meeting with the holy God, and the burial of idols was part of that preparation as in the ancient Near East.

Chapter 8

CONCLUSION

A distinct pattern of patriarchal religion emerges from the above investigation into patriarchal worship and cultic practices as portrayed in the
patriarchal narratives. One may suggest that altars, prayer and pillars
reflect patriarchal worship, while tithes, vows and purification their religious practices. In both sets, a pattern peculiar to patriarchal religion
emerges from my study. In the ancient Near East and Israel, worship
was highly organized with an established cult and cultic personnel, and
with the occasion, purpose and procedures of sacrifices elaborately prescribed. By contrast, the patriarchal cultic practices were informal, with
no fixed cult place or cult personnel and with no prescribed sacrifices or
procedures.

Patriarchal altars were usually outside the settled communities and
probably distinct from their public shrines. The occasions for their sacrifices were prompted by theophany, relocation, covenant and guidance.
Unlike the ancient Near East and Israel, they had no festivals or sacrifices for healing or for battle. The purpose of patriarchal sacrifice is less
clear, though it seems mainly to have been for worship, and occasionally for the fulfilment of vows or for thanksgiving.

Similarly, prayer in the patriarchal narratives occurs in the family
and other informal contexts, unlike the ancient Near East and, to a large
extent, Israel. Prayer is preserved entirely as a conversation between the
patriarchs and God. The intercession of Abraham is the most telling
example of this. Thus the content, setting and theology of prayer in the
patriarchal narratives are distinct from that of both the ancient Near
East and Israel. This fits well with the practice and concept of sacrifice
in the patriarchal narratives. While the form of patriarchal prayer is
similar to that of the ancient Near East and Israel, the range of problems
for which the latter approached the deity are surprisingly lacking in the
former, in that there is no prayer regarding sin and guilt, oppression by

enemies or abandonment by the deity, although the patriarchs experienced all these problems. While the similarity of form reflects a universal pattern of prayer, the problems mentioned or ignored are distinctive to the lifestyle and religion of the patriarchs. It is unlikely that patriarchs going through such problems would not have turned to their God for help, but to record and preserve such experiences would be a concern for an organized cult and society. The fact that such problems are not recorded in the patriarchal narratives suggests the lack of an organized cult or society. The most revealing of all their prayers is the prayer of blessing. While the occasions for blessing in all the cultures, including patriarchal, were identical, the setting of patriarchal blessing is distinct from the others in that it was never cultic. Another distinctive aspect of patriarchal blessing is the possession of land. Whereas this was singularly important for their nomadic lifestyle, it is not found elsewhere. Further, while prayer is assumed in the context of building altars and offering sacrifices, prayer or sacrifice is not used to manipulate the deity, as was common in the organized cults of the ancient Near East and Israel.

The most distinctive feature of patriarchal religion is the raising of pillars by Jacob in response to theophanies. Patriarchal sacrifices and prayers display at least some similarities to ancient Near Eastern and Israelite practices, although their occasion and purpose in most cases were distinct for the patriarchs. But pillars were strongly condemned in later Israel, while in the ancient Near East they were found only in cultic areas or were promised by the devotees. They are not attested as being raised in response to theophanies. Jacob's pillars are unique in that they signify not only worship and commemoration of God and his theophanies but also the establishment of a contractual bond with him. Nevertheless, they are not to be identified with either *baetylia* or the sacred stones which embody the deities they represent, and Jacob's worship was not to the *numen* dwelling in the stone.

The patriarchs' practices of tithes, vow-making and purificatory rites were similarly distinct, and compatible with their lifestyle and worship. The unvowed tithe paid by Abraham to the Canaanite priest-king Melchizedek and the unpaid tithe vowed to God by Jacob were not regular, annual, obligatory tithes, but single, voluntary tithes in contrast to the tithe practices in the ancient Near East and Israel. It is uncertain whether Abraham's tithe reflects his religious beliefs, although he was following ancient custom attested both in the ancient Near East and

Israel where a portion of the booty was paid to the deity. This single activity does not establish his allegiance to the Canaanite deity but rather his exigent circumstance. His normal pattern of worship was to build an altar or plant a tree and call on the name of Yahweh. Jacob's tithe, however, was part of his vow, and thus certainly a religious obligation. There is no mention of its payment, although it was probably subsumed in his religious feast at Bethel, given the lack of priests or organized cult to receive it. Thus the patriarchs' tithes, while resembling ancient Near Eastern and Israelite practice, were distinct from it and compatible with their own wandering lifestyle and non-localized religion.

The familiar custom of vow-making appears to be as old as prayer and is attested in all cultures of the ancient Near East from the early second millennium. The objects vowed in Jacob's vow, such as tithes, loyalty and a shrine, are very common in the vows of the ancient Near East. This suggests that the patriarchs were familiar with the practice, though not all of them made use of the custom. In contrast to tithing, which is attested with both Abraham and Jacob, vow-making occurs only with Jacob. Apart from the fact that this practice reveals his religious beliefs, the element of bargain involved in vow-making particularly suited Jacob's situation and character. While Abraham and Isaac encountered critical moments such as childlessness, famine and enforced travel in their lives, they did not resort to vows. They prayed in some cases and used other methods in others. But the fact that Jacob made use of this form suggests that it suited not only his critical situation when facing uncertain future, but also his character. Therefore Jacob's vow was a matter of his choice, in conformity with his character as portrayed in the narrative. Further, in contrast to the ancient Near East and Israel, Jacob made a vow at an obscure place where there was not even a sanctuary. The fact that Jacob did not bother to fulfil his vow even long after his safe arrival in the land of promise, a condition stipulated in his vow, suggests that he did not know legislation common in the ancient Near East and Israel that vows once made must not be delayed, even less deferred. When Jacob finally arrives at Bethel, he merely builds an altar, offers sacrifices and raises a pillar, but there is no mention of either payment of tithes or raising a sanctuary. The narrator was probably more concerned with Jacob's escape from Shechem than with his fulfilment of the vow. Or he was deliberately vague, if not silent, about the fulfilment of his vow, because it involved an established cult and priests which are incompatible with the patriarchal religion and lifestyle that he had portrayed thus far. Therefore Jacob's vow was only partially fulfilled, in that he offered worship and pledged his loyalty to the God who had been with him. Thus, just as his payment of tithes, Jacob's fulfilment of his vow is compatible with his nomadic lifestyle and religion.

Similarly, the ideas of purity and defilement attested in the patriarchal narratives are compatible with patriarchal lifestyle and religion, and are unlike those attested in the ancient Near East and Israel. The idea of pollution by death is not very significant in the patriarchal stories. Although death, burial and mourning customs are frequently attested, there is only one possible allusion to uncleanness by death, and that in the Joseph cycle set in Egypt. We are not certain if the author was alluding to the peculiar patriarchal custom or to the Egyptian practice, since Joseph was married to the daughter of an Egyptian priest. The idea of pollution by contact with the dead is probably present, but there is no record of purification from it. The fact that this idea is given little or no significance, in contrast to its paramount importance in the Priestly system, suggests that the author himself thought that pollution from death for the patriarchs was just a social custom at the least, and could affect only the individuals at the most. As in Israel, there is no sanctuary in the threat of pollution since they had no sanctuary or ritual laws. In contrast, death pollution in the Priestly system is a serious defilement, and the human corpse is the greatest pollutant that could threaten the defilement of the sanctuary. The high priest who serves in the inner sanctuary is protected by every means from corpse contamination, even though he enters there only once a year. Even the ritual law of the ancient Near East is nowhere near as strict as the Priestly law regarding corpse contamination. However, the only time the concepts occur with any religious importance in the patriarchal narratives is in the Jacob stories. But even here they do not have the same import as in the Priestly texts. Their background is to be sought in the ancient Near Eastern cultures. Thus Jacob's call for purification and renunciation of foreign gods has closer similarities with the practices of the ancient Near East, since purification is called for before approaching a holy place and foreign gods are carefully buried to affirm loyalty to one's own God. That Jacob was following such a practice is demonstrated from his own experience at Bethel, in Paddan-aram and at Shechem. Therefore Jacob's practice is distinct from Israel's. In some sense it is also distinct from the ancient Near East, because the place where Jacob went to meet with God had no organized cult or priests. By himself he called for purification, buried the idols and other tokens of foreign gods, and on arrival at the holy place built an altar, offered sacrifices and worshipped God. Thus, though his practices reflect ancient Near Eastern ones, the pattern of his worship is his own, compatible with his lifestyle and religion.

Thus the patriarchal religious practices are compatible with their worship pattern and their belief in a family God who went along with them wherever they went. Their worship and religious practices are distinct from both ancient Near Eastern and Israelite practices, although they reflect elements of both at several points. The patriarchal religion is family oriented, clan based and compatible with the semi-nomadic lifestyle of the patriarchs. Thus the Genesis account of patriarchal religion is feasible, not likely a product of later imagination. Further, the patriarchs appear not only to be living as aliens in the land but also as aliens to the indigenous cult. Their social and political relations with the native inhabitants were usually harmonious, but only on the basis that they were still aliens. This means that their ethnic difference made them distinct as much as their religious practices. This probably had a large effect on their religious observances. The problem of religious syncretism became an issue only after Israel claimed the land as her own and wanted to become like the native inhabitants, but this does not seem to have been a problem for the patriarchs. Thus their religion was probably less syncretistic than that of Israel at other periods.

BIBLIOGRAPHY

Aalders, G.C.
    1981   *Genesis* (2 vols.; BSC; Grand Rapids: Zondervan).
Abel, E.L.
    1973   'The Nature of the Patriarchal God "El Šadday" ', *Numen* 20: 48-59.
Abusch, T.
    1974   'The Nature of *Maqlû*: Its Character, Divisions, and Calendrical Setting',
                JNES 33: 251-62.
Aejmelaeus, A.
    1986   *The Traditional Prayer in the Psalms* (BZAW, 167; Berlin: W. de
                Gruyter).
Aharoni, Y.
    1967   'Excavations at Tel Arad: Preliminary Report on the Second Season,
                1963', *IEJ* 17: 233-49.
Aharoni, Y.
    1979   *The Land of the Bible: Historical Geography* (Philadelphia: Westminster
                Press, rev. edn).
Aharoni, Y. (ed.)
    1973   *Beer-Sheba I: Excavations at Tel Beer-Sheba* (Tel Aviv: Institute of
                Archaeology).
Ahlström, G.W.
    1993   *The History of Ancient Palestine from the Palaeolithic Period to
                Alexander's Conquest* (JSOTSup, 146; Sheffield: JSOT Press).
Albertz, R.
    1978   *Persönliche Frömmigkeit und offizielle Religion: Religionsinterner
                Pluralismus in Israel und Babylon* (CTM, 9; Stuttgart: Calwer Verlag).
    1994   *A History of Israelite Religion in the Old Testament Period. I. From the
                Beginnings to the End of the Exile* (London: SCM Press, 1992).
Albright, W.F.
    1932   *The Archaeology of Palestine and the Bible* (New York: Revell).
    1935   'The Names Shaddai and Abram', *JBL* 54: 173-93.
    1940   'The Ancient Near East and the Religion of Israel', *JBL* 59: 85-112.
    1942   'A Votive Stele Erected by Ben-Hadad I of Damascus to the God
                Melcarth', *BASOR* 87: 23-29.
    1950   *The Biblical Period* (Pittsburgh: repr. from L. Finkelstein [ed.], *The Jews:
                Their History, Culture and Religion* [New York: Harper, 1949]).
    1957a   *From Stone Age to Christianity: Monotheism and the Historical Process*
                (New York: Doubleday, 2nd edn).
    1957b   'A High Place in Ancient Palestine', in G.W. Anderson *et al.* (eds.),
                Volume du Congres (VTSup, 4; Leiden: E.J. Brill): 242-58.

1961 'Abram the Hebrew: A New Interpretation', *BASOR* 163: 36-54.

1963 *The Biblical Period from Abraham to Ezra* (New York: Harper & Row).

1968 *Yahweh and the Gods of Canaan: A Historical Analysis of Two Contrasting Faiths* (London: Athlone Press).

Alexander, T.D.

1983 'Gen 22 and the Covenant of Circumcision', *JSOT* 25: 17-22.

1986 'The Old Testament View of Life after Death', *Themelios* 11: 41-46.

Alfrink, B.

1948 'L'expression נאסף אל־עמיו', *OTS* 5: 118-31.

Alt, A.

1953 'Die Wallfahrt von Sichem nach Bethel', in A. Alt, *Kleine Schriften zur Geschichte des Volkes Israel*, I (Munich: Beck): 79-88.

1989a 'The God of the Fathers', in A. Alt, *Essays on Old Testament History and Religion* (BSS; Sheffield: JSOT Press): 1-77. ET of *Der Gott der Väter* (BWANT, 3.12; Stuttgart: W. Kohlhammer, 1929); reissued in A. Alt, *Kleine Schriften zur Geschichte des Volkes Israel*, I (Munich: Beck, 1953): 1-78.

1989b 'The Settlement of the Israelites in Palestine,' in A. Alt, *Essays on Old Testament History and Religion* (BSS; Sheffield: JSOT Press): 133-69.

Alter, R.

1981 *The Art of Biblical Narrative* (London: George Allen & Unwin).

Andersen, F.I.

1969 'Note on Genesis 30:8', *JBL* 88: 200.

Anderson, B.W.

1983 *Out of the Depths: The Psalms Speak for Us Today* (Philadelphia: Westminster Press, 2nd edn).

Anderson, G.A.

1987 *Sacrifices and Offerings in Ancient Israel: Studies in their Social and Political Importance* (HSM, 41; Atlanta: Scholars Press).

Ap-Thomas, D.R.

1956 'Notes on Some Terms Relating to Prayer', *VT* 6: 225-41.

Ashley, T.R.

1993 *The Book of Numbers* (NICOT; Grand Rapids: Eerdmans).

Assman, J.

1975 *Ägyptische Hymnen und Gebete* (Munich: Artemis).

Astour, M.C.

1980 'The Nether World and its Denizens at Ugarit', in B. Alster (ed.), *Death in Mesopotamia: Papers Read at the XXVIe Rencontre Assyriologique Internationale* (Copenhagen: Akademisk): 227-38.

Avner, U.

1984 'Ancient Cult Sites in the Negev and Sinai Deserts', *Tel Aviv* 11: 115-31.

1993 'Mazzebot Sites in the Negev and Sinai and their Significance', in A. Biran and J. Aviram (eds.), *Biblical Archaeology Today, 1990: Proceedings of the Second International Congress on Biblical Archaeology* (Jerusalem: Israel Exploration Society): 166-81.

Baal, J. van

1976 'Offering, Sacrifice and Gift', *Numen* 23: 161-78.

Bailey, L.R.
    1968   'Israelite 'El Šadday and Amorite Bêl Šadê,' *JBL* 87: 434-38.
    1979   *Biblical Perspectives on Death* (OBT; Philadelphia: Fortress Press).
Balentine, S.E.
    1984   'The Prophet as Intercessor: A Reassessment', *JBL* 103: 161-73.
    1993   *Prayer in the Hebrew Bible: The Drama of Divine-Human Dialogue* (OBT; Minneapolis: Fortress Press).
Banks, J.
    1873   *The Works of Hesiod and Callimachus and Theognis* (London: Bell & Daldy).
Barnett, R.D.
    1948   'Hittite Hieroglyphic Texts at Aleppo', *Iraq* 10: 122-37.
Barr, J.
    1974   'Philo of Byblos and his "Phoenician History"', *BJRL* 57: 17-68.
Barrick, W.B.
    1975   'The Funerary Character of "High Places" in Ancient Palestine: A Reassessment', *VT* 25: 565-95.
Baudissin, W.W.
    1878   *Studien zur semitischen Religionsgeschichte*, II (Leipzig: Grunow).
    1925   'El Bet-el (Gen. 31,13; 35,7)', in Karl Budde (ed.), *Marti-Festschrift* (BZAW, 41; Giessen: Alfred Töpelmann): 1-11.
Baumgarten, A.I.
    1981   *The Phoenician History of Philo of Byblos: A Commentary* (Leiden: E.J. Brill).
Bayliss, M.
    1973   'The Cult of the Dead Kin in Assyria and Babylonia', *Iraq* 3: 115-24.
Bertholet, A.
    1930   'Zum Verständnis des alttestamentlichen Opfergedankens', *JBL* 49: 218-33.
Bimson, J.J.
    1980   'Archaeological Data and the Dating of the Patriarchs,' in A.R. Millard and D.J. Wiseman (eds.), *Essays on the Patriarchal Narratives* (Leicester: Inter-Varsity Press): 59-92.
Blank, S.H.
    1948   'The Confession of Jeremiah and the Meaning of Prayer', *HUCA* 21: 331-54.
    1961   'Some Observations Concerning Biblical Prayer', *HUCA* 32: 75-90.
Bloch-Smith, E.
    1992a   *Judahite Burial Practices and Beliefs about the Dead* (JSOTSup, 123; Sheffield: JSOT Press).
    1992b   'The Cult of the Dead in Judah: Interpreting the Material Remains', *JBL* 111: 213-24.
Blum, E.
    1984   *Die Composition der Vätergeschichte* (Neukirchen–Vluyn: Neukirchener Verlag).
Boadt, L.
    1973   'Isaiah 41:8-13: Notes on Poetic Structure and Style', *CBQ* 35: 20-34.

Bochart, S.
    1707   *Geographia sacrea* (Holland: Cornelium Bontesteyn & Jordanum Lucht-mans).

Boer, P.A.H. de
    1972   'An Aspect of Sacrifice', in G.W. Anderson *et al.* (eds.), *Studies in the Religion of Ancient Israel* (VTSup, 23; Leiden: E.J. Brill): 27-47.

Bourdillon, M.F.C., and M. Fortes
    1980   *Sacrifice* (London: Academic Press).

Boyce, R.
    1989   *The Cry to God in the Old Testament* (Atlanta: Scholars Press).

Boyd, J.L.
    1986   'The Etymological Relationship between *ndr* and *nzr* Reconsidered', *UF* 17: 61-75.

Bray, J.S.
    1993   'Genesis 23: A Priestly Paradigm for Burial', *JSOT* 60: 69-73.

Brichto, H.C.
    1963   *The Problem of 'Curse' in the Hebrew Bible* (SBLMS, 13; Philadelphia: SBL).
    1973   'Kin, Cult, Land and Afterlife: A Biblical Complex', *HUCA* 44: 1-54.

Bright, J.
    1981   *A History of Israel* (OTL; Philadelphia: Westminster Press, 3rd edn).

Broyles, C.C.
    1989   *The Conflict of Faith and Experience in the Psalms: A Form-Critical and Theological Study* (JSOTSup, 52; Sheffield: JSOT Press).

Buck, F.
    1975   'Prayer in the Old Testament', in J. Plevnik (ed.), *Word and Spirit: Essays in Honor of David Michael Stanley on his 60th Birthday* (Willow-dale: Regis College Press): 61-110.

Buis, P.
    1966   'Les formulaires d'alliance', *VT* 16: 396-411.

Burkert, W.
    1985   *Greek Religion* (Cambridge, MA: Harvard University Press).

Burrows, M.
    1934   'From Pillar to Post', *JPOS* 14: 42-51.

Campbell, E.F., and G.E. Wright
    1969   'The Tribal League Shrines in Amman and Shechem', *BA* 32: 104-16.

Caplice, R.
    1965   'Namburbi Texts in the British Museum I', *Or* 34: 105-31.
    1967   'Namburbi Texts in the British Museum III', *Or* 36: 5-36; 273-98.
    1970   'Namburbi Texts in the British Museum IV', *Or* 39: 111-51.
    1971   'Namburbi Texts in the British Museum V', *Or* 40: 133-83.

Carmichael, C.M.
    1969   'Some Sayings in Genesis 49', *JBL* 88: 435-44.

Carroll, R.P.
    1969   'The Elijah-Elisha Sagas: Some Remarks on Prophetic Succession in Ancient Israel', *VT* 19: 401-15.

Cartledge, T.W.
1992   *Vows in the Hebrew Bible and the Ancient Near East* (JSOTSup, 147; Sheffield: JSOT Press).

Cassuto, U.
1950   'The Seven Wives of King Keret', *BASOR* 119: 18-20.
1961   *The Documentary Hypothesis and the Composition of the Pentateuch* (Jerusalem: Magnes Press, 1941).
1964   *A Commentary on the Book of Genesis*, I (Jerusalem: Hebrew University).

Cazelles, H.
1951   'Le dîme israélite et les textes de Ras Shamra', *VT* 1: 131-34.
1975   'La religion des patriarches', *DBS* 7: 141-56.

Childs, B.S.
1974   *Exodus* (OTL; London: SCM Press).

Clements, R.E.
1965   *God and Temple* (Oxford: Basil Blackwell).
1967   *Abraham and David: Genesis XV and its Meaning for Israelite Tradition* (London: SCM Press).
1986   *The Prayers of the Bible* (London: SCM Press).
1989   'Israel in its Historical and Cultural Setting', in R.E. Clements (ed.), *The World of Ancient Israel: Sociological, Anthropological and Political Perspectives* (Cambridge: Cambridge University Press): 3-16.

Coats, G.W.
1976   *From Canaan to Egypt: Structural and Theological Context for the Joseph Story* (CBQMS, 5; Washington: Catholic Biblical Association).
1983   *Genesis: With an Introduction to Narrative Literature* (Grand Rapids: Eerdmans).

Contenau, G.
1959   *Everyday Life in Babylon and Assyria* (London: Edward Arnold).

Cooke, G.A.
1936   *The Book of Ezekiel* (ICC; Edinburgh: T. & T. Clark).

Cooke, S.A.
1930   *The Religion of Ancient Palestine in the Light of Archaeology* (London: Oxford University Press).

Costecalde, C.-B.
1985   'La racine *qdš* et ses dérivés en milieu ouest-sémitique et dans les cunéiformes', *DBS* 10: 1346-415.

Cross, F.M.
1962   'Yahweh and the God of the Patriarchs', *HTR* 55: 225-59.
1973   *Canaanite Myth and Hebrew Epic: Essays in the History of the Religion of Israel* (Cambridge, MA: Harvard University Press).

Crüsemann, F.
1969   *Studien zur Formgeschichte von Hymnus und Danklied in Israel* (WMANT, 32; Neukirchen–Vluyn: Neukirchener Verlag).

Dalglish, E.R.
1962   *Psalm Fifty-One: In the Light of Ancient Near Eastern Patternism* (Leiden: E.J. Brill).

Dandamajew, M.A.
1969   'Der Tempelzehnte in Babylonien während des 6.-4. Jh. v. u. Z.', in
          R. Steihl and H.E. Stier (eds.), *Beiträge zur Alten Geschichte und deren*
          Nachleben: Festschrift für Franz Altheim zum 6. 10. 1968, I (Berlin:
          W. de Gruyter): 82-90.

Davies, G.H.
1962   'Vows', *IDB* 4: 792-93.

Day, J.
1986   'Asherah in the Hebrew Bible and Northwest Semitic Literature', *JBL*
          105: 385-408.

Delitzsch, F.
1888   *A New Commentary on Genesis*, I (Edinburgh: T. & T. Clark, 5th edn
          [1887]).
1889   *A New Commentary on Genesis*, II (Edinburgh: T. & T. Clark, 5th edn
          [1887]).

Dever, W.G.
1977   'The Patriarchal Traditions,' in J.H. Hayes and J.M. Miller (eds.), *Israel-*
          ite and Judaean History (London: SCM Press): 70-148.
1987   'The Contribution of Archaeology to the Study of Canaanite and Early
          Israelite Religion', in P.D. Miller, P.D. Hanson and S.D. McBride (eds.),
          Ancient Israelite Religion (Philadelphia: Fortress Press): 209-47.

Dillmann, A.
1897   *Genesis: Critically and Exegetically Expounded*, II (Edinburgh: T. & T.
          Clark, 6th edn [1892]).

Dhorme, E.
1949   *Les religions de babylonie et d'assyrie* (Paris: Presses Universitaires de
          France).

Donner, H.
1962   'Zu Genesis 28,22', *ZAW* 74: 68-70.

Douglas, M.
1966   *Purity and Danger: An Analysis of Concepts of Pollution and Taboo*
          (London: Routledge & Kegan Paul).
1975   *Implicit Meanings: Essays in Anthropology* (London: Routledge & Kegan
          Paul).
1993   'The Forbidden Animals in Leviticus', *JSOT* 59: 5-23.

Draffkorn, A.
1959   'Was King Abba-AN of Yamḫad a Vizier for the King of Ḫattusa?', *JCS*
          13: 94-97.

Driver, G.R., and J.C. Miles
1952   *The Babylonian Laws*, I (Oxford: Clarendon Press).
1924   *The H. Weld-Blundell Collection*. III. *Letters of the First Babylonian*
          Dynasty (OECT; London: Oxford University Press).

Driver, S.R.
1902   *Deuteronomy* (ICC; Edinburgh: T. & T. Clark).
1911   *The Book of Exodus* (Cambridge: Cambridge University Press).
1948   *The Book of Genesis* (London: Methuen, 15th edn).

Dupont-Sommer, A.
1958   *Les inscriptions araméennes de Sfiré* (Paris: Imprimerie Nationale).

Eichholz, D.E.
     1962   *Pliny: Natural History* (LCL, 10; London: Heineman; Cambridge, MA:
                   Harvard University Press).
Eichrodt, W.
     1961   *Theology of the Old Testament*, I (OTL; London: SCM Press).
     1967   *Theology of the Old Testament*, II (OTL; London: SCM Press).
Eissfeldt, O.
     1956   'El and Yahweh', *JSS* 1: 25-37.
     1962a   'Der Gott Bethel', in KlSchr, I: 206-33: (= *ARW* 28 [1930]: 1-30).
     1962b   'Genesis', *IDB*, II: 366-80.
     1965   *The Old Testament: An Introduction* (Oxford: Basil Blackwell; German,
                   1964).
     1968   'Yahwe, der Gott der Väter,' in KlSchr, IV: 79-91.
     1973   'Der kanaanäische El als Geber der den israelitischen Erzvätern geltenden
                   Nachkommenschaft- und Landbesitzverheissungen', in *KlSchr*, V: 50-62.
Eliade, M.
     1958   *Patterns of Comparative Religion* (London: Sheed & Ward).
Emerton, J.A.
     1971a   'Some False Clues in the Study of Genesis xiv', *VT* 21: 24-47.
     1971b   'The Riddle of Genesis xiv', *VT* 21: 407-39.
     1990a   'The Site of Salem, the City of Melchizedek (Genesis xiv 18)', in J.A.
                   Emerton (ed.), *Studies in the Pentateuch* (VTSup, 41; Leiden: E.J. Brill):
                   45-71.
     1990b   'Some Problems in Genesis xiv', in J.A. Emerton (ed.), *Studies in the
                   Pentateuch* (VTSup, 41; Leiden: E.J. Brill): 78-91.
     1991   'T.J. Lewis' *Cults of the Dead in Ancient Israel*', *VT* 41: 383-84.
Evans, A.J.
     1901   'Mycenaean Tree and Pillar Cult and its Mediterranean Relations', *JHS*
                   21: 99-204.
Evans-Pritchard, E.E.
     1956   *Nuer Religion* (Oxford: Clarendon Press).
Evelyn-White, H.G. (ed.)
     1982   *Hesiod: The Homeric Hymns and Homerica* (LCL; London: Heinemann).
Exum, J.C.
     1973   'A Literary and Structural Analysis of the Song of Songs', *ZAW* 85: 47-
                   79.
Falkenstein, A., and W. von Soden
     1953   *Sumerische und akkadische Hymnen und Gebete* (Zürich: Artemis).
Faulkner, R.O.
     1969   *The Ancient Egyptian Pyramid Texts* (Oxford: Clarendon Press).
Feldman, E.
     1977   *Biblical and Post-Biblical Defilement and Mourning: Law as Theology*
                   (New York: Ktav).
Finkelstein, J.J.
     1966   'The Genealogy of the Hammurapi Dynasty', *JCS* 20: 95-118.

Firmage, E.

    1990   'The Biblical Dietary Laws and the Concept of Holiness,' in J.A. Emerton (ed.), *Studies in the Pentateuch* (VTSup, 41, Leiden: E.J. Brill): 177-208.

Fishbane, M.

    1975   'Composition and Structure in the Jacob Cycle (Gen. 25:19–35:22)', *JJS* 26: 15-38.

    1979   *Text and Texture: Close Readings of Selected Biblical Texts* (New York: Schocken Books).

    1983   'Form and Formulation of Biblical Priestly Blessing', *JAOS* 103: 115-21.

Fisher, L.R

    1962   'Abraham and his Priest-King', *JBL* 81: 264-70.

    1973   'The Patriarchal Cycles', in H.A. Hoffner (ed.), *Orient and Occident: Festschrift to C.H. Gordon* (Kevelaer: Butzon & Becker; Neukirchen–Vluyn: Neukirchener Verlag): 59-65.

    1975   'Literary Genres in the Ugaritic Texts', in L.R. Fisher (ed.), *Ras Shamra Parallels*, II (AnOr, 50; Rome: Pontificio Istituto Biblico): 131-52.

Fitzmyer, J.A.

    1967   *The Aramaic Inscriptions of Sefire* (BibOr, 19; Rome: Pontifical Biblical Institute).

Fohrer, G.

    1970   *Introduction to the Old Testament* (ET; London: SPCK).

    1973   *History of Israelite Religion* (London: SPCK [1968]).

Fokkelman, J.

    1975   *Narrative Art in Genesis* (Assen: Van Gorcum).

Fontaine, C.R.

    1987   'Queenly Proverb Performance: The Prayer of Puduḫepas (KUB XXI, 27)', in K.G. Hoglund *et al.* (eds.), *The Listening Heart: Essays in Wisdom and the Psalms in Honour of Roland E. Murphy, O. Carm* (JSOTSup, 58; Sheffield: JSOT Press): 95-126.

Fowler, J.D.

    1988   *Theophoric Personal Names in Ancient Hebrew: A Comparative Study* (JSOTSup, 49; Sheffield: JSOT Press).

Fowler, M.D.

    1982a   'The Excavation of Tell Beer-Sheba and the Biblical Record', *PEQ* 114: 7-11.

    1982b   'The Israelite *bāmâ*: A Question of Interpretation', *ZAW* 94: 203-13.

Frankena, R.

    1961   'New Materials for the *Tākultu Ritual: Additions and Corrections*', *BibOr* 18: 199-207.

Frazer, J.G.

    1969   'Jacob at Bethel', in T.H. Gaster (ed.), *Myth, Legend and Custom in the Old Testament* (London: Gerald Duckworth): 182-93.

Freedman, D.N.

    1961   'The Chronology of Israel and the Ancient Near East: A. Old Testament Chronology', in G.E. Wright (ed.), *The Bible and the Ancient Near East: Essays in Honour of W.F. Albright* (London: Routledge & Kegan Paul): 203-14.

1975   'The Aaronic Benediction', in J.W. Flanagan and A.W. Robinson (eds.),
            No Famine in the Land: Festschrift to John L. McKenzie (Missoula, MT:
            Scholars Press): 35-48.

1985   'Who Asks (or Tells) God to Repent?', *BR* 1: 56-59.

Fretheim, T.E.

1972   'The Jacob Tradition: Theology and Hermeneutic', *Int* 26: 419-36.

Furlani, G.

1938   'The Basic Aspect of Hittite Religion', *HTR* 31: 352-62.

Gammie, J.G.

1979   'Theological Interpretation by Way of Literary and Tradition Analysis:
            Genesis 25–35', in Martin J. Buss (ed.), *Encounter with the Text: Form
            and History in the Hebrew Bible* (Philadelphia: Fortress Press; Missoula,
            MT: Scholars Press): 117-34.

Garcia-Treto, F.O.

1967   'The History and Traditions of an Israelite Sanctuary' (PhD Dissertation,
            Princeton University).

Gaster, T.H.

1966   *Thespis: Ritual, Myth, and Drama in the Ancient Near East* (New York:
            Harper & Row).

Gemser, B.

1958   'God in Genesis', *OTS* 12: 1-21.

Gerstenberger, E.S.

1980   *Der bittende Mensch: Bittritual und Klaglied des Einzelnen im Alten
            Testament* (Neukirchen–Vluyn: Neukirchener Verlag).

1988   *The Psalms: Part I with an Introduction to Cultic Poetry* (FOTL, 14;
            Grand Rapids: Eerdmans).

Gevirtz, S.

1975a   'The Issachar Oracle in the Testament of Jacob', *EI* 12: 104-12.

1975b   'Of Patriarchs and Puns: Joseph at the Fountain, Jacob at the Ford',
            HUCA 46: 33-54.

Gifford, E.H. (ed.)

1903   *Eusebius: Preparation for the Gospel*, I (Oxford: Clarendon Press); Greek
            text may be found in G. Dindorfius, *Eusebii Caesariensis: Preaepa-
            rationis Evangelicae*, I (Leipzig: Teubner, 1867).

Goetze, A., and J. Pedersen

1934   *Mursilis Sprachlähmung* (Copenhagen: Levin & Munksgaard).

Goetze, A., and E.H. Sturtevant

1938   *The Hittite Ritual of Tunnawi* (New Haven: American Oriental Society).

Goldingay, J.

1980   'The Patriarchs in History and Tradition', in A.R. Millard and D.J. Wise-
            man (eds.), *Essays on the Patriarchal Narratives* (Leicester: Inter-Varsity
            Press).

Good, E.M.

1963   'The "Blessing" on Judah, Gen 49:8-12', *JBL* 82: 427-32.

Gordon, C.H.

1935   'אלהים in its Reputed Meaning of Rulers, Judges', *JBL* 54: 139-44.

1940   'Biblical Customs and the Nuzi Tablets', *BA* 3: 1-12.

1953	*Introduction to Old Testament Times* (Ventnor: Ventnor Publishers).
1954	'The Patriarchal Narratives', *JNES* 13: 56-59.
1963	'Abraham of Ur', in D.W. Thomas and W.D. McHardy (eds.), *Hebrew and Semitic Studies Presented to G.R. Driver* (Oxford: Clarendon Press): 77-84.
1965	*Ugaritic Textbook* (Rome: Pontifical Biblical Institute).

Gorman, F.H.

1990   *The Ideology of Ritual: Space, Time and Status in the Priestly Theology* (JSOTSup, 91; Sheffield: JSOT Press).

Graesser, C.F.

1972   'Standing Stones in Ancient Palestine', *BA* 35: 34-63.

Gray, G.B.

1903   *Numbers* (ICC; Edinburgh: T. & T. Clark).

1912   *The Book of Isaiah I–XXVII* (ICC; Edinburgh: T. & T. Clark).

1925   *Sacrifice in the Old Testament: Its Theory and Practice* (Oxford: Clarendon Press).

Gray, J.

1957   *The Legacy of Canaan: The Ras Shamra Texts and their Relevance to the Old Testament* (VTSup, 5; Leiden: E.J. Brill).

1964   *I and II Kings: A Commentary* (OTL; London: SCM Press).

Grayson, A.K.

1987   *Assyrian Rulers of the Third and Second Millennia BC: Royal Inscriptions of Mesopotamia, Assyrian Periods*, I (Toronto: Toronto University Publication).

Greenberg, M.

1977–78   'Moses' Intercessory Prayer', *TY*: 21-36.

1983   *Biblical Prose Prayer as a Window to the Popular Religion of Ancient Israel* (Berkeley: University of California Press).

Greenwood, D.

1970   'Rhetorical Criticism and Formgeschichte: Some Methodological Considerations', *JBL* 89: 418-26.

Gressmann, H.

1934   'Sage und Geschichte in den Patriarchen-Erzählungen', *ZAW* 30: 1-34.

Gunkel, H.

1902   *Genesis: Übersetzt und erklärt* (Göttingen: Vandenhoeck & Ruprecht).

1928   *What Remains of the Old Testament and Other Essays* (London: George Allen & Unwin).

1964   *The Legends of Genesis: The Biblical Saga and History* (New York: Schocken Books).

Gunkel, H., and J. Begrich

1933   *Einleitung in die Psalmen: Die Gattungen der religiösen Lyrik Israels* (HAT; Göttingen: Vandenhoeck & Ruprecht).

Gunn, D.M.

1987   'New Directions in the Study of Biblical Hebrew Narrative', *JSOT* 39: 65-75.

Gurney, O.R.

1935   'Babylonian Prophylactic Figures and their Rituals', *AAA* 22: 31-96.

1952   *The Hittites* (London: Penguin Books).

1960   'A Tablet of Incantation against Slander', *Iraq* 22: 221-27.
1977   *Some Aspects of Hittite Religion* (Oxford: Oxford University Press).
Hallo, W.W.
1968   'Individual Prayer in Sumerian: The Continuity of a Tradition', *JAOS* 88:
              71-89.
1983   'Lugalbanda Excavated', *JAOS* 103: 165-80.
Hamilton, V.P.
1990   *The Book of Genesis 1–17* (NICOT; Grand Rapids: Eerdmans).
Haran, M.
1961   'The Complex of Ritual Acts Performed inside the Tabernacle', *SH* 8:
              272-302.
1965   'The Religion of the Patriarchs: An Attempt at a Synthesis', *ASTI* 4: 30-
              55.
1972   'The Passover Sacrifice', in G.W. Anderson *et al.* (eds.), *Studies in the
              Religion of Ancient Israel* (VTSup, 23; Leiden: E.J. Brill): 86-116.
1978   *Temples and Temple-Service in Ancient Israel* (Oxford: Clarendon Press).
Harper, W.R.
1936   *Amos and Hosea* (ICC; Edinburgh: T. & T. Clark).
Harris, R.
1960   'Temple Loans', *JCS* 14: 126-37.
Hasel, G.F.
1981   'The Meaning of the Animal Rite in Genesis 15', *JSOT* 19: 61-78.
Hayes, W.C.
1953   *The Scepter of Egypt: From the Earliest Times to the End of the Middle
              Kingdom: Part I* (Cambridge, MA: Harvard University Press).
Head, B.V.
1909   *A Guide to the Principal Gold and Silver Coins of the Ancients* (London:
              British Museum, 5th edn).
Heck, J.D.
1990   'A History of Interpretation of Genesis 49 and Deuteronomy 33', *BSac*
              147: 16-31.
Heiler, F.
1923   *Das Gebet: Eine religionsgeschichtliche und religionspsychologische
              Untersuchung* (Munich: E. Reinhardt, 5th edn).
1958   *Prayer: A Study in the History and Psychology of Religion* (New York:
              Galaxy).
Heimerdinger, J.-M.
1992   'The God of Abraham', *VE* 22: 41-55.
Heltzer, M.
1976   *The Rural Community in Ancient Ugarit* (Wiesbaden: Ludwig Reichert).
Herman, M.
1991   *Tithe as Gift: The Institution in the Pentateuch and in Light of Mauss's
              Prestation Theory* (San Francisco: Mellen Research University Press).
Hermisson, H.-J.
1965   *Sprache und Ritus im altisraelitischen Kult* (Neukirchen–Vluyn: Neu-
              kirchener Verlag).
Herzog, Z.
1980   'Beer-sheba of the Patriarchs', *BARev* 6: 12-28.

Hess, R.S.
1993   'The Slaughter of the Animals in Genesis 15', in R.S. Hess, P.E. Satterth-
        waite and G.J. Wenham (eds.), *He Swore an Oath: Biblical Themes from
        Genesis 12–50* (Cambridge: Tyndale House): 55-65.
Hill, G.F.
1899   *A Hand Book of Greek and Roman Coins* (London: Macmillan).
Hillers, D.R.
1970   'Ugaritic *šnpt* "Wave-Offering" ', *BASOR* 198: 42.
1972   'Paḥad Yiṣḥāq', *JBL* 91: 90-92.
Hoenig, S.B.
1962   'Circumcision: The Covenant of Abraham', *JQR* 53: 322-34.
Hoffner, H.A.
1965   'The Elkunirsa Myth Reconsidered', *RHA* 23: 5-16.
1973   'Incest, Sodomy and Bestiality in the Ancient Near East', in H.A. Hoffner
        (ed.), *Orient and Occident* (AOAT, 22; Neukirchen–Vluyn: Neukirchener
        Verlag): 81-90.
Hoftijzer, J.
1956   *Die Verheissungen an die drei Erzväter* (Leiden: E.J. Brill).
Holladay, J.S.
1987   'Religion in Israel and Judah under the Monarchy: An Explicitly Archae-
        ological Approach', in P.D. Miller, P.D. Hanson and S.D. McBride
        (eds.), *Ancient Israelite Religion: Festschrift to F.M. Cross* (Philadelphia:
        Fortress Press): 249-99.
Holladay, W.L.
1989   *Jeremiah*, II (Minneapolis: Fortress Press).
Holmgren, F.
1988   'Remember Me; Remember Them', in C. Osiek and D. Senior (eds.),
        Scripture and Prayer: A Celebration for Carroll Stuhlmueller (Wilm-
        ington, DE: Michael Glazier).
Holzinger, H.
1898   *Genesis* (Leipzig, Tübingen: J.C.B. Mohr).
1903   *Numeri, erklärt* (KHAT, 4; Tübingen: J.C.B. Mohr).
Hornung, E.
1983   *Conception of God in Ancient Egypt* (London: Routledge & Kegan Paul).
Horwitz, L.K.
1987   'Animal Offerings from Two Middle Bronze Age Tombs', *IEJ* 37: 251-
        55.
House, P.R.
1992   'The Rise and Current Status of Literary Criticism of the Old Testament',
        in P.R. House (ed.), *Beyond Form Criticism: Essays in Old Testament
        Literary Criticism* (Winona Lake, IN: Eisenbrauns): 3-22.
Houston, W.
1993   *Purity and Monotheism: Clean and Unclean Animals in Biblical Law*
        (JSOTSup, 140; Sheffield; JSOT Press).
Houtman, C.
1977   'What did Jacob See in his Dream at Bethel', *VT* 27: 337-51.

Hubert, H., and M. Mauss
    1898   *Sacrifice: Its Meaning and Function* (Chicago: University of Chicago Press).
Hughes, G.R.
    1958   'A Demotic Letter to Thoth', *JNES* 17: 1-12.
Hyatt, J.P.
    1937   'A Neo-Babylonian Parallel to Bethel-Šar-ezer, Zech. 7:2,' *JBL* 56: 387-94.
    1939   'The Deity Bethel and the Old Testament', *JAOS* 59: 81-98.
    1955   'Yahweh as "The God of my Father" ', *VT* 5: 130-36.

Illman, K.-J.
    1979   *Old Testament Formulas about Death* (Åbo: Åbo Akademi).
Isaac, E.
    1964   'Circumcision as a Covenant Rite', *Anthropos* 59: 444-56.
Jacob, B.
    1934   *Das erste Buch der Tora Genesis: Übersetzt und erklärt* (New York: Ktav).
Jacobsen, T.
    1976   *The Treasures of Darkness: A History of Mesopotamian Religion* (New Haven: Yale University Press).
Jacobson, R.
    1974   'The Structuralists and the Bible', *Int* 28: 146-64.
Jagersma, H.
    1981   'Tithes in the Old Testament', *OTS* 21: 116-28.
James, E.O.
    1938–39 'Aspects of Sacrifice in the OT', *ExpTim* 50: 151-55.
Japhet, S.
    1993   *I and II Chronicles: A Commentary* (OTL; London: SCM Press; Louisville, KY: Westminster/John Knox Press).
Jastrow, M.
    1898   *The Religion of Babylonia and Assyria* (Boston: Ginn).
    1905   *Die Religion Babyloniens und Assyriens*, I (Giessen: J. Ricker'sche Verlagsbuchhandlung).
Jenson, P.
    1992   *Graded Holiness: A Key to the Priestly Conception of the World* (JSOTSup, 106; Sheffield: JSOT Press).
Jenni, E.
    1952   'Das Wort 'ōlām im AT', *ZAW* 64: 197-248.
    1953   'Das Wort 'ōlām im AT', *ZAW* 65: 1-35.
Johnston, P.S.
    1993   'The Underworld and the Dead in the Old Testament' (PhD Dissertation, Cambridge University).
Jones, W.H.S.
    1935   *Pausanias: Description of Greece* (London: Heinemann; Cambridge, MA: Harvard University Press).

Kaiser, O.
    1958   'Traditionsgeschichtliche Untersuchung von Gen 15', *ZAW* 70: 107-26.
    1974   *Isaiah 13–39* (OTL; ET; London: SCM Press [1973]).
Kallai, Z.
    1986   *Historical Geography of the Bible* (Jerusalem: Magnes Press; Leiden: E.J. Brill).
Kapelrud, A.S.
    1966   'The Role of the Cult in Old Israel', in J.P. Hyatt (ed.), *The Bible and Modern Scholarship* (London: Carey Kingsgate): 44-56.
Kaufmann, Y.
    1961   *The Religion of Israel: From its Beginnings to the Babylonian Exile* (London: George Allen & Unwin [1937–48]).
Keel, O.
    1973   'Das Vergraben der "fremden Götter" in Genesis xxxv 4b', *VT* 23: 305-36.
Keil, C.F.
    1869   *The Book of Numbers* (Edinburgh: T. & T. Clark).
    1878   *Genesis und Exodus* (Giessen/Basel: Brunnen Verlag, 3rd edn).
Keller, C.A.
    1954   ' "Die Gefährdung der Ahnfrau": Ein Beitrag zur gattungs- und motivgeschichtlichen Erforschung alttestamentlicher Erzählungen', *ZAW* 66: 181-91.
Kelso, J.L.
    1968   *Excavations of Bethel 1934–60* (Cambridge, MA: American Schools of Oriental Research).
Kidner, D.
    1967   *Genesis* (TOTC; London: Tyndale Press).
King, L.W.
    1916   *A History of Sumer and Akkad* (London: Chatto & Windus).
Kitchen, K.A.
    1977   'The King List of Ugarit', *UF* 9: 131-42.
Kittel, R.
    1925   *The Religion of the People of Israel* (London: George Allen & Unwin).
Kline, M.
    1968   *By Oath Consigned: A Reinterpretation of the Covenant Signs of Circumcision and Baptism* (Grand Rapids: Eerdmans).
Knight, D.A.
    1973   *Rediscovering the Traditions of Israel: The Development of the Traditio-Historical Research of the Old Testament, with Special Consideration of Scandinavian Contributions* (SBLDS, 9; Missoula, MT: SBL).
Knoppers, G.N.
    1992   ' "The God in his Temple": The Phoenician Text from Pyrgi as a Funerary Inscription', *JNES* 51: 105-20.
Koch, K.
    1976   'Šaddaj', *VT* 26: 299-332.
Köckert, M.
    1988   *Vätergott und Väterverheißungen* (FRLANT, 142; Göttingen: Vandenhoeck & Ruprecht).

König, E.
    1919   *Die Genesis* (Gütersloh: C. Bertelsmann).
Kosmala, H.
    1963   'The Name of God (YHWH and HU')', *ASTI* 2: 103-106.
Kramer, S.N.
    1955   ' "Man and his God": A Sumerian Variation of the "Job" Motif', *VT* 3: 170-82.
Kraus, H-J.
    1966   *Worship in Israel: A Cultic History of the Old Testament* (Oxford: Basil Blackwell [1962]).
Kutsch, E.
    1963   *Salbung als Rechtsakt im Alten Testament und im alten Orient* (BZAW, 87; Berlin: Alfred Töpelmann).
Lack, R.
    1962   'Les origines de *Elyon*, le très-haut, dans la tradition cultuelle d'Israël', *CBQ* 24: 44-64.
Lambert, W.G.
    1960   *Babylonian Wisdom Literature* (Oxford: Clarendon Press).
    1974   '*Dingir.ša.dib.ba* Incantations', *JNES* 3: 267-322.
    1990   'Ancient Mesopotamian Gods: Superstition, Philosophy, Theology', *RHR* 207: 115-30.
    1993   'Donations of Food and Drink to the Gods in Ancient Mesopotamia', in J. Quaegebeur (ed.), *Ritual and Sacrifice in the Ancient Near East* (OLA, 55; Leuven: Peeters): 191-201.
Lambert, W.G., and A.R. Millard
    1969   *Attra-ḫasīs: The Babylonian Story of the Flood* (Oxford: Clarendon Press).
Langdon, S.
    1923a   *The H. Weld-Blundell Collection in the Ashmolean Museum. I. Sumerian and Semitic Religious Texts* (OECI; London: Oxford University Press).
    1923b   *The H. Weld-Blundell Collection. II. Historical Inscriptions, Containing Principally the Chronological Prism, W-B. 444* (OECT, 2; London: Oxford University Press).
    1927   *Babylonian Penitential Psalms* (OECT, 4; Paris: Paul Geuthner).
Lemaire, A.
    1977   'Les inscriptions de Kirbet el-Qôm et l'Asherah de YHWH', *RB* 84: 595-608.
Levine, B.A.
    1963   'Ugaritic Descriptive Rituals', *JCS* 17: 105-111.
    1965   'The Descriptive Tabernacle Texts of the Pentateuch', *JAOS* 85: 307-18.
    1974   *In the Presence of the Lord: A Study of Cult and some Cultic Terms in Ancient Israel* (Leiden: E.J. Brill).
    1993   *Numbers 1–20* (AB; New York: Doubleday).
Lewis, T.J.
    1989   *Cults of the Dead in Ancient Israel and Ugarit* (HSM, 39; Atlanta: Scholars Press).
Lewy, J.
    1934   'Les textes paléo-assyriens et l'Ancien Testament', *RHR* 110: 29-65.

Lichtheim, M.
    1975   *Ancient Egyptian Literature: A Book of Readings*, I (Berkeley: University
            of California Press).
    1976   *Ancient Egyptian Literature: A Book of Readings*, II (Berkeley: Univer-
            sity of California Press).
    1980   *Ancient Egyptian Literature: A Book of Readings*, III (Berkeley: Univer-
            sity of California Press).
Lods, A.
    1938   'The Religion of Israel: Origins', in H.W. Robinson (ed.), *Record and
            Revelation* (Oxford: Clarendon Press): 187-215.
Løkkegaard, F.
            1954   'Some Comments on Sanchuniaton Tradition', *ST* 8: 51-76.
Luckenbill, D.D.
    1924   *The Annals of Sennacherib* (Chicago: University of California Press).
Luke, J.T.
    1977   'Abraham and the Iron Age: Reflections on the New Patriarchal Studies',
            JSOT 4: 35-47.
Maclaurin, E.C.B.
    1962   'YHWH, the Origin of the Tetragrammaton', *VT* 12: 439-63.
Maimonides, M.
    1956   *The Guide for the Perplexed* (New York: Dover).
Mair, A.W.
    1908   *Hesiod: The Poems and Fragments* (Oxford: Clarendon Press).
Manley, G.T.
    1964   'The God of Abraham', *TynBul* 14: 3-7.
Margalit, B.
    1976   'Studia Ugaritica II: Studies in Krt and Aqht', *UF* 8: 137-92.
    1986   'Why King Mesha of Moab Sacrificed his Oldest Son', *BAR* 12: 62-63.
May, H.G.
    1941a   'The Patriarchal Idea of God', *JBL* 60: 113-28.
    1941b   'The God of My Father: A Study of Patriarchal Religion', *JBR* 9: 155-58.
Mayer, W.
    1976   *Untersuchungen zur Formensprache der babylonischen 'Gebetsbe-
            schwörungen'* (Rome: Biblical Institute Press).
Mays, A.D.H.
    1979   *Deuteronomy* (NCB; London: Marshall, Morgan & Scott).
Mays, J.L.
    1969a   *Hosea: A Commentary* (OTL; London: SCM Press).
    1969b   *Amos: A Commentary* (OTL: London: SCM Press).
Mazar, A.
    1990   *Archaeology of the Land of the Bible 10,000–586 BCE* (New York:
            Doubleday).
McCarthy, D.J.
    1964   'Three Covenants in Genesis', *CBQ* 26: 179-89.
    1978   *Treaty and Covenant: A Study in Form in the Ancient Oriental Docu-
            ments and in the Old Testament* (AnBib, 21A; Rome: Pontifical Biblical
            Institute).

McConville, J.G.
1984   *Law and Theology in Deuteronomy* (JSOTSup, 33; Sheffield: JSOT Press).
1993   'Abraham and Melchizedek', in R.S. Hess, P.E. Satterthwaite and G.J. Wenham (eds.), *He Swore an Oath: Biblical Themes from Genesis 12–50* (Cambridge: Tyndale House): 93-118.

McEvenue, S.E.
1971   *The Narrative Style of the Priestly Writer* (AnBib, 50; Rome: Biblical Institute Press).

McFadyen, J.E.
1921   'Vows' (Hebrew), *ERE* 12: 654-56.

McNeile, A.H.
1908   The Book of Exodus (London: Methuen).

Meier, G.
1937   *Die assyrische Beschwörungssammlung Maqlu* (AfO, 2; Berlin: Ernst F. Weidner).

Meier, S.
1989   'House Fungus: Mesopotamia and Israel (Lev. 14: 33-53)', *RB* 96: 184-92.

Mendelsohn, I.
1956   'Samuel's Denunciation of Kingship in the Light of the Akkadian Documents from Ugarit', *BASOR* 143: 17-22.
1959   'A Ugaritic Parallel to the Adoption of Ephraim and Manasseh', *IEJ* 9: 180-88.

Mettinger, T.N.D.
1976   *King and Messiah* (Lund: C.W.K. Gleerup).
1988   *In Search of God: The Meaning and Message of the Everlasting Names* (Philadelphia: Fortress Press).
1995   *No Graven Image? Israelite Aniconism in its Ancient Near Eastern Context* (Stockholm: Almqvist & Wiksell).

Meyers, E.M.
1970   'Secondary Burials in Palestine', *BA* 33: 2-29.
1971   *Jewish Ossuaries: Rebirth and Reburial* (Rome: Biblical Institute Press).

Michalowski, P.
1987   'On the Early History of the Ershahunga Prayer', *JCS* 39: 37-48.

Milgrom, J.
1970   *Studies in Levitical Terminology. I. The Enchroacher and the Levite, The Term 'Aboda* (Berkeley: University of California Press).
1971a   'A Prolegomenon to Leviticus 17:11', *JBL* 90: 149-56.
1971b   'Sin-Offering or Purification-Offering?', *VT* 21: 237-39.
1973   'The Cultic אשם—A Philological Analysis', in A. Shinan (ed.), *Proceedings of the Sixth World Congress of Jewish Studies* (Jerusalem: Magnes Press): 299-308.
1976   *Cult and Conscience: The Asham and the Priestly Doctrine of Repentance* (Leiden: E.J. Brill).
1990   'Ethics and Ritual: The Foundations of the Biblical Dietary Laws', in E.B. Firmage, B.G. Weiss and J.W. Welch (eds.), *Religion and Law: Bib-*

lical-Judaic and Islamic Perspectives (Winona Lake, IN: Eisenbrauns): 176-91.

1991   *Leviticus 1–16* (AB, 3; New York: Doubleday).

Milik, J.T.

1967   'Les papyrus araméens d'Hemoupolis et les cultes syro-phéniciens en Egypte perse', *Bib* 48: 546-622.

Millard, A.R.

1974   'The Meaning of the Name Judah', *ZAW* 86: 216-18.

1980   'Methods of Studying the Patriarchal Narratives as Ancient Texts', in A.R. Millard and D.J. Wiseman (eds.), *Essays on the Patriarchal Narratives* (Leicester: Inter-Varsity Press): 43-58.

1990   'The Homeland of Zakkur', *Semitica* 39: 47-52.

Miller, J.M.

1977   'The Patriarchs and the Extra-Biblical Sources: A Response', *JSOT* 2: 62-66.

Miller, P.D.

1975   'The Blessing of God: An Interpretation of Numbers 6:22-27', *Int* 29: 240-51.

1988   'Prayer and Sacrifice in Ugarit and Israel', in W. Claassen (ed.), *Text and Context: Old Testament and Semitic Studies for F.C. Fensham* (JSOTSup, 48; Sheffield: JSOT Press): 139-55.

1994   *They Cried to the Lord: The Form and Theology of Biblical Prayer* (Minneapolis: Fortress Press).

Mitchel, L.L.

1977   *The Meaning of Ritual* (New York: Paulist Press).

Moberly, R.W.L.

1990   'Abraham's Righteousness (Gen. xv 6)', in J.A. Emerton (ed.), *Studies in the Pentateuch* (VTSup, 41; Leiden: E.J. Brill): 103-30.

1992a   *The Old Testament of the Old Testament: Patriarchal Narratives and Mosaic Yahwism* (Minneapolis: Fortress Press).

1992b   *Genesis 12–50* (OTG; Sheffield: JSOT Press).

Moor, J.C. de

1971   *The Seasonal Pattern in the Ugaritic Myth of Ba'lu* (AOAT, 16; Neukirchen–Vluyn: Neukirchener Verlag).

Moore, G. F.

1902   'Massebah', *EnBib* 3: 2974-2983.

1903a   'Baetylia', *AJA* 7: 198-208.

1903b   'Vow, Votive Offerings', *EnBib* 4: 5252-55.

Moran, W.L. (ed. and trans.)

1992   *The Amarna Letters* (Baltimore: The Johns Hopkins University Press).

Morenz, S.

1973   *Egyptian Religion* (London: Methuen [1960]).

Muffs, Y.

1982   'Abraham the Noble Warrior: Patriarchal Politics and Laws of War in Ancient Israel', *JJS* 33: 81-107.

Muilenburg, J.

1992   'Form Criticism and Beyond', *JBL* 88: 1-18.

Nelson, H.H.
    1949   'Certain Reliefs at Karnak and Medinet Habu and the Ritual of
                Amenophis I', *JNES* 8: 201-32, 310-45.
Newlands, D.L.
    1972   'Sacrificial Blood at Bethel?', *PEQ* 104: 155.
Nielsen, E.
    1954–55   'The Burial of the Foreign Gods', *ST* 8: 103-22.
    1955   *Shechem: A Traditio-Historical Investigation* (Copenhagen: G.E.C. Gad).
Noth, M.
    1928   *Die israelitischen Personennamen im Rahmen der gemeinsemitischen
                Namengebung* (Stuttgart: W. Kohlhammer).
    1961   *Exodus* (OTL; London: SCM Press).
    1968   *Numbers* (OTL; London: SCM Press).
    1972   *A History of Pentateuchal Traditions* (Englewood Cliffs, NJ: Prentice–
                Hall).
O'Callaghan, R.T.
    1949   'The Great Phoenician Portal Inscription from Karatepe', *Or* 18: 173-205.
Oesterley, W.O.E., and T.H. Robinson
    1937   *Hebrew Religion, its Origin and Development* (London: SPCK, 2nd edn).
Oesterley, W.O.E.
    1937   *Sacrifices in Ancient Israel: Their Origin, Purposes and Development*
                (London: Hodder & Stoughton).
Oppenheim, A.L.
    1956   *The Interpretation of Dreams in the Ancient Near East* (Philadelphia: The
                Americal Philosophical Society).
    1964   *Ancient Mesopotamia: Portrait of a Dead Civilisation* (Chicago: Univer-
                sity of Chicago Press).
Otto, E.
    1976   'Jacob in Bethel: Ein Beitrag zur Geschichte der Jakobüberlieferung',
                ZAW 88: 165-90.
Ottosson, M.
    1980   *Temples and Cult Places in Palestine* (Boreas, 12; Uppsala: Almqvist &
                Wiksell).
Ouellette, J.
    1969   'More on ʾÊl Šaddai and Bêl Šadê', *JBL* 88: 470-71.
Parker, S.B.
    1977   'The Historical Composition of KRT and the Cult of El', *ZAW* 88: 161-
                75.
    1979   'The Vow in Ugaritic and Israelite Narrative Literature', *UF* 11: 693-700.
Parpola, S.
    1983   *Letters from Assyrian Scholars to the Kings Esarhaddon and Assur-
                banipal*, II (Neukirchen–Vluyn: Neukirchener Verlag).
Pedersen, J.
    1940   *Israel: Its Life and Culture*, III; IV (London: Oxford University Press).
Petrie, F.
    1924   *Religious Life in Ancient Egypt* (London: Constable).
Pitard, W.T.
    1994   'The "Libation Installations" of the Tombs at Ugarit', *BA* 57: 20-37.

Pope, M.H.
 1955 *El in the Ugaritic Texts* (VTSup, 2; Leiden: E.J. Brill).
 1981 'The Cult of the Dead at Ugarit', in G. D. Young (ed.), *Ugarit in Retrospect* (Winona Lake, IN: Eisenbrauns): 159-79.
Porten, B.
 1968 *Archives from Elephantine* (Berkeley: University of California Press).
Procksch, O.
 1924 *Die Genesis* (Leipzig: Deichert).
Pury, A. de
 1975 *Promèsse divine et légende cultuelle dans le cycle de Jacob*, I; II (Paris: J. Gabalda).
Rad, G. von
 1958 'The Form-Critical Problem of the Hexateuch', in *The Problem of the Hexateuch and Other Essays* (Edinburgh: Oliver & Boyd [1938]): 1-78.
 1965 *Genesis: A Commentary* (OTL; London: SCM Press [1949]).
 1966 *Deuteronomy* (OTL; London: SCM Press [1964]).
 1967 *Old Testament Theology*, I (OTL; London: SCM Press [1957]).
Rainey, A.F.
 1970a 'The Order of Sacrifices in Old Testament Ritual Texts', *Bib* 51: 485-98.
 1970b 'Compulsory Labour Gangs in Ancient Israel', *IEJ* 20: 191-202.
 1976 'Institutions: Family, Civil, and Military', in L.R. Fisher (ed.), *Ras Shamra Parallels*, II (AnOr, 50; Rome: Pontifical Biblical Institute): 69-107.
Redford, D.B.
 1970 *A Study of the Biblical Story of Joseph* (VTSup, 20; Leiden: E.J. Brill).
Reider, J.
 1937 *Deuteronomy* (Philadelphia: Jewish Publication Society of America).
Reiner, E.
 1956 'Lipšur Litanies', *JNES* 15: 129-49.
 1958 *Šurpu: A Collection of Sumerian and Akkadian Incantations* (AfO, 2; Graz).
Rendtorff, R.
 1966 'El, Ba'al, und Yahwe. Erwägungen zum Verhältnis von kanaanäischer und israelitischer Religion', *ZAW* 78: 277-92.
 1967 *Studien zur Geschichte des Opfers im alten Israel* (Neukirchen–Vluyn: Neukirchener Verlag).
 1979 *The Problem of the Process of Transmission in the Pentateuch* (JSOTSup, 89; Sheffield: JSOT Press [1977]).
 1982 'Jakob in Bethel: Beobachtungen zum Aufbau und zur Quellenfrage in Gen 28:10-22', *ZAW* 94: 511-23.
 1985 *The Old Testament: An Introduction* (London: SCM Press).
Richter, W.
 1967 'Das Gelübde als theologische Rahmung der Jakobsüberlieferungen', *BZ* 11: 21-52.
Rist, M.
 1938 'The God of Abraham, Isaac and Jacob: A Liturgical and Magical Formula', *JBL* 57: 289-303.

Roberts, J.J.M.
      1972   *The Earliest Semitic Pantheon* (Baltimore: The Johns Hopkins University
                    Press).
      1988   'The Bible and the Literature of Antiquity: The Ancient Near East', in
                    J.L. Mays *et al.* (eds.), *Harper's Bible Commentary* (San Francisco:
                    Harper & Row): 33-41.
Rodriguez, A.M.
      1979   *Substitution in the Hebrew Cultus* (Berrien Springs: Andrews University
                    Press).
Rosenberg, R.A.
      1965   'The God Ṣedeq', *HUCA* 36: 161-77.
Rowley, H.H.
      1950   *From Joseph to Joshua* (London: British Academy).
      1952   'Recent Discovery and the Patriarchal Age', in *The Servant of the Lord
                    and Other Essays* (London: Lutterworth): 269-305.
      1967   *Worship in Ancient Israel* (London: SPCK).
Rowton, M.B.
      1965   'The Topological Factor in the Ḥabiru Problem', in H.G. Güterbock and
                    T. Jacobsen (eds.), *Studies in Honor of Benno Landsberger on his
                    Seventy-Fifth Birthday* (Assyriological Studies, 16; Chicago: University
                    of Chicago Press): 375-87.
Rudolph, W.
      1971   *Joel–Amos–Obadja–Jona* (Gütersloh: Gütersloher Verlagshaus).
Saggs, H.W.F.
      1962   *The Greatness that was Babylon: A Sketch of the Ancient Civilization of
                    the Tigris-Euphrates Valley* (London: Sidgwick & Jackson).
Salonen, E.
      1972   'Über den Zehnten in Alten Mesopotamien: Ein Beitrag zur Geschichte
                    der Besteuerung', *StudOr* 43.4: 1-62.
Sarna, N.M.
      1989   *Genesis* בראשית (The JPS Torah Commentary; Philadelphia: Jewish Pub-
                    lication Society of America).
Sasson, J.M.
      1966   'Circumcision in the Ancient Near East', *JBL* 85: 473-76.
Sauneron, S.
      1960   *The Priests of Ancient Egypt* (New York: Grove).
Sayce, A. H.
      1902   *The Religions of Ancient Egypt and Babylonia* (Edinburgh: T. & T.
                    Clark).
Segal, M.H.
      1967   *The Pentateuch: Its Composition and its Authorship and other Biblical
                    Studies* (Jerusalem: Magnes Press).
Selman, M.J.
      1976   'The Social Environment of the Patriarchs', *TB* 27: 114-36.
      1980   'Comparative Customs and the Patriarchal Age', in A.R. Millard and D.J.
                    Wiseman (eds.), *Essays on the Patriarchal Narratives* (Leicester: Inter-
                    Varsity Press): 93-138.

Selms, A. van
1958 'The Canaanites in Genesis', *OTS* 12: 182-213.
Seyrig, H.
1933 'Altar Dedicated to Zeus Betylos', in P.V.C. Baur, M.I. Restovtzeff and A.R. Bellinger (eds.), *Excavations at Dura Europas, Preliminary Report of the Fourth Season of Work, October 1930–March 1931*, IV (New Haven: Yale University Press): 68-71.
Skinner, J.
1930 *Genesis* (ICC; Edinburgh: T. & T. Clark, 2nd edn).
Smith, R.H.
1965 'Abram and Melchizedek (Gen 14:18-20)', *ZAW* 77: 129-53.
Smith, W.R.
1927 *The Religion of the Semites* (London: A. & C. Black, 3rd edn).
Snaith, N.H.
1957 'Sacrifice in the Old Testament', *VT* 7: 308-17.
1965 'The Sin-Offering and the Guilt-Offering', *VT* 15: 73-80.
1967 *Leviticus and Numbers* (NCB; London: Nelson).
1975 'The Verbs *zābaḥ* and *šāḥat*', *VT* 25: 242-46.
1978 'The Altar at Gilgal: Joshua xxii 23-29', *VT* 28: 330-35.
Snijders, L.A.
1958 'Genesis 15: The Covenant with Abram', *OTS* 12: 261-79.
Soden, W. von
1994 *The Ancient Orient: An Introduction to the Study of the Ancient Near East* (Grand Rapids: Eerdmans [1985]).
Soggin, J.A.
1987 *Judges* (OTL; London: SCM Press, 2nd edn).
Speiser, E.A.
1955 'I Know Not the Day of my Death', *JBL* 74: 252-56.
1963a 'The Stem *PLL* in the Hebrew Bible', *JBL* 82: 301-306.
1963b 'The Wife–Sister Motif in the Patriarchal Narratives', in A. Altmann (ed.), *Biblical and Other Studies* (Cambridge, MA: Harvard University Press): 15-28.
1964 *Genesis* (AB, 1; New York: Doubleday).
Spronk, K.
1986 *Beatific Afterlife in Ancient Israel and in the Ancient Near East* (AOAT, 219; Kevelaer: Butzon & Backer; Neukirchen–Vluyn: Neukirchener Verlag).
Steinmueller, J.E.
1959 'Sacrificial Blood in the Bible', *Bib* 40: 556-67.
Stockton, E.
1972 'Sacred Pillars in the Bible', *ABR* 20: 16-32.
Strus, A.
1978 'Etymologies des noms pryopres dans Gen 29:32–30:24: Valeurs littéraires et functionelles', *Salesianum* 40: 57-72.
Sweeney, D.
1985 'Intercessory Prayer in Ancient Egypt and the Bible', in S. Israelit-Groll (ed.), *Pharaohnic Egypt: The Bible and Christianity* (Jerusalem: Magnes Press): 213-30.

Talmon, S.
    1977   'The "Comparative Method" in Biblical Interpretation: Principles and
                Problems', in J.A. Emerton *et al.* (eds.), *Congress Volume* (VTSup, 29;
                Leiden: E.J. Brill): 320-56.
Taylor, J.B.
    1969   *Ezekiel* (TOTC; London: Tyndale Press).
Teixidor, J.
    1977   *The Pagan God: Popular Religion in the Greco-Roman Near East*
                (Princeton, NJ: Princeton University Press).
Terrien, S.
    1970   'The Omphalus Myth and the Hebrew Religion', *VT* 20: 315-38.
Thomas, D.W.
    1960   '*Kelebh* "Dog": Its Origin and some Usage of it in the Old Testament',
                VT 10: 410-27.
Thompson, R.C.
    1903   *The Devils and Evil Spirits of Babylonia*, I (London: Luzac).
    1904   *The Devils and Evil Spirits of Babylonia*, II (London: Luzac).
Thompson, T.L.
    1974   *The Historicity of the Patriarchal Narratives: The Quest For the
                Historical Abraham* (BZAW, 133; Berlin: W. de Gruyter).
    1987   *The Origin Tradition of Ancient Israel. I. The Literary Tradition of Gen-
                esis and Exodus 1-23* (JSOTSup, 55; Sheffield: JSOT Press).
    1992   *Early History of the Israelite People: From the Written and Archaeo-
                logical Sources* (Leiden: E.J. Brill).
Tigay, J.
    1982   *The Evolution of the Gilgamesh Epic* (Philadelphia: University of Penn-
                sylvania).
    1986   *You Shall Have No other Gods before Me: Israelite Religion in the Light
                of Hebrew Inscriptions* (HSS, 31; Atlanta: Scholars Press).
    1987   'Israelite Religion: The Onomastic and Epigraphic Evidence', in P.D.
                Miller, P.D. Hanson and S.D. McBride (eds.), *Ancient Israelite Religion:
                Festschrift F.M. Cross* (Philadelphia: Fortress Press): 157-94.
Tobin, V.A.
    1989   *Theological Principles of Egyptian Religion* (New York: Peter Lang).
Toombs, L.E.
    1962   'Clean and Unclean', *IDB*, I: 641-48.
Toombs, L.E., and G.E. Wright
    1969   'Tribal League Shrines in Amman and Shechem', *BA* 32: 104-16.
Toorn, K. van der
    1985   *Sin and Sanction in Israel and Mesopotamia: A Comparative Study*
                (Assen: Van Gorcum).
Towner, W.S.
    1968   ' "Blessed Be Yahweh" and "Blessed art Thou, Yahweh": The Modu-
                lation of a Biblical Formula', *CBQ* 30: 386-99.
Tucker, G.M.
    1966   'The Legal Background of Genesis 23', *JBL* 85: 77-84.
Urie, D.M.L.
    1949   'Sacrifice among the West Semites', *PEQ* 26: 67-82.

Ussishkin, D.
1971   'The "Ghassulian" Temple in En Gedi and the Origin of the Hoard from Nahal Mishmar', *BA* 34: 23-39.
Van Seters, J.
1968   'The Problem of Childlessness in Near Eastern Law and the Patriarchs of Israel', *JBL* 87: 401-408.
1969   'Jacob's Marriages and Ancient Near Eastern Customs: A Reexamination', *HTR* 62: 377-95.
1975   *Abraham in History and Tradition* (New Haven: Yale University Press).
1980   'The Religion of the Patriarchs in Genesis', *Bib* 61: 220-33.
1992   *Prologue to History: The Yahwist as Historian in Genesis* (Louisville, KY: Westminster/John Knox Press).
Vaughan, P.H.
1974   *The Meaning of 'bāmâ' in the Old Testament* (SOTSMS, 3; Cambridge: Cambridge University Press).
Vaux, R. de
1949   'Les patriarches hébreux et les découvertes modernes', *RB* 56: 5-36.
1961   *Israel: Its Life and Institutions* (London: Darton, Longman & Todd).
1964   *Studies in Old Testament Sacrifice* (Cardiff: University of Wales Press).
1978   *The Early History of Israel: To the Exodus and Covenant of Sinai* (London: Darton, Longman & Todd [1971]).
Veenhof, K.R.
1966   'Ernest Kutsch "Salbung als Rechtsakt" ', *BibOr*: 305-11.
Vida, G.L. della
1944   ' 'El 'Elyon in Genesis 14:18-20', *JBL* 63: 1-9.
Vida, G.L. della, and W.F. Albright
1943   'Some Notes on the Stele of Ben-Hadad', *BASOR* 90: 30-34.
Vos, H.F.
1977   *Archaeology in Bible Lands* (Chicago: Moody Press).
Walton, J.H.
1989   *Ancient Israelite Literature in its Cultural Context: A Survey of Parallels between Biblical and Ancient Near Eastern Texts* (Grand Rapids: Zondervan).
Warner, S.M.
1977   'The Patriarchs and Extra-Biblical Sources', *JSOT* 2: 50-61.
Weidmann, H.
1968   *Die Patriarchen und ihre Religion im Lichte der Forschung seit Julius Wellhausen* (FRLANT, 94; Göttingen: Vandenhoeck & Ruprecht).
Weidner, E.I.
1930–31   'Eine Bauinschrift des Königs Assurnadinapli von Assyrien', *AfO* 6: 11-17.
Weinfeld, M.
1970   'The Covenant of Grant in the Old Testament and in the Ancient Near East', *JAOS* 90: 184-204.
1972a   'Tithe', in *EncJud*, XV: 1156-62.
1972b   *Deuteronomy and the Deuteronomic School* (Oxford: Clarendon Press).
1983   'Social and Cultic Institutions in the Priestly Source against their Ancient

Near Eastern Background', in *Proceedings of the Eighth World Congress of Jewish Studies* (Jerusalem: World Union of Jewish Studies): 95-129.

Weippert, M.
1961   'Erwägungen zur Etymologie des Gottesnamens '*El Shaddaj*', *ZDMG* 111: 42-62.

1971   'Abraham der Hebräer?: Bemerkungen zu W.F. Albrights Deutung der Väter Israels', *Bib* 52: 407-32.

Wellhausen, J.
1885   *Prolegomena to the History of Israel* (Edinburgh: A. & C. Black [1878]).

1889   *Die Composition des Hexateuchs und der historischen Bücher des Alten Testaments* (Berlin: Georg Reimer, 2nd edn).

1897   *Reste arabischen Heidentum* (Berlin: Georg Reimer).

Wendel, A.
1931   *Das israelitisch-judische Gelübde* (Berlin: Philo).

Wenham, G.J.
1979   *The Book of Leviticus* (NICOT; Grand Rapids: Eerdmans).

1980   'The Religion of the Patriarchs', in A.R. Millard and D.J. Wiseman (eds.), *Essays on the Patriarchal Narratives* (Leicester: Inter-Varsity Press): 157-88.

1981a   *Numbers* (TOTC; Leicester: Inter-Varsity Press).

1981b   'The Theology of Unclean Food', *EvQ* 53: 6-15.

1982   'The Symbolism of the Animal Rite in Genesis 15: A Response to G.F. Hasel, *JSOT* 19 (1981) 61-78', *JSOT* 22: 134-37.

1983   'Why Does Sexual Intercourse Defile (Lev 15:18)?', *ZAW* 95: 432-34.

1985   'Were David's Sons Priests?', *ZAW* 87: 79-82.

1987   *Genesis 1–15* (WBC, 1; Dallas: Word Books).

1994   *Genesis 16–50* (WBC, 2; Dallas: Word Books).

Westermann, C.
1960   'Die Begriffe für Fragen und Suchen', *KD* 6: 2-16.

1965   *The Praise of God in the Psalms* (Atlanta: John Knox Press).

1980a   *The Promises to the Fathers* (Philadelphia: Fortress Press [1976]).

1980b   *The Psalms: Structure, Content, and Message* (Minneapolis: Augsburg).

1981   *Praise and Lament in the Psalms* (Edinburgh: T. & T. Clark).

1985   *Genesis 12–36* (London: SPCK; Minneapolis: Augsburg [1981]).

1986   *Genesis 37–50* (London: SPCK; Minneapolis: Augsburg [1985]).

1989   *The Living Psalms* (Edinburgh: T. & T. Clark [1984]).

Whybray, R.N.
1987   *The Making of the Pentateuch: A Methodological Study* (JSOTSup, 53; Sheffield: JSOT Press).

Widengren, G.
1937   *The Accadian and Hebrew Psalms of Lamentation as Religious Documents: A Comparative Study* (Uppsala: Almqvist & Wiksell).

Wilcoxen, J.A.
1974   'Narrative,' in J.H. Hayes (ed.), *Old Testament Form Criticism* (San Antonio: Trinity University Press): 57-98.

Williamson, H.G.M.
1982   *1 and 2 Chronicles* (NCBC; London: Marshall, Morgan & Scott).

Wilson, I.
    1992   'Divine Presence in Deuteronomy' (PhD Dissertation, Cambridge University).

Wilson, J.A.
    1948   'The Oath in Ancient Egypt', *JNES* 7: 129-56.

Wiseman, D.J.
    1958   'Abban and Alalaḫ', *JCS* 12: 124-29.

Witney, J.T.
    1979   'Bamoth in the Old Testament', *TynBul* 30: 125-47.

Woolley, L.
    1939/40   'The Iron-Age Graves of Carchemish', *AAA* 26: 11-37.

Wright, D.P.
    1987   *The Disposal of Impurity: Elimination Rites in the Bible and in Hittite and Mesopotamian Literature* (SBLDS, 101; Atlanta: Scholars Press).

Wright, G.E.
    1962   *Biblical Archaeology* (Philadelphia: Westminster Press).
    1965   *Shechem* (London: Gerald Duckworth).

Wright, G.R.H.
    1968   'Temples at Shechem', *ZAW* 80: 1-35.

Yardeni, A.
    1991   'Remarks on the Priestly Blessings on Two Ancient Amulets from Jerusalem', *VT* 41: 176-85.

Yaron, R.
    1988   *The Laws of Eshnunna* (Jerusalem: Magnes Press, 2nd edn).

Yerkes, R.K.
    1953   *Sacrifice in Greek and Roman Religions and Early Judaism* (London: A. & C. Black).

Young, E.J.
    1969   *The Book of Isaiah*, II (Grand Rapids: Eerdmans).

Zimmerli, W.
    1983   *Ezekiel* (Philadelphia: Scholars Press).

Zintzen, C. (ed.)
    1967   *Damascii: Vitae Isidori Reliquiae* (Hildesheim: Georg Olms).

Zuntz, G.
    1945   'Baitylos and Bethel', *CM* 8: 169-219.

INDEXES

INDEX OF REFERENCES

BIBLICAL REFERENCES

Wenham, G.J. 9, 17, 19, 23, 28, 30, 31,
      45, 46, 48, 55, 56, 61-63, 65, 68,
      69, 71, 73, 75, 76, 79, 80, 83, 109,
      110, 114, 117, 120-22, 127-31,
      132, 184, 186, 189, 210, 225, 226,
      235-38
Westermann, C. 17, 18, 22-24, 27, 55,
      58, 61-69, 71-74, 79, 80, 83, 89,
      99, 108-12, 114, 115, 120, 122,
      124, 125-29, 131, 132, 149, 158-
      62, 164-68, 184, 186, 187, 193,
      194, 205, 208, 210, 230, 231, 234-
      40
Whybray, R.N. 27, 28
Widengren, G. 91
Wilson, I. 222
Wilson, J.A. 196

Wiseman, D.J. 64
Witney, J.T. 156
Woolley, L. 149
Wright, D.P 45, 51, 217, 219, 224, 227,
      228, 236
Wright, G.E. 20, 72
Wright, G.R.H. 58

Yardeni, A. 105
Yaron, R. 48
Yerkes, R.K. 34
Young, E.J. 153

Zimmerli, W. 154
Zintzen, C. 139
Zuntz, G. 137, 142

JOURNAL FOR THE STUDY OF THE OLD TESTAMENT
SUPPLEMENT SERIES